# THE
# SUBDIVISION
# AND
# SITE PLAN
# HANDBOOK

CONSULTING TECHNICAL STAFF

*Engineering*

HOWARD M. SCHOOR AND WILLIAM F. NERO
SCHOOR DEPALMA & CANGER GROUP, INC.

*Legal*

DANIEL BERNSTEIN, ESQ.
BERNSTEIN, HOFFMAN & CLARK

*Design*

CARL G. LINDBLOOM, P.P., A.I.C.P.

ANTON NELESSEN
HINTZ-NELESSEN ASSOCIATES

# THE
# SUBDIVISION
# AND
# SITE PLAN
# HANDBOOK

David Listokin

AND

Carole Walker

CENTER
FOR URBAN
POLICY RESEARCH

Copyright © 1989 by Rutgers, The State University of New Jersey

Second printing 1990
Published by the Center for Urban Policy Research
Building 4051—Kilmer Campus
New Brunswick, New Jersey 08903

Library of Congress Cataloging-in-Publication Data

Listokin, David.
    The subdivision and site plan handbook / David Listokin and Carole
Walker.
        p.    cm.
    Bibliography: p.
    Includes index.
    ISBN 0-88285-123-3
    1. Land subdivision—Law and legislation—United States.
2. Zoning law—United States.     I. Walker, Carole.    II. Rutgers
University. Center for Urban Policy Research.    III. Title.
KF5698.L57 1989
346.7304′5—dc19                                           88-31633
[347.30645]                                                CIP

To my family
D.L.

To Susannah and Sally
C.W.

# CONTENTS

Acknowledgments    ix

Introduction    xv

## Part I
## Model Ordinance and Commentary

| | | |
|---|---|---|
| Article One | General Provisions | 1 |
| Article Two | Definitions | 4 |
| Article Three | Administration | 10 |
| Article Four | Procedure | 13 |
| Article Five | Design and Improvement Standards | 23 |
| Article Six | Off-Tract Improvements | 81 |
| Article Seven | Specification of Documents To Be Submitted | 87 |
| Appendix | Construction Details | 97 |

# Part II
## Reference

Introduction                                                           127

Chapter 1    Background: Evolution of                    129
             Subdivision Regulation

Chapter 2    Procedure                                        175

Chapter 3    Site Design                                      189

Chapter 4    Improvement Standards                  293

Bibliography                                                        395

Credits                                                               423

Index                                                                  431

# ACKNOWLEDGMENTS

*The Subdivision and Site Plan Handbook* benefited from the contributions of many people. The original work for the Rutgers model ordinance was carried out for the New Jersey Department of Community Affairs. We would like to thank, first, the Department for providing the financial support to undertake this study, and, in particular, William M. Connolly, whose vision provided the impetus for the project; Arthur Bernard, who was project manager and provided invaluable assistance and comments; Stuart L. Bressler, who contributed in the initial phases of the work; Arthur R. Kondrup, under whose leadership the model ordinance was completed; and Richard N. Binetsky, who assisted in the dissemination of the ordinance.

Our work on the model ordinance in New Jersey was supported by an advisory committee whose members provided technical expertise and comments on numerous preliminary drafts. Preparation of *The Handbook* would not have been possible without their assistance on the original work. Members of the engineering, legal, planning, and builders subcommittees are listed following these acknowledgments. We would particularly like to thank A. Lee Talbot for his engineering expertise and James Jager for his legal oversight. Carl Lindbloom was so helpful in making design recommendations that we asked him to join us in working on *The Handbook*. We would also extend our appreciation to Bruce Shepherd, Guliet Hirsch, George Yankowich, and David Fisher—all of whom reviewed extra drafts, offered improvements, and supplied us with materials.

Our consulting technical staff contributed significant sections and helped us refine standards. Howard M. Schoor, of Schoor DePalma & Canger Group, Inc., must be singled out for his work on engineering specifications. The model ordinance is in no small measure a tribute to his technical expertise and practical development experience. Howard also put members of his staff of engineers and planners at our disposal. Carolyn Neighbor was particularly helpful; she researched specific standards and oversaw the assembling of final drawings and technical submissions for *The Handbook*. William F. Nero acted as project manager during the original work; in addition, he co-drafted the background section on storm water management and provided the answers to numerous engineering questions. Robert Lawrence, George Broberg, and Daniel C. McSweeney also reviewed and commented on the technical standards for streets, water, sewers, and storm water management.

Our legal consultant, Daniel S. Bernstein, Esq., deserves special thanks for his careful examination of the model ordinance. Dan tirelessly advised us on the legality of various provisions, polished language, and helped draft the articles on procedure and administration. Dan's legal expertise and commitment to fairness to the many partners involved in the subdivision and site plan process were essential in shaping the model ordinance.

Finally, our consultant on design in the original model ordinance, Anton Nelessen, of Hintz/Nelessen Associates, provided useful comments and focused our attention on an often-neglected aspect of subdivision development: its design. We would also like to thank Carl E. Hintz for contributions to the landscaping section.

David J. Frizell, Esq., and Harry S. Pozycki, Esq., Frizell & Pozycki, Metuchen, New Jersey, reviewed later drafts of the ordinance, pointing out potential legal pitfalls and refining the language. Their legal expertise and experience in the land-use approval and development process were invaluable in improving the model ordinance. We are also indebted to Robert B. Heibell, Van Cleef Engineering Associates, who provided additional expertise and whose comments helped clarify engineering specifications.

The model ordinance also benefited from the comments of state officials and regional planning officials who reviewed sections relevant to their area of responsibility or jurisdiction. New Jersey officials responding to our request for comments included Vincent Pedicini, Department of Energy; Joseph A. Miri, Office of Water Policy, and John R. Weingart, Division of Coastal Resources; Feather O'Connor, New Jersey Housing and Mortgage Finance Agency (now State Treasurer); Perry E. Frenzel, Hackensack Meadowlands Development Commission; and Terrence D. Moore, The Pinelands Commission.

To ensure its applicability in the field, we submitted a final draft of the model ordinance to a number of practicing planners who reviewed it and offered suggestions. We would like to thank in particular Harvey S. Moskowitz, who took the time to edit and help us clarify significant portions of the text, and Alan Mallach, whose detailed comments on a number of sections led to more balanced requirements. Nicholas Bellizzi, Philip B. Caton, Richard T. Coppola, John J. Lynch, Lester L. Nebenzahl, Creigh Rahenkamp, John Rahenkamp, and George Raymond must also be singled out for sharing their expertise with us and providing helpful advice. Gary W. Davies, Garmen Associates, and Henry Ney, Abbington-Ney, deserve special appreciation for insightful recommendations on street and parking standards.

Land-use experts nationally were also gracious enough to read and comment on a series of drafts. We would like to extend our appreciation to Lee E. Koppelman, Long Island Regional Planning Board, for his encouraging words and constructive comments. The comments of both Joseph R. Molinaro, of the National Association of Home Builders, and Joseph Sherman, United States Department of Housing and Urban Development, were invaluable in suggesting provisions to help eliminate unnecessary costs. We would also like to thank Welford Sanders, of the American Planning Association, for his support of our work on the model ordinance.

A number of people and organizations were particularly helpful to us in tracking down photographs and other materials. The

American Planning Association generously made available its extensive photograph collection. We thank Dennis McClendon of the APA for his assistance in this regard. Numerous slides were provided by John Rahenkamp Consultants, Inc. Creigh Rahenkamp and David Golab were most generous in making available this firm's photographic resources. John Rahenkamp Consultants, Inc. emphasizes good design—and it shows in the quality of the developments they have planned.

Others also provided photographs. Lloyd Bookout willingly shared photos on subdivision design from The Urban Land Institute's collection, as did Susan Bradford, Director of Publications, National Association of Home Builders. In addition, the staffs at the Department of Agriculture, the Soil Conservation Service, the Department of Transportation, and the Department of Housing and Urban Development made their collections of photographs available. These are, indeed, a wonderful public resource. We also appreciated the efforts of Jon Reis and his staff, who found illustrations of specific points in the design section.

Finally, we would especially like to thank Carl Lindbloom for his significant contributions to *The Handbook*. Carl gave generously of his time, shared photographs, and did the drawings for the book.

These words of acknowledgment would not be complete without recognizing our debt to our colleagues at the Center for Urban Policy Research. Our thanks to Dr. Robert W. Burchell for his guidance and probing questions—he made us refine our thinking on numerous occasions. Our librarians, Edward Duensing and Azar Aryanpour, brought literally hundreds of books, reports, and studies on the subject of subdivision development and regulation to our attention. Heather MacDonald, Keith Hawkins, and Siobhon Maroney, graduate students at Rutgers University, researched portions of the reference section and organized the bibliography.

We pause for a final and special note of thanks. With their usual skill, Arlene Pashman edited the manuscript and Mary Picarella guided the book through publication. They personify professionalism. Mary Jane Hicks tirelessly persisted in obtaining permissions for the many materials included in the study; we thank her. Dahk Muhammad reformatted most of the original manuscript, and Yvonne Hardie handled numerous inquiries about publication with patience and good spirits. Finally, to Lydia Lombardi, we owe a tremendous debt of gratitude. Lydia typed and retyped and somehow kept track of 30 disks of model ordinance and commentary sections through countless revisions. Our thanks and appreciation to her cannot be exaggerated.

David Listokin
Carole Walker

## ADVISORY COMMITTEE MEMBERS

### ENGINEERS SUBCOMMITTEE

David B. Fisher
New Jersey Builders Association
Woodbridge, New Jersey

Eugene Golub
New Jersey Institute of Technology
Newark, New Jersey

James Kovacs
Abbington-Ney Associates
Freehold, New Jersey

Robert Lorentz
Consulting Engineers Council of New Jersey
Flemington, New Jersey

David Stem
New Jersey Association of County Engineers
Flemington, New Jersey

A. Lee Talbot
New Jersey Society of Municipal Engineers
Richard A. Alaimo Associates
Mount Holly, New Jersey

### LEGAL SUBCOMMITTEE

Thomas Collins, Esq.
Vogel and Chait
Morristown, New Jersey

Guliet Hirsch, Esq.
Brenner, Wallack & Hill
Princeton, New Jersey

James Jager, Esq.
Bureau of Housing Services
Department of Community Affairs
Trenton, New Jersey

Glenn C. Kienz, Esq.
Richard H. Downes, Esq.
Sparta, New Jersey

Robert F. Rogers, Esq.
Rogers & Smith
Burlington, New Jersey

### PLANNING SUBCOMMITTEE

Barry Bourquin
Hunterdon County Planning Board
Flemington, New Jersey

Rob Goodwin
John Rahenkamp and Associates
Philadelphia, Pennsylvania

Ray Hodnett
Hodnett/Abbington-Ney
Red Bank, New Jersey

Carl Lindbloom
Princeton, New Jersey

John Madden
Bridgewater Township Planning Board
Bridgewater, New Jersey

Judith Schleicher
New Jersey Federation of Planning Officials
Denville, New Jersey

### BUILDERS SUBCOMMITTEE

William Bowman
William Bowman Associates
Atco, New Jersey

Craig Hamilton
Lanid Corporation
Parsippany, New Jersey

Michael Merkle
The Linpro Developers
Marlton, New Jersey

Bruce Shepherd
Shepherd Engineering Associates
Toms River, New Jersey

George Yankowich
K. Hovnanian Companies
Red Bank, New Jersey

# INTRODUCTION

## Background

Few issues have dominated the planning field to the degree that excessive land-use regulations have. The rising cost of housing through the 1970s and early 1980s focused attention on outmoded requirements that added unnecessary costs to housing. Initially, local zoning practices—minimum lot size and frontage, mandatory bedroom ratios, and limitations on multifamily development—came under attack as "the exclusionary zoning problem." Next under review came overrestrictive subdivision regulations and excessively complicated permitting procedures.

By the 1980s, subdivision and site plan submission requirements and standards governing street widths, sidewalks, parking, off-site improvements, drainage, and water systems were increasingly being questioned and their revision proposed to help remedy the situation. National commissions studied the effect of subdivision controls; land-use treatises examined the emerging regulations; and professional and research organizations analyzed the impacts of excessive controls as a prelude to developing state and local land-use policy.[1]

Local governments were also becoming increasingly concerned with improving their development controls. Municipalities enacted land-use regulations to protect the public health, safety, and welfare; yet, these regulations have not always proved effective, and there have been recurring examples of developers who have not provided a physically sound and well-designed product.

Thus, there was a growing recognition on the part of both public and private participants in the development process that improvement in standards and procedures was needed. In response, groups such as the American Planning Association, National Association of Home Builders, Urban Land Institute, and the Institute of Transportation Engineers published model subdivision guidelines.[2] Additionally, a number of counties and states developed model statutes.[3] The recommended standards were field-tested. For instance, demonstrations of cost-reducing subdivision techniques were attempted by the Joint Venture for Affordable Housing and other groups; these efforts were highlighted in numerous case-study descriptions.[4]

## The Rutgers *Subdivision and Site Plan Handbook*

*OBJECTIVE AND PROCESS*

The Rutgers *Subdivision and Site Plan Handbook*, which is contained in two sections (Ordinance and Reference), follows and builds upon the rich model subdivision literature. It also reflects the experience of developing a model ordinance for the State of New Jersey.

In 1984, the New Jersey Department of Community Affairs commissioned Rutgers University, Center for Urban Policy Research to draft a model subdivision and site plan ordinance. The goal in developing the model ordinance was to adopt standards that would result in quality municipal improvements and protect the public, without adding unnecessary costs to development. The mandate was not to produce guidelines applicable only to low- and moderate-cost housing developments, but rather to produce a model ordinance for site plan and subdivision development with more universal applicability. In a similar vein, the model ordinance was not intended to straitjacket development into a uniform mold. Given the wide disparity in local needs and differences in development sites, it aimed to incorporate design flexibility and permit a variety of approaches. The purpose, in short, was to arrive at a uniform set of standards that would ensure a measure of consistency and predictability, yet at the same time allow flexibility in order to avoid design monotony and accommodate variations due to local site conditions.

In developing balanced standards, innovations in both the research community and field-level practice were considered. To arrive at state-of-the-art recommendations, the Center for Urban Policy Research conducted an in-depth study of subdivision and site plan requirements from the model subdivision literature. To ensure that the recommended standards would be practicable, advisory committees of planners, engineers, attorneys, and developers were formed and consulted; in addition, drafts of the recommendations were commented upon by state and national development and professional organizations.

The model ordinance was published by the State of New Jersey in 1987;[5] it was well-received by practitioners. This document was then revised for a national audience. The revisions include addition of commentary notes on the ordinance, changes to the reference (background) section, and substitution of generic review procedures for the New Jersey-specific requirements. In addition, modifications in some of the model's standards have been introduced in response to feedback from the field concerning the implementation of the recommended subdivision specifications. The end result of these many changes is *The Subdivision and Site Plan Handbook*.

## Contents and Emphasis

*The Handbook* consists of two parts—the model ordinance with a commentary that explains ordinance provisions, and a reference section that covers all aspects of subdivision development in depth. Both sections of the book follow the sequence of articles in the model ordinance shown below.

| | |
|---|---|
| Article One | General Provisions |
| Article Two | Definitions |
| Article Three | Administration |
| Article Four | Procedure |
| Article Five | Design and Improvement Standards |

Article Six     Off-Tract Improvements
Article Seven   Specification of Documents
                to be Submitted

These articles reflect a comprehensive perspective of what subdivision and site plan regulation encompasses. The first four articles—General Provisions, Definitions, Administration, and Procedure—consist of introductory and procedure-related provisions. Article Five covers design and improvement standards, including site design, site preparation, landscaping, open space, streets, off-street parking, water supply, sanitary sewers, storm water management, and improvement guarantees. Article Six addresses the equitable allocation of off-tract improvement costs. Article Seven defines the documents that must be submitted as part of an application package. In addition, to set the context, the reference section opens with a background chapter on land-use regulations.

The model ordinance incorporates a number of improvements to subdivision controls that the authors believe are critical. These include:

1. Functional standards
2. Performance standards
3. Design integration
4. Procedural improvement

**Functional standards.** Since the origin of subdivision controls in the United States, there has been an effort to determine those standards that are "functionally necessary." *The Subdivision and Site Plan Handbook* continues this tradition: it incorporates today's technology, information, and practice to define what is functionally required. To illustrate, engineering advances permit the utilization of PVC pipe. The downsizing of cars in the 1970s allows for smaller parking spaces. Demographic changes are also incorporated. More accurate water and sewer standards for residential units can be formulated by taking into account the reduction in the American household size in general, as well as the fact that attached units, in particular, tend to house smaller households.

The philosophy of functional standards is one of the reasons why *The Subdivision and Site Plan Handbook* contains the reference section in addition to the ordinance section. The reference section explains the issues involved in determining model standards. To use a legal term from exactions, the discussion in the reference section constitutes the "rational nexus" between public controls and the furtherance of public health, safety, and welfare. The reference materials should be carefully reviewed: as technology and demographics change, and where local conditions differ, revisions to the standards will have to be made.

**Performance standards.** Performance standards were first used in the 1950s when minimum levels of "performance" were specified to regulate noise, smoke, dust, and other nuisances associated with industry. Performance standards are designed to provide a desired result without specifying exactly what must be done to achieve this result.[6]

The advantage of performance standards is that they provide flexibility and avoid arbitrary regulations. The problem with performance standards, however—especially the more technical ones—is that municipalities often do not possess the expertise or equipment to measure performance. Because of this, many communities prefer specific standards rather than performance standards. Most recent model ordinances attempt to deal with this problem by blending precise requirements with performance criteria when the latter can be handled by smaller- and mid-size communities.[7]

*The Subdivision and Site Plan Handbook* follows this practice. Wherever practicable, it uses a performance approach, establishing general objectives to be met, rather than rigid numerical criteria. For example, in drafting buffering standards, instead of attempting to dictate the design of a buffer area by specifying the exact placement and spacing of trees and shrubs, *The Handbook* requires that buffer materials be placed so that they will provide maximum protection to adjacent properties. In addition, the buffer must become a screen at least eight feet high within three growing seasons. This approach allows for a variety of designs and plant materials, as long as the desired effect is achieved.

Physical improvement standards also incorporate a performance approach. Different categories of streets are defined and standards tailored accordingly. In addition, the developer can utilize a variety of street paving materials as long as their "relative strengths" meet the indicated performance standard. Similarly, the developer is given the leeway to design an appropriate storm water management system, as long as specified velocities in both open and closed channels are not exceeded.

Thus, wherever possible, performance standards are given. Where this cannot be accomplished, precise requirements are established.

**Design integration.** An underlying philosophy of *The Subdivision and Site Plan Handbook* is the need to integrate design sensitivity into the core of the subdivision process, which traditionally has been the domain of physical engineering and planning. The realization of this goal requires articulation in terms of specifying what is "good design." To illustrate, a fundamental planning and design principle is the need to preserve "sensitive areas." It is important for an ordinance to go beyond generalities and to define precisely what is "sensitive." Thus, *The Subdivision and Site Plan Handbook* identifies the specific areas—wetlands, severe slope locations, historic sites, etc.—where development should be avoided.

The emphasis throughout the design standards in *The Handbook* is on flexibility within the context of local conditions and desires. Flexibility is the optimal approach, for more often than not, good design is arrived at through a process of negotiation between the developer and the planning board members.

**Procedural improvement.** One of the less obvious but still major costs involved in American subdivision practice is the time consumed in review. Much of the recent literature bemoans this new area of unnecessary cost inflation. *The Subdivision and Site Plan Handbook* emphasizes the need for the expeditious review of applications. To this end, it encourages developers and communities to meet and work with each other early on so that concept plans can be agreed upon before formal and detailed submissions are made. Additionally, *The Handbook's* specification of documents to be submitted is keyed to functional need. Thus, fewer submission items are required for preliminary and/or smaller-size applications.

## Conclusion

Subdivision regulation and practice in the United States have undergone a long process of change and refinement.[8] A half-century ago, the lack of subdivision controls contributed to widespread failed subdivisions and foreclosure. Today, the state of the art is much improved. However, constant reevaluation is imperative to foster economical and well-designed development. It is hoped that *The Subdivision and Site Plan Handbook* will contribute to the ongoing process of refining American subdivision controls.

## Notes

1. Stephen R. Seidel, *Housing Costs and Government Regulations* (New Brunswick, NJ: Center for Urban Policy Research, 1978); U.S. Department of Housing and Urban Development, *Reducing the Development Costs of Housing: Actions for States and Local Governments* (Washington, D.C.: U.S. Government Printing Office, 1979); Welford Sanders and David Mosena, *Changing Development Standards for Affordable Housing* (Chicago, IL: American Planning Association, 1982); International City Management Association, *Streamlining Local Regulations: A Handbook for Reducing Housing and Development Costs* (Washington, D.C.: ICMA, 1983).

2. Robert H. Freilich and Peter S. Levi, *Model Subdivision Regulations: Text and Commentary* (Chicago, IL: American Society of Planning Officials, 1975); Michael B. Brough, *A Unified Development Ordinance* (Chicago, IL: American Planning Association, 1985); Urban Land Institute, National Association of Home Builders, and American Society of Civil Engineers, *Residential Streets: Objectives, Principles, and Design Considerations* (Washington, D.C.: ULI, 1976); National Association of Home Builders, *Subdivision Regulation Handbook: NAHB Land Development Series* (Washington, D.C.: National Association of Home Builders, 1978); Institute of Transportation Engineers, *Recommended Guidelines for Subdivision Streets* (Washington, D.C.: ITE, 1984).

3. University of Oregon, Bureau of Governmental Research, *A Model Land Subdivision Ordinance Format* (Eugene, OR: University of Oregon, Bureau of Governmental Research, 1979); Pennsylvania Department of Transportation, *Guidelines for Design of Local Roads and Streets* (Harrisburg, PA: Pennsylvania Department of Transportation, 1972), PDT Publi-

cation 190; Bucks County Planning Commission, *Performance Streets: A Concept and Model Standards for Residential Streets* (Doylestown, PA: Bucks County Planning Commission, 1980).

4. See, for instance, *The Affordable Housing Demonstration: Case Studies* in Phoenix, Arizona; Christian County, Kentucky; Everett, Washington; and Mesa County, Colorado (Washington, D.C.: Government Printing Office, 1984). Studies prepared by the NAHB Research Foundation, Inc., for the U.S. Department of Housing and Urban Development.

5. David Listokin and Carole W. Baker, *Model Subdivision and Site Plan Ordinance,* prepared for the New Jersey Department of Community Affairs, January 1987.

6. Marilyn Spigel Schultz and Vivian Loeb Kasen, *Encyclopedia of Community Planning and Environmental Management* (New York, NY: Facts on File Publications, 1984), p. 293.

7. See, for example, Brough, *A Unified Development Ordinance,* p. xvii.

8. See chapter 1 in the reference section.

# Part I

# Model Ordinance
# and Commentary

# Article One
# General Provisions

## A. Short Title

Ordinances are typically given an abbreviated title for reference purposes. While subdivision and site plan standards usually constitute a chapter within a larger land development ordinance which contains zoning and other regulations, in this study the subdivision and site plan provisions are referred to as an "ordinance."

All material in the model ordinance appearing between brackets is to be filled in by the jurisdictions adopting the ordinance. In some sections of the ordinance, standards have been suggested and are indicated within brackets. It is recommended that these standards be adopted. Revised standards may, however, be substituted after careful consideration and review of local characteristics and needs.

## B. Authority and Purpose

These and similar enumerated purposes would typically be found in the purpose section of the overall land use development ordinance which includes both zoning and subdivision regulations.

1. The statutory authority for land use regulations in general, and subdivision and site plan controls in particular, should be cited.

2. Balance is a central theme of this ordinance. Improvement standards must be keyed to protect the public welfare, where welfare encompasses both the design and physical improvements associated with development. Excessive standards which do not further the public welfare, and therefore unnecessarily add to construction costs, should be avoided.

The general statement of purpose in the model ordinance is brief. Not uncommonly, a series of more specific statements will be added such as the "prevention of traffic hazards" or "protection from flooding."

3. The purpose of this section is not to stipulate a technical legal requirement that subdivision and site plan regulations be "in accordance with" the indicated land use documents, but rather to encourage the integration of land use controls. For instance,

# Article One
# General Provisions

## A. Short Title

This ordinance shall be known and may be cited as: The Subdivision and Site Plan Chapter of the Land Development Ordinance of [municipality or other jurisdiction].

## B. Authority and Purpose

1. This ordinance is adopted pursuant to the authority delegated to [municipality or other jurisdiction] under [cite relevant enabling state/other land use regulations] and to promote good planning practice.

2. The purpose of this ordinance is to protect the public health, safety, and general welfare while allowing for cost-saving efficiencies.

3. The provisions in this ordinance shall be administered to ensure orderly growth and development and shall supplement and facilitate the provisions in the master or comprehensive plan, zoning ordinance, official map, and capital budget.

*C. Jurisdiction*

*1. The provisions in this ordinance shall be applicable in [specify area].*

*2. This ordinance shall become effective on [specify date].*

*3. When necessary to further its purposes, this ordinance shall be amended [specify amending agency and procedure].*

**D. Fees**

*Reasonable fees sufficient to recover incurred costs may be charged.*

**E. Enforcement and Penalties**

*1. It shall be the duty of the [specify agency or individual, such as the administrative officer] to enforce the provisions of this ordinance and to bring to the attention of [specify agency or individual] any violations or lack of compliance.*

*2. Violation of the provisions of this ordinance shall be deemed a misdemeanor, punishable as provided by law and with each day such violation continues constituting a separate offense. The [specify agency or individual] shall have recourse to such remedies in law and equity as may be necessary to ensure compliance with the provisions of these regulations.*

"capped" water and sewer lines ("dry" lines designed to ultimately tap into a future public water and sewer system) should be required only if there is official indication in the public capital facilities plan that public water and sewer service will be extended to the site in question in the future.

## C. Jurisdiction

1. It is recommended that the ordinance have a comprehensive spatial scope. At minimum, it should apply to the full corporate limits of the municipality, county, or other applicable jurisdiction. Where a jurisdiction controls development outside these boundaries, such as in nearby unincorporated areas, then the ordinance should apply in these extraterritorial areas as well.

It is recommended that separate regulations not be allowed for privately maintained facilities. An example is a street within a development that is not dedicated to the municipality, but instead is the responsibility of a homeowners association. The question of what is a proper street standard should be determined by engineering considerations based on the street's function and use (i.e., subcollector or collector) as specified in Article Five of this ordinance—not on the basis of public or private dedication of the improvement.

3. An ordinance should be a living document to be amended when necessary.

## D. Fees

The power to levy processing fees may be derived from state statute or implied in the authority to regulate land use. The specifics should be checked.

In general, a fee schedule will be accepted by the courts if the charges bear a reasonable relationship to the costs of administering the regulation in question. See, for instance, Vranicar, *Setting Zoning and Subdivision Fees: Making Ends Meet*, 1981.

## E. Enforcement and Penalties

1. and 2. This provision is intended to ensure that subdivision standards are enforced by stating clearly that there will be penalties for violations. See Freilich and Levi, *Model Subdivision Regulations*, 1975.

## F. Interpretation, Conflict, and Separability

1. While a jurisdiction should be permitted the flexibility to require standards over and above those stipulated in an ordinance if necessitated by special site conditions, such modification should be limited to only that specific case.

2. Where "dual" standards are found, prudence dictates that the more stringent provisions should govern until it can be determined which standard should rule.

3. A separability provision is often included in an ordinance to protect the whole if a section is declared invalid.

## F. Interpretation, Conflict, and Separability

*1. In their interpretation and application, the provisions of this ordinance shall be held to be the minimum requirements. More stringent provisions may be required if it is demonstrated that different standards are necessary to promote the public health, safety and welfare.*

*2. Where the conditions imposed by any provisions of this ordinance are either more restrictive or less restrictive than comparable conditions imposed by any other provisions of this ordinance or of any other applicable law, ordinance, resolution, rule or regulation of any kind, the regulations which are more restrictive and impose higher standards or requirements shall govern.*

*3. The provisions of this ordinance are separable. If a section, sentence, clause, or phrase of this ordinance is adjudged by a court of competent jurisdiction to be invalid, the decision shall not affect the remaining portions of this ordinance.*

# Article Two
# Definitions

## A. Purpose

Unless otherwise expressly stated, the following terms shall, for the purposes of this ordinance, have the meaning herein indicated. (See bibliography for sources.)

## B. Definitions

**Administrative Officer.** The governmental officer charged with administering development regulations.

**ADT (Average Daily Traffic).** The average number of cars per day that pass over a given point.

**Aggressive Soils.** Soils that may be corrosive to cast iron and ductile iron pipe. These soils represent approximately five percent (5%) of the soils found within the United States and include dump areas, swamps, marshes, alkaline soils, cinder beds, polluted river bottoms, etc., which are considered to be potentially corrosive.

**Aisle.** The traveled way by which cars enter and depart parking spaces.

**Alley.** A public or private street primarily designed to serve as secondary access to the side or rear of those properties whose principal frontage is on some other street.

**Applicant.** A developer submitting an application for development.

**Application for Development.** The application form and all accompanying documents required by ordinance for approval of a subdivision plat or site plan.

**Approving Authority.** The planning board, unless a different agency is designated by ordinance.

**ASCE.** American Society of Civil Engineers.

**ASTM.** American Society for Testing Materials.

**AWWA.** American Water Works Association.

**Barrier Curb.** A steep-faced curb intended to prevent encroachments. See Curb.

**Belgian Block Curb.** A type of paving stone generally cut in a truncated, pyramidal shape, laid with the base of the pyramid down. See Curb.

**Berm.** A mound of soil, either natural or manmade, used to obstruct views.

**Bicycle-Compatible Roadway.** A road designed to accommodate the shared use of the roadway by bicycles and motor vehicles.

**Bicycle Lane.** A lane at the edge of a roadway reserved and marked for the exclusive use of bicycles.

**Bicycle Path.** A pathway usually separated from the roadway, designed specifically to satisfy the physical requirements of bicycling.

**Bikeway.** A pathway designed to be used by bikers.

**Blow-Off.** An outlet in a pipe through which water or sediment can be discharged from a lower sewer.

**Board of Adjustment.** The zoning board of adjustment established pursuant to [          ].

**Buffer.** An area within a property or site, generally adjacent to and parallel with the property line, either consisting of natural existing vegetation or created by the use of trees, shrubs, fences, and/or berms, designed to limit continuously the view of and/or sound from the site to adjacent sites or properties.

**Caliper.** The diameter of a tree trunk measured in inches, six (6) inches above ground level for trees up to four (4) inches in diameter and twelve (12) inches above ground level for trees over four (4) inches in diameter.

**Capital Improvements Program.** A proposed schedule of all future projects listed in order of construction priority together with cost estimates and the anticipated means of financing each project.

**Capped System.** A completed water supply and/or sewerage system put in place for future use (contingent upon expansion), rather than to meet immediate development needs.

**Cartway.** The actual road surface area from curbline to curbline, which may include travel lanes, parking lanes, and deceleration and acceleration lanes. Where there are no curbs, the cartway is that portion between the edges of the paved, or hard surface, width.

**Centerline Offset of Adjacent Intersections.** The gap between the centerline of roads adjoining a common road from opposite or same sides.

**Channel.** The bed and banks of a natural stream which convey the constant or intermittent flow of the stream.

**Channelization.** The straightening and deepening of channels and/or the surfacing thereof to permit water to move rapidly and/or directly.

**Cluster Development.** A development approach in which building lots may be reduced in size and buildings sited closer together, usually in groups or clusters, provided that the total development density does not exceed that which could be constructed on the site under conventional zoning and subdivision regulations. The additional land that remains undeveloped is then preserved as open space and recreational land.

**Common Lateral.** A lateral serving more than one (1) unit.

**Common Open Space.** Land within or related to a development, not individually owned or dedicated for public use, which is designed and intended for the common use or enjoyment of the residents of the development. It may include complementary structures and improvements.

**Concept Plan.** A preliminary presentation and attendant documentation of a proposed subdivision or site plan of sufficient accuracy to be used for the purpose of discussion and classification.

**Conventional Development.** Development other than planned development.

**Corporation Stop.** Also known as corporation cock. A valve which is placed in a building's water or gas service pipe near its junction with the public water or gas main.

**Cul-de-Sac.** A local street with only one outlet and having the other end for the reversal of traffic movement. See Street.

**Culvert.** A structure designed to convey a water course not incorporated in a closed drainage system under a road or pedestrian walk.

**Curb.** A vertical or sloping edge of a roadway. See also Belgian Block Curb, Barrier Curb, Mountable Curb.

**Cushions.** Supportive or protective bedding materials placed underneath piping.

**Dedication.** An act transmitting property or interest thereto.

**Density.** The permitted number of dwelling units per gross acre of land to be developed.

**Design Flood.** The relative size or magnitude of a major flood of reasonable expectancy, which reflects both flood experience and flood potential and is the basis of the delineation of the floodway, the flood hazard area, and the water surface elevations.

**Design Standards.** Standards that set forth specific improvement requirements.

**Detention Basin.** A man-made or natural water collector facility designed to collect surface and sub-surfaced water in order to impede its flow and to release the same gradually at a rate not greater than that prior to the development of the property, into natural or man-made outlets.

**Developer.** The legal or beneficial owner or owners of a lot or of any land included in a proposed development. Also, the holder of an option or contract to purchase, or any other person having enforceable proprietary interest in such land.

**Development.** A planning or construction project involving substantial property improvement and, usually, a change of land-use character within the site; the act of using land for building or extractive purposes.

**Development Regulation.** Zoning, subdivision, site plan, official map, flood plain regulation, or other governmental regulation of the use and development of land.

**Divided Street.** A street having an island or other barrier separating moving lanes.

**Drainage.** The removal of surface water or groundwater from land by drains, grading, or other means.

**Drainage Facility.** Any component of the drainage system.

**Drainage System.** The system through which water flows from the land, including all watercourses, waterbodies and wetlands.

**Driveway.** A paved or unpaved area used for ingress or egress of vehicles, and allowing access from a street to a building or other structure or facility.

**Drop Manhole.** A manhole provided for inspection and maintenance of sewers where an incoming sewer is considerably higher than the outgoing.

**Drop Pipe.** A vertical pipe used to convey sewage from a higher to a lower elevation.

**Dry Lines.** See Capped System.

**Easement.** A right-of-way granted, but not dedicated, for limited use of private land for a public or quasi-public purpose and within which the owner of the property shall not erect any permanent structures.

**Environmental Constraints.** Features, natural resources, or land characteristics that are sensitive to improvements and may require conservation measures or the application of creative development techniques to prevent degradation of the environment, or may require limited development, or in certain instances may preclude development.

**Erosion.** The detachment and movement of soil or rock fragments, or the wearing away of the land surface by water, wind, ice, or gravity.

**Escrow.** A deed, a bond, money, or a piece of property delivered to a third person to be delivered by him to the grantee only upon fulfillment of a condition.

**Exempt Subdivision.** See Subdivision.

**Fence.** An artificially constructed barrier of wood, masonry, stone, wire, metal, or any other manufactured material or combination of materials.

**Final Approval.** The official action of the planning board taken on a preliminarily approved major subdivision or site plan, after all conditions, engineering plans, and other requirements have been completed or fulfilled and the required improvements have been installed, or guarantees properly posted for their completion, or approval conditioned upon the posting of such guarantee.

**Final Plat.** The final map of all or a portion of a subdivision which is presented for final approval.

**Floor Area.** *Area of all floors of buildings or structures.*

**Flushing.** *The cleaning out of debris and sediment from pipes by force of moving liquid, usually water.*

**Frontage.** See Lot Frontage.

**General Development Plan.** *A plan outlining general, rather than detailed, development intentions. It describes the basic parameters of a major development proposal, rather than giving full engineering details. As such, it allows general intentions to be proposed and discussed without the extensive costs involved in submitting a detailed proposal.*

**Governing Body.** *The chief legislative body of the municipality.*

**Grade.** *The slope of a street, or other public way, specified in percentage (%) terms.*

**Ground Cover.** *A planting of low-growing plants or sod that in time forms a dense mat covering the area, preventing soil from being blown or washed away and the growth of unwanted plants.*

**Gutter.** *A shallow channel usually set along a curb or the pavement edge of a road for purposes of catching and carrying off runoff water.*

**Hardy Cross Method.** *Method of controlled trial and error by which a water distribution system can be analyzed, first introduced in 1936 by Hardy Cross, Professor of Civil Engineering, University of Illinois.*

**Historic District.** *An area related by historical events or themes, by visual continuity or character, or by some other special feature that helps give it a unique historical identity. May be designated a historic district by local, state, or federal government and given official status and protection.*

**Historic Site.** *A structure or place of historical significance. May be designated*

as such by local, state, or federal government.

**Hydrologic Response.** *The properties, distribution, and circulation of water.*

**IES.** *Illuminating Engineering Society.*

**Impervious Surface.** *A surface that has been compacted or covered with a layer of material so that it is highly resistant to infiltration by water.*

**Impoundment.** *A body of water, such as a pond, confined by a dam, dike, floodgate, or other barrier.*

**Improvement.** *Any man-made, immovable item which becomes part of, placed upon, or is affixed to, real estate.*

**Individual Sewage Disposal System.** *A septic tank, seepage tile sewage disposal system, or any other approved sewage treatment device serving a single unit.*

**Island.** *In street design, a raised area, usually curbed, placed to guide traffic and separate lanes, or used for landscaping, signing, or lighting.*

**ITE.** *Institute of Transportation Engineers.*

**Lateral Sewers.** *Pipes conducting sewage from individual buildings to larger pipes called trunk or interceptor sewers that usually are located in street rights-of-way.*

**Lot.** *A designated parcel, tract, or area of land established by a plat or otherwise as permitted by law and to be used, developed, or built upon as a unit.*

**Lot Area.** *The size of a lot measured within the lot lines and expressed in terms of acres or square feet.*

**Lot Frontage.** *That portion of a lot extending along a street line.*

**Main.** *In any system of continuous piping, the principal artery of the system to which branches may be connected.*

**Maintenance Guarantee.** *Any security which may be required and accepted by a governmental agency to ensure that*

necessary improvements will function as required for a specific period of time.

**Major Site Plan.** *Any site plan not classified as a minor site plan.*

**Major Subdivision.** *Any subdivision not classified as a minor subdivision.*

**Manhole.** *An inspection chamber whose dimensions allow easy entry and exit and working room for a person inside.*

**Manning Equation.** *A method for calculating the hydraulic capacity of a conduit to convey water.*

**Marginal Access Street.** *A service street that runs parallel to a higher-order street which, for purposes of safety, provides access to abutting properties and separation from through traffic. May be designed as a residential access street or subcollector as anticipated daily traffic dictates.*

**Master Plan.** *A comprehensive long-range plan intended to guide the growth and development of a community or region. Includes analysis, recommendations, and proposals for the community's population, economy, housing, transportation, community facilities and land use.*

**Median.** *That portion of a divided highway separating lanes of traffic proceeding in opposite directions.*

**Minor Site Plan.** *A development plan for less than [          ] square feet of floor area and less than [          ] square feet of impervious surface, provided that such site plan does not involve planned development.*

**Minor Subdivision.** *A subdivision of land of not more than [          ] lots, provided that such subdivision does not involve a planned development, any new street, or the extension of a utility or other municipal facility.*

**Mountable Curb.** *A low curb with a flat slope designed to be crossed easily without discomfort.*

**Moving Lane.** Any traffic lane where traffic movement is the primary if not sole function. (Compare with Parking Lane.)

**Mulch.** A layer of wood chips, dry leaves, straw, hay, plastic, or other materials placed on the surface of the soil around plants to retain moisture, prevent weeds from growing, hold the soil in place, or aid plant growth.

**Off-Site.** Located outside the lot lines of the lot in question but within the property (of which the lot is a part) that is the subject of a development application, or on a contiguous portion of a street or right-of-way.

**Off-Street Parking Space.** A parking space provided in a parking lot, parking structure, or private driveway.

**Off-Tract.** Not located on the property that is the subject of a development application nor on a contiguous portion of a street or right-of-way.

**On-Site.** Located on the lot in question.

**On-Street Parking Space.** A parking space that is located on a dedicated street right-of-way.

**On-Tract.** Located on the property that is the subject of a development application or on a contiguous portion of a street or right-of-way.

**Open Space.** Any parcel or area of land or water essentially unimproved and set aside, dedicated, designated, or reserved for the public or private use or enjoyment or for the use and enjoyment of owners and occupants of land adjoining or neighboring such open space.

**Parking Lane.** A lane usually located on the sides of streets, designed to provide on-street parking for vehicular traffic.

**Parking Space.** An area provided for the parking of a motor vehicle.

**Pavement.** See Cartway.

**Perc Test.** (Percolation Test.) A test designed to determine the ability of ground to absorb water, and used to determine the suitability of a soil for drainage or for the use of a septic system.

**Performance Guarantee.** Any security that may be accepted by a municipality as a guarantee that the improvements required as part of an application for development are satisfactorily completed.

**Pervious Surface.** A surface that permits full or partial absorption of storm water.

**Planned Unit Development.** An area of a minimum contiguous size, as specified by ordinance, to be planned, developed, operated, and maintained as a single entity containing one or more structures to accommodate commercial or office uses, or both, and appurtenant common areas and other uses incidental to the predominant uses.

**Planning Board.** The duly designated planning board of the municipality, county, or region.

**Plat.** A map or maps of a subdivision or site plan.

**Potable Water Supply.** Water suitable for drinking or cooking purposes.

**Pre-Application Conference.** An initial meeting between developers and municipal representatives which affords developers the opportunity to present their proposals informally.

**Preliminary Approval.** The conferral of certain rights prior to final approval after specific elements of a development plan have been agreed upon by the planning board and the applicant.

**Preliminary Subdivision Plat.** A map indicating the proposed layout of a development and related information that is submitted for preliminary approval.

**Public Open Space.** An open space area conveyed or otherwise dedicated to a municipality, municipal agency, board of education, state or county agency, or other public body for recreational or conservational uses.

**PUD.** See Planned Unit Development.

**Rational Method.** A method of runoff calculation.

**Residential Access Street.** The lowest order of residential street (see Street Hierarchy). Provides frontage for access to private lots, and carries traffic having destination or origin on the street itself. Designed to carry traffic at slowest speed. Traffic volume should not exceed 250 ADT at any point of traffic concentration. The maximum number of housing units should front on this class of street.

**Residential Collector.** The highest order of residential street (see Street Hierarchy). Conducts and distributes traffic between lower-order residential streets and higher-order streets (arterials and expressways). Since its function is to promote free traffic flow, access to homes and parking should be prohibited. Collectors should be designed to prevent use as shortcuts by non-neighborhood traffic. Total traffic volume should not exceed 3,000 ADT.

**Residential Density.** The number of dwelling units per gross acre of residential land area including streets, easements, and open space portions of a development.

**Residential Subcollector.** Middle order of residential streets (see Street Hierarchy). Provides frontage for access to lots and carries traffic to and from adjoining residential access streets. Traffic should have origin or destination in the immediate neighborhood. Traffic volume should not exceed 500 ADT at any point of traffic concentration.

**Retaining Wall.** A structure erected between lands of different elevation to protect structures and/or to prevent the washing down or erosion of earth from the upper slope level.

**Retention Basin.** A pond, pool, or basin used for the permanent storage of water runoff.

**Right-of-Way.** A strip of land occupied or intended to be occupied by a street, crosswalk, railroad, road, electric transmission line, gas pipeline, water main, sanitary or storm sewer main, shade trees, or for another special use.

**Screen.** A structure or planting consisting of fencing, berms, and/or evergreen trees or shrubs providing a continuous view obstruction within a site or property.

**SCS.** Soil Conservation Service.

**Sedimentation.** A deposit of soil that has been transported from its site of origin by water, ice, wind, gravity, or other natural means as a product of erosion.

**Septic System.** An underground system with a septic tank used for the decomposition of domestic wastes.

**Septic Tank.** A watertight receptacle that receives the discharge of sewage.

**Setback.** The distance between the street right-of-way line and the front line of a building or any projection thereof, excluding uncovered steps.

**Sewer.** Any pipe conduit used to collect and carry away sewage or storm water runoff from the generating source to treatment plants or receiving streams.

**Shade Tree.** A tree in a public place, street, special easement, or right-of-way adjoining a street.

**Shoulder.** The graded part of the right-of-way that lies between the edge of the main pavement (main traveled way) and the curbline.

**Sidewalk (area).** A paved path provided for pedestrian use and usually located at the side of a road within the right-of-way.

**Sight Triangle.** A triangular-shaped portion of land established at street intersections in which nothing is erected, placed, planted, or allowed to grow in such a manner as to limit or obstruct the sight distance of motorists entering or leaving the intersection.

**Site Plan.** An accurately scaled development plan that illustrates the existing conditions on a land parcel as well as depicting details of a proposed development.

**Site Plan, Major.** See Major Site Plan.

**Site Plan, Minor.** See Minor Site Plan.

**Sketch Plan.** A rough plan of a proposed subdivision or other development.

**Soil Cement.** A mixture of portland cement and locally available soil. It serves as a soil stabilizer.

**Stabilized Turf or Earth.** Turf, or earth (soil), strengthened usually by the mixing of cement or lime with the original material to achieve increased strength, thereby reducing shrinkage and movement.

**Storm Water Detention.** A provision for storage of storm water runoff and the controlled release of such runoff during and after a flood or storm.

**Storm Water Retention.** A provision for storage of storm water runoff.

**Street.** Any street, avenue, boulevard, road, parkway, viaduct, drive, or other roadway. See, also: Cul-de-Sac; Divided Street; Marginal Access Street; Residential Access Street; Residential Collector; Residential Subcollector; Stub Street.

**Street Furniture.** Man-made, aboveground items that are usually found in street rights-of-way, including benches, kiosks, plants, canopies, shelters, and phone booths.

**Street Hardware.** The mechanical and utility systems within a street right-of-way, such as hydrants, manhole covers, traffic lights and signs, utility poles and lines, and parking meters.

**Street Hierarchy.** The conceptual arrangement of streets based upon function. A hierarchical approach to street design classifies streets according to function, from high-traffic arterial roads down to streets whose function is residential access. Systematizing street design into a road hierarchy promotes safety, efficient land use, and residential quality.

**Street Loop.** A street that has its only ingress and egress at two points on the same subcollector or collector street.

**Stub Street.** A portion of a street for which an extension has been proposed and approved. May be permitted when development is phased over a period of time, but only if the street in its entirety has been approved in the preliminary plan.

**Subdivision.** The division of a lot tract or parcel of land into two or more lots, tracts, parcels or other divisions of land for sale or development. The following shall not be considered subdivision within the meaning of this ordinance if no new streets are created: (1) divisions of land found by the planning board or subdivision and site plan committee to be for agricultural purposes where all resulting parcels are [        ] acres or larger in size, (2) divisions of property by testamentary or intestate provisions, (3) divisions of property upon court order including but not limited to judgments of foreclosure, (4) consolidation of existing lots by deed or other recorded instrument, and (5) other activities as specified.

**Subdivision and Site Plan Committee.** A committee appointed by the chairperson of the planning board for the purpose of reviewing, commenting, and making recommendations with respect to subdivision and site plan applications and having the power to approve minor site plans and subdivisions.

**Subgrade.** The natural ground lying beneath a road.

**Topsoil.** The original upper layer of soil material to a depth of six inches which is usually darker and richer than the subsoil.

**Trip.** A single or one-way vehicle movement to or from a property or study area. "Trips" can be added together to calculate the total number of vehicles expected to enter and leave a specific land use or site over a designated period of time.

**ULI.** Urban Land Institute.

**USCGS.** (Also **USC&G** and **USC&GS**). United States Coast and Geodetic Survey.

**Variance.** A waiver from compliance with a specific provision of the zoning ordinance granted to a particular property owner because of the practical difficulties or unnecessary hardship that would be imposed by the strict application of that provision of the ordinance. The granting of variances traditionally is the responsibility of the zoning board of appeals.

**Wye.** A Y-branch or Y-fitting. In a plumbing system, a branch in the shape of the letter Y.

**Wye Connections.** A Y-fitting or connection. See Wye.

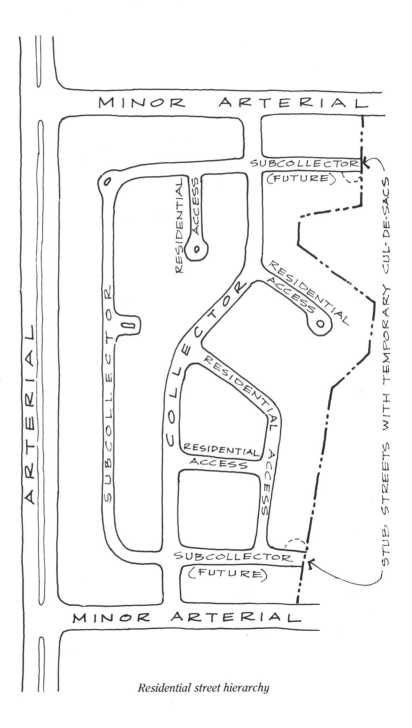

*Residential street hierarchy*

## Article Three
## Administration

### A. Planning Board and
####    Zoning Board of Adjustment

*1. A planning board is hereby established pursuant to [specify state or other applicable enabling legislation] and amendments thereto and Section [      ] of the Land Development Ordinance of [       ].*

*2. A zoning board of adjustment is hereby established pursuant to [specify state or other applicable enabling legislation] and amendments thereto and Section [      ] of the Land Development Ordinance of [      ].*

*3. The [mayor and governing body or other relevant entity] shall appoint an administrative officer whose tasks are specified herein. In addition, the administrative officer shall be given the responsibility for ensuring orderly and expeditious processing of subdivision and site plan applications.*

### B. Jurisdiction

*Pursuant to [specify state or other applicable land use regulation], approval of subdivision plats by resolution of the planning board is hereby required as a condition for the filing of such plats with [specify agency], and approval of site plans by resolution of the planning board is hereby required as a condition for the issuance of a permit for any development [specify any exemptions], except that subdivision or individual lot applications for detached one- or two-dwelling-unit buildings shall be exempt from such site plan review and approval. The resolution of the board of adjustment shall substitute for that of the planning board whenever the board of adjustment has jurisdiction over a subdivision or site plan pur-*

# Article Three
# Administration

## A.  Planning Board
##     and Zoning Board of Adjustment

1. and 2. One of the difficulties in formulating a model ordinance concerns the variation in the specific public entities charged with administering land use regulations in different states and attendant varying administrative procedures. The governing statutes in each state should therefore be carefully checked; what is presented here is an outline.

It should further be noted that the provisions in the model ordinance concerning the establishment of the planning board and zoning board of adjustment and the procedures that the boards should follow would typically be found in the administration and procedure sections of the overall land use development ordinance which includes both zoning and subdivision regulations. The administration and procedure provisions in the model ordinance are therefore abbreviated.

3. The designated officer is given the responsibility for the practical tasks of administration and is also charged with facilitating the administrative flow. All too often development costs escalate because of delays. See Reference section.

## B.  Jurisdiction

In the spirit of reducing unnecessary administrative responsibilities by the planning board and the zoning board of adjustment, provision is made for exempting certain types of development from site plan review where such action is deemed unnecessary. Such exemptions may be stipulated in the state or other applicable land use regulations. Similarly, to avoid duplicative review, provision is made for the planning board and zoning board of adjustment to act independently as opposed to requiring sequential action by both boards.

These provisions reduce submission review expenses by the applicant—savings which ideally translate into a better development.

## C. Waiver and Exception

The waiver and exception provisions are added to avoid unnecessary review by the planning board and zoning board of adjustment and unnecessary expense by the developer.

1. It is difficult to specify the exact conditions under which a waiver should be granted. The model ordinance outlines the parameters which should be considered; the planning board and zoning board of adjustment have the authority to decide on a case-by-case basis when a site plan application should be waived.

2. Not all requirements for subdivision and site plan approval are necessary in all cases. For example, the documents to be submitted, shown in Article Seven, are recommended for general applications. The specific submissions that are appropriate for each application should be decided on a case-by-case basis. (See also commentary for Article Four, Section C.2, below.)

suant to [specify state or other applicable land use regulation]. Where the board of adjustment has such jurisdiction, references in this ordinance to the planning board refer as well to the board of adjustment.

### C. Waiver and Exception

1. WAIVER OF SITE PLAN APPLICATION

A planning board may waive the requirement for site plan approval where there is a change in use or occupancy and no extensive construction or improvements (or de minimis construction or improvements) is sought. The waiver may be granted only upon a resolution by the planning board finding that the use will not affect existing drainage, circulation, relationship of buildings to each other, landscaping, buffering, lighting, and other considerations of site plan approval, and that the existing facilities do not require upgraded or additional site improvements. The application for a waiver of site plan shall include a discussion of the prior use of the site, the proposed use, and its impact.

2. EXCEPTION OF SPECIFIC SUBDIVISION AND SITE PLAN REQUIREMENTS

The planning board, when acting upon applications for preliminary or minor subdivision approval, shall have the power to grant such exceptions from the requirements for subdivision approval as may be reasonable and within the general purpose and intent of the provisions for subdivision review and approval of this ordinance, if the literal enforcement of one or more provisions of the ordinance is impracticable or will exact undue hardship because of peculiar conditions pertaining to the land in question.

The planning board, when acting upon applications for preliminary or minor site plan approval, shall have the *power to grant such exceptions from the requirements for site plan approval as may be reasonable and within the general purpose and intent of the provisions for site plan review and approval of this ordinance, if the literal enforcement of one or more provisions of the ordinance is impracticable or will exact undue hardship because of peculiar conditions pertaining to the land in question.*

### D. Subdivision and Site Plan Committee

*The chairperson of the planning board may appoint a subdivision and site plan committee. The subdivision and site plan committee shall consist of at least [          ] board members along with technical and other staff members such as the planner and/or engineer as deemed appropriate. The purpose of the subdivision and site plan committee is to review, comment, and make recommendations with respect to subdivision and site plan applications, and to perform other duties conferred on this committee by the board through a motion duly adopted and recorded.*

## D.  Subdivision and Site Plan Committee

The establishment of a committee by the full board is a further mechanism to facilitate the board's efficient operation. Some of the tasks which can be performed by a committee are specified in Article Four of the model ordinance.

# Article Four
# Procedure

## A. Purpose

As was noted with respect to administration, the governing statutes in each state should be checked with respect to the specific procedures to be followed.

What is universal, however, is the need for expeditious review of subdivision and site plan applications. Delay is costly to the developer and the host community.

## B. Pre-Application

The objective of both a pre-application conference and concept plan presentation is to foster informal plan review between the applicant and the municipality (or other review jurisdiction). A pre-application conference is envisioned as a forum for the technical staffs of both the developer and municipality to meet informally; the concept plan presentation is a forum for an informal presentation to the planning board.

The model ordinance makes both the pre-application conference and concept plan optional on the part of the applicant. A concept plan may not be appropriate for routine or minor applications, but an informal meeting in the form of a pre-application conference is generally encouraged.

The conduct of a pre-application conference and a concept plan presentation should reflect their purpose—informal review and exchange. Requiring a formal and detailed format would defeat the intended function and add to the length and expense of the review process. No one is served by repeated, nearly identical presentations of pre-application, concept plan, preliminary approval, and final approval.

*1. PRE-APPLICATION CONFERENCE*

a. and b. The informal presentation provides an invaluable forum for eliciting reactions from the jurisdiction's planner, engineer, and other professionals.

*Article Four*
*Procedure*

*A. Purpose*

*The purpose of this article is to establish the procedure for planning board review and action on applications for subdivisions and/or site plans. The procedure is intended to provide orderly and expeditious processing of such applications.*

*B. Pre-Application*

*For the purpose of expediting applications and reducing subdivision and site plan design and development costs, the developer may request a pre-application conference and/or concept plan in accordance with the following requirements:*

1. PRE-APPLICATION CONFERENCE

*a. At the request of the applicant, the planning board shall authorize a pre-application conference.*

*b. The pre-application conference shall allow the applicant to meet with appropriate [municipal/county/other] representatives. These individuals, who shall be designated by the [mayor and governing body/the planning board/other] may include:*

*1) [municipal/county] engineer;*

*2) [municipal/county] planner;*

*3) [municipal/county] construction officer and zoning officer;*

*4) representative(s) from the planning board and the board of adjustment;*

*5) representative(s) from environmental, historic preservation, and other commissions, as deemed appropriate;*

*6) subdivision and site plan committee or representative(s) if this committee is established;*

*7) any other representative(s) invited by the planning board chairperson.*

*c. Applicants seeking a pre-application conference shall submit the information stipulated in Article Seven of this ordinance [10] days prior to the pre-application conference.*

*d. If requested and paid for by the applicant, a brief written summary of the pre-application conference shall be provided within [10] working days of the final meeting.*

*e. The applicant may be charged reasonable fees for a pre-application conference.*

*f. The applicant shall not be bound by the determination of the pre-application conference, nor shall the planning board or subdivision and site plan committee be bound by any such review.*

2. CONCEPT PLAN

*a. In addition or as an alternative to the pre-application conference, at the request of the applicant, the planning board or the subdivision and site plan committee shall grant an informal review of a concept plan for a development for which the applicant intends to prepare and submit an application for development.*

*The purpose of the concept plan is to provide planning board or subdivision and site plan committee input in the formative stages of subdivision and site plan design.*

*b. Applicants seeking concept plan informal review shall submit the items stipulated in Article Seven of this ordinance [10] days before the concept plan meeting. These items provide the subdivider and planning board or subdivision and site plan committee with an opportunity to discuss the development proposal in its formative stages.*

*c. If requested and paid for by the applicant, a brief written summary of the concept plan review shall be provided*

c. The purpose of the meeting is defeated if the technical staff does not have the preliminary plat and other conceptual plans far enough in advance to study them.

d. A written summary is useful for clarifying the results of the discussion.

e. As with other charges, in establishing fees for a pre-application conference, state statutes possibly governing the levying of such fees and their amount should be checked. Fees must be reasonable, however. While a public body understandably wishes to recover the costs incurred for its technical staff participation, the levying of too high a charge will discourage developers from participating in the pre-application conference and concept plan presentation.

f. This underscores the function of the pre-application conference and concept plan presentation—informal review rather than final decision-making and the conferring of rights.

2. *CONCEPT PLAN*
   See Pre-Application Conference section.

## C. Application

### 1. ASSIGNMENT

However clearly statutes are written, it is not uncommon for uncertainty to arise concerning the proper board to be approached and the appropriate procedure to follow. This is an issue which can be discussed at the pre-application conference. To provide further clarification, the model ordinance allows for assistance on this matter by the administrative officer.

### 2. CONTENT

The checklist in Article Seven is for general application; the list of documents to be submitted should be reviewed on a case-by-case basis to determine which submissions are appropriate. Article Seven allows for such flexibility. It provides that "in specific cases and for documented reasons, the approving authority may waive the submission of a particular document."

### 3. COMPLETE APPLICATION

As with other provisions concerning procedure, governing state statutes should be checked. Where state law does not specify whether the planning board or administrative officer determines completeness, then the choice should be made on the basis of local conditions. Is the board "detail oriented," in which case it should be assigned responsibility? On the other hand, where the board is facing a heavy volume of applications, then the determination of completeness should perhaps best be left to the administrative officer.

On another note, the indicated time periods for completion are designed to foster movement in the administrative flow; an applicant should be able to obtain a response within a reasonable period of time. Yet, time limits should be adequate for proper consideration by the municipal planning, engineering, and other review staff.

It is also important that the institution of time limits not be thwarted by applicants being asked, as a matter of course, to waive this right. The length of the time periods should be workable and adhered to.

*within [10] working days of the final meeting.*

*d. The applicant may be charged reasonable fees for concept plan review.*

*e. The applicant shall not be bound by any concept plan for which review is requested, nor shall the planning board or subdivision and site plan committee be bound by any such review.*

### C. Application

1. ASSIGNMENT

*The applicant shall have the option of seeking the direction of the administrative officer as to which approvals are required and the appropriate board for hearing same, or of filing an application and proceeding before the board which the applicant believes to be appropriate. The administrative official's determination shall be presumed to be correct. The following applications may be filed:*

*a) exempt subdivision*
*b) minor subdivision*
*c) major subdivision*
*d) minor site plan*
*e) major site plan*

*(Note: Certain applications may involve a combination of actions.)*

2. CONTENT

*An application for development shall include the items specified in Article Seven of this ordinance which constitutes a checklist of items to be submitted for subdivision and site plan review.*

3. COMPLETE APPLICATION

*A subdivision and site plan application shall be complete for purposes of commencing the applicable time period for action when so certified by the [administrative officer/planning board]. In the event such certification of the application is not made within [45] days of the date of its submission, the application shall be deemed complete upon the expiration of the [45]-day period for purposes of commencing the applicable time period unless (1) the application lacks information indicated on the checklist of items to be submitted specified in Article Seven and provided in writing to the applicant, and (2) the [administrative officer/planning board] has notified the applicant, in writing, of the deficiencies in the application within [45] days of submission of the application. The planning board may subsequently require correction of any information found to be in error and submission of additional information not specified in the ordinance, as is reasonably necessary to make an informed decision. The application shall not be deemed incomplete for lack of any such additional information or any revisions in the accompanying documents so required by the planning board.*

### D. Minor Subdivision and Minor Site Plan Procedure

*1. Any applicant requesting approval of a proposed minor subdivision or minor site plan as defined in this ordinance shall submit to the administrative officer [          ] copies of the items required in Article Seven of this ordinance, together with an executed application form, the prescribed fee, and evidence that no taxes or assessments are outstanding against the property.*

*2. The application shall be declared complete or incomplete within a [45]-day period from the date of its submission according to the provisions of Article Four, Section C.3, of this ordinance.*

*3. If the subdivision or site plan is unanimously approved with at least [ ] members of the subdivision and site plan committee present and voting (only those who are members or alternates of the board having jurisdiction to act, may vote), no further action shall be required*

## D. Minor Subdivision and Minor Site Plan Procedure

1. The model ordinance does not define what is a "minor" versus a "major" application. The distinction may be stipulated in the state statute. Where it is not, then a local definition, sensitive to local conditions, should rule. What is a significant development in a small community will often be viewed as minor in a larger jurisdiction.

2. The concept of time limits, incorporated with respect to the completeness of an application, is found here as well concerning the action on the application.

3. and 4. These provisions incorporate a middle ground with respect to the powers of the subdivision and site plan committee versus those of the full planning board. If the former unanimously approves a minor application, then it is sensible to defer to the committee and let its approval stand. Where the committee itself disagrees, then the matter should be referred to the board. Again, as with other procedural provisions, possible state statutory stipulations should be checked.

5. The specific endorsements, plat details, and related requirements will often be indicated in state statute.

6. On the one hand, an applicant should be able to expect that the conditions of approval will continue to prevail for a reasonable period of time. On the other hand, the municipality or county should not be locked into an agreement for an indefinite period of time, as conditions and the sense of development direction change over time. The provisions in the model ordinance attempt to balance these two concerns.

of the planning board as a whole. If the vote is not unanimous, or if such committee has not been established, the minor subdivision or site plan shall be referred to the planning board. If a variance within the jurisdiction of the planning board is requested, the subdivision or site plan shall not be referred to the committee but instead to the planning board as a whole.

4. The action of the subdivision and site plan committee or the planning board under this article must be taken within [45] days, or [90] days if a variance is involved, of a complete application as defined in Article Four, Section C.3, of this ordinance or within such further time as is agreed to by the subdivider and the board. Failure of the planning board or committee to act within the period prescribed shall constitute minor subdivision or site plan approval and a certificate of the administrative officer as to the failure of the planning board or committee to act shall be issued on request of the applicant.

5. Approval of a minor subdivision shall expire [90] days from the date of approval unless within such period a plat in conformity with such approval and the provisions of [map filing law/other regulations] or a deed clearly describing the approved minor subdivision is filed by the developer with [specify agency/individuals]. Any such plat or deed accepted for such filing shall have been signed by the chairperson and secretary of the planning board. The planning board may for good cause shown, extend the period for recording for an additional period not to exceed [       ] days from the date of signing of the plat.

6. The zoning requirements and general terms and conditions, whether conditional or otherwise, upon which minor subdivision and site plan approval

*was granted, shall not be changed for a period of [two years] after the date of minor subdivision and site plan approval.*

**E. Major Subdivision and Major Site Plan Procedure**

1. GENERAL DEVELOPMENT PLAN

*a. Applicants of planned-unit developments, major site plans, or major subdivisions of at least [      ] acres·containing a minimum of [      ] dwelling units, or [      ] square feet of nonresidential building area, shall have the option of bifurcating preliminary approval into two phases: Phase One—General Development Plan, and Phase Two—Preliminary Approval.*

*b. An applicant requesting General Development Plan approval shall first submit to the administrative officer of the planning board [      ] copies of the materials stipulated in Article Seven of this ordinance.*

*c. The application shall be declared complete within a [45]-day period from date of its submission according to the provisions of Article Four, Section C.3, of this ordinance.*

*d. The planning board shall, within [90] days or within such further time as may be consented to by the applicant, either grant approval of the General Development Plan as submitted or with changes and/or conditions, or deny approval.*

*e. Phase One—General Development Plan, shall confer upon the applicant the following rights for a period of at least [      ] years, or for a longer period if determined by the planning board:*

*1) The total number of residential dwelling units, and the general type (single-family detached residences, townhouses, garden apartments, etc.).*

# E. Major Subdivision and Major Site Plan Procedure

## 1. GENERAL DEVELOPMENT PLAN

The General Development Plan (GDP) is a mechanism designed to permit the developer of a large-scale project to go before the planning board with a description, but not full engineering details of the project, and secure formal approval of basic development parameters such as the total number of residential units and nonresidential square footage. Once having secured such approval, the developer proceeds with full engineering plans to be considered at the preliminary subdivision and site plan review stages.

The GDP offers economies to the developer. It is a wasteful outlay to prepare full engineering details on a major project before basic project parameters are settled upon. There is also a benefit to the host jurisdiction: the GDP permits review of project fundamentals which are sometimes lost in the details of the project engineering and planning which accompany preliminary major subdivision and site plan review.

a. As with the case of the definition of a major versus minor application, the local jursidiction is called upon to define the threshold conditions appropriate for a GDP submission.

b. A balance is especially critical with respect to the GDP submission items; the project should be adequately described, yet excessive detail is to be avoided.

c. A period of five to ten years is recommended depending on the size and nature of the major project. Unlike the pre-application conference and concept plan presentation, the GDP process confers a vested right: the planning board is empowered to approve the project's size and composition. It also can indicate its preference for major project siting elements—the location of collector roads and the location and density of the different land uses—although this is not a vested right.

## 2. PRELIMINARY APPROVAL OF MAJOR
##    SUBDIVISION AND SITE PLANS

a. and c. While the subdivision and site plan committee cannot act on major applications, it can serve an invaluable role by reviewing, commenting on, and making recommendations on applications.

b. and d. Any time period is difficult to specify (i.e., 30 versus 45 days) and, moreover, may be already governed by state law. Where local specification of time limits is permitted, the time period should be formulated on the basis of functional considerations. For instance, the model ordinance provides for a longer review period for larger subdivision and site plans. Similarly, where a variance is involved, and additional deliberation is necessary, then the nominal time span for official response is extended.

*2) The amount and type of non-residential gross floor area, i.e., commercial, office, institutional, industrial.*

*The planning board shall indicate the following which shall not vest, but still be presumed to be valid at Phase Two—Preliminary Approval, subject to engineering and environmental considerations:*

*1) The location of the collector roads.*

*2) The general location of the different uses and density by land-use area.*

2. PRELIMINARY APPROVAL OF MAJOR
   SUBDIVISION AND SITE PLANS

*a. Following approval of the General Development Plan (or if the applicant does not choose to seek General Development Plan approval), the applicant seeking preliminary major subdivision or preliminary major site plan approval shall submit to the administrative officer of the planning board [ ] copies of the materials stipulated in Article Seven of this ordinance.*

*b. The application shall be declared complete within a [45]-day period from the date of its submission according to the provisions of Article Four, Section C.3, of this ordinance.*

*c. The subdivision and site plan committee, if established, shall review the application and shall comment and make recommendations to the planning board.*

*d. A complete application for a major subdivision or site plan of fewer than [          lots/acres/units] shall be acted upon within [45] days of the date of such submission, or [90] days if a variance is required, or within such further time as may be consented to by the developer. A major subdivision or site plan of more than [          lots/acres/ units] shall be acted upon within [90] days of the date of such submission, or [120] days if a variance is required, or within such further time as may be consented to by the developer. Otherwise, the planning board shall be deemed to have granted preliminary subdivision or site plan approval.*

3. EFFECT OF PRELIMINARY APPROVAL
   OF MAJOR SUBDIVISIONS AND SITE
   PLANS

*Preliminary approval of a major subdivision and site plan shall confer upon the applicant the following rights for a [3]-year period from the date of the preliminary approval:*

*a. That the general terms and conditions on which preliminary approval was granted shall not be changed.*

*b. That the applicant may submit for final approval on or before the expiration date of preliminary approval the whole, or a section, or sections of the preliminary subdivision plat or site plan, as the case may be; and*

*c. That the applicant may apply for and the planning board may grant extension on such preliminary approval for additional periods of at least [1] year but not to exceed a total extension of [2] years.*

*d. In the case of a subdivision or site plan of more than [          lots/acres/ units], the planning board may grant the rights referred to in Subsections a., b., and c. above for such period of time longer than [3] years as shall be determined by the planning board to be reasonable.*

4. FINAL APPROVAL OF MAJOR
   SUBDIVISIONS AND SITE PLANS

*a. An applicant requesting final approval of a proposed major subdivision and site plan shall submit to the administrative officer of the planning board, or other designee, [          ] copies of the*

## 3. EFFECT OF PRELIMINARY APPROVAL OF MAJOR SUBDIVISIONS AND SITE PLANS

a. Given the more significant nature of a major versus minor application, a slightly longer protective time period—three versus two years—is conferred.

b. Not uncommonly, a major approved application will be developed in stages.

c. and d. Again, these provisions attempt to strike a balance between the need of an applicant for time extensions because of market, financing, and other factors and the right of a community not to be locked into approvals which have not been acted upon for a long period of time.

## 4. FINAL APPROVAL OF MAJOR SUBDIVISIONS AND SITE PLANS

a. and b. The transition from preliminary to final approval consists mainly of the submission of technical as-built plans, ensuring that infrastructure improvements have been provided or guaranteed, etc. Given the routine nature of the tasks at this stage, the administrative officer can monitor compliance and give approval—where allowed by state law.

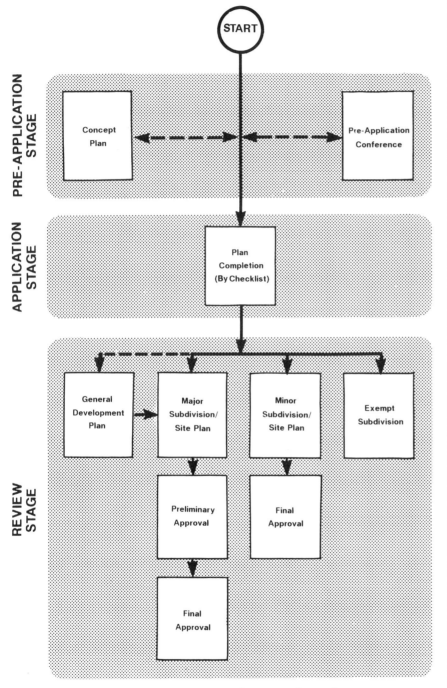

*Subdivision and site plan approval procedure*

materials specified in Article Seven of this ordinance. The final plat shall be accompanied by a statement from the [municipal/county] engineer that the [municipality/county] is in receipt of as-built plans showing all streets and utilities in exact location and elevation and identifying those portions already installed and those to be installed, and/or certified in the amount of performance guarantees required to assure completion of those improvements not yet installed as stipulated in Article Five of this ordinance.

b. The application for final subdivision or site plan approval shall be declared complete within a [45]-day period from the date of its submission according to the provisions of Article Four, Section C.3, of this ordinance.

c. Final approval shall be granted or denied within [45] days after submission of a complete application to the administrative officer, or other designee, or within such further time as may be consented to by the applicant. Failure of the [administrative officer/planning board] to act within the period prescribed shall constitute final approval, and a certificate of the administrative officer as to the failure of the planning board to act shall be issued on request of the applicant.

d. Final approval of a major subdivision shall expire [90] days from the date of the signing of the plat by the chairman and secretary of the planning board unless within such period the plat shall have been duly filed by the developer with the [specify agency/individual]. The planning board may for good cause shown, extend the period for recording for an additional period not to exceed [          ] days from the date of signing of the plat.

e. No subdivision plat shall be accepted for filing by the [specify agency/individual] until it has been approved by the planning board as indicated on the instrument by the signature of the chairperson and secretary of the planning board or a certificate has been issued. The signatures of the chairperson and secretary of the planning board shall not be affixed until the developer has posted the guarantees required pursuant to Article Five of this ordinance.

5. EFFECT OF FINAL APPROVAL OF MAJOR SUBDIVISIONS AND SITE PLANS

*a. The zoning requirements applicable to the preliminary approval granted and all other rights conferred upon the developer pursuant to preliminary approval whether conditionally or otherwise shall not be changed for a period of [three] years after the date of final approval.*

*b. If the developer has followed the standards prescribed for final approval and in the case of a subdivision has duly recorded the plat, the planning board may extend such period of protection for extensions of [one] year, but not to exceed [three] extensions.*

*c. In the case of a subdivision or site plan of more than [ lots/acres/ units], the planning board may grant the rights referred to in Subsections a. and b. above for such period of time, longer than [3] years, as shall be determined by the planning board to be reasonable.*

5. *EFFECT OF FINAL APPROVAL OF MAJOR SUBDIVISIONS AND SITE PLANS*

See comments with respect to the "Effects of Final Approval," Article Four, Section D and Article Four, Section E.3, for minor and preliminary major applications.

# Article Five
# Design and Improvement Standards

Article Five consists of standards to regulate subdivision design and improvements. Overall, these standards deal with the arrangement and engineering of site details, such as buildings, roads, utilities, and plantings, with design standards specifying how to approach planning and laying out a development, and improvement standards specifying the standards a development must meet or the methods of construction that must be adhered to. A design standard, for example, might require that roads be fitted into the natural contours of the site; an improvement standard, by contrast, would specify maximum and minimum road grade. Both types of standards, however, share the same objective: the flexible regulation of development, with standards based on function and responsive to the unique character of the specific development site and to local needs and objectives.

## A.  Purpose

The stated purpose of the design and improvement standards reflects the tension that exists in drafting equitable standards: striking a balance between requirements that are excessive and those that are inadequate. The former add unnecessary costs to development, but the latter may threaten public safety and welfare. The intent in applying the standards is to promote quality development. They are not to be used to exclude housing for persons with low and moderate incomes.

## B.  Site Design Standards

Site design standards consist of the steps that should be followed in designing developments. They are meant to be used both by developers in preparing subdivision and site plans and by planning boards in reviewing and evaluating developments. The objective is to design the proposed project in light of data collected about the site and the surrounding area. The physical characteristics of the site, adjacent land character and patterns, unique visual qualities, street patterns, and the scale and design of nearby buildings are all taken into consideration. The larger the site, the greater the role played by the natural features and development

## Article Five
## Design and Improvement Standards

### A. Purpose

*The purpose of good subdivision and site design is to create a functional and attractive development, to minimize adverse impacts, and to ensure a project will be an asset to a community. To promote this purpose, the subdivision and/or site plan shall conform to the following standards which are designed to result in a well-planned community without adding unnecessarily to development costs.*

### B. Site Design Standards

1. SITE ANALYSIS

*An analysis shall be made of characteristics of the development site, such as site context; geology and soil; topography; climate; ecology; existing vegetation, structures, and road networks; visual features; and past and present use of the site.*

2. SUBDIVISION AND SITE DESIGN

*a. Design of the development shall take into consideration all existing local and regional plans for the surrounding community.*

*b. Development of the site shall be based on the site analysis. To the maximum extent practicable, development shall be located to preserve the natural features of the site, to avoid areas of environmental sensitivity, and to minimize negative impacts and alteration of natural features.*

*c. The following specific areas shall be preserved as undeveloped open space, to the extent consistent with the reasonable utilization of land, and in accordance with applicable state or local regulations:*

*1) Unique and/or fragile areas, including wetlands as defined in Sec.*

*404, Federal Water Pollution Control Act Amendments of 1972, and delineated on wetlands maps prepared by the U.S. Fish and Wildlife Service, field verified by on-site inspection;*

*2) Significant trees or stands of trees, defined as the largest known individual trees of each species in the state, large trees approaching the diameter of the known largest tree, or species or clumps of trees that are rare to the area or of particular horticultural or landscape value;*

*3) Lands in the flood plain, as defined by state or local regulations;*

*4) Steep slopes in excess of 20 percent as measured over a 10-foot interval unless appropriate engineering measures concerning slope stability, erosion, and resident safety are taken;*

*5) Habitats of endangered wildlife, as identified on federal or state lists; and*

*6) Historically significant structures and sites, as listed on federal or state lists of historic places.*

*d. The development shall be laid out to avoid adversely affecting ground water and aquifer recharge; to reduce cut and fill; to avoid unnecessary impervious cover; to prevent flooding; to provide adequate access to lots and sites; and to mitigate adverse effects of shadow, noise, odor, traffic, drainage, and utilities on neighboring properties.*

suitability of the site itself; the smaller the site, the greater the importance of the pattern, character, and scale of existing adjacent development.

After data about the site are gathered, unique and fragile areas are protected by and woven into an open space system, and areas that are obviously suitable for building lots, such as level or slightly sloping land, are blocked out for buildings. Next, access points and circulation patterns are integrated with building locations. If a site has few development constraints, the site designer looks to the surrounding pattern of streets and the rhythm, scale, and intensity of adjacent buildings to help provide the geometry of the site design. These general steps to laying out a development are described in further detail below and in the Reference section.

## 1. SITE ANALYSIS

The first step in designing a development is to gather and evaluate information about the project site and its surrounding area. The checklist included in the Reference section provides a guide to the types of data that can be collected about a development site. Each site is, of course, unique, and the data collected will vary by site depending on the nature of the site itself, the purpose and design of the development, and available resources. Some information may be required for one site and not another; and no data should be collected unless it has a significant bearing on the design.

## 2. SUBDIVISION AND SITE DESIGN

The purpose of the subdivision and site design standards is to ensure that the design of new development will respect the site environment, give appropriate consideration to the scale and character of the existing neighborhood, and be an asset to the community.

a. A development's design should conform to relevant local and state plans, such as master plans, county transportation plans, and regional storm water management plans. To cite two elementary examples, widths of new roads should correspond to the widths of planned or existing roads, and drainage should tie into regional systems.

b. These restrictions guiding the design of a development are widely accepted and promoted in the planning literature. The language, "[t]o the maximum extent practicable," is intended to protect developers from unreasonable restrictions that might be imposed by a community wishing to stop development of any kind. The planning literature recommends that as a general rule, placement of lots, buildings, and roads should complement and preserve the natural and historical features of the site, such as existing stands of trees, scenic views, and bodies of water. Land unsuitable for development and of a fragile environmental nature should be protected—a restriction that can be justified on the grounds of protecting the health, safety, and welfare of the public. In view of the 1987 Supreme Court *First Evangelical Lutheran Church v. County of Los Angeles* decision on takings, however, restrictions for environmental reasons must be carefully determined (see Reference section for further discussion of this case and its implications). Open space and scenic areas can be planned for portions of the site unsuitable for development, yet usable for recreational purposes. Cluster development is recommended: instead of spreading development over environmentally sensitive lands, at similar gross densities cluster development offers the opportunity to preserve special site characteristics.

c. This section attempts to define as precisely as possible the areas that should be preserved and where development should be avoided. Precise definition is important: the delineation between developable and undevelopable areas must be clear, consistent, and based on sound—not capricious—reasons in order to avoid legal challenges and so that all parties understand exactly where development is proscribed.

1) Developers generally prefer the delineation of wetlands as defined by the Federal Water Pollution Control Act Amendments of 1972, whereas environmentalists prefer the more liberal inclusion of lands shown on maps prepared by the Fish and Wildlife Service. The model ordinance includes both as parameters to be verified by an inspection of the site itself. Some states may regulate development in wetlands, and these state regulations should, of course, be complied with.

2) Defining "significant stands of trees" so that on the one hand, the definition won't be overly burdensome to builders and

3. RESIDENTIAL DEVELOPMENT DESIGN

*a. In conventional developments, the planning board may vary lot areas and dimensions, yards, and setbacks for the purpose of encouraging and promoting flexibility, economy, and environmental soundness in layout and design, provided that the average lots' areas and dimensions, yards, and setbacks within the subdivision conform to the minimum requirements of the municipal development regulations, and provided that such standards shall be appropriate to the type of development permitted.*

*b. Residential lots shall front on residential access or subcollector streets, not on collector streets.*

*c. Every lot shall have sufficient access to it for emergency vehicles as well as for those needing access to the property in its intended use.*

*d. The placement of units in residential developments shall take into consideration topography, privacy, building height, orientation, drainage, and aesthetics.*

*e. Buildings shall be spaced so that adequate privacy is provided for units.*

excessively restrict development, yet on the other hand, will protect recognizable community assets, is particularly difficult. Many states maintain lists of the largest known individual trees of each species; the public has an interest in preserving these trees and ones that approach them in size. However, it should also be pointed out that diseased and dying trees should not be saved, even if they are approaching the size of the largest trees. The wording of the provision to save rare, horticulturally significant trees, and trees with particular landscape value, is intended to introduce flexibility in the negotiating process between municipality and developer—allowing a community to work with a developer in saving trees that may not be the largest of their species, but are still an asset to a community.

3) Municipalities adopting this ordinance should define "flood plain" according to local and state regulations.

4) The figure 20 percent is a compromise between the more restrictive 10- to 15-percent slope usually favored by engineers, and the reality that steeper slopes are being, and have been, developed without endangering the public safety. In fact, as long as proper engineering measures are taken, building on steeper slopes is permissible.

5) Federal and state governments maintain lists and regulate the protection of endangered species. Many states also keep records of where their habitats may be found.

6) Both the federal government and the states maintain registers of historic places. Some communities may wish to protect especially significant local structures and sites as well.

d. These provisions are minimum considerations in laying out a development to protect the public.

*3. RESIDENTIAL DEVELOPMENT DESIGN*

Standards for the design of residential projects build on the general subdivision and site design standards, but include provisions that apply specifically to residential development.

a. This provision permits some of the flexibility in laying out conventional subdivisions that is available in cluster and planned-unit developments.

b. Residential lots should front on lower order streets because they have less traffic and are safer and quieter.

c.–e. Refer to the Reference section for recommended guidelines on the spacing of residential buildings.

## 4. COMMERCIAL AND INDUSTRIAL DEVELOPMENT DESIGN

The principles for good design are standard and cover commercial and industrial developments as well as residential developments. In addition, the special requirements of commercial and industrial developments should be taken into consideration when planning and laying out such developments. For example, the size and configuration of lots and blocks should be adequate to provide for off-street parking and loading facilities for large vehicles.

## 5. CIRCULATION SYSTEM DESIGN

a. and b. The importance of a development's circulation system can hardly be overemphasized. It is a key factor in the safety, social workings, and visual impact of a development. In residential developments, as traffic and speeds increase, the road becomes a barrier, safety becomes a problem, and the sense of neighborhood is lost. The pattern of streets or paths can provide or destroy a sense of coherence in the neighborhood. In addition, views along the road help give a development its identity and the designer an opportunity to highlight special features of the site. The circulation system design standards presented in the model ordinance are intended to promote safety, flexibility, and design based on function.

c. In planned developments, experience has shown that walks are needed at the point of street access to the housing units: this point is used as the principal foot access to the units, as the close-to-home play area for children, and as a social focus. It should, therefore, be linked with the main walkway system of the development.

d. Bikeways add to development costs and should be required only as part of an overall system.

## 6. LANDSCAPE DESIGN

Landscaping is extremely important for ensuring the quality of a development. Trees, shrubs, and other plantings add greatly to the aesthetic appeal of a community. Landscaping, however,

### 4. COMMERCIAL AND INDUSTRIAL DEVELOPMENT DESIGN

*Commercial and industrial developments shall be designed according to the same principles governing the design of residential developments; namely, buildings shall be located according to topography, with environmentally sensitive areas avoided to the maximum extent practicable; factors such as drainage, noise, odor, and surrounding land uses considered in siting buildings; sufficient access shall be provided; and adverse impacts buffered.*

### 5. CIRCULATION SYSTEM DESIGN

*a. The road system shall be designed to permit the safe, efficient, and orderly movement of traffic; to meet, but not exceed the needs of the present and future population served; to have a simple and logical pattern; to respect natural features and topography; and to present an attractive streetscape.*

*b. In residential subdivisions, the road system shall be designed to serve the needs of the neighborhood and to discourage use by through traffic.*

*c. The pedestrian system shall be located as required for safety. In conventional developments, walks shall be placed parallel to the street, with exceptions permitted to preserve natural features or to provide visual interest. In planned developments, walks may be placed away from the road system, but they may also be required parallel to the street for safety reasons.*

*d. Bikeways shall be required only if specifically indicated in the master plan.*

### 6. LANDSCAPE DESIGN

*a. Reasonable landscaping should be provided at site entrances, in public areas, and adjacent to buildings. The type and amount of landscaping required shall be allowed to vary with type of development.*

*b. The plant or other landscaping material that best serves the intended function shall be selected. Landscaping materials shall be appropriate for the local environment, soil conditions, and availability of water. The impact of the proposed landscaping plan at various time intervals shall also be considered.*

### C. Open Space and Recreation

1. PURPOSE

*Planned-unit developments, planned-unit residential developments, and residential cluster developments shall be required to provide open space. Developed open space shall be designed to provide active recreational facilities to serve the residents of the development. Undeveloped open space shall be designed to preserve important site amenities and environmentally sensitive areas. (See Section B, Subsection 1.c, for areas to be preserved as undeveloped open space.)*

serves a number of functions besides aesthetic ones: it controls erosion, reduces glare, lowers temperature, buffers sounds, removes pollutants from the air, and blocks and diverts winds. Some landscaping requirements can be justified on these grounds. Furthermore, most state enabling acts give municipalities the authority to require plantings for buffering, or, at a minimum, shade trees. In general, however, landscaping is viewed as an aesthetic concern and the regulations are phrased accordingly.

a. "Reasonable" and "should" are key words in this provision. The amount and type of landscaping at site entrances, in public areas, and adjacent to buildings, unless required for buffering or some similar grounds, are usually matters for discussion and negotiation between the municipality and developer. No single landscaping plan can be prescribed for all developments—some sites already contain plantings, while others do not. Requirements should be flexible and plantings allowed to vary with each development.

b. Landscape design must also be sensitive to the characteristics and maintenance requirements of the plantings selected. Plants assume a variety of forms depending on their environment and age. Growth rate, eventual size, color, life span, scent, and seasonal effect must be taken into consideration in the design. Species must be chosen that are hardy for the climate and soil conditions, that can tolerate expected traffic, that are resistant to disease and insects, and whose maintenance needs can be met.

### C. Open Space and Recreation

In recent years there has been a shift in the responsibility for providing open space and recreation facilities. Traditionally, local government has been responsible for providing open space, usually in the form of public parks and playgrounds. However, rising costs, limited public resources, and strained facilities have increasingly compelled governments to turn over the task of providing outdoor recreation space to the private sector. Local ordinances now generally require builders of planned-unit developments to provide some kind of open space and/or recreational facilities.

This shift of responsibility in providing park space has coincided with the trend toward arranging residential subdivisions in clusters as an alternative to the conventional single-family housing layout on individual lots. The arrangement of buildings in closely related groups, or clusters, is based on the concept of concentrating development in physically suitable locations, thus freeing up open areas and preserving environmentally sensitive areas. The private developer can use the open space as part of an amenities package aimed at attracting buyers.

## 1.  PURPOSE

The model ordinance requires a developer to provide open space only for certain developments and to serve the residents of the development only. State and other prevailing statutes should be checked in this regard. Furthermore, where statutory authority exists, some municipalities may wish to require a developer to contribute in lieu fees to a recreational fund so that the municipality will have the resources to provide recreational facilities on a wider basis for multiple developments.

## 2.  MINIMUM REQUIREMENTS

a. Ordinances typically require that major developments provide a certain minimum percentage of total open space (either gross or net project area), with some also specifying the portion of total open space that should be provided as developed open space and the portion that should be provided as undeveloped open space. The approach taken in this model ordinance is to recognize that no matter what minimum percentage is specified, it will probably have to be adjusted on a case-by-case basis, depending on the factors listed in the ordinance, among others. For example, a development designed for senior citizens will have recreational needs very different from one designed for young singles or families. Similarly, the recreational facilities designed for a development on flat land would not necessarily be appropriate for a development built on hills. These and other numerous factors influencing decisions about the specific percentage of land that should be set aside are detailed in the Reference section.

An alternative approach for a municipality is to specify the minimum percentage of open space that is required, with the understanding that the amount may be adjusted depending on the specific site and development. For a developer, this approach has the advantage of at least having a ball park estimate of how much open space will be required. Minimum standards from various sources that can be used by municipalities as guidelines are

2. MINIMUM REQUIREMENTS

*a. Amount of open space required.*
[          ] *percent of the tract proposed for development shall be set aside for developed and undeveloped open space, adjusted, as appropriate, for conditions such as population density, existing municipal facilities, topography, socio-economic characteristics of the prospective population, and other appropriate site- and development-specific factors.*

*b. Size of open space parcels. The area of each parcel of open space designed for active recreational purposes shall be of such minimum dimensions as to be functionally usable.*

*c. Location of open space parcels. Open space parcels shall be convenient to the dwelling units they are intended to serve. However, because of noise generation, they shall be sited with sensitivity to surrounding development.*

3. IMPROVEMENT OF OPEN SPACE
   PARCELS

*a. **Developed open space.** The planning board or other approving authority may require the installation of recreational facilities, taking into consideration:*

*1) The character of the open space land;*

*2) The estimated age and the recreation needs of persons likely to reside in the development;*

*3) Proximity, nature, and excess capacity of existing municipal recreation facilities; and*

*4) The cost of the recreational facilities.*

*b. **Undeveloped open space.** As a general principle, undeveloped open space should be left in its natural state. A developer may make certain improvements such as the cutting of trails for walking or jogging, or the provision of picnic areas, etc. In addition, the planning board may require a developer to make other improvements, such as removing dead or diseased trees, thinning trees or other vegetation to encourage more desirable growth, and grading and seeding.*

4. EXCEPTIONS TO THE STANDARDS

*The planning board may permit minor deviations from open space standards when it can be determined that: a) the objectives underlying these standards can be met without strict adherence to them; and/or b) because of peculiarities in the tract of land or the facilities proposed, it would be unreasonable to require strict adherence to these standards.*

5. DEED RESTRICTIONS

*Any lands dedicated for open space purposes shall contain appropriate covenants and deed restrictions approved*

presented in the Reference section, but these should be adapted to fit local needs.

b. Some reference to the dimensions of the open space is generally included in ordinances in order to ensure the open space is functional and to protect the community from the dedication of numerous non-functional small parcels of land. The model ordinance uses a performance standard to guide size requirements, but specific sizes can be included. Municipalities can refer to the Reference section for dimensions suggested by some sources.

c. Open space should be distributed equitably throughout a development so that it is easily accessible. Linking open space parcels also enlarges the area available for recreation.

3.  IMPROVEMENT OF OPEN SPACE PARCELS

To ensure that the open space will be usable and have value as an amenity, most ordinances include some level of site-preparation requirements. Typically, the improvements are ones that would be undertaken by the developer in any case, since it is in the interests of the developer to provide the recreational amenities that will appeal to the target market. For example, a builder of homes targeted to young families would want to include tot lots or playgrounds; those targeted to senior citizens might offer golf courses, shuffleboard courts, or walking trails.

4.  EXCEPTIONS TO THE STANDARDS

The model ordinance recognizes that in some cases the objectives underlying the open space standards can be met without strict adherence to them, or a particular parcel of land may be so unusual that application of the open space standards becomes unreasonable. The planning board is therefore given the authority to permit minor deviations from the open space standards.

5.  DEED RESTRICTIONS

This provision is intended to ensure that the open space will always be available for the use and enjoyment of the population it is intended to serve.

## 6. OPEN SPACE OWNERSHIP

In order to assign responsibility for a development's open space, it is important to clarify its ownership at the outset. The model ordinance lists five alternative arrangements for the ownership of commonly owned open spaces, but the current trend has been away from municipal ownership towards a privatization of common open space. Usually the developer is responsible for deciding on the type of ownership. The developer is also responsible for setting up the homeowners organization or corporation—the preferred technique for managing commonly owned property. Nevertheless, to ensure the continuing maintenance of the open space, the type of ownership and the formation of the homeowners association should be subject to the approval of the municipality.

## 7. HOMEOWNERS ASSOCIATION

These provisions are designed to ensure that a viable association is established with authority to obtain sufficient resources to maintain the open space and any of its recreational facilities.

*by the municipal attorney ensuring that:*

*a. The open space area will not be further subdivided in the future;*

*b. The use of the open space will continue in perpetuity for the purpose specified;*

*c. Appropriate provisions will be made for the maintenance of the open space; and*

*d. Common undeveloped open space shall not be turned into a commercial enterprise admitting the general public at a fee.*

## 6. OPEN SPACE OWNERSHIP

*The type of ownership of land dedicated for open space purposes shall be selected by the owner, developer, or subdivider, subject to the approval of the planning board. Type of ownership may include, but is not necessarily limited to, the following:*

*a. The municipality, subject to acceptance by the governing body of the municipality;*

*b. Other public jurisdictions or agencies, subject to their acceptance;*

*c. Quasi-public organizations, subject to their acceptance;*

*d. Homeowner, condominium, or cooperative associations or organizations; or*

*e. Shared, undivided interest by all property owners in the subdivision.*

## 7. HOMEOWNERS ASSOCIATION

*If the open space is owned and maintained by a homeowner or condominium association, the developer shall file a declaration of covenants and restrictions that will govern the association, to be submitted with the application for the preliminary approval. The provisions shall include, but are not necessarily limited to, the following:*

*a. The homeowners association must be established before the homes are sold;*

*b. Membership must be mandatory for each homebuyer and any successive buyer;*

*c. The open space restrictions must be permanent, not just for a period of years;*

*d. The association must be responsible for liability insurance, local taxes, and the maintenance of recreational and other facilities;*

*e. Homeowners must pay their pro rata share of the cost, and the assessment levied by the association can become a lien on the property if allowed in the master deed establishing the homeowners association; and*

*f. The association must be able to adjust the assessment to meet changed needs.*

8. MAINTENANCE OF OPEN SPACE AREAS

*The person or entity identified in Section C.6 as having the right of ownership or control over the open space shall be responsible for its continuing upkeep and proper maintenance.*

### D. Landscaping Standards

1. PURPOSE

*a. Landscaping shall be provided as part of site plan and subdivision design. It shall be conceived in a total pattern throughout the site, integrating the various elements of site design, preserving and enhancing the particular identity of the site, and creating a pleasing site character.*

*b. Landscaping may include plant materials such as trees, shrubs, ground covers, perennials, and annuals, and other materials such as rocks, water, sculpture, art, walls, fences, paving materials, and street furniture.*

8. *MAINTENANCE OF COMMON OPEN SPACE AREAS*

It is important that the cost of maintaining common (as opposed to public) open space is borne by the people benefitting, not the community as a whole, especially considering the reality of the limited resources usually available to most local governments.

### D. Landscaping Standards

Since landscaping more than anything else can tie together the components of a design, it plays a critical role in site planning. Because landscaping involves aesthetic judgments, however, standards concerning landscaping raise legal issues. Yet, landscaping regulations can be justified on a number of grounds, depending on the particular function being performed by the landscaping. It is thus useful to think of landscaping as falling into two categories: 1) landscaping that fulfills a specific purpose, which is authorized and for which fairly unambiguous regulations can be drafted; and 2) general site landscaping for which it is difficult, it not impossible, to draft specific standards. The first can be justified on the grounds that state enabling acts generally give municipalities the power to make regulations regarding certain aspects of landscaping, such as shade trees. Other landscaping, such as buffering, can be justified as safeguarding public health, safety, and welfare. General landscaping, however, is usually thought of as an aesthetic concern, and regulations regarding general landscaping are often legally suspect, unless they, too, can be justified on health and safety grounds.

1. *PURPOSE*

a. In good site design, landscaping will fulfill the purpose expressed in the model ordinance; in practice, however, this goal is often unrealized. By stating the purpose of the landscaping standards, it is hoped that more thought will be given to how landscaping can help ensure the quality of developments that most communities are looking for.

b. Landscaping elements are commonly thought to consist of plant materials, yet all of the items listed in the model ordinance affect the appearance of the landscape and should be considered in the landscape design. Nevertheless, plants remain the fundamental landscaping material, and much of the language in the model ordinance regarding landscaping concerns plantings and their requirements.

## 2. LANDSCAPE PLAN

For large developments, the landscape plan is likely to be quite extensive, including location and planting details for street trees, buffering, and the landscaping of public areas and parking lots. For smaller subdivisions, the plan will be more limited, consisting of the number and type of foundation plantings and street trees.

## 3. SITE PROTECTION
### AND GENERAL PLANTING REQUIREMENTS

a. Some municipalities may wish to require six inches of topsoil; this ordinance suggests four inches in order to save on development costs. If a development site does not have four inches of topsoil initially, this provision requires the developer to truck in sufficient topsoil to satisfy the four-inch requirement.

b. This provision is intended to ensure that the development site is clean and presents no safety hazards. In addition, it allows landscaping to be installed properly, which will in turn help lower future maintenance costs.

c. When development sites contain existing vegetation, preservation can be the best method of landscaping. Fine specimens in particular should be retained whenever possible. A "fine" specimen can be defined as one that is large for its species, rare to the area, or of special horticultural or landscape value. This provision outlines the steps that must be taken to protect trees and shrubs during construction.

## 2. LANDSCAPE PLAN

*A landscape plan prepared by a certified landscape architect shall be submitted with each site plan application, unless an exception is granted pursuant to Article Three, Section C.2, of this ordinance. The plan shall identify existing and proposed trees, shrubs, and ground covers; natural features such as rock outcroppings; and other landscaping elements. The plan shall show where they are or will be located and planting and/or construction details. Where existing plantings are to be retained, the applicant shall include in the plans proposed methods of protecting them during construction.*

## 3. SITE PROTECTION AND GENERAL PLANTING REQUIREMENTS

*a. **Topsoil preservation.** Topsoil moved during the course of construction shall be redistributed on all regraded surfaces so as to provide at least [4] inches of even cover to all disturbed areas of the development and shall be stabilized by seeding or planting.*

*b. **Removal of debris.** All stumps and other tree parts, litter, brush, weeds, excess or scrap building materials or other debris shall be removed from the site and disposed of in accordance with the law. No tree stumps, or portions of tree trunks or limbs shall be buried anywhere in the development. All dead or dying trees, standing or fallen, shall be removed from the site. If trees and limbs are reduced to chips, they may be used as mulch in landscaped areas, subject to approval by the municipal engineer.*

*c. **Protection of existing plantings.** Maximum effort should be made to save fine specimens. No material or temporary soil deposits shall be placed within four (4) feet of shrubs or ten (10) feet of trees designated on the landscape* *plan to be retained. Protective barriers or tree wells shall be installed around each plant and/or group of plants that are to remain on the site. Barriers shall not be supported by the plants they are protecting, but shall be self-supporting. They shall be a minimum of four (4) feet high and constructed of a durable material that will last until construction is completed. Snow fences and silt fences are examples of acceptable barriers.*

*d. **Slope plantings.** Landscaping of all cuts and fills and/or terraces shall be sufficient to prevent erosion, and all roadway slopes steeper than one (1) foot vertically to three (3) feet horizontally shall be planted with ground cover appropriate for the purpose and for soil conditions, water availability, and environment.*

*e. **Additional landscaping.** In residential developments, besides the screening and street trees required, additional plantings or landscaping elements may be required throughout the subdivision where necessary for climate control, privacy, or other reasons in accordance with the landscape plan approved by the planning board and taking into consideration cost constraints. In non-residential developments, all areas of the site not occupied by buildings and required improvements shall be landscaped by the planting of grass or other ground cover, shrubs, and trees as part of the landscape plan approved by the planning board.*

*f. **Planting specifications.** Deciduous trees shall have at least a two-inch caliper at planting. Size of evergreens and shrubs shall be allowed to vary depending on setting and type of shrub. Only nursery-grown plant materials shall be acceptable, and all trees, shrubs, and ground covers shall be planted according to accepted horticultural standards. Dead and dying plants shall by replaced by the developer during the following planting season.*

e. Although this ordinance allows a municipality the flexibility to require more plantings where necessary, it should be emphasized that caution should be used in exercising this option. First, as stated at the outset of this section, there is the legal issue. Landscaping requirements can be justified only if there is enabling language that allows them, or if they can be justified on the basis of public health and safety. Secondly, even where there is legal justification for the requirement, aesthetic concerns arise and can become an issue. From a design point of view, for example, some sites may not require additional plantings—a site may already be heavily wooded, or adding plantings would not be appropriate to the design. Sometimes developments are over-landscaped, with buildings lost in a jungle of plantings. These are aesthetic judgments, however, and cannot be imposed on a developer, but only suggested and discussed.

f. Many ordinances include size requirements for evergreens and shrubs. Because size varies so much by species, however, this model ordinance uses a performance standard instead. Balled and burlapped plant materials are usually preferred in landscaping and often required by ordinances, but in some cases bare-root plants are perfectly acceptable (see Reference section for details). For this reason, balled and burlapped plants are not required in the model ordinance. Since the developer is required to replace dead and dying plants, it is in the developer's interest to use appropriate and healthy plant materials in landscaping, and the municipality is protected.

g. "Climatic zone" refers to the division of the country into temperature zones according to average minimum winter temperature. Plants are hardy depending on the climate of each zone—the plant hardiness zones in the United States are depicted on a map shown in the Reference section. Any number of standard reference books on trees and shrubs can be consulted for lists of plants appropriate for each zone and comments on the advantages and disadvantages of each species.

### 4. SHADE TREES

It is standard practice in subdivisions to plant shade trees along streets. Shade trees help lower the temperature and provide interest along the street and sidewalk. When planted between the street and the sidewalk, they provide a measure of protection for pedestrians, help buffer traffic noise, and filter pollution.

a. Location of shade trees along streets can be allowed to vary, depending on the kind of development, municipal preferences, topography, street width, and so on. These considerations and others are detailed in the Reference section.

The model ordinance ties the spacing standard to tree size, but builds in the flexibility to permit variations in spacing for different effects, as long as the design has the approval of a landscape architect.

b. Although disease can obliterate a species, sources recommend restricting trees to a few species, both for economy and the power of effect.

*g. **Plant species.** The plant species selected should be hardy for the particular climatic zone in which the development is located and appropriate in terms of function and size.*

*4. SHADE TREES*

*a. **Location.** Shade trees shall be installed on both sides of all streets in accordance with the approved landscape plan. Trees shall be either massed or spaced evenly along the street, or both.*

*When trees are planted at predetermined intervals along streets, spacing shall depend on tree size, as follows:*

| Tree Size (in feet) | Planting Interval (in feet) |
|---|---|
| Large trees (40+) | 50–70 |
| Medium trees (30–40) | 40–50 |
| Small trees (to 30) | 30–40 |

*When the spacing interval exceeds 40 feet, small ornamental trees can be placed between the larger trees. If a street canopy effect is desired, trees may be planted closer together, following the recommendations of a certified landscape architect. The trees shall be planted so as not to interfere with utilities, roadways, sidewalks, sight easements, or street lights. Tree location, landscaping design, and spacing plan shall be approved by the planning board as part of the landscape plan.*

*b. **Tree type.** Tree type may vary depending on overall effect desired, but as a general rule, all trees on a street shall be the same kind except to achieve special effects. Selection of tree type shall be approved by the planning board.*

*c. **Planting specifications.** All trees shall have a caliper of two (2) inches and be nursery grown, of substantially uniform size and shape, and have straight trunks. Trees shall be properly planted* and staked and provision made by the applicant for regular watering and maintenance until they are established. Dead and dying trees shall be replaced by the applicant during the next planting season.

5. BUFFERING

*a. **Function and materials.** Buffering shall provide a year-round visual screen in order to minimize adverse impacts. It may consist of fencing, evergreens, berms, rocks, boulders, mounds, or combinations thereof to achieve the same objectives.*

*b. **When required.** Every development shall provide sufficient buffering when topographical or other barriers do not provide reasonable screening and when the planning board determines that there is a need (1) to shield neighboring properties from any adverse external effects of a development; or (2) to shield the development from negative impacts of adjacent uses such as streets or railroads. In high-density developments, when building design and siting do not provide privacy, the planning board may require landscaping, fences, or walls to screen dwelling units for privacy. Buffers shall be measured from side and rear property lines, excluding driveways.*

*c. **Amount required.***

*1) Where more-intensive land uses abut less-intensive uses, a buffer strip [twenty-five (25) feet] in width shall be required.*

*2) Parking lots, garbage collection and utility areas, and loading and unloading areas should be screened around their perimeters by a buffer strip a minimum of [five (5) feet] wide.*

*3) Where residential subdivisions abut higher-order streets (collectors or arterials), adjacent lots shall front on lower-order streets, and a landscaped buffer area shall be provided along the property line abutting the road. The*

5. BUFFERING

a. Buffering is often required by ordinances to screen land uses that create nuisances, to divert or soften glare, to filter noise, to modify climatic conditions, or to create privacy. The model ordinance is flexible in the materials allowed for buffering, as long as the screening objective is met.

b. The determination by the planning board of when buffering is required is not as straightforward as it may sound. In more urban areas, for example, municipalities may prefer a mix of uses, with minimal or no buffering. Buffering, like so many other things, should not be done automatically, but rather when there is an identified need.

c. Municipalities may revise the figures shown in brackets if they wish, although these requirements are fairly standard among ordinances.

d. The model ordinance allows flexibility of design. Every buffer need not look like every other to be functional.

e. Again, a performance approach is used, with the method for achieving the buffering objective left flexible.

f. These ordinance provisions are intended to protect the municipality and ensure that it is in the best interests of the developer to plant healthy specimens.

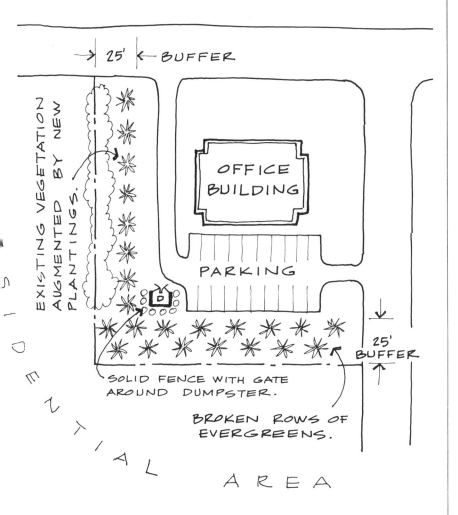

25' ← BUFFER

EXISTING VEGETATION AUGMENTED BY NEW PLANTINGS.

RESIDENTIAL

OFFICE BUILDING

PARKING

D

25' BUFFER

SOLID FENCE WITH GATE AROUND DUMPSTER.

BROKEN ROWS OF EVERGREENS.

AREA

*Buffering between residential area and office development*

buffer strip shall be a minimum of *[twenty-five (25) feet wide]* or wider where necessary for the health and safety of the residents. It shall include both trees and shrubs.

d. **Design.** Arrangement of plantings in buffers shall provide maximum protection to adjacent properties and avoid damage to existing plant material. Possible arrangements include planting in parallel, serpentine, or broken rows. If planted berms are used, the minimum top width shall be four (4) feet, and the maximum side slope shall be 2:1.

e. **Planting specifications.** Plant materials shall be sufficiently large and planted in such a fashion that a year-round screen at least eight (8) feet in height shall be produced within three (3) growing seasons. All plantings shall be installed according to accepted horticultural standards.

f. **Maintenance.** Plantings shall be watered regularly and in a manner appropriate for the specific plant species through the first growing season, and dead and dying plants shall be replaced by the applicant during the next planting season. No buildings, structures, storage of materials, or parking shall be permitted within the buffer area; buffer areas shall be maintained and kept free of all debris, rubbish, weeds, and tall grass.

6. PARKING LOT LANDSCAPING

*a. **Amount required.** In parking lots, at least five percent (5%) of the interior parking area shall be landscaped with plantings, and one (1) tree for each ten (10) spaces shall be installed. Parking lot street frontage screening and perimeter screening shall be a minimum of five (5) feet wide. Planting required within the parking lot is exclusive of other planting requirements, such as for shade trees planted along the street.*

*b. **Location.** The landscaping should be located in protected areas, such as along walkways, in center islands, at the ends of bays, or between parking stalls. All landscaping in parking areas and on the street frontage shall be placed so that it will not obstruct sight distance.*

*c. **Plant type.** A mixture of hardy flowering and/or decorative evergreen and deciduous trees may be planted. The evergreens should be used along the perimeter of the lot for screening, and the deciduous trees for shade within the lot. The area between trees shall be mulched, planted with shrubs or ground cover, or covered with paving material. Any area that will be under the overhang of vehicles shall be mulched or covered with paving material.*

## 6.  *PARKING LOT LANDSCAPING*

Landscaping can play a significant role in minimizing and moderating many adverse effects of parking lots. It breaks up the broad expanse of pavement and screens the lot from the street and surrounding properties. Planting strips and islands help guide the circulation of vehicles and pedestrians, creating a safe environment for both. Visual barriers minimize the hazard of nighttime glare from headlights, and plants moderate the microclimate on hot days and provide a buffer to winter winds.

a. Although 1 tree for every 10 spaces is a reasonable standard to meet the goal of shading a parking lot, these requirements can be modified by a municipality based on its own preferences.

b. It should be noted that some kind of car stops should also be provided to prevent cars from driving over the landscaping.

c. Plants appropriate for the plant hardiness zone and ones that will be able to withstand the often adverse conditions of a parking lot should be selected. The portion of the island that will be under the car overhang should be mulched or covered with paving material because the heat from car engines will usually kill plantings in this area.

## 7. PAVING MATERIALS

Paving serves a number of functions. On sidewalks or in courtyards, it creates a firm, level surface to facilitate passage. It can be used to define areas by varying materials, colors and textures—highlighting a crosswalk with a different paving surface from that of the street would be an example of this use. Paving also stabilizes surfaces by preventing erosion. Finally, it provides visual interest to a landscape.

a. These considerations are important when choosing paving materials. Tanbark, for example, might be appropriate for a jogging trail, but not where there is heavy pedestrian or bicycle traffic. Brick often ices up in cold climates, and this should be taken into consideration. Smooth pavement, rather than decorative pavers which can result in an uneven surface, might be more appropriate in a development designed for the elderly.

## 8. WALLS AND FENCES

a. Walls and fences serve a number of important functions in site planning. They provide enclosure, separate areas, provide security, screen areas from view, serve as a backdrop, focus a view, aid in climate control as a wind barrier or sun screen, and retain water or earth.

b. It should be pointed out that walls and fences often become a dominant spatial feature of the landscape and the wall or fence materials must work with the site itself. Design is often part of a regional tradition, but principles guiding design and choice of materials are detailed in the Reference section.

## 9. STREET FURNITURE

Most of the man-made objects located on plazas, sidewalks, or in other pedestrian areas can be considered street furniture. These objects are usually associated with amenities for pedestrians and may be freestanding or fixed. Besides the items listed in the model ordinance, street furniture includes bollards, kiosks, drinking fountains, planters, bus shelters, information signs, bike racks, game tables, and notice boards.

Because of the number and variety of components, street furniture often accumulates without design, resulting in a cluttered and discordant streetscape. To overcome visual chaos, site details

## 7. PAVING MATERIALS

*a. Design and choice of paving materials used in pedestrian areas shall consider such factors as function, climate, characteristics of users, availability, cost, maintenance, glare, drainage, noise, appearance, and compatibility with surroundings.*

*b. Acceptable materials shall include, but are not limited to, concrete, brick, cement pavers, asphalt, and stone.*

## 8. WALLS AND FENCES

*a. Walls and fences shall be erected where required for privacy, screening, separation, security, erosion control, or to serve other necessary and reasonable functions.*

*b. The design and materials used shall be functional and compatible with existing and proposed site architecture.*

*c. No fence or wall shall be so constructed or installed as to constitute a hazard to traffic or safety.*

## 9. STREET FURNITURE

*a. Street furniture, such as—but not limited to—trash receptacles, benches, and phone booths, shall be located and sized in accordance with function.*

*b. The different street furniture components shall be compatible in form, material, and finish. Design and materials shall be coordinated with existing and proposed site architecture. Selection of street furniture shall take into consideration function, durability, maintenance, and long-term cost.*

*E. Streets*

1. GENERAL

*a. The arrangement of streets shall conform to the circulation plan of the master plan or official map for the community.*

*b. For streets not shown on the master plan or official map, the arrangement shall provide for the appropriate extension of existing streets.*

*c. Residential streets shall be arranged so as to discourage through traffic and provide for maximum privacy.*

2. STREET HIERARCHY

*a. Streets shall be classified in a street hierarchy system with design tailored to function.*

*b. The street hierarchy system shall be defined by road function and average daily traffic (ADT), calculated by trip generation rates prepared by the Institute of Transportation Engineers as indicated in Exhibit 1. Trip generation rates from other sources may be used if the applicant demonstrates that these sources better reflect local conditions.*

*c. Each residential street shall be classified and designed for its entire length to meet the standards for one of the street types defined in Exhibit 2.*

*d. The applicant shall demonstrate to the planning board's satisfaction that the distribution of traffic to the proposed street system will not exceed the ADT thresholds indicated in Exhibit 2 for any proposed street type.*

should be coordinated with each other and with their setting. Other principles guiding selection of street furniture are detailed in the Reference section.

## E.  Streets

### 1.  GENERAL

Authorities have approached the regulation of residential streets in one of two ways: they have adopted the traditional standards usually adapted from state highway design requirements, or more recently, they have advocated a new approach embodying the concept that residential streets should be designed to serve the needs of the neighborhood rather than through traffic. This ordinance follows the second approach in the belief that overdesigned roads are unnecessarily wide, costly, and unsafe for residents. In accordance with good planning practices, streets in new subdivisions should conform to all official municipal plans.

### 2.  STREET HIERARCHY

a. Residential streets can be described in terms of serving different functions. Some provide access to a limited number of homes; others are designed to collect and move traffic to major highway arteries. Because the design of streets differs depending on the function served, streets in this model ordinance are classified into a street hierarchy.

b. The street hierarchy system is defined by road function as measured by average daily traffic (ADT). The ADT for a particular street can be estimated by calculating number of trips by housing type or land-use category. A "trip" is a single or one-way vehicle movement to or from a property or study area. "Trips" can be added together to calculate for each street the total number of trips entering and leaving a specific land use or site over a designated period of time. The ITE trip generation rates are widely accepted, but the ordinance permits rates from other sources to be used.

## EXHIBIT 1

### ITE TRIP GENERATION RATES BY MAJOR LAND USE CATEGORIES

| Land Use Type* | Average Weekday Trip Generation Rates |
|---|---|
| *Residential* | Trips Per Indicated Measure: Dwelling Unit |
| Single-family detached | 10.06 |
| Condominium/townhouse** | 5.86 |
| Low-rise apartment | 6.60 |
| High-rise apartment | 4.20 |
| Mobile home park | 4.81 |
| Retirement community | 3.30 |
| Recreational home (owner) | 3.16 |
| *Office Building* | Trips Per Indicated Measure: 1,000 gross ft.$^2$ of building area |
| General office, 10,000 gross ft.$^2$ | 24.39 |
| General office, 50,000 gross ft.$^2$ | 16.31 |
| General office, 100,000 gross ft.$^2$ | 13.72 |
| General office, 200,000 gross ft.$^2$ | 11.54 |
| General office, 500,000 gross ft.$^2$ | 9.17 |
| General office, 800,000 gross ft.$^2$ and over | 8.16 |
| Medical office building | 34.17 |
| Office park | 11.40 |
| Research center | 6.09 |
| *Retail* | Trips Per Indicated Measure: 1,000 gross ft.$^2$ of leasable area |
| Specialty retail | 40.67 |
| Discount store | 71.16 |
| Shopping center | |
| 10,000 ft.$^2$ gross leasable area | 166.35 |
| 50,000 ft.$^2$ gross leasable area | 94.71 |
| 100,000 ft.$^2$ gross leasable area | 74.31 |
| 200,000 ft.$^2$ gross leasable area | 58.93 |
| 500,000 ft.$^2$ gross leasable area | 39.81 |
| 1,000,000 ft.$^2$ gross leasable area | 33.44 |
| 1,600,000 ft.$^2$ gross leasable area | 31.05 |

## EXHIBIT 1 (continued)

| Land Use Type* | Average Weekday Trip Generation Rates | |
|---|---|---|

| Industrial | Trips Per Indicated Measure: | |
|---|---|---|
| | Employee | 1,000 gross ft.$^2$ of building area |
| Light industrial | 3.02 | 6.97 |
| Heavy industrial | 2.05 | 1.50 |
| Industrial park | 3.41 | 6.97 |
| Manufacturing | 2.09 | 3.85 |
| Warehousing | 3.89 | 4.88 |
| Mini-Warehouse | 56.28 | 2.61 |

| Lodging | Trips Per Indicated Measure: | |
|---|---|---|
| | Employee | Room |
| Hotel | 14.34 | 8.70 |
| Motel | 12.81 | 10.19 |

| Institutional | Trips Per Indicated Measure: | |
|---|---|---|
| | Employee | Student |
| Elementary school | 13.10 | 1.03 |
| High school | 16.79 | 1.39 |
| Junior/community college | 10.06 | 1.55 |
| Library | 49.50 | 45.50 (per 1,000 gross ft.$^2$) |

Notes:
  *For definitions, see below.
** High-rise condominium (>2 stories) = 4.18

## EXHIBIT 1 (continued)

### ITE DEFINITIONS OF LAND USES

*Single-Family Detached*
A single-family detached home on an individual lot.

*Condominium/Townhouse*
Single-family ownership units that have at least one other single-family owned unit within the same building structure. Both condominiums and townhouses are included in this category.

*Low-Rise Apartment*
Apartments in buildings that are only one or two levels (floors).

*High-Rise Apartment*
Apartments in buildings three or more levels high.

*Mobile Home Park*
Trailers shipped, sited, and installed on a permanent foundation.

*Retirement Community*
Residential units similar to apartments or condominiums usually located in self-contained villages, and restricted to adult or senior citizens.

*Recreational Homes*
Homes usually contained in a resort together with local services and complete recreation facilities.

*General Office Building*
Houses one or more tenants and is the location where the affairs of a business, commercial, or industrial organization, professional person, or firm are conducted.

*Medical Office Building*
A facility that provides diagnoses and outpatient care on a routine basis but which is unable to provide prolonged in-house medical/surgical care.

*Office Park*
Subdivisions or planned-unit developments containing general office buildings and support services such as banks, savings and loan institutions, restaurants, and service stations arranged in a park or campus-like atmosphere.

*Research Center*
Facilities or groups of facilities devoted nearly exclusively to research and development activities.

*Specialty Retail Center*
Small shopping centers which contain shops specializing in quality apparel or hard goods.

*Discount Stores*
Freestanding stores with off-street parking.

*Light Industrial*
Usually employs less than 500 persons with an emphasis on other than manufacturing.

*Heavy Industrial*
Encompasses the manufacturing of large items.

*Industrial Park*
Areas containing a number of industrial or related facilities. They are characterized by a mix of manufacturing, service, and warehouse facilities with a wide variation in the proportion of each type of use from one location to another.

## EXHIBIT 1 (continued)

*Manufacturing*
Places where the primary activity is the conversion of raw materials or parts into finished products.

*Warehousing*
Facilities that are all or largely devoted to storage of materials.

*Mini-Warehouse*
A building in which a storage unit or vault is rented for the storage of goods.

*Hotel*
A place of lodging providing sleeping accommodations, restaurants, cocktail lounges, meeting and banquet rooms or convention facilities, and other retail and service shops.

*Motel*
A place of lodging offering only sleeping accommodations and possibly a restaurant.

*Elementary School*
School serving students between kindergarten and high school levels.

*High School*
School serving students between the elementary and junior college or university levels.

*Junior/Community College*
Includes all two- and four-year educational institutions that call themselves a junior college, community college, or college.

*Library*
Includes those at universities and other public and private facilities.

*Source: Trip Generation,* 1987 edition. Washington, D.C.: Institute of Transportation Engineers. Data reprinted with permission of Institute of Transportation Engineers, 525 School Street, SW, Suite 410, Washington, D.C. 20024. *Note:* The 1987 edition of *Trip Generation* provides a graphic presentation of the fitted curve and the data points of the trip information. It also provides a fitted curve equation and $R^2$ values.

The ITE trip generation data should be used as a general guideline. Trip generation rates from other sources may be used if the applicant demonstrates that these sources better reflect local conditions.

# EXHIBIT 2

## RESIDENTIAL STREET HIERARCHY: DEFINITION

| Residential Street Type | Function | Guideline Maximum ADT |
|---|---|---|
| 1) Residential Access Street | Lowest order of residential streets. Provides frontage for access to lots, and carries traffic having destination or origin on the street itself. Designed to carry the least amount of traffic at the lowest speed. All, or the maximum number of housing units, shall front on this class of street. An east-to-west orientation is considered desirable to allow for maximum solar lot configuration.<br><br>Residential access streets should be designed so that no section conveys an ADT greater than 250. Each half of a loop street may be classified as a single residential access street, but the total traffic volume generated on the loop street should not exceed 500 ADT, nor should it exceed 250 ADT at any point of traffic concentration. | 250 (each loop) 500 (total) |
| 2) Residential Subcollector | Middle order of residential street. Provides frontage for access to lots, and carries traffic of adjoining residential access streets. Designed to carry somewhat higher traffic volumes with traffic limited to motorists having origin or destination within the immediate neighborhood. Is not intended to interconnect adjoining neighborhoods or subdivisions and should not carry regional through traffic.<br><br>Subcollectors shall be designed so that no section conveys an ADT greater than 500. Each half of a loop subcollector may be classified as a single subcollector street, but the total traffic volume conveyed on the loop street should not exceed 1,000 ADT, nor should it exceed 500 ADT at any point of traffic concentration. | 500 (each loop) 1,000 (total) |
| 3) Residential Collector | Highest order of residential streets. Conducts and distributes traffic between lower-order residential streets and higher-order streets—arterials and expressways. Carries the largest volume of traffic at higher speeds. Function is to promote free traffic flow; therefore, parking and direct access to homes from this level of street should be prohibited. Collectors should be designed so that they cannot be used as shortcuts by non-neighborhood traffic. | 3,000 (total) |
| 4) Arterial | A higher order, interregional road in the street hierarchy. Conveys traffic between centers; should be excluded from residential areas. | 3,000+ |

## EXHIBIT 2 (continued)

| Residential Street Type | Function | Guideline Maximum ADT |
|---|---|---|
| **5) Special Purpose Streets** | | |
| a) Rural Residential Lane | A street serving a very low-density area [minimum 2-acre zoning]. The maximum ADT level limits the number of single-family homes on this road to 20. | 200 |
| b) Alley | A service road that provides secondary means of access to lots. On same level as residential access street, but different standards apply. Used in cases of narrow lot frontages. No parking shall be permitted; should be designed to discourage through traffic. ADT level corresponds to that of residential access street. Number of units served should not exceed 76. | 250 (each loop) 500 (total) |
| c) Cul-de-Sac | A street with a single means of ingress and egress and having a turnaround. Design of turnaround may vary. Cul-de-sacs shall be classified and designed according to anticipated ADT level: a residential access cul-de-sac will have a maximum ADT level of 250, and a subcollector cul-de-sac will have a maximum ADT level of 500. Cul-de-sacs may also be classified as alleys depending on function. | 250 (residential access) 500 (subcollector) |
| d) Marginal Access Street | A service street that runs parallel to a higher-order street and provides access to abutting properties and separation from through traffic. May be designed as residential access street or subcollector according to anticipated daily traffic. | 500 (residential access total) 1,000 (subcollector total) |
| e) Divided Street | Municipalities may require streets to be divided in order to provide alternate emergency access, to protect environmental features, or to avoid grade changes. Design standards should be applied to the combined dimensions of the two-street segments as required by the street class. | 500 (residential access total) 1,000 (subcollector total) 3,000 (collector total) |
| f) Stub Street | A portion of a street which has been approved in its *entirety.* Permitted as part of phased development; may be required if part of overall adopted master plan of the municipality. | 500 (residential access total) 1,000 (subcollector total) 3,000 (collector total) |

*3.   CARTWAY WIDTH*

The cartway is the area of the street within which vehicles are permitted. It includes moving and parking lanes, but not shoulders, curbs, sidewalks, or swales. Minimum cartway width must be sufficient to allow safe passage of moving traffic and is computed by adding up the number of traffic and parking lanes required by the intensity and form of development. Two issues arise, however: 1) the dimensions of the parking and moving (or traffic) lanes—or lane width; and 2) the number of parking and moving lanes that should be required for each street in the street hierarchy.

**Lane width.** *Parking lane* widths must be large enough to accommodate the vehicle, allow room for maneuvering, and permit the opening of doors without impeding traffic flow. In most residential subdivisions, on-street parking consists of parallel parking, in 8-foot parking lanes. *Moving lane* widths differ according to the function of the road. For minor roads, narrower widths are adequate, but as traffic and truck volume increase, the width of the moving lane also increases.

**Number of lanes.** Number of lanes is a function of intensity of development and volume of traffic. Fewer lanes are required and cartway dimensions are narrower for minor streets that serve areas with less concentrated development and where on-street parking lanes are not needed. More lanes are required and the cartway surface is wider for streets that must accommodate a greater volume of traffic and where on-street parking is needed.

The standards specified in this ordinance, while narrower than those in some municipal ordinances, are based on recommendations by many authorities and are sufficient to meet the functional needs of each street category. Streets are among the most costly of development improvements, and excessive requirements—while not the only reason—have been a contributing element to rising housing prices. As in other areas of subdivision control, local officials must weigh the costs and benefits in setting minimum pavement width requirements.

a. Cartway widths should vary for the same classification of street depending on the form and intensity of development. For example, a development that consists of houses widely spread out on two- or three-acre lots is less likely to require parking lanes on

3. CARTWAY WIDTH

*a. Cartway width for each street classification shall be determined by parking and curbing requirements which are based on form and intensity of development.*

*b. Intensity of development shall be based on lot frontage as follows:*

INTENSITY OF DEVELOPMENT

|  | Low | Medium | High |
|---|---|---|---|
| Lot | more | 75 | less |
| Frontage | than | to | than |
| (in feet): | 150 | 150 | 75 |

*c. Cartway width shall also consider possible limitations imposed by sight distances, climate, terrain, and maintenance needs. In order to minimize street costs, the minimum width assuring satisfaction of needs shall be selected.*

*d. Cartway widths for each street classification are shown in Exhibit 3.*

the street than a development of townhouses, even though the streets carry the same amount of traffic. Parking is more likely to be accommodated on-site in the large-lot development, and narrower streets without parking lanes are adequate to handle the needs of the large-lot development.

b. Lot frontage is used to measure intensity of development. Development density is not used because density figures are averages of housing units by number of acres. If the density of a proposed development of 40 units is two units to the acre, on a 20-acre tract it could mean that each unit is on a half-acre lot; but it could also mean that development is clustered, with all the units clustered on three acres and the rest remaining as open space. Density on those three acres would then be 13 to 14 units to the acre. Although overall density is identical in the two hypothetical cases, provision of parking lanes would be less pressing in the former development configuration than in the latter.

The frontage figures for different development intensities that are suggested in this ordinance reflect New Jersey development patterns. Other states or municipalities may wish to adopt figures that more accurately reflect the local situation.

c. This provision is intended to introduce some flexibility into setting minimum cartway standards in different localities. Municipalities in cold climates may need wider cartways, for example, to accommodate snow storage. Similarly, as terrain becomes hilly, curves increase, and wider cartways are required.

d. The cartway widths shown in Exhibit 3 are computed by adding up the number of traffic and parking lanes required by the intensity and form of development. Minimum moving lane width, with one exception, is 10 feet. While some authorities recommend 9-foot lanes, most find 10-foot lanes more satisfactory, especially since most residential subdivision streets will provide some on-street parking. Curbing is recommended where there is parking, and the presence of curbs tends to make cars veer towards the center of the roadway, making 10-foot lane widths necessary. As traffic volume increases up the street hierarchy, lane widths increase. Nine-foot moving lane widths are considered adequate, however, for rural residential lanes since they serve very low-density development with limited traffic.

The cartway widths shown in Exhibit 3 are explained below in more detail for each street in the street hierarchy.

# EXHIBIT 3

## CARTWAY WIDTH

| Street Classification* | Travel/Moving Lane | Subtotal | Parking [a] Lane | Subtotal | Total Cartway Width |
|---|---|---|---|---|---|
| *RESIDENTIAL ACCESS STREET* | | | | | |
| *Intensity of Development* | | | | | |
| Low | two 10' | 20' | none | 0 | 20' |
| Medium | two 10' | 20' | one 8' | 8' | 28' |
| High | | | | | |
| On-street parking | two 10' | 20' | one 8' | 8' | 28' [b] |
| Off-street parking | two 10' | 20' | none | 0 | 20' |
| *RESIDENTIAL SUBCOLLECTOR* | | | | | |
| *Intensity of Development* | | | | | |
| Low | two 10' | 20' | none | 0 | 20' |
| Medium | two 10' | 20' | one 8' | 8' | 28' |
| High | | | | | |
| One-side parking | two 10' | 20' | one 8' | 8' | 28' |
| Two-side parking | two 10' | 20' | two 8' | 16' | 36' |
| Off-street parking | two 11' | 22' | none | 0 | 22' |
| *RESIDENTIAL COLLECTOR* | | | | | |
| *Intensity of Development* | | | | | |
| Low | two 12' | 24' | none | 0 | 24' |
| Medium and high | two 12' | 24' | none | 0 | 24' |
| *SPECIAL PURPOSE STREETS* | | | | | |
| Rural residential lane | two 9' | 18' | none | 0 | 18' |
| Alley | two 9' | 18' | none | 0 | 18' |
| Cul-de-sac (stem) [c] | | | | | |
| Marginal access street [d] | | | | | |
| Divided street [e] | | | | | |
| Stub street [f] | | | | | |

*Notes:* *See Exhibit 2 for definition of street hierarchy and Article Five, Section E.3.b. for definition of low, medium, and high intensity of development.

a. Refers to parallel parking.

b. The 28' cartway also would accommodate two 8-foot parking lanes and one 12-foot moving lane.

c. Cartway widths of cul-de-sacs should conform to standards of either residential access or subcollector streets as dictated by anticipated average daily traffic. Cul-de-sac turnarounds shall have a minimum cartway radius of 40 feet.

d. Cartway widths of marginal access streets should conform to standards of either residential access or subcollector streets as dictated by anticipated daily traffic. If the classification is a subcollector requiring a 36-foot cartway, cartway width may be reduced to 28 feet since frontage is restricted to one side of street.

e. Cartway widths of divided streets should conform to standards of street classification as dictated by anticipated average daily traffic and be applied to aggregate dimensions of the two street segments.

f. Cartway widths of stub streets should conform to the standards of the street classification as dictated by anticipated daily traffic.

## Residential Access Streets

**Lane widths.** Moving lanes should be 10-feet wide—a dimension not overly wide, yet adequate for the low traffic volume and 25-mph speed limit typical on residential access streets. An additional 8 feet of cartway should be added when a parking lane is provided.

**Low development intensity (lot widths 150+ feet).** In subdivisions with large lots and where average daily traffic will be low, there will be little to no demand for on-street parking. A 20-foot cartway width is specified (two 10-foot moving lanes). In the rare cases a vehicle must park on the street, the low traffic volume will allow other vehicles to pull around it with little inconvenience.

**Medium development intensity (lot widths 75–150 feet).** Generally, the demand for on-street parking increases as lot size decreases. To accommodate occasional parking, a 28-foot minimum width is specified for minor residential roads at this density (one 8-foot parking lane and two 10-foot moving lanes).

**High development intensity (lot widths less than 75 feet).** For subdivision lots less than 75 feet in width and where off-street parking is not provided, residential access streets should be designed to anticipate a demand for on-street parking. A 28-foot wide cartway is specified. This width allows the flexibility to accommodate one 8-foot parking lane and two 10-foot moving lanes, or two 8-foot parking lanes and one 12-foot moving lane. Even where parking occurs on both sides of the street, there is curbside room for one car to pull over to let another pass. On-lot parking should also be required for each housing unit. Where ample off-street parking is provided, a narrower 20-foot cartway width will be sufficient, providing two 10-foot moving lanes.

## Subcollectors

**Lane widths.** As with residential access streets, subcollector moving lanes should generally be 10 feet wide. Parking lanes, where necessary, are an additional 8 feet in width each for parallel parking.

**Low development intensity (lot widths 150+ feet).** A 20-foot pavement width is recommended for two 10-foot moving lanes.

**Medium development intensity (lot widths 75–150 feet).** A pavement width of 28 feet is recommended for two 10-foot moving lanes and one 8-foot parallel parking lane.

High development intensity (lot widths less than 75 feet). A pavement width of 28 feet is specified for two 10-foot moving lanes and one 8-foot parallel parking lane; if parallel parking on both sides of the street is anticipated, a 36-foot cartway is recommended for two 10-foot moving lanes and two 8-foot parking lanes. Where off-street parking is available, a 22-foot cartway width is needed, providing two 11-foot moving lanes (a wider width is necessary since there are no parking lanes to provide added space where the lane is not occupied).

## Residential Collectors

**Lane width.** Collectors should be designed to promote free traffic flow with minimum interruption or curb cuts. Moving lanes should be 12 feet wide for maximum safety. Because of the high volume of traffic, parking should not be allowed on collectors.

**All development intensities.** A 24-foot minimum cartway width is specified providing for two 12-foot moving lanes.

## Special Purpose Streets

**Rural residential lanes.** Rural residential lanes require a minimum cartway width of 18 feet providing two 9-foot lanes. The low traffic volume on this type of road permits a narrower cartway.

**Alleys.** Alleys also require a minimum cartway width of 18 feet providing two 9-foot lanes. A narrower cartway would be appropriate for one-way alleys, however.

**Cul-de-sacs: stems.** Cartway widths correspond to the width specified for the appropriate classification.

**Cul-de-sacs: turnarounds.** Minimum cartway radius of a round turnaround should be 40 feet. This minimum standard should also be viewed, however, as the maximum standard, since a turning radius of more than 40 feet creates large expanses of pavement. Parking is not recommended because of the large amount of pavement required, but where necessary, parking should be provided on the inside of the turnaround. For "T" or hammerhead turnarounds, the width of the "T" should be 60 feet, and all dimensions should provide adequate turnaround for garbage trucks. (This type of turnaround should be used only in very low traffic situations and to provide access to no more than 5 lots because of the hazardous movements required for backing.)

### 4. CURBS AND GUTTERS

*a. Curbing shall be required for the purposes of drainage, safety, and delineation and protection of pavement edge.*

*b. Curb requirements shall vary according to street hierarchy and intensity of development in accordance with the requirements shown in Exhibit 4. Curbing may also be required:*

*1) For storm water management;*

*2) To stabilize pavement edge;*

*3) To delineate parking areas;*

*4) Ten (10) feet on each side of drainage inlets;*

*5) At intersections;*

*6) At corners; and*

*7) At tight radii.*

*c. Where curbing is not required, some sort of edge definition and stabilization shall be furnished for safety reasons and to prevent pavement unraveling.*

*d. Where curbing is required, this requirement may be waived and shoulders and/or drainage swales used when it can be shown that:*

*1) Shoulders are required by state regulations;*

*2) Soil or topography make the use of shoulders and/or drainage swales preferable; or*

*3) It is in the best interests of the community to preserve its rural character by using shoulders and/or drainage swales instead of curbs.*

*e. At medium development intensity, the curbing requirement may be waived where front setbacks exceed 40 feet and it can be demonstrated that sufficient on-site parking exists.*

*f. Flexibility regarding curb type shall be permitted as long as the curb type accommodates the system of drainage proposed.*

**Marginal access streets.** Cartway widths of marginal access streets are required to conform to the standards of their classification as either residential access or subcollector streets as indicated by anticipated daily traffic. If the classification is that of a subcollector which requires a 36-foot cartway, cartway width may, however, be reduced to 28 feet since lot frontage is restricted to one side of the street, and parking demands should be less.

**Divided streets.** Cartway widths of divided streets conform to the standards of their street classification as indicated by anticipated average daily traffic. Width requirements are applied to the aggregate dimensions of the two street segments.

**Stub streets.** Cartway widths of stub streets should conform to the standards of their street classification indicated by anticipated daily traffic.

### 4. CURBS AND GUTTERS

Curbing is used for drainage control and for delineation and protection of the pavement edge, but because it is expensive and can aggravate storm water runoff, the benefits must be weighed against the costs. Many authorities recommend minimizing the use of curbs and using shoulders and swales instead, but municipalities should recognize that swales can be costly in terms of future maintenance. In addition, shoulders and swales may add to right-of-way dimensions.

Curb requirements vary according to the street hierarchy and intensity of development. As one ascends the street hierarchy, speeds increase, and at higher travel speeds, curbs are needed to delineate the pavement edge.

The intensity of development is also a factor in curbing requirements. With greater intensity of development, the impervious surface increases which, in turn, increases the problem of storm water runoff. Curbs and gutters are often needed to manage runoff in these situations. Higher densities are also usually accompanied by a greater number of curb cuts. Frequent curb cuts increase the need for curbs to protect the pavement edge. In addition, on-street parking at higher densities requires curbs because curbs serve to limit the encroachment of vehicles off the pavement edge and minimize erosion of planted areas.

In residential subdivisions with very large lots or where there is adequate off-street parking, however, curbs are not necessary.

## EXHIBIT 4

## RIGHT-OF-WAY REQUIREMENTS AND DIMENSIONS

| Street Category [a] | Cartway Width | Curb or Shoulder | Sidewalk or Graded Area | Total Right-of-Way Width |
|---|---|---|---|---|
| RESIDENTIAL ACCESS | | | | |
| Low intensity | 20' | Not Required | Graded Area (1 each side) [f] | 40' |
| Medium intensity | 28' | Curb | Graded Area (1 each side) [f] | 40' |
| High intensity | | | | |
|   On-street parking | 28' | Curb | Sidewalk (1 side) Graded Area (1 side) | 50' |
|   Off-street parking | 20' | Not Required | Sidewalk (1 side) Graded Area (1 side) | 40' |
| RESIDENTIAL SUBCOLLECTOR | | | | |
| Low intensity | 20' | Not Required | Graded Area (1 each side) [f] | 40' |
| Medium intensity | 28' | Curb | Sidewalk (1 side) Graded Area (1 side) | 50' |
| High intensity | | | | |
|   One-side parking | 28' | Curb | Sidewalk (1 each side) | 50' |
|   Two-side parking | 36' | Curb | Sidewalk (1 each side) | 60' |
|   Off-street parking | 22' | Curb or Shoulder | Sidewalk (1 each side) | 40' (with curb) 50' (with shoulder) |
| RESIDENTIAL COLLECTOR | | | | |
| Low intensity | 24' | Not Required | Graded Area (1 each side) [f] | 40' |
| Medium intensity | 24' | Curb or Shoulder | Sidewalk (1 each side) | 50' |
| High intensity | 24' | Curb or Shoulder | Sidewalk (1 each side) | 50' |
| SPECIAL PURPOSE | | | | |
| Rural Residential Lane | 18' | Not Required | Graded Area (1 each side) [f] | 40' |
| Alley | 18' | Not Required | Graded Area (1 each side) | 22' |
| Cul-de-Sac [b] | | | | |
| Marginal Access [c] | | | | |
| Divided Street [d] | | | | |
| Stub Street [e] | | | | |

*g. Curbing shall be designed to provide a ramp for bicycles and/or wheelchairs as required by state law.*

*h. Curbing shall be constructed according to the specifications set forth in the Appendix.*

Furthermore, where a specific site permits a natural, open drainage system of swales and recharge or retention basins, curbing may be a hindrance to the storm water management system.

The curbing requirements shown in Exhibit 4 are explained below in more detail for each street in the street hierarchy.

**Residential access streets.** In areas with low development intensity, curbing is optional. In medium-intensity developments, curbs are recommended because there is on-street parking and curbs help keep cars on the cartway surface. In high-intensity developments, curbing is recommended for a number of reasons, including: 1) with a great deal of impervious cover, a closed drainage system is likely, and curbs facilitate storm water management in such systems; 2) driveways may be constructed at frequent intervals and curbs serve to delineate the cartway and protect the pavement edge.

**Subcollectors.** Except in areas of low development intensity, subcollector streets should have curbs because of their higher traffic volume.

## EXHIBIT 4 (continued)

*Notes:*

a. See Exhibit 2 for definition of street hierarchy and Article Five, Section E.3.b. for definition of low, medium, and high intensity of development.

b. Cartway and right-of-way widths of cul-de-sac stems and right-of-way requirements should conform to standards of either residential access or subcollector streets as dictated by anticipated average daily traffic. Cul-de-sac turnarounds shall have a minimum cartway radius of 40 feet and a minimum right-of-way radius of 48 feet.

c. Cartway and right-of-way widths of marginal access streets and right-of-way requirements should conform to the standards of either residential access or subcollector streets as dictated by anticipated daily traffic. If the classification is a subcollector requiring a 36-foot cartway, cartway width may be reduced to 28 feet since frontage is restricted to one side of the street.

d. Cartway and right-of-way widths of divided streets and right-of-way requirements should conform to the standards of street classification as dictated by anticipated average daily traffic and be applied to aggregate dimensions of the two street segments.

e. Cartway and right-of-way widths of stems and right-of-way requirements should conform to the standards of street classification as dictated by anticipated daily traffic.

f. A separate graded area is *not* required where shade tree and utility strips are provided (see Exhibit 5).

Collectors. Curbs or shoulders should be required along residential collectors, except in areas with low development intensity.

Special purpose streets. In general, rural residential lanes and alleys should not be provided with curbs, but for alleys with numerous driveways, curbs should be required. Curb requirements for cul-de-sacs, marginal access, divided streets, and stub streets conform to those required for the appropriate street class and development intensity.

e. This provision is intended to permit flexibility in curbing requirements.

f. Communities should allow the most economical curb types, and developers should be permitted to install more costly alternatives as long as drainage requirements are satisfied. Asphalt curbs, however, are not recommended because they deteriorate rapidly.

## 5. SHOULDERS

a. Shoulders are used in case of emergency use, to accommodate stopped vehicles, and for lateral support of the pavement. They also provide additional width for a narrow cartway, allowing a driver meeting or passing other vehicles an extra margin of pavement surface.

b. Shoulders are an option to curbs at higher levels of the street hierarchy and at higher intensities of development. As traffic speed increases, so does the necessity to provide an area for cars to clear the cartway. With greater development intensity, there is more need to provide a strip for cars and service vehicles to pull off the traveled way and to stop safely for deliveries. At higher development intensities where open drainage systems are used, the shoulder can be an integral part of the open system.

c. Four-foot shoulders may be considered somewhat narrow for collectors, but since no parking is permitted and the moving lanes are 12 feet each, a vehicle making an emergency stop can pull off and the width of the remaining pavement should be adequate to allow vehicles safe passage.

d. Materials used to surface shoulders include gravel, crushed stone, stabilized turf, bituminous treatments, and other forms of pavement.

5. SHOULDERS

*a. Shoulders and/or drainage swales shall be required instead of curbs when:*

*1) Shoulders are required by state law;*

*2) Soil or topography make the use of shoulders and/or drainage swales preferable; or*

*3) It is in the best interest of the community to serve its rural character by using shoulders and/or drainage swales instead of curbs.*

*b. Shoulder requirements shall vary according to street hierarchy and intensity of development in accordance with the requirements set forth in Exhibit 4.*

*c. Shoulders shall measure four (4) feet in width on each side for all streets and shall be located within the right-of-way as shown in Exhibit 5. The width of swales shall be determined by site-specific conditions.*

*d. Shoulders shall consist of stabilized turf or other material acceptable to the planning board.*

# EXHIBIT 5

## RIGHT-OF-WAY (R.O.W.) PROFILES

NOTE: The individual components shown in the non-travel-way portion of the right-of-way—utility and shade tree areas, sidewalks and graded areas—are indicated for illustrative purposes only. Municipalities may vary the placement and dimensions of these individual items depending on utility company requirements and local practice and preferences. For instance, the shade trees may be planted next to the cartway to provide a canopy effect; or, the shade trees may be planted outside the right-of-way. These variations may be accommodated within the total right-of-way widths indicated for each street type.

### RESIDENTIAL ACCESS STREETS

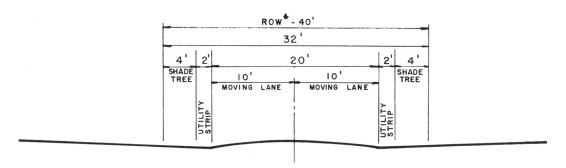

**LOW INTENSITY**

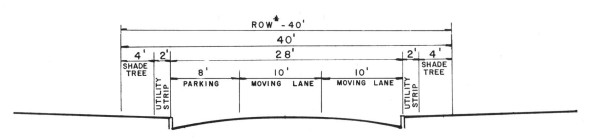

**MEDIUM INTENSITY
ONE-SIDE PARKING**

*ROW figures are rounded from the sum of the right-of-way components into a limited number of dimensions in order to reduce multiple street right-of-way requirements.

## EXHIBIT 5 (continued)

### RESIDENTIAL ACCESS STREETS (continued)

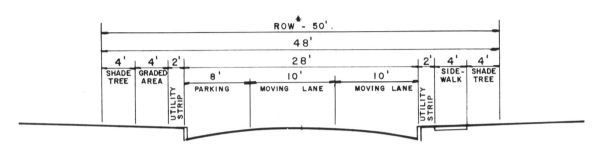

**HIGH INTENSITY
WITH ON-STREET PARKING**

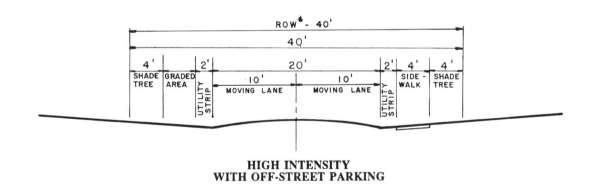

**HIGH INTENSITY
WITH OFF-STREET PARKING**

*ROW figures are rounded from the sum of the right-of-way components into a limited number of dimensions in order to reduce multiple street right-of-way requirements.

**EXHIBIT 5 (continued)**

## RESIDENTIAL SUBCOLLECTORS

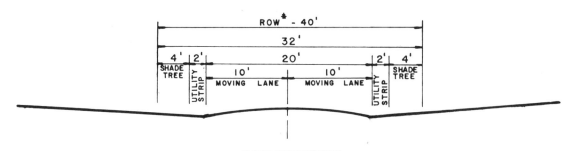

**LOW INTENSITY**

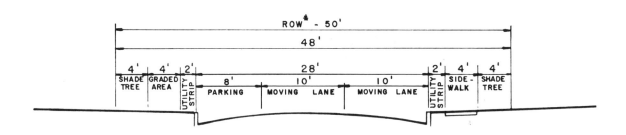

**MEDIUM INTENSITY
ONE-SIDE PARKING**

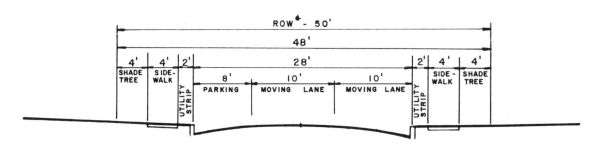

**HIGH INTENSITY
ONE-SIDE PARKING**

*ROW figures are rounded from the sum of the right-of-way components into a limited number of dimensions in order to reduce multiple street right-of-way requirements.

## EXHIBIT 5 (continued)

## RESIDENTIAL SUBCOLLECTORS (continued)

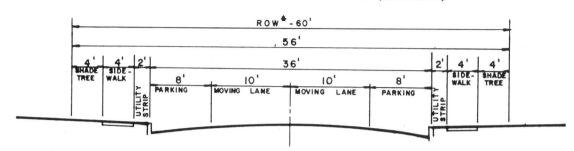

**HIGH INTENSITY
TWO-SIDE PARKING**

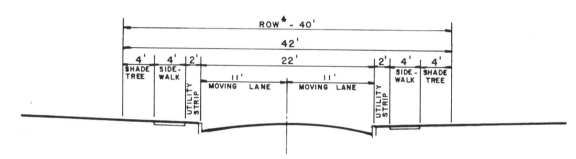

**HIGH INTENSITY
OFF-STREET PARKING—WITH CURB**

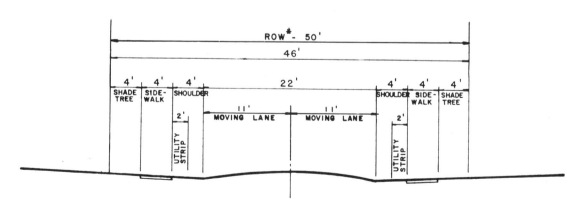

**HIGH INTENSITY
OFF-STREET PARKING—WITH SHOULDER**

*ROW figures are rounded from the sum of the right-of-way components into a limited number of dimensions in order to reduce multiple street right-of-way requirements.

The Schoor DePalma & Canger Group Inc.
SCHOOR & DePALMA
Consulting and Municipal Engineers

**EXHIBIT 5 (continued)**

## RESIDENTIAL COLLECTORS

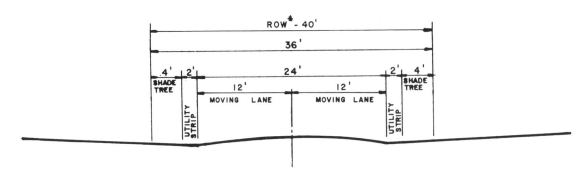

**LOW INTENSITY**

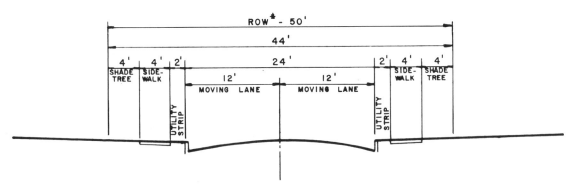

**MEDIUM AND HIGH INTENSITY
WITH CURB**

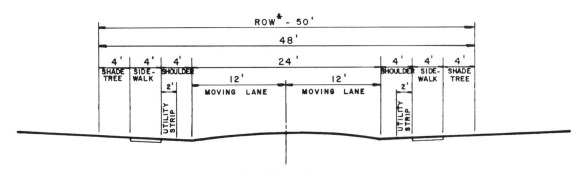

**MEDIUM AND HIGH INTENSITY
WITH SHOULDER**

*ROW figures are rounded from the sum of the right-of-way components into a limited number of dimensions in order to reduce multiple street right-of-way requirements.

The Schoor DePalma & Canger Group Inc.
SCHOOR & DePALMA
Consulting and Municipal Engineers

## 6. SIDEWALKS AND GRADED AREAS

The elimination of unnecessary sidewalks in residential subdivisions has been espoused as a way of reducing development costs and lowering housing costs. The debate, of course, centers on which sidewalks can be considered unnecessary and therefore dispensable. There is general agreement that sidewalks in low-density developments with large frontages are less necessary than those in high-density developments with narrow frontages, although some authorities question requiring sidewalks even in the latter case.

As in so many other areas of subdivision control, sidewalk requirements are a matter for municipal authorities to discuss with the costs incurred weighed against the benefits received. The model ordinance has tried to present balanced sidewalk standards, although its authors must confess to a bias towards sidewalks in medium- and high-density developments as a place for children to play and adults to walk. Where sidewalks are required on one side of the street only, a graded area is required on the other, partly so that the right-of-way will be symmetrical on both sides of the cartway centerline, and partly so that if the need for a sidewalk arises in the future, there will be space for it.

c. The advantage of allowing flexible placement of sidewalks in conventional residential developments in order to preserve topographical or natural features is illustrated in the Reference section.

d. In planned-unit developments, in addition to the internal pedestrian system, it may be necessary to require sidewalks parallel to the street for access to schools, bus stops, shopping, or other facilities.

## 6. SIDEWALKS

*a. Sidewalks and/or graded areas shall be required depending on road classification and intensity of development in accordance with the requirements set forth in Exhibit 4.*

*b. Where sidewalks are optional, they may be required if close to pedestrian generators, to continue a walk on an existing street, to link areas, or depending on probable future development as indicated in applicable master plans.*

*c. In conventional developments, sidewalks shall be placed in the right-of-way, parallel to the street as shown in Exhibit 5, unless an exception has been permitted to preserve topographical or natural features or to provide visual interest, or unless the applicant shows that an alternative pedestrian system provides safe and convenient circulation. In commercial and in high-density residential areas, sidewalks may abut the curb.*

*d. In planned developments, sidewalks may be located away from the road system to link dwelling units with other dwelling units, the street, and on-site activity centers such as parking areas and recreational areas. They may also be required parallel to the street for safety and other reasons.*

*e. Pedestrian-way easements ten (10) feet wide may be required by the planning board through the center of blocks more than 600 feet long to provide circulation or access to schools, playgrounds, shopping, or other community facilities.*

*f. Sidewalks shall measure four (4) feet in width; wider widths may be necessary near pedestrian generators and employment centers. Where sidewalks abut the curb and cars overhang the sidewalk, widths shall be five (5) feet. The width of graded areas shall be the same as for sidewalks.*

*g. Sidewalks and graded areas shall be constructed according to the specifications set forth in the Appendix.*

### 7. BIKEWAYS

*a. Separate bicycle paths shall be required only if such paths have been specified as part of a municipality's adopted master plan.*

*b. Bicycle lanes, where required, shall be placed in the outside lane of a roadway, adjacent to the curb or shoulder. When on-street parking is permitted, the bicycle lane shall be between the parking lane and the outer lane of moving vehicles. Lanes shall be delineated with markings, preferably striping. Raised reflectors or curbs shall not be used.*

*c. Bikeways shall be constructed according to the specifications set forth in the Appendix.*

### 8. UTILITY AND SHADE TREE AREAS

*a. Utilities and shade trees shall generally be located within the right-of-way on both sides of and parallel to the street as shown in Exhibit 5. Shade trees may also be placed outside the public right-of-way.*

*b. Utility and shade tree areas shall be planted with grass or ground cover, or treated with other suitable cover material.*

### 9. RIGHT-OF-WAY

*a. The right-of-way shall be measured from lot line to lot line and shall be sufficiently wide to contain the cartway, curbs, shoulders, sidewalks, graded areas, utilities, and shade trees (if they are placed within the right-of-way). Right-of-way requirements are shown in Exhibit 4 and displayed graphically in the street profiles in Exhibit 5.*

*b. The right-of-way width of a new street that is a continuation of an exist-*

## 7. BIKEWAYS

The three types of bikeways are described in detail in the Reference section. The most important consideration in subdivision requirements for bikeways is that they be based on overall planning for an area. Some municipalities in the past have been known to extract elaborate bicycle path systems from developers as one of the costs of doing business in the town when there has been no regional bikeway plan. Bikeways should be part of a network, just like streets and sidewalks. A large subdivision could, however, support its own internal system of bike paths.

## 8. UTILITY AND SHADE TREE AREAS

Placement of utility lines is usually determined by the utility company—some prefer placement under the cartway, others in a strip within the right-of-way and parallel to the street. The former placement is less convenient for maintenance or replacement of obsolete systems, but local companies will generally set the policy.

Placement of shade trees is another one of those issues about which there is some debate. After decades of requiring shade trees within the right-of-way, there has been a trend in recent years to place them on private property where they become the responsibility of the homeowner. Again, each municipality has to determine its own preference for placement: trees planted within the right-of-way and next to the cartway will eventually form a canopy over the street, but their roots may also buckle the sidewalk if the planting strip is not wide enough. Trees planted on private property will save the municipality maintenance responsibilities, but the street will not be shaded as effectively. In addition, some mechanism enforcing maintenance by the homeowner may be required.

## 9. RIGHT-OF-WAY

Since excessive right-of-way requirements raise development costs, right-of-way dimensions should be the minimum necessary to contain all required street components. It seems logical that one would simply add up the required components to find the right-of-way dimensions for each street in the street hierarchy. Some standardization and rounding off are necessary, however, in order to avoid a multiplicity of right-of-way requirements. The right-of-way dimensions set forth in this ordinance, like those for the cartway, are somewhat narrower than those required by some municipalities. They are, however, adequate and comport with national recommendations.

## 10. STREET GRADE AND INTERSECTIONS

As with the other sections, the guiding principle is cost-efficient performance standards.

## 11. PAVEMENT SECTION

The thickness of the pavement should be adequate for the level of usage placed on the pavement, the strength properties of the subgrade supporting the surface, and the type of pavement. The text accompanying the Appendix explains these considerations in greater detail. The main concern in setting standards is that excessive pavement requirements be avoided. Developers in New Jersey like to refer to the pavement section requirements of some municipalities for minor residential access streets that exceed the requirements for airport jet landing strips. Clearly, such requirements are excessive for the purpose and raise costs unnecessarily.

## 12. LIGHTING

Municipal street light requirements should be sensitive to the street hierarchy and character of the area. Roads that carry greater traffic volumes and have wider rights-of-way and cartways need better lighting. Commercial areas—especially those with heavy nighttime traffic—need more lighting than residential areas. The standards recommended by the Illuminating Engineering Society (IES) (see Exhibit A-8) are intended to guide municipalities in situations where the utility company does not provide a lighting plan.

ing street shall in no case be continued at a width less than that of the existing street.

*c. The right-of-way shall reflect future development as indicated by the master plan.*

### 10. STREET GRADE AND INTERSECTIONS

*Street grade and intersection requirements are specified in the Appendix.*

### 11. PAVEMENT SECTION

*a. Street pavement thickness shall vary by street hierarchy, subgrade properties, and pavement type.*

*b. Pavement design for residential access streets, subcollectors, and collectors shall conform to the specifications shown in the Appendix.*

### 12. LIGHTING

*a. Lighting shall be provided in accordance with a plan designed by the utility company, or using as a guideline the standards set forth by the* IES *Lighting Handbook shown in the Appendix, Exhibit A-8.*

*b. Lighting for safety shall be provided at intersections, along walkways, at entryways, between buildings, and in parking areas.*

*c. Spacing of standards shall be equal to approximately four times the height of the standard.*

*d. The maximum height of standards shall not exceed the maximum building height permitted, or 25 feet, whichever is less.*

*e. The height and shielding of lighting standards shall provide proper lighting without hazard to drivers or nuisance to residents, and the design of lighting standards shall be of a type appropriate to the development and the municipality.*

*f. Spotlights, if used, shall be placed on standards pointing toward the build-*

*ing and positioned so as not to blind the residents, rather than on the buildings and directed outwards which creates dark shadows adjacent to the buildings.*

13. UNDERGROUND WIRING

*a. All electric, telephone, television, and other communication lines, both main and service connections, servicing new developments shall be provided by underground wiring within easements or dedicated public rights-of-way, installed in accordance with the prevailing standards and practices of the utility or other companies providing such services.*

*b. Lots that abut existing easements or public rights-of-way where overhead electric or telephone distribution supply lines and service connections have previously been installed may be supplied with electric and telephone service from those overhead lines, but the service connections from the utilities' overhead lines shall be installed underground. In the case of existing overhead utilities, should a road widening, or an extension of service, or other such condition occur as a result of the subdivision and necessitate the replacement or relocation of such utilities, such replacement or relocation shall be underground.*

*c. Where overhead lines are permitted as the exception, the placement and alignment of poles shall be designed to lessen the visual impact of overhead lines. Alignments and pole locations shall be carefully routed to avoid locations along horizons; clearing swaths through treed areas shall be avoided by selective cutting and a staggered alignment; trees shall be planted in open areas and at key locations to minimize the view of the poles and the alignments; and alignments shall follow rear lot lines and other alignments.*

*13. UNDERGROUND WIRING*

The placement of wiring—overhead or underground—varies among municipalities, with many local ordinances requiring new developments to place wiring underground. In addition, some states have a policy of requiring underground wiring in all new developments.

c. This provision allows for the possibility that overhead lines may be permitted as an exception—to lower development costs in order to provide affordable housing, for example.

*14.  SIGNS*

State regulations generally govern the design and placement of traffic control signs. Street name signs and site information signs in planned developments are generally regulated by municipalities. Some municipalities have elaborate requirements as well for commercial signs. Since this ordinance is primarily concerned with residential development, commercial sign regulations are not covered here.

## F.  Off-Street Parking

Before the 1970s, subdivision and site plan ordinances did not contain off-street parking standards. The growth of cluster and multifamily residential developments, which often do not have garages or driveways attached to individual units, has led to a need to include parking standards with other subdivision requirements.

*1.  NUMBER OF SPACES*

a. This performance standard sets forth the objective of the quantitative standards that are usually specified in ordinances: to supply an adequate number of parking spaces to accommodate need. Need is determined by comparing demand (based on such factors in residential developments, for example, as dwelling unit type, household characteristics, and availability of mass transit) with existing parking (available on-street parking, or possibly, nearby nonresidential parking that can be shared).

b. This provision presents a quantitative standard for the number of parking spaces required for residential developments. Parking requirements are based on vehicle ownership by housing unit, information that is available for each state from the Bureau of the Census, Public Use Sample. One parking space for each vehicle, plus visitor parking (.5 spaces per unit), yield the total parking requirement. Calculated in this fashion, the parking standard varies by housing type and size. Since the vehicle ownership figures used in this model ordinance apply to New Jersey, the parking standards are presented to illustrate the method. They should be adjusted on a state-by-state basis to reflect the applicable ownership figures.

c. Parking standards for nonresidential developments are presented as a guideline, primarily because there is no authorita-

*d. Year-round screening of any utility apparatus appearing above the surface of the ground, other than utility poles, shall be required.*

14. SIGNS

*a. Design and placement of traffic signs shall follow state regulations or the requirements specified in the* Manual on Uniform Traffic Control Devices for Streets and Highways, *published by the U.S. Department of Transportation.*

*b. At least two street name signs shall be placed at each four-way street intersection, and one at each "T" intersection. Signs shall be installed under light standards and free of visual obstruction. The design of street name signs shall be consistent, of a style appropriate to the community, and of a uniform size and color.*

*c. Site information signs in planned developments shall follow a design theme that is related and complementary to other elements of the overall site design.*

*F. Off-Street Parking*

1. NUMBER OF SPACES

*a. An adequate number of off-street parking spaces shall be required in all developments to accommodate residents and visitors.*

*b. For residential developments, off-street parking shall be provided as set forth in Exhibit 6.*

*c. For nonresidential developments, the parking standards shown in Exhibit 7 shall be used as a guideline.*

# EXHIBIT 6

## OFF-STREET PARKING REQUIREMENTS [1]
## FOR RESIDENTIAL LAND USES

| Housing Unit Type and Size [2] | Off-Street Parking Requirements | Housing Unit Type and Size | Off-Street Parking Requirements |
|---|---|---|---|
| *Single-Family Detached* | | *High-Rise* | |
| 2 Bedroom | 1.5 | Studio | .8 |
| 3 Bedroom | 2.0 | 1 Bedroom | 1.3 |
| 4 Bedroom | 2.5 | 2 Bedroom | 1.9 |
| 5 Bedroom | 3.0 | | |
| | | *Mobile Home* | |
| *Garden Apartment* | | 1 Bedroom | 1.8 |
| 1 Bedroom | 1.8 | 2 Bedroom | 2.0 |
| 2 Bedroom | 2.0 | | |
| 3 Bedroom | 2.1 | | |
| *Townhouse* | | | |
| 1 Bedroom | 1.8 | | |
| 2 Bedroom | 2.3 | | |
| 3 Bedroom | 2.4 | | |

*Notes:*

1. When determination of the number of parking spaces required by this exhibit results in a requirement of a fractional space, any fraction of one-half or less may be disregarded, while a fraction in excess of one-half shall be counted as one parking space.

2. Requirements for attached units include provision for guest parking.

*Source:* See Reference section.

## EXHIBIT 7

## GUIDELINES FOR OFF-STREET PARKING REQUIREMENTS
## FOR NONRESIDENTIAL LAND USES

| Nonresidential Land Use | Required Off-Street Parking Spaces Per Indicated Area |
|---|---|
| Assembly operations | 1 per 800 sq.ft. GFA |
| Bar | 1 per 2 seats |
| Bowling alley | 4 per alley |
| Car wash | 10 per washing lane |
| Church/Synagogue | 1 per 3 seats |
| Fiduciary institutions | 1 per 300 sq.ft. GFA |
| Finishing operations | 1 per 800 sq.ft. GFA |
| Hotel | .7 per guest room plus 10 per 1,000 sq.ft. GFA non-room area |
| Industrial | 1 per 800 sq.ft. GFA |
| Library | 1 per 300 sq.ft. GFA |
| Manufacturing | 1 per 800 sq.ft. GFA |
| Medical center | 1 per 250 sq.ft. GFA |
| Neighborhood convenience center | |
|     Under 400,000 sq.ft. GLA | 4 per 1,000 sq.ft. GLA |
| Nightclub | 1 per 3 seats |
| Offices | |
|     Under 49,999 sq.ft. GFA | 4.5 per 1,000 sq.ft. GFA |
|     50,000-99,999 sq.ft. GFA | 4 per 1,000 sq.ft. GFA |
|     100,000+ sq.ft. GFA | 3.5 per 1,000 sq.ft. GFA |
| Receiving | 1 per 5,000 sq.ft. GFA |
| Research | 1 per 1,000 sq.ft. GFA |
| Restaurant | 1 per 3 seats |
|     Quick-food establishments | 1 per 30 sq.ft. GFA |
| Retail store | 1 per 200 sq.ft. GFA |
| Schools | |
|     Elementary | 2 per classroom; but not less than 1 per teacher & staff |
|     Intermediate | 1.5 per classroom; but not less than 1 per teacher & staff |
|     Secondary | 2.5 per classroom; but not less than 1 per teacher & staff |
| Service station | 4 per bay & work area |
| Shipping | 1 per 5,000 sq.ft. GFA |
| Shopping center | |
|     Under 400,000 sq.ft. GLA | 4 per 1,000 sq.ft. GLA |
|     400,000-599,999 sq.ft. GLA | 4.5 per 1,000 sq.ft. GLA |
|     600,000+ sq.ft. GLA | 5 per 1,000 sq.ft. GLA |
| Storage areas | 1 per 5,000 sq.ft. GLA |
| Theater | 1 per 3 seats |
|     In shopping center | 1 per 4 seats |
| Warehouse | 1 per 5,000 sq.ft. GFA |

*Notes:* GFA = Gross floor area
GLA = Gross leasable area
*Source:* See Reference section.

*d. Alternative off-street parking standards to those shown in Exhibit 6 and Exhibit 7 shall be accepted if the applicant demonstrates that such standards better reflect local conditions.*

*e. A one-car garage and driveway combination shall count as 1.75 off-street parking spaces, provided the driveway measures a minimum of 25 feet in length between the face of the garage door and the sidewalk, or 30 feet to the curbline. A two-car garage and driveway combination shall count as 3.5 off-street parking spaces, provided the minimum width of the driveway is 20 feet and its minimum length is as specified above for a one-car garage.*

*f. For mixed-use developments, a shared parking approach to the provision of off-street parking shall be permitted.*

*g. Where the total number of off-street parking spaces required are not immediately required for a particular use, a staged development plan may be permitted requiring that only a portion of the parking area, but not less than sixty-five percent (65%) of the required spaces, be completed initially, subject to the following regulations:*

*1) The site plan shall clearly indicate both that portion of the parking area to be paved initially and the total parking needed to provide the number of spaces required.*

*2) The site plan shall provide for adequate drainage of both the partial and total parking areas.*

*3) The portion of the parking area not to be paved initially shall be landscaped with a ground cover to prevent erosion. The ground cover shall be appropriate for soil conditions, water availability, and the environment.*

*4) The applicant shall post separate performance guarantees, in addition to the performance guarantees*

tive, reliable source on which to base them. Unfortunately, there has been little research on the parking needs for many land uses, and even the standards of the Institute of Transportation Engineers (ITE) are often based on as few as one or two observations.

d. Because some of the parking requirements offered as guidelines are informed estimates at best, the model ordinance permits alternative parking requirements to be used. In addition, factors such as household characteristics, availability of mass transit, urban versus suburban location, and existing parking can also affect the number of parking spaces that should be required for a development. The burden of proof is, however, on the applicant to show that the alternative requirements better reflect local needs.

e. By not allowing full credit for each parking space in a garage and driveway, the ordinance recognizes that many garages are used to store assorted large objects almost as often as vehicles. It does assume, however, that most garages and driveways will be available for parking vehicles under the stipulated conditions (i.e., when the driveway length is such that parking in the driveway will generally occur).

f. The methodology outlined in the Urban Land Institute and Barton Aschman Associates' publication, *Shared Parking* (Urban Land Institute, 1984), is a recognized approach that can be used to calculate the number of parking spaces required for mixed-use developments.

g. Permitting a staged development plan when not all the parking spaces are needed immediately allows cost savings and decreases runoff—at least initially. It is also possible that in practice not all of the parking spaces originally required will be necessary. This provision provides the flexibility to determine after a period of 18 months whether the parking area already provided is sufficient to meet the needs of the development. The provision also includes safeguards to protect the community in case a developer defaults on building the remainder of the spaces if it is determined that they are necessary.

## 2. SIZE OF SPACES

As the size of cars has decreased, so has the required size of parking spaces, especially in residential developments. Nine-foot widths are adequate, and if curbs are used as bumpers, up to two feet of a vehicle will overhang the curb, making stalls 18 feet in length long enough. Some authorities recommend setting aside a separate area in the lot for compact cars with spaces measuring 7½ feet in width by 15 feet in length. Other authorities comment that these separate areas do not work well in practice and are often filled with full-size cars. The decision of whether to provide separate areas is one of the many policy issues that municipalities must resolve for themselves.

*required under Article Five, Section J, which shall reflect the cost of installing the additional parking facilities necessary to provide the total number of parking spaces required.*

*5) In lieu of a permanent certificate of occupancy, a temporary certificate of occupancy shall be issued for a period of two (2) years. Prior to the expiration of the two-year period, the applicant may either install the additional parking shown on the site plan and apply for issuance of a permanent certificate of occupancy, or apply to the planning board after the use has been in operation a minimum of eighteen (18) months for a determination as to whether or not the initial parking area provided is adequate. If the planning board determines that the parking facility is adequate as originally constructed, the performance guarantees shall be released and a permanent certificate of occupancy issued. If, however, the planning board determines that the partial off-street parking area is not adequate, the applicant shall be required to install the additional parking facilities in accordance with the terms of the performance guarantees prior to issuance of a permanent certificate of occupancy.*

*6) Any change of use on a site for which the planning board may have approved a partial paving of off-street parking areas to a use which requires more parking spaces than are provided on the site shall require submission of a new site plan.*

### 2. SIZE OF SPACES

*Each off-street parking space shall measure nine (9) feet in width by eighteen (18) feet in length. Parking spaces for the physically handicapped shall measure twelve (12) feet in width.*

3. PARKING AREAS

*a. Off-street parking areas shall be oriented to and within a reasonable walking distance of the buildings they are designed to serve.*

*b. Access to parking areas shall be designed so as not to obstruct free flow of traffic. There shall be adequate provision for ingress to and egress from all parking spaces to ensure ease of mobility, ample clearance, and safety of vehicles and pedestrians.*

*c. The width of all aisles providing direct access to individual parking stalls shall be in accordance with the requirements specified below. Only one-way traffic shall be permitted in aisles serving single-row parking spaces placed at an angle other than ninety degrees.*

| Parking Angle (degrees) | Aisle Width (feet) |
|---|---|
| 30 | 12 |
| 45 | 13 |
| 60 | 18 |
| 90 | 24 |

*d. Where sidewalks occur in parking areas, parked vehicles shall not overhang the sidewalk unless an additional one (1) foot is provided in order to accommodate such overhang.*

*e. Parking areas shall be suitably landscaped to minimize noise, glare, and other nuisance characteristics as well as to improve the environment of the site and surrounding area. Large parking lots shall be broken down into sections as appropriate for the type and size of the development. Sections shall be separated by landscaped dividing strips, berms, and similar elements.*

*3. PARKING AREAS*

a. A "reasonable walking distance" between parking areas and buildings can be defined in various ways. The Reference section presents standards from the national literature. There is general agreement that 200–250 feet is the maximum reasonable distance for residents to walk and 300 feet the distance for guests.

b. Rather than include detailed diagrams of acceptable parking lot entrance and exit design, the model ordinance substitutes a performance standard on the presumption that the planning board engineer will determine the safety of the site plan design.

e. No precise standard can be specified for the size of the sections; that will depend on factors that must be decided on a case-by-case basis. Further landscaping requirements for parking lots are detailed in Section D.6.

## G. Water Supply

*1. GENERAL*

a. Where a public or community water supply system is available, developments should connect to such systems.

b. Where a public water system is available but is not immediately accessible to the development site, then the question arises as to how distant a connection should be required. While linkage to the system is desirable, a lengthy connection can be quite expensive. The model ordinance attempts to balance these considerations by taking into account such factors as development size and distance to the public system. It is more feasible, for example, for a larger project to amortize the expense of a longer water connection.

c. Again, there are economic issues concerning the development to consider. If a public water supply system is planned within a reasonable period of time for the area in which a development is located, then it makes sense to provide the groundwork for connection to such a system by installing a capped system or "dry lines." Such construction, however, does not make much sense if the likelihood of a public water supply is remote or will not take place for many years. The model ordinance attempts to balance these considerations by calling for "dry lines" only if provision of the public water system is officially indicated (i.e., in a capital master plan) and is planned for the near future (i.e., within six years).

d. Water supply systems may be regulated by numerous governmental agencies. The proposed water source for a development must meet applicable regulations.

## *G. Water Supply*

1. GENERAL

*a. All installations shall be properly connected with an approved and functioning public community water system.*

*b. Depending on the number of housing units, residential subdivisions shall be connected to an existing public water supply system if public service is available within the following distances:*

| Size of Development | Distance |
|---|---|
| 1 unit | 200 feet |
| 2 units | 400 feet |
| 3 units | 600 feet |
| 4 units | 800 feet |
| 5-15 units | 1,000 feet |

*For developments with more than 15 units and located within one mile of an existing public water system, adequate justification shall be provided as to why they shall not provide a connection to the existing public water supply system. For developments with more than 15 units and located more than one mile from an existing system, the water supply system strategy shall be determined on a case-by-case basis taking into consideration density of the development, costs, and ground water availability and quality.*

*c. If a public water supply system is to be provided to the area within a six-year period as indicated in a municipal water master plan, official map, or other official document, a municipality may require installation of a capped system, or dry lines (mains only), within the road right-of-way; or a municipality may require a payment in lieu of the improvement.*

*d. All proposals for new public community water supplies or extensions to existing public water systems, or the installation of dry lines, or use of wells and other water sources, shall be approved by the officially designated agency of local, state, or other unit of government.*

2. CAPACITY

*a. The water supply system shall be adequate to handle the necessary flow based on complete development.*

*b. The demand rates for all uses shall be considered in computing the total system demand. Where fire protection is provided, the system shall be capable of providing the required fire demand plus the required domestic demand.*

*c. Average daily residential demand can be computed in accordance with the housing unit type and size data shown in Exhibit 8.*

*d. Nonresidential demand can be computed in accordance with the data shown in Exhibit 9.*

*e. Fire protection shall be furnished for any development connected to the municipal water supply system, and minimum fire flows shall be based on recommendations by the American Insurance Association and the National Board of Fire Underwriters, as indicated in Exhibit 10.*

*2. CAPACITY*

a. The model ordinance uses a performance approach in specifying water capacity standards, with supply determined by need.

b. A sufficient water supply must be available to satisfy the demands of both residential and nonresidential uses, to provide for adequate fire protection, to respond to the "peaked" nature of water use, and to provide for sufficient quantities of water at these peaked periods of high demand (see Reference section).

c. and d. The water consumption of a residential unit is influenced by the number of persons in that unit. The number of people, in turn, varies by unit type (single-family, townhouse, garden) and size (number of bedrooms). The model ordinance, therefore, differentiates water supply standards by type and size of the housing being provided. Similarly, nonresidential water demand varies by type of use, and this factor is incorporated in the ordinance.

**EXHIBIT 8**

**WATER AND SEWER DEMAND/GENERATION BY
TYPE AND SIZE OF HOUSING UNIT**

| Housing Type and Size | Number of Residents | Residential Water Demand [1] (daily) | Sewer Flow [2] (daily) | Peak Sewer Flow [3] (daily) |
|---|---|---|---|---|
| *Single-Family Detached* | | | | |
| 2 Bedroom | 2.13 | 215 | 140 | 560 |
| 3 Bedroom | 3.21 | 320 | 210 | 840 |
| 4 Bedroom | 3.93 | 395 | 255 | 1,020 |
| 5 Bedroom | 4.73 | 475 | 310 | 1,240 |
| *Garden Apartment* | | | | |
| 1 Bedroom | 1.57 | 120 | 100 | 400 |
| 2 Bedroom | 2.33 | 175 | 150 | 600 |
| 3 Bedroom | 3.56 | 270 | 230 | 920 |
| *Townhouse* | | | | |
| 1 Bedroom | 1.69 | 125 | 110 | 440 |
| 2 Bedroom | 2.02 | 150 | 130 | 520 |
| 3 Bedroom | 2.83 | 210 | 185 | 740 |
| 4 Bedroom | 3.67 | 275 | 240 | 960 |
| *High-Rise* | | | | |
| Studio | 1.07 | 80 | 70 | 280 |
| 1 Bedroom | 1.34 | 100 | 90 | 360 |
| 2 Bedroom | 2.14 | 160 | 140 | 560 |
| *Mobile Home* | | | | |
| 1 Bedroom | 1.73 | 130 | 115 | 460 |
| 2 Bedroom | 2.01 | 150 | 130 | 520 |
| 3 Bedroom | 3.47 | 260 | 225 | 900 |

*Notes:*

1. Based on 100 gallons per day (gpd) per person for single-family detached units and 75 gpd for other housing types (rounded).

2. Based on 65 gpd per person (rounded). *Note:* These figures do not include allowance for infiltration/inflow. Determination of infiltration/inflow should be made and added to the sewer flow figures shown in this exhibit.

3. Based on four times daily sewer flow (rounded). (This factor is not constant throughout the range of system sizes; for large systems, consult state and industry guidelines.)

*Source:* U.S. Census, Public Use File—New Jersey (units built 1975–1980 and monitored by 1980 Census).

## EXHIBIT 9

## NONRESIDENTIAL WATER DEMAND

| NONRESIDENTIAL USES (SELECTED) | | EXPECTED WATER CONSUMPTION | |
|---|---|---|---|
| *COMMERCIAL–INSTITUTIONAL* [1] | *Parameter* | *Mean Annual Gallons/Day Per Unit of Parameter* | *Peak Hour* |
| Office building | square foot | 0.093 | 0.521 |
| Medical office | square foot | 0.618 | 4.970 |
| Retail | square foot | 0.106 | 0.271 |
| Hotel | square foot | 0.256 | 0.433 |
| Motel | square foot | 0.224 | 1.550 |
| Restaurant | seat | 24.200 | 167.000 |
| Drive-in restaurant | car stall | 100.000 | 547.000 |
| School, elementary | student | 3.830 | 37.400 |
| School, high | student | 8.020 | 79.900 |
| Service station | inside sq. foot | 0.251 | 4.890 |
| Theater | seat | 3.530 | 3.330 |

| *INDUSTRIAL* [2] | *Parameter* | *Gallons Per Day Per Employee* | *Peak Hour* |
|---|---|---|---|
| Bakery | employee | 220 | NA |
| Textile-finishing | employee | 810 | NA |
| Home furniture | employee | 122 | NA |
| Basic chemicals | employee | 2,744 | NA |
| Drugs | employee | 457 | NA |
| Agriculture chemicals | employee | 449 | NA |
| Petroleum refining | employee | 3,141 | NA |
| Plastic products | employee | 527 | NA |
| Cement | employee | 353 | NA |
| Engines | employee | 197 | NA |
| Metalwork | employee | 196 | NA |
| Electronic components | employee | 203 | NA |
| Motor vehicles | employee | 318 | NA |
| Scientific instruments | employee | 181 | NA |
| Medical instruments | employee | 506 | NA |

*Notes:*

NA = Information not available

1. *Source:* Michael Greenberg et al., *A Primer on Industrial Environmental Impact* (New Brunswick, NJ: Center for Urban Policy Research, 1979), p. 116.

2. *Source:* Hittman Associates, Inc., *Forecasting Municipal Water Requirements* (Columbia, MD, 1969).

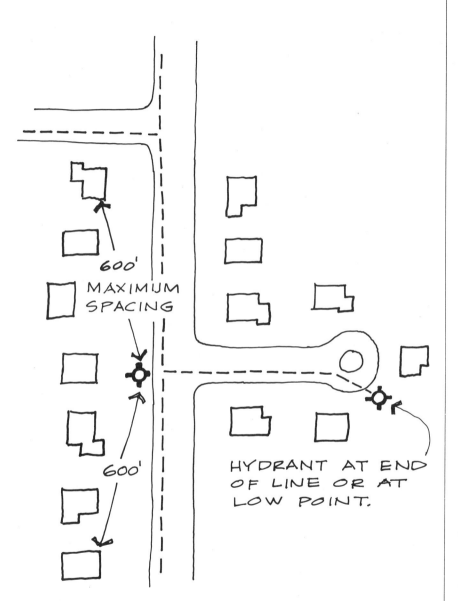

*Example of fire hydrant location and spacing*

600'
MAXIMUM
SPACING

600'

HYDRANT AT END
OF LINE OR AT
LOW POINT.

## EXHIBIT 10

## FIRE FLOWS

| Population | Flow (gpm)* | Duration of Flow (hours) |
|---|---|---|
| Under 100 | 500 | 4 |
| 1,000 | 1,000 | 4 |
| 1,500 | 1,250 | 5 |
| 2,000 | 1,500 | 6 |
| 3,000 | 1,750 | 7 |
| 4,000 | 2,000 | 8 |
| 5,000 | 2,250 | 9 |
| 6,000 | 2,500 | 10 |
| 10,000 | 3,000 | 10 |

*Note:* *gpm = gallons per minute

f. The water system shall be designed to carry peak-hour flows and be capable of delivering the peak hourly demands indicated in Exhibit 11.

g. For developments of one- and two-family dwellings, not exceeding two stories in height, the short method indicated in Exhibit 12 may be used.

## EXHIBIT 11

## DESIGN STANDARDS FOR PEAK HOUR FLOW

| Total Houses Served | Peak Hourly Rates (gpm per house) |
|---|---|
| 5 | 8.0 |
| 10 | 5.0 |
| 50 | 3.0 |
| 100 | 2.0 |
| 250 | 1.3 |
| 500 | 0.8 |
| 750 | 0.7 |
| 1,000 or more | 0.6 |

## EXHIBIT 12

### SHORT METHOD FOR CALCULATING FIRE FLOWS

| Distance Between Buildings* | Required Fire Flow |
|---|---|
| over 100 feet | 500 gpm |
| 31 feet–100 feet | 750 gpm – 1,000 gpm |
| 11 feet–30 feet | 1,000 gpm – 1,500 gpm |
| 10 feet or less | 1,500 gpm – 2,000 gpm |

*Note:* * For contiguous buildings (attached dwelling units of two or more two-family units and/or multi-family units), a minimum of 2,500 gpm may be used.

#### 3. SYSTEM DESIGN AND PLACEMENT

*System design and placement shall comply with the construction specifications set forth in the Appendix.*

#### 4. FIRE HYDRANTS

*a. Hydrants shall be spaced to provide necessary fire flow. The average area per hydrant shall not exceed 120,000 square feet. In addition, hydrants shall be spaced so that each residence shall be within 600 feet of a hydrant.*

*b. A hydrant shall be located at all low points and at all high points with adequate means of drainage provided.*

*c. Hydrants shall be located at the ends of lines, and valves of full line size shall be provided after hydrant tees at the ends of all dead lines that may be extended in the future.*

*d. Size, type, and installation of hydrants shall conform to the specifications set forth in the Appendix.*

### 3. *SYSTEM DESIGN AND PLACEMENT*
See Reference section.

### 4. *FIRE HYDRANTS*

a. Rather than specifying minimum fire hydrant spacing, the model ordinance uses a performance standard, i.e., spacing between hydrants should provide the required fire flow. Certain maximum standards are specified, however, such as the 600-foot distance between a residence and a hydrant. These are established for functional reasons. The maximum length of a fire hose, for example, is typically 500 to 600 feet.

b. and c. The location of fire hydrants is similarly determined by functional requirements. Hydrants, for example, are needed at low points to flush out accumulated sediment particles.

## H. Sanitary Sewers

### 1. *GENERAL*

a. A properly functioning sanitary sewer system—whether an on-lot septic system, a private system designed to serve a particular development, or a public community-wide system—is an essential prerequisite to development occupancy.

b. Where a public sanitary sewer system is available but not immediately accessible to the development site, the question arises as to how distant a connection should be required. While linkage to a public system is desirable, a lengthy connection can be quite expensive. The model ordinance attempts to balance these considerations by taking into account such factors as development size and distance to the public system. It is more feasible for a larger project, for example, to amortize the expense of longer sewer hookup. The standards indicated here parallel those for water supply connection to a public system.

c. Many jurisdictions are attempting to discourage the use of individual lot septic systems. In practice, however, there may be no economically viable alternative to such a strategy. On-site septic systems should be permitted in lower-density developments as long as soil, slope, and other physical conditions are suitable for septic systems. In addition, installation must comply with state and local regulations.

d. Public purpose and the economics of a development project must be balanced. If a public sanitary sewer system is planned within a reasonable period of time for the area in which a development is located, then it makes sense to provide the groundwork for connection to such a system by installing a capped system or "dry lines." Such construction, however, does not make much sense if the likelihood of public sewers is remote or will not take place for many years. The model ordinance attempts to balance these considerations by calling for "dry lines" only if provision of the public sewer system is officially indicated (i.e., in a capital master plan) and is planned for the near future (i.e., within six years). Again, this section parallels the strategy indicated for water supply "dry lines."

## 2. SYSTEM DESIGN AND PLACEMENT

a. The model ordinance uses a performance approach in specifying sanitary sewer standards, with requirements determined by need. Sufficient system capacity must be available to satisfy the demands placed on it by residential and nonresidential uses.

b. The sewage generation of a residential unit is linked to its water consumption, with the latter influenced by the number of people in that unit. The number of people, in turn, varies by unit type (single-family, townhouse, garden) and size (number of bedrooms). The model ordinance, therefore, differentiates sanitary sewer needs by type and size of the housing being provided.

c. These are explained in the Reference section.

### H. Sanitary Sewers

1. GENERAL

*a. All installations shall be properly connected to an approved and functioning sanitary sewer system prior to the issuance of a certificate of occupancy.*

*b. Depending on the number of housing units, residential subdivisions shall be connected to an existing public water supply system if public service is available within the following distances:*

| Size of Development | Distance |
| --- | --- |
| 1 unit | 200 feet |
| 2 units | 400 feet |
| 3 units | 600 feet |
| 4 units | 800 feet |
| 5-15 units | 1,000 feet |

*For developments with more than 15 units and located within one mile of an existing public sanitary sewer system, adequate justification shall be provided as to why they should not provide a connection to the existing public water supply system. For developments with more than fifteen units and located more than one mile from an existing system, the sanitary sewer system strategy shall be determined on a case-by-case basis, taking into consideration the density of development and cost.*

*c. If a public system is not in place or cannot be extended, the developer must provide individual subsurface disposal systems where appropriate, given site density, soil, slope, and other conditions and subject to applicable state and other prevailing regulations.*

*d. If a public sanitary sewer system will be provided to the area within a six-year period as indicated in a municipal sewer master plan, official map, or other official document, a municipality may require installation of a capped system,* or "dry lines" (mains only), within the road right-of-way; or the municipality may require a payment in lieu of the improvement.

*e. All proposals for new public sanitary sewer systems, or extensions to existing public sewer systems or the installation of "dry lines," or the use of individual subsurface disposal systems, shall be approved by the officially designated agency of local, state, or other unit of government.*

2. SYSTEM DESIGN AND PLACEMENT

*a. The sanitary sewer system shall be adequate to handle the necessary flow based on complete development.*

*b. Average daily residential sewer flow shall be calculated as shown in Exhibit 8.*

*c. System design and placement shall comply with the specifications set forth in the Appendix.*

## I. Storm Water Management

1. GENERAL

*a. Design of the storm water management system shall be consistent with general and specific concerns, values, and standards of the municipal master plan and applicable county, regional, and state storm drainage control programs, including mosquito commission control standards, if applicable. Design shall be based on environmentally sound site planning and engineering techniques.*

*b. The best available technology shall be used to minimize off-site storm water runoff, increase on-site infiltration, encourage natural filtration functions, simulate natural drainage systems, and minimize off-site discharge of pollutants to ground and surface water. Best available technology may include measures such as retention basins, recharge trenches, porous paving and piping, contour terraces, and swales.*

## I.  Storm Water Management

*1.  GENERAL*

a. It is especially critical that storm water management be approached from a regional perspective. There should be an emphasis on designing systems for an entire drainage basin rather than just specific sites.

b. There has been a change in drainage design. For years there was an emphasis on eliminating excess water at an individual site by containing and disposing of that water through a closed system. While such a strategy may function, it requires costly infrastructure. Today, the emphasis has changed to non-structural systems which combine natural storage, percolation, and channeling techniques.

*2. SYSTEM STRATEGY AND DESIGN*
    a. See Reference section.

## J.  Improvement Guarantees

*1. PURPOSE*

The nature and amount of improvement guarantees should reflect a balancing of interests. Developers should not be required to provide guarantees which are excessive in amount, duration, and cost. Yet, the public must be protected by ensuring proper provision of subdivision improvements.

*2. APPLICATION*

a. While the planning board could require that all improvements be completed before, or as a condition of, final site plan approval, this up-front provision is an economic burden to developers, especially with larger projects. Consequently, completion of all improvements is usually not required, but to protect the community, improvement guarantees are provided.

There are two types of guarantees: *performance* and *maintenance*. The former ensures that the improvements are constructed properly; the latter ensures that the improvements are operationally sound (i.e., they perform adequately for a stated period of time). To illustrate, a performance bond would guarantee that a retention basin was constructed as specified, while a maintenance bond would guarantee that the retention facility performed its storm water management functions.

The amounts and time periods of guarantees that are required in the model ordinance are based on a number of considerations. The performance guarantee is for an amount not to exceed 120 percent of the cost of installing the improvements. The added 20-percent factor is included to: 1) provide for a margin of error; and 2) factor for inflation and institutional costs if the municipality, upon developer default, is forced to provide improvements some years in the future.

The maintenance bond time and security parameters are guided by practicality. A two-year period is reasonable for determining if an improvement is functioning properly; a 15-percent-of-cost factor is generally adequate for correcting the deficiencies of a poorly functioning improvement.

2. SYSTEM STRATEGY AND DESIGN

*Storm water management system strategy and design shall comply with the specifications set forth in the Appendix.*

### J. Improvement Guarantees

1. PURPOSE

*Improvement guarantees shall be provided to ensure the proper installation and maintenance of required street, utility, and other improvements. The nature and duration of the guarantee shall be structured to achieve this goal without adding unnecessary costs to the developer.*

2. APPLICATION

*a. Before the recording of final subdivision plats, or as a condition of final site plan approval, the planning board may require and shall accept in accordance with the standards adopted by ordinance the following guarantees:*

*1) The furnishing of a performance guarantee in an amount not to exceed [120] percent of the cost of installation for improvements;*

*2) Provision for a maintenance guarantee for a period not to exceed [2] years after final acceptance of the improvement, in an amount not to exceed [15] percent of the cost of the improvement. In the event that other governmental agencies or public utilities automatically will own the utilities to be installed, or the improvements are covered by a performance or maintenance guarantee to another governmental agency, no performance or maintenance guarantee, as the case may be, shall be required by the planning board for such utilities or improvements.*

*b. The time allowed for installation of the improvements for which the performance guarantee has been provided may be extended by the planning board by resolution.*

*c. Upon substantial completion of all required improvements, the developer may notify the planning board in writing, by certified mail, of the completion or substantial completion of improvements, and shall send a copy to the municipal engineer. The municipal engineer shall inspect all improvements of which such notice has been given and shall file a detailed report, in writing, with the planning board indicating either approval, partial approval, or rejection of such improvements with a statement of reasons for any rejection. The cost of the improvements as approved or rejected shall be set forth.*

*d. The governing body shall either approve, partially approve, or reject the improvements on the basis of the report of the municipal engineer, and shall notify the developer in writing, by certified mail, of the contents of the report and the action not later than [30] days after receipt of the notice from the developer of the completion of the improvements. Failure of the governing body to send or provide such notification to the developer within [30] days shall be deemed to constitute approval of the improvements, and the obligor and surety, if any, shall be released from all liability pursuant to such performance guarantee for such improvements.*

*e. Where partial approval is granted, the developer shall be released from all liability except for that portion of improvements not yet approved.*

3. PERFORMANCE AND MAINTENANCE
   MECHANISMS

*Performance and maintenance guarantees shall be provided by a variety of means including, but not limited to, the following:*

*a. **Security bond.** The applicant may obtain a security bond from a*

b. Not uncommonly, there is slippage in the development delivery schedule. This ordinance provision allows flexibility by permitting an extension to the time given to the developer for making improvements. There should be a limit, however, to the number and length of extensions which are granted.

c. and d. A clear procedure is necessary for determining which improvements have been made and, correspondingly, which guarantees can be released. If the municipality does not respond within a reasonable period of time to the developer's clarification of status with respect to the improvements, then the improvements will automatically be accepted. This provision is included to spur expeditious review.

e. In practice, improvements are usually made on an incremental basis. This is especially the case with larger projects. Given this reality, it is unfair to require that the full bond be maintained until all work is completed; instead, partial release of the guarantee should be allowed—reflecting the pace of the improvements which have been made.

3. *PERFORMANCE AND MAINTENANCE*
   *MECHANISMS*

The premise of this section is that a variety of guarantee mechanisms should be allowed; limitation to a security bond is unnecessary and expensive. See Reference section for details.

# Article Six
# Off-Tract Improvements

## A. Purpose

This section considers the proper allocation of off-tract improvement costs. Off-tract improvements encompass the off-tract infrastructure and other public facility additions or expansions made as a consequence of growth. A key issue is how to distribute off-tract improvement costs fairly among a community's existing, entering, and future residents. This section provides the direction for achieving an equitable allocation.

## B. Definition and Principles

The issue of when an off-site improvement can be charged to a developer has generated considerable litigation. The courts have decided the question by reference to one of three "tests" related to the needs created by new development and the benefits conferred by infrastructure investment. These three tests are "reasonable relationship," "specific and unique attribution," and "rational nexus."

The reasonable relationship test permits an exaction if there is any relationship, however general and long-term, between the requested improvement and an entering new development.

The specifically and uniquely attributable test places a stringent burden of proof on the public body; exactions are justified only if they arise out of a need "specifically and uniquely" caused by the new development.

The rational nexus test adopts a midway position; while a "specific and unique" linkage is not required for imposing an exaction, a closer association between development and improvements—a "rational" or reasonable linkage—must be shown, rather than just a generalized "reasonable relationship."

The model ordinance embodies the "rational nexus" test. (Prevailing state court opinion on the appropriate test should be checked.) To further foster the "reasonableness" of the exactions, the model ordinance calls for a demonstrated linkage between the off-tract improvements and the community's overall capital facilities plan.

*surety bonding company authorized to do business in the state.*

*b. Letter of credit. The applicant may provide an irrevocable letter of credit from a bank or other reputable institution.*

*c. Escrow account. The applicant shall deposit cash, or other instruments readily convertible into cash at face value, either with the municipality, or in escrow with a bank.*

*d. Property. The applicant may provide as a guarantee land or other property.*

*e. Subdivision improvement guarantee. An applicant may provide as a guarantee a subdivision improvement agreement between the applicant, lender, and local government.*

## *Article Six*
## *Off-Tract Improvements*

### *A. Purpose*

*This article is intended to ensure a pro rata share allocation of the costs for off-tract improvements necessitated by new development.*

### *B. Definition and Principles*

*As a condition of final subdivision or site plan approval, the planning board may require an applicant to pay a pro rata share of the cost of providing reasonable and necessary circulation improvements and water, sewerage, drainage facilities and other improvements, including land and easements, located off-tract of the property limits of the subdivision or development but necessitated or required by the development. "Necessary" improvements are those clearly and substantially related to the development in question. The planning board shall provide in its resolution of approval the basis of the required* improvements. *The capacity and design of proposed improvements shall be based upon the circulation plan element and utility service plan element of the adopted master plan. The proportionate or pro rata amount of the cost of such facilities within a related or common area shall be based on the following criteria.*

### C. Cost Allocation

1. FULL ALLOCATION

*In cases where off-tract improvements are necessitated by the proposed development, and where no other property owner(s) receive(s) a special benefit thereby, the applicant may be required at his sole expense and as a condition of approval, to provide and install such improvements.*

2. PROPORTIONATE ALLOCATION

*a. Where it is determined that properties outside the development will also be benefitted by the off-tract improvement, the following criteria shall be utilized in determining the proportionate share of the cost of such improvements to the developer.*

*b.* Allocation Formula

*1)* Sanitary Sewers. *The applicant's proportionate share of distribution facilities including the installation, relocation, or replacement of collector, trunk, and interceptor sewers, and associated appurtenances, shall be computed as follows:*

*a) The capacity and the design of the sanitary sewer system shall be based on the standards specified in Article Five of this ordinance;*

*b) The municipal engineer or planner shall provide the applicant with the existing and reasonably anticipated peak hour flows as well as capacity limits of the affected sewer system;*

## C. Cost Allocation

Once having established a "rational nexus," there is the further issue of determining the share of the costs of the required improvements that may be allocated to the proposed development. The model ordinance considers different situations in this regard.

### 1. FULL ALLOCATION

Provision is made in the ordinance for cases when needs and benefits apply *only* to the proposed subdivision; in such cases no proportionate allocation of cost is required, and the developer bears full responsibility for any improvements.

### 2. PROPORTIONATE ALLOCATION

It is important, however, that the developer not be required to bear the full costs for improvements if the benefits of the improvements will be shared by others. The calculation of proportionate share of benefit in cases where benefits are distributed among more than one property owner is handled by the model ordinance through the following formula:

$$\frac{\text{Total cost of enlargement or improvement}}{\text{Developer's Cost}} = \frac{\text{Capacity of enlargement or improvement}}{\text{Development share of capacity of enlargement or improvement}}$$

In short, a development's off-tract exactions should be proportionate to its share of the benefit realized from the off-tract improvement. "Benefit" is defined by the model ordinance in terms of capacity—both the total capacity of the improvement and the fractional share of the capacity utilized by a specific development.

The model ordinance includes the exaction formula for four specific categories of improvements (sanitary sewers, water supply, drainage improvements, and roadways) as well as a general category. In calibrating the formula, the exhibits contained in Article Five of the ordinance can prove useful. These include automobile trips and road capacity, water consumption by type and size of housing unit, sewage generation by type and size of housing unit, drainage figures, etc.

To illustrate, suppose a developer wishes to construct 500 single-family units (250 four-bedroom, 250 five-bedroom) which will "clearly and substantially" require the construction of an off-tract water main with 2 MGD (million of gallons per day) total capacity. The water main will cost $1,000,000. It would be unfair to demand a $1,000,000 exaction from the developer as other developments will likely tap into the main and thus benefit from the utility extension. What then, is a fair share?

An answer is suggested by Exhibit 8 in Article Five of the model ordinance. It specifies that residential water demand for a four-bedroom, single-family home is 395 gallons per day; for a five-bedroom unit, the figure is 475 gallons daily. On this basis, the 500-unit development will exert the following water demand:

| Unit Size/Type | No. of Units | Water Demand | Total Project Share (Gal.) |
|---|---|---|---|
| 4 Bedroom SFU | 250 | 395 | 98,750 |
| 5 Bedroom SFU | 250 | 475 | 118,750 |
| | | | 217,500 |

Of the water main's total 2 MGD capacity, the development will be using 217,500 gallons per day, or 10.9 percent. A fair exaction would therefore be calculated as 10.9 percent of the $1,000,000 total utility-main expenditure, or $109,000. The formula according to the model ordinance would be as follows:

$$\frac{\$1,000,000}{\text{development share}} = \frac{2,000,000 \text{ gallons/day}}{217,500 \text{ gallons/day}}$$

Thus, the improvement standards found in Article Five of the model ordinance can be used for assigning off-tract costs. It should be noted, however, that for apportioning off-tract roadway improvements, peak hour trips (PHT) rather than average daily trips (ADT) is applied as a measure. While ADT is useful for defining the road hierarchy as indicated in Article Five, PHT is a better measure of road capacity. The latter is therefore used for determining exactions.

*c) If the existing system does not have adequate capacity to accommodate the applicant's flow given existing and reasonably anticipated peak-hour flows, the pro rata share shall be computed as follows:*

$$\frac{\text{Total cost of enlargement or improvement}}{\text{Developer's Cost}} = \frac{\text{Capacity of enlargement or improvement (gal. per day)(gpd)}}{\text{Development-generated gallons per day to be accommodated by the enlargement or improvement}}$$

*2) Water Supply. The applicant's proportionate share of water distribution facilities including the installation, relocation, or replacement of water mains, hydrants, valves, and associated appurtenances shall be computed as follows:*

*a) The capacity and the design of the water supply system shall be based on the standards specified in Article Five of this ordinance;*

*b) The municipal engineer or planner shall provide the applicant with the existing and reasonably anticipated capacity limits of the affected water supply system in terms of average demand, peak demand, and fire demand;*

*c) If the existing system does not have adequate capacity as defined above to accommodate the applicant's needs, the pro rata share shall be computed as follows:*

$$\frac{\text{Total cost of enlargement or improvement}}{\text{Developer's Cost}} = \frac{\text{Capacity of enlargement or improvement (gal. per day)(gpd)}}{\text{Development-generated gallons per day to be accommodated by the enlargement or improvement}}$$

*3)* Roadways. *The applicant's proportionate share of street improvements, alignment, channelization, barriers, new or improved traffic signalization, signs, curbs, sidewalks, trees, utility improvements not covered elsewhere, the construction or reconstruction of new or existing streets, and other associated street or traffic improvements shall be as follows:*

*a) The municipal engineer or planner shall provide the applicant with the existing and reasonably anticipated future peak-hour flows for the off-tract improvement;*

*b) If the existing system does not have adequate capacity as defined above, the pro rata share shall be computed as follows:*

$$\frac{\text{Total cost of enlargement or improvement}}{\text{Developer's Cost}} = \frac{\text{Capacity of enlargement or improvement (peak-hour traffic)}}{\text{Development peak-hour traffic to be accommodated by the enlargement or improvement}}$$

*4)* Drainage improvements. *The applicant's proportionate share of storm water and drainage improvements including the installation, relocation, or replacement of storm drains, culverts, catch basins, manholes, riprap, improved drainage ditches and appurtenances, and relocation or replacement of other storm drainage facilities or appurtenances, shall be determined as follows:*

*a) The capacity and the design of the drainage system to accommodate storm water runoff shall be based on the standards specified in Article Five of this ordinance, computed by the developer's engineer and approved by the municipal engineer.*

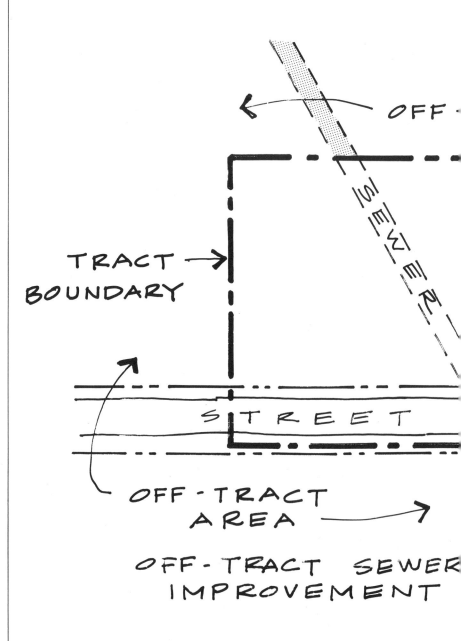

*On-tract and off-tract infrastructure improvements*

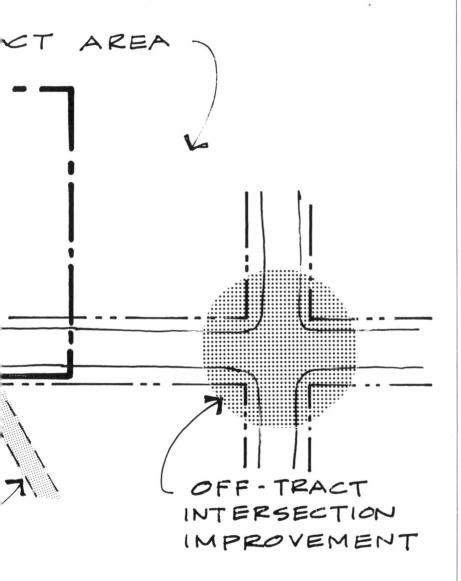

CT AREA

OFF - TRACT
INTERSECTION
IMPROVEMENT

*b) The capacity of the enlarged, extended, or improved system required for the subdivision and areas outside of the developer's tributary to the drainage system shall be determined by the developer's engineer subject to approval of the municipal engineer. The plans for the improved system shall be prepared by the developer's engineer and the estimated cost of the enlarged system calculated by the municipal engineer. The pro rata share for the proposed improvement shall be computed as follows:*

$$\frac{\text{Total cost of enlargement or improvement}}{\text{Developer's Cost}} = \frac{\text{Capacity of enlargement (total capacity expressed in cubic feet per second)}}{\text{Development-generated peak rate of runoff expressed in cubic feet per second to be accommodated by the enlargement or improvement}}$$

5) Other Improvements. *The applicant's proportionate share of other capital improvements shall be computed as follows:*

$$\frac{\text{Total cost of enlargement or improvement}}{\text{Developer's Cost}} = \frac{\text{Capacity of enlargement or improvement}}{\text{Development share of enlargement or improvement}}$$

### D. Escrow Accounts

*Where the proposed off-tract improvement is to be undertaken at some future date, the monies required for the improvement shall be deposited in a separate interest-bearing account to the credit of the municipality until such time as the improvement is constructed. If the off-tract improvement is not begun within [　　　] years of deposit, all monies and interest shall be returned to the applicant.*

## D. Escrow Accounts

If an off-tract improvement is not made coterminously with the construction of a specific development, an exaction using the formula described above is calculated, but funds are deposited in an escrow account.

If an improvement is not made within a reasonable number of years, then the basis of the exaction—a capital improvement made in response to growth—is called into question. In such an instance, the monies paid into the escrow account are returned.

# Article Seven
# Specification of Documents
# to be Submitted

## A.  Purpose and Requirements

The model ordinance's requirements for documents to be submitted organizes and lists submission items. Three categories of information are required:

1) *basic project and plat description* (i.e., applicant's name, block and lot number, zoning district, monumentation, signature blocks, etc.);

2) *setting and environmental information* (i.e., key map, location of flood plains, wetlands, and other sensitive areas, drainage calculations, perc test and soil-boring results, etc.); and

3) *project improvement and construction information* (circulation, parking, landscaping, etc.)

To help the expeditious and "rational" consideration of development applications, the model ordinance's list of documents to be submitted is keyed to the different development steps incorporated in the ordinance: preliminary pre-application and concept plan stages, followed by final review of applications according to their category—minor or major. For the pre-application and concept plan stages, only preliminary project and area information, which for the most part is readily obtainable, is required. Examples include: a tax map sheet, north arrow, and topographic features from the United States Coast & Geodetic Survey (U.S.C. & G.S.). More detailed information is requested at the later review stages, especially for the major subdivision and site plan category of development applications. To illustrate, a tighter contour line specification is required for major subdivision and site plans than for minor subdivision and site plan applications.

This same philosophy is incorporated in the specification of items to be submitted for a General Development Plan (GDP). A GDP is designed to allow review of major projects, such as PUDs, without immediately necessitating all detailed project engineering plans. Given this objective for the GDP, the model ordinance calls

## Article Seven
## Specification of Documents
## to be Submitted

### A. Purpose

The documents to be submitted are intended to provide the approving authority with sufficient information and data to assure compliance with all municipal codes and specifications and ensure that the proposed development meets the design and improvement standards contained in this ordinance. The specification of documents to be submitted is based on the type of development and particular stage of development application.

### B. Requirements

The documents to be submitted are shown on the following pages. In specific cases and for documented reasons, the approving authority may waive the submission of a particular document. The reasons for the waiver shall be indicated in the minutes of the approving authority.

for only those submission items which are appropriate for overall project consideration, such as a key map and the general project circulation pattern. Deliberately not required at the GDP stage are detailed engineering specifications, such as drainage calculations, a soil erosion plan, and road cross-sections and profiles. It makes little sense to submit these items when the planning board has yet to decide on the exact size and land-use mix of a major project. Once this determination is made at the GDP stage, detailed engineering specifications are then appropriately submitted at the preliminary major site plan and preliminary major subdivision stage reviews (see Article Four).

It should further be noted that the model ordinance permits a waiver of a submission item if it is deemed unnecessary. Documents should be required only if functionally necessary for proper subdivision and site plan review.

## Documents To Be Submitted

I. *PROJECT—PLAT INFORMATION*
1. Basic, readily available information.
2. Authorship of documents should be indicated.
3. Basic, readily available information.
4. Describes setting; may be less detailed in pre-application concept plan and GDP stages.
5. Schedule may be less detailed in pre-application–concept plan stages.
6. Item necessary for orientation.
7. Basic, readily available information.
8. Not relevant at pre-application–concept plan stages.
9. Often required by statute.
10. Monumentation required only for final subdivision.
11. May be specified by state statute.
12. Such detail is unnecessary for pre-application–concept plan, minor site plan, and GDP; it is also unnecessary for preliminary major subdivision because the information will be shown at the final subdivision plat.
13. May be required by state map filing laws; GDP does not require detail because of its conceptual focus.

14. Item necessary for continuity and history of project.

15. Item important for detailed planning.

16. Item important for detailed planning.

17. Unnecessary for preliminary–concept or GDP stages.

18. Item basic to planning.

19. Basic, readily available information.

20. Not applicable at pre-application–concept plan stage; minor plans usually not built in stages.

21. Basic planning information.

22. Basic planning information.

23. Basic planning information.

24. Required by ordinance; should reflect locally incurred review costs.

II. *SETTING—*
   *ENVIRONMENTAL INFORMATION*

25. Describes location of all adjacent structures; not necessary at pre-application–concept plan stages; required at site plan only if notice is required by ordinance.

26. While detailed specification of environmentally sensitive areas may not be necessary at pre-application–concept plan and GDP stages, general specification of and sensitivity to such conditions are important planning considerations.

27. Rights-of-way and easements are often unknown at the pre-application–concept stages (see however, item 26).

28. More detailed topographic information is needed for major subdivision.

29. Major site plan and subdivision require level of detail of item 29 as opposed to item 28.

30. Basic for good planning.

31. See item 29. Extensive level of detail required only for major subdivision and site plan.

32. Necessary for major applications; inapplicable at GDP stage.

33. Required for minor applications if deemed necessary by planning board; not required at GDP stage because

storm water management evaluated at major subdivision and site plan stage.

*III.*   *IMPROVEMENTS AND*
     *CONSTRUCTION INFORMATION*

34.   Necessary where using septic systems.

35.   Information necessary for minor site plan because of potential effect on utility systems. Only general location required for telephone, electric, and cable TV.

36.   Required for soil disturbance of over 5,000 sq. ft.

37.   Not required for minor subdivision because construction of buildings is not involved.

38.   Such level of detail necessary only for major applications.

39.   See item 38.

40.   Applicable only when new road is proposed.

41.   Needed whenever a new lot is created.

42.   Not applicable because minor subdivision merely creates lots.

43.   Required for site plans because of magnitude of required landscaping.

44.   Site plan consideration only; see item 42.

45.   See item 42.

46.   Necessary even for minor applications because sight triangle easement created.

47.   See item 42.

48.   See item 42.

49.   Not required where building is not proposed.

## REQUIRED SUBMISSION DOCUMENTS

| Item Number | Description | Preapplication Concept Plan | Minor Application Subdivision | Minor Application Site Plan | Major Application General Development Plan | Major Application Subdivision Preliminary | Major Application Subdivision Final | Major Application Site Plan Preliminary | Major Application Site Plan Final |
|---|---|---|---|---|---|---|---|---|---|
| | | | | | DEVELOPMENT STAGE | | | | |
| I. | **PROJECT–PLAT INFORMATION** | | | | | | | | |
| 1. | Name, address of owner and applicant. | X | X | X | X | X | X | X | X |
| 2. | Name, signature, license number, seal and address of engineer, land surveyor, architect, planner, and/or landscape architect, as applicable, involved in preparation of plat. | X | X | X | X | X | X | X | X |
| 3. | Title block denoting type of application, tax map sheet, county, name of municipality, block and lot, and street location. | X | X | X | X | X | X | X | X |
| 4. | A key map at specified scale showing location of tract with reference to surrounding properties, streets, municipal boundaries, etc., within 500'; date of current survey. | X | X | X | X | X | X | X | X |
| 5. | A schedule of required and provided zone district(s) requirements including lot area, width, depth, yard setbacks, building coverage, open space, parking, etc. | X | X | X | X (vested items only) | X | X | X | X |
| 6. | North arrow and scale. | X | X | X | X | X | X | X | X |
| 7. | Proof that taxes are current. | | X | X | X | X | X | X | X |
| 8. | Signature blocks for Chairman, Secretary, and Municipal Engineer. | | X | X | X | X | X | X | X |
| 9. | Appropriate certification blocks. | | X | | | X | X | | |

## REQUIRED SUBMISSION DOCUMENTS

| Item Number | Description | Preapplication Concept Plan | Minor Application Subdivision | Minor Application Site Plan | Major Application General Development Plan | Major Application Subdivision Preliminary | Major Application Subdivision Final | Major Application Site Plan Preliminary | Major Application Site Plan Final |
|---|---|---|---|---|---|---|---|---|---|
| 10. | Monumentation. | | X | | | | X | | |
| 11. | One (1) of four (4) standardized sheets:<br>30" x 42"<br>24" x 36"<br>15" x 21"<br>8.5" x 13" | | X | | | X | X | | |
| 12. | Metes and bounds description showing dimensions, bearings, curve data, length of tangents, radii, arcs, chords and central angles for all centerlines and rights-of-way, and centerline curves on streets. | | X | X | | | X | | X |
| 13. | Acreage of tract to the nearest tenth of an acre (for GDP, to nearest acre). | | X | X | X (general) | | X | | X |
| 14. | Date of original and all revisions. | | X | X | X | X | X | X | X |
| 15. | Size and location of any existing or proposed structures with all setbacks dimensioned (for GDP and preapplication-concept plan, general location but not setbacks). | X (general) | X | X | X (general) | X | X | X | X |
| 16. | Location and dimensions of any existing or proposed streets (for GDP and preapplication-concept plan, general locations). | X (general) | X | X | X (general) | X | X | X | X |
| 17. | All proposed lot lines and area of lots in square feet. | | X | X | | X | X | X | X |

## REQUIRED SUBMISSION DOCUMENTS

| Item Number | Description | Preapplication Concept Plan | Minor Application Subdivision | Site Plan | Major Application General Development Plan | Subdivision Preliminary | Final | Site Plan Preliminary | Final |
|---|---|---|---|---|---|---|---|---|---|
| | | | | | *DEVELOPMENT STAGE* | | | | |
| 18. | Copy and/or delineation of any existing or proposed deed restrictions or convenants. | X (existing) | X | X | X (existing) | X | X | X | X |
| 19. | Any existing or proposed easement or land reserved for or dedicated to public use.[1] | X | X | X | X | X | X | X | X |
| 20. | Development stages or staging plans (for GDP, general staging). | | | | X (general) | X | X | X | X |
| 21. | List of required regulatory approvals or permits.[2] | | X | X | X (vested items only) | | X | | X |
| 22. | List of variances required or requested.[1] | | X | X | | X | X | X | X |
| 23. | Requested or obtained design waivers or exceptions.[2] | | X | X | | X | X | X | X |
| 24. | Payment of application fees. | X | X | X | X | X | X | X | X |
| II. | *SETTING–ENVIRONMENTAL INFORMATION* | | | | | | | | |
| 25. | Property owners and lines of all parcels within 200' identified on most recent tax map sheet. | | | X | X | X | X | X | X |

## REQUIRED SUBMISSION DOCUMENTS

| | | | | | DEVELOPMENT STAGE | | | | |
| | | Preapplication | Minor Application | | Major Application | | | | |
| Item Number | Description | Concept Plan | Subdivision | Site Plan | General Development Plan | Subdivision Preliminary | Subdivision Final | Site Plan Preliminary | Site Plan Final |
|---|---|---|---|---|---|---|---|---|---|
| 26. | All existing streets, water courses, flood plains, wetlands or other environmentally sensitive areas on and within 200' of site. | X (general) | | X | X (general) | X | X | X | X |
| 27. | Existing rights-of-way and/or easements on and within 200' of tract. | X | | X | X (vested items only) | X | X | X | X |
| 28. | Topographical features of subject property from U.S.C.&G.S. map. | X | | X | X | | | | X |
| 29. | Existing and proposed contour intervals based on U.S.C.&G.S. data. Contours to extend at least 200' beyond subject property as follows: up to 3% grade = 1' 3% + grade = 2' | | | | | X | X | X | X |
| 30. | Boundary, limits, nature and extent of wooded areas, specimen trees, and other significant physical features (details may vary). | X (general) | X | X | X (general) | X | X | X | X |
| 31. | Existing system of drainage of subject site and of any larger tract or basin of which it is a part. | | | | | X | X | X | X |
| 32. | Drainage Area Map. | | | | | X | X | X | X |
| 33. | Drainage calculations. | | | | | X | X | X | X |
| 34. | Perc tests. | | X | X | | X | X | X | X |

## REQUIRED SUBMISSION DOCUMENTS

| Item Number | Description | Preapplication Concept Plan | Minor Application Subdivision | Minor Application Site Plan | Major Application General Development Plan | Major Application Subdivision Preliminary | Major Application Subdivision Final | Major Application Site Plan Preliminary | Major Application Site Plan Final |
|---|---|---|---|---|---|---|---|---|---|
| | **DEVELOPMENT STAGE** | | | | | | | | |
| III. | IMPROVEMENTS AND CONSTRUCTION INFORMATION | | | | | | | | |
| 35. | Proposed utility infrastructure plans, including sanitary sewer, water, storm water management, telephone, electric, and cable TV. | | | X | X (general availability) | X | X | X | X |
| 36. | Soil Erosion and Sediment Control Plan. | | | X | | X | X | X | X |
| 37. | Spot and finished elevations at all property corners, corners of all structures or dwellings, existing or proposed first floor elevations. | | | X | X (general location of buildings) | X | X | X | X |
| 38. | Construction details as required by ordinance. | | | | | X | X | X | X |
| 39. | Road and paving cross-sections and profiles. | | | | | X | X | X | X |
| 40. | Proposed street names. | | | | | X | X | X | X |
| 41. | New block and lot numbers confirmed with local assessor or municipal designee. | X | | | | | X | | |
| 42. | Lighting plan and details. | | | X | | X | X | X | X |
| 43. | Landscape plan and details. | | | X | | X | X | X | X |
| 44. | Solid waste management plan. | | | X | | | | X | X |

## REQUIRED SUBMISSION DOCUMENTS

| | | | | | DEVELOPMENT STAGE | | | | |
|---|---|---|---|---|---|---|---|---|---|
| | | Preapplication | Minor Application | | Major Application | | | | |
| Item | | Concept | | Site | General | Subdivision | | Site Plan | |
| Number | Description | Plan | Subdivision | Plan | Development Plan | Preliminary | Final | Preliminary | Final |
| 45. | Site identification signs, traffic control signs, and directional signs. | | | X | | X | X | X | X |
| 46. | Sight triangles. | | X | X | | X | X | X | X |
| 47. | Vehicular and pedestrian circulation patterns (less detail necessary for preapplication-concept plan and GDP stages). | X (general) | | X | X (general) | X | X | X | X |
| 48. | Parking plan showing spaces, size and type, aisle width, curb cuts, drives, driveways, and all ingress and egress areas and dimensions. | | | X | | X | X | X | X |
| 49. | Preliminary architectural plan and elevations. | | | X | | | | X | X |

Notes:

X = item required at indicated development stage.

1. Proposed restrictions or convenants do not have to be included for preapplication-concept plan and GDP.
2. Conditional approval may be granted subject to other regulatory approvals.

# Appendix

## EXHIBIT A-1

## SPECIFICATIONS FOR ACCEPTABLE CURB TYPES

### VERTICAL CONCRETE CURB

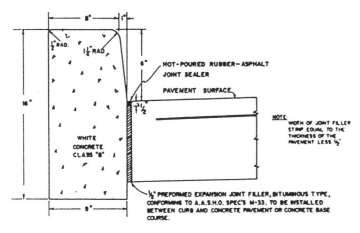

9" x 18" WHITE CONCRETE VERTICAL CURB

### MOUNTABLE CONCRETE CURB

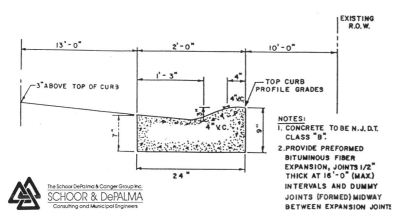

# Appendix
# Improvement Standards:
# Construction Specifications

## A. Curbs

*1. The standard curb section used shall be twenty (20) feet in length. All concrete used for curbs shall be prepared in accordance with applicable state or other regulatory standard specifications for road construction. The twenty-eight day compressive strength of the concrete used shall be not less than the following:*

| Type of Concrete | Average Strength (Pounds per Square Inch) |
|---|---|
| Class P | 6,500 |
| Class A | 5,500 |
| Class B, B-1 | 5,000 |
| Class C, C-1 | 4,500 |

*2. Curbs and/or combination curbs and gutters shall be constructed of Class B concrete, air-entrained (5,000 p.s.i.). Where bituminous concrete is used, the pavement, curb, and/or curb and gutter shall be constructed prior to the construction of the pavement.*

*3. Where drainage inlets are constructed, but curbs are not required, curbing must be provided at least ten (10) feet on each side of the inlet, set back one (1) foot from the extension of the pavement edge.*

*4. Acceptable curb types are shown in Exhibit A-1.*

## B. Sidewalks and Bikeways

1. SIDEWALKS AND GRADED AREAS

*a. Sidewalks shall be four inches thick except at points of vehicular crossing where they shall be at least six inches thick. At vehicular crossings, sidewalks shall be reinforced with welded wire fabric mesh or an equivalent.*

b. *Concrete sidewalks shall be Class C concrete, having a twenty-eight day compressive strength of 4,500 p.s.i. Other paving materials, such as gravel, crushed stone, brick, etc., may be permitted depending on the design of the development.*

c. *Graded areas shall be planted with grass or treated with other suitable ground cover, and their width shall correspond to that of sidewalks.*

2. BIKEWAYS

a. **Bicycle paths.** *Dimensions and construction specifications of bicycle paths shall be determined by the number and type of users and the location and purpose of the bicycle path. A minimum 8-foot paved width should be provided for two-way bicycle traffic and a 5-foot width for one-way traffic.*

   *1) Choice of surface materials, including bituminous mixes, concrete, gravel, soil cement, stabilized earth and wood planking, shall depend on use and users of the path.*

   *2) Gradients of bike paths should generally not exceed a grade of 5 percent, except for short distances.*

b. **Bicycle lanes.** *Lanes shall be 4 feet wide, or wide enough to allow safe passage of bicycles and motorists.*

c. **Drainage grates.** *Bicycle-safe drainage grates shall be used in the construction of all residential streets.*

### C. Street Grade, Intersections, Pavement, and Lighting

1. STREET GRADE

a. *Minimum street grade permitted for all streets shall be 0.5 percent; but streets constructed at this grade shall be closely monitored and strict attention paid to construction techniques to avoid ponding. Where topographical conditions permit, grades in excess of 0.5 percent shall be used.*

**EXHIBIT A-1** (continued)

## VERTICAL GRANITE BLOCK CURB

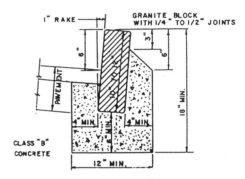

## MOUNTABLE GRANITE BLOCK CURB

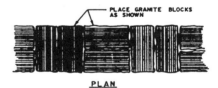

PLAN

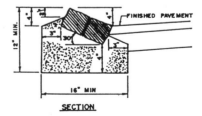

SECTION

The Schoor DePalma & Canger Group Inc.
SCHOOR & DePALMA
Consulting and Municipal Engineers

# EXHIBIT A–2

## STREET GRADE AND INTERSECTION STANDARDS

*Local Street Hierarchy*

| Intersection Standards | Special Purpose Streets | | Residential Access Street | Residential Subcollector | Residential Collector |
|---|---|---|---|---|---|
| | Alley | Cul-de-Sac | | | |
| Minimum Grade | 0.5% | 0.5% | 0.5% | 0.5% | 0.5% |
| Maximum Grade | 15% | 12% | 12% | 10% | 8% |
| Maximum Grade Within 50' of Intersection | 5% | 5% | 5% | 5% | 3% |
| Minimum Centerline Radius | 100' | 100' | 100' | 150' | 300' |
| Minimum Tangent Length Between Reverse Curves | 0' | 50' | 50' | 100' | 150' |
| Curb Radii | 20' | 25' | 25' | 30' | 35' |

*b. Maximum street grade shall vary by road hierarchy, with flatter grades required for roads with higher ADTs, in accordance with the requirements shown in Exhibit A-2.*

2. INTERSECTIONS

*a. **Minimum intersection angle.** Street intersections shall be as nearly at right angles as possible and in no case shall be less than 75 degrees.*

*b. **Minimum centerlines offset of adjacent intersections.** New intersections along one side of an existing street shall, if possible, coincide with any existing intersections on the opposite side of each street. Use of "T" intersections in subdivisions shall be encouraged. To avoid corner-cutting when inadequate offsets exist between adjacent intersections, offsets shall measure at least 175 to 200 feet between centerlines.*

*c. **Minimum curb radius.** Intersections shall be rounded at the curbline, with the street having the highest radius requirement as shown in Exhibit A-2 determining the minimum standard for all curblines.*

*d. **Grade.** Intersections shall be designed with a flat grade wherever practicable. Maximum grade within intersections shall be 5 percent except for collectors which shall be 3 percent.*

*e. **Minimum centerline radius; minimum tangent length between reverse curves; and curb radii.** Requirements shall be as shown in Exhibit A-2.*

*f. **Sight triangles.** Sight triangle easements shall be required and shall include the area on each street corner that is bounded by the line which connects the sight or "connecting" points located on each of the right-of-way lines of the intersecting street. The planting of trees or other plantings or the location of structures exceeding thirty (30) inches in height that would obstruct the clear sight* *across the area of the easements shall be prohibited, and a public right-of-entry shall be reserved for the purpose of removing any object, material or otherwise, that obstructs the clear sight.*

*The distances shown in Exhibit A-3 between the connecting points and the intersection of the right-of-way lines shall be required.*

## EXHIBIT A–3

## SIGHT TRIANGLES

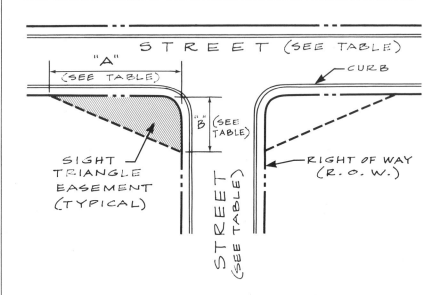

TYPICAL REQUIREMENTS BY STREET TYPE
(MEASURED ALONG R.O.W. LINE)

| "A" (DISTANCE IN FEET) | | RESIDENTIAL ACCESS | RESIDENTIAL SUBCOLLECTOR | RESIDENTIAL COLLECTOR | ARTERIAL |
|---|---|---|---|---|---|
| | | "B" (DISTANCE IN FEET) | | | |
| 30 | RESIDENTIAL ACCESS | 30 | 100 | 120 | 130 - 150 |
| 100 | RESIDENTIAL SUBCOLLECTOR | 30 | 100 | 120 | 130 - 150 |
| 120 | RESIDENTIAL COLLECTOR | 30 | 100 | 120 | 130 - 150 |
| 130 - 150 | ARTERIAL | 30 | 100 | 120 | 130 - 150 |

The Schoor DePalma & Canger Group Inc.
SCHOOR & DePALMA
Consulting and Municipal Engineers

Graphic by Carl Lindbloom, P.P., A.I.C.P.

## EXHIBIT A-4

## PAVEMENT SECTIONS FOR LOCAL STREETS
### (Residential Access and Subcollector Streets)

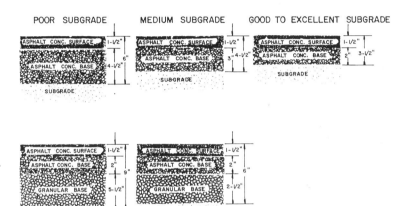

*Source:* New Jersey Society of Municipal Engineers, *Asphalt Handbook for County and Municipal Engineers* (Edison, NJ: NJSME, 1966). Handbook is currently under revision, as it is outdated. Questions as to specifications should be directed to the Municipal Engineer.

*Notes:*

1. The granular base shall be soil aggregate designated I-5 conforming to subsection 901.09 and shown in Table 901-2 of the N.J. State Highway Department standard specifications for road and building construction (1983).

2. All subgrades shall be considered "poor" unless the applicant proves otherwise through CBR testing. Test results shall be reviewed by the Municipal Engineer.

3. Subgrade compaction shall be approved by the Municipal Engineer.

### 3. PAVEMENT

*a. Pavement design for residential access streets, subcollectors, and collectors shall follow the specifications shown in Exhibits A-4 and A-5.*

*b. Subgrade categories are shown in Exhibit A-6.*

*c. If substitutions of paving materials are proposed, the relative strength ratings shown in Exhibit A-7 should be consulted to ensure appropriate substitutions.*

### 4. LIGHTING

*Lighting shall be designed in accordance with a plan designed by the utility company; or the standards recommended in the* IES Lighting Handbook, *shown in Exhibit A-8, shall be used as a guideline.*

The Schoor DePalma & Canger Group Inc.
SCHOOR & DePALMA
Consulting and Municipal Engineers

# EXHIBIT A-5

# PAVEMENT SECTIONS FOR COLLECTOR STREETS

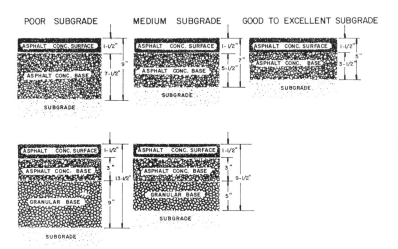

*Source:* New Jersey Society of Municipal Engineers, *Asphalt Handbook for County and Municipal Engineers* (Edison, NJ: NJSME, 1966). Handbook is currently under revision, as it is outdated. Questions as to specifications should be directed to the Municipal Engineer.

*Notes:*

1. The granular base shall be soil aggregate designated I-5 conforming to subsection 901.09 and shown in Table 901-2 of the N.J. State Highway Department standard specifications for road and building construction (1983).

2. All subgrades shall be considered "poor" unless the applicant proves otherwise through CBR testing. Test results shall be reviewed by the Municipal Engineer.

3. Subgrade compaction shall be approved by the Municipal Engineer.

## EXHIBIT A–6

## SUBGRADE CATEGORIES

| A. BASED ON STRENGTH TEST | |
|---|---|
| Subgrade Category | California Bearing Ratio (CBR) |
| Very good/excellent | +10 |
| Good/medium | +6 to 10 |
| Poor | 3 to 6 |

| B. BASED ON SOIL CLASSIFICATION* | | | |
|---|---|---|---|
| Subgrade Category | Material | Unified System* | AASHO System* |
| Very good/excellent | Gravels and sandy gravels | GW, GP, GM, GC | A–1, A–2-4, A–2-5 A–2-6, A–2-7, A–3 |
| Good or Poor | Silts and clays | ML, CL, OL, MH, CH, OH | A–4, A–5, A–6 A–7-5, A–7-6 |

*Note:* * Refers to categories of soil types and properties.

*Source:* Derived from the Asphalt Institute, *Thickness Design Manual* MS–1, 8th edition, August 1970, in Robert F. Baker et al. (ed.), *Handbook of Highway Engineering.* Note: Eighth edition out of print since 1981. This table is not included in ninth edition.

## EXHIBIT A-7

## RELATIVE STRENGTHS OF PAVING MATERIALS

| Type of Material | Coefficient Per Inch | Thickness Equivalency |
|---|---|---|
| *Surface or Binder Course* | | |
| Plant mix, high stability | 0.44 | 3.14 |
| *Base Course* | | |
| Bituminous treated, coarse aggregate | 0.34 | 2.43 |
| Sand asphalt | 0.30 | 2.14 |
| Old bituminous concrete | 0.84 | 1.00 |
| Cement-treated, 650 psi+ | 0.23 | 1.64 |
| 400–650 psi | 0.20 | 1.43 |
| less than 400 psi | 0.15 | 1.07 |
| Waterbound macadam | 0.15–0.30 | 1.07–2.14 |
| Lime treated | 0.15–0.30 | 1.07–2.14 |
| Crushed stone | 0.14 | 1.00 |
| Old bituminous concrete scarified and mixed with old base | 0.14 | 1.00 |
| Sand gravel | 0.07 | 0.50 |
| Sandy gravel | 0.11 | 0.79 |
| Sand or sandy clay | 0.05–0.10 | 0.36–0.72 |

*Source:* New Jersey Society of Municipal Engineers, *Asphalt Handbook for County and Municipal Engineers* (Edison, NJ: NJSME, 1966), p. 32. Handbook is currently under revision, as it is outdated. Questions as to specifications should be directed to the Municipal Engineer.

## EXHIBIT A–8

## ILLUMINATION GUIDELINES FOR STREETS, PARKING, AND PEDESTRIAN AREAS

### A. STREET ILLUMINATION

| | AREA CLASSIFICATION | | | | | |
| | Commercial | | Intermediate | | Residential | |
| Street Hierarchy | Lux | Footcandles | Lux | Footcandles | Lux | Footcandles |
|---|---|---|---|---|---|---|
| "Major" | 12 | 1.2 | 9 | 0.9 | 6 | 0.6 |
| "Collector" | 8 | 0.8 | 6 | 0.6 | 4 | 0.4 |
| "Local" | 6 | 0.6 | 5 | 0.5 | 3 | 0.3 |

### B. PARKING ILLUMINATION (OPEN PARKING FACILITIES)

| | ILLUMINATION OBJECTIVE | | | |
| | Vehicular Use Area Only | | General Parking & Pedestrian Safety | |
| Level of Activity | Lux | Footcandles | Lux | Footcandles |
|---|---|---|---|---|
| Low activity | 5 | 0.5 | 2 | 0.2 |
| Medium activity | 11 | 1 | 6 | 0.6 |
| High activity | 22 | 2 | 10 | 0.9 |

### C. PEDESTRIAN WAY ILLUMINATION

| | Minimum Average Horizontal Levels | Average Levels for Special Pedestrian Security |
| Walkways & Bikeway Classification | Lux | Lux |
|---|---|---|
| Sidewalks (roadside) and Type A bikeways | | |
|    Commercial areas | 10 | 22 |
|    Intermediate areas | 6 | 11 |
|    Residential areas | 2 | 5 |
| Walkways distant from roadways and Type B bikeways | | |
|    Walkways, bikeways and stairways | 5 | 5 |
| Pedestrian tunnels | 43 | 54 |

## EXHIBIT A-8 (continued)

*Notes:*

*IES Lighting Handbook* definitions:

1. STREET HIERARCHY

These are the terms utilized by the IES and defined as follows:

*Major.* The part of the roadway system that serves as the principal network for through traffic flow. The routes connect areas of principal traffic generation and important rural highways entering the city.

*Collector.* The distributor and collector roadways serving traffic between major and local roadways. These are roadways used mainly for traffic movements within residential, commercial and industrial areas.

*Local.* Roadways used primarily for direct access to residential, commercial, industrial, or other abutting property. They do not include roadways carrying through traffic. Long local roadways will generally be divided into short sections by collector roadway systems.

2. AREA CLASSIFICATION

1. *Commercial.* A business area of a municipality where ordinarily there are many pedestrians during night hours.

2. *Intermediate.* Those areas of a municipality often characterized by moderately heavy nighttime pedestrian activity such as in blocks having libraries, community recreation centers, large apartment buildings, industrial buildings, or neighborhood retail stores.

3. *Residential.* A residential development, or a mixture of residential and small commercial establishments, characterized by few pedestrians at night. This definition includes areas with single family homes, town houses, and/or small apartment buildings.

3. ACTIVITY LEVEL

*High activity.* Examples include major-league athletic events, major cultural or civic events, regional shopping centers, and fast food facilities.

*Medium activity.* Examples include community shopping centers, office parks, hospital parking areas, transportation parking (airports, etc.), cultural, civic or recreational events, and residential complex parking.

*Low activity.* Examples include neighborhood shopping, industrial employee parking, educational facility parking, and church parking.

4. BIKEWAY CLASSIFICATION

1. Type A bikeway — *Designated bicycle lane.* A portion of roadway or shoulder which has been designated for use by bicyclists. It is distinguished from the portion of the roadway for motor vehicle traffic by a paint stripe, curb, or other similar device.

2. Type B bikeway — *Bicycle trail.* A separate trail or path from which motor vehicles are prohibited and which is for the exclusive use of bicyclists or the shared use of bicyclists and pedestrians. Where such a trail or path forms a part of a highway, it is separated from the roadways for motor vehicle traffic by an open space or barrier.

*Source:* Illuminating Engineering Society of North America, *IES Lighting Handbook — Application Volume* (New York, NY: IES, 1987). Note: The IES reference volumes should be consulted for details.

## D. Water Supply: System Design and Placement

*1.* System design and placement *shall comply with all applicable state, American Water Works Association (AWWA), and municipal standards, with the strictest standards governing.*

*2.* Water and sewer mains *generally shall be separated a distance of at least 10 feet horizontally. If such lateral separation is not possible, the pipes shall be in separate trenches with the sewer at least 18 inches below the bottom of the water main; or such other separation as approved by the state or other regulatory body shall be made. In general, the vertical separation at a crossing of water and sewer line shall be at least 18 inches. Where this is not possible, the sewer shall be constructed of cast iron pipe using mechanical or slip-on joints, or hot poured lead joints for a distance of at least 10 feet on either side of the crossing; or other suitable protection shall be provided.*

*3.* Distribution mains *shall be connected into loops so that the supply may be brought to the consumer from more than one direction. In balancing loops in a design, the Hardy Cross method or an equivalent method shall be used.*

*4.* Valves *shall be located on distribution mains so that no more than one street or block would be out of service for a single break. They shall be located in all small branches off larger mains; and where 8-inch or larger lines intersect, a valve shall be located in each branch. At street intersections, valves shall be located in line with the property line for ease in finding in the event of a break, or as per local practice.*

*5.* Arteries and secondary feeder mains *shall be valved so that not more than one-quarter of a mile would be affected by a single break. Geared valves on 16-inch mains or larger shall be furnished.*

*6. Dead ends shall not be allowed without permission of the municipality and, in any case, shall not be permitted in excess of 400 feet. If dead-end lines are permitted, they shall be provided with a hydrant as a means of flushing.*

*7. No pipe shall be placed on private property unless the owner of the land is to own or operate the pipe, or an easement deeded to the municipality is obtained. All easements shall be unrestricted, and a minimum of 20 feet wide or wider if necessary unless otherwise specified by utility companies.*

*8.* House service connections. *A service connection consists of the pipe and appurtenances between the municipal street main and any customer's property line. A house service connection shall be comprised of a corporation stop at the main, a curb stop, and an inside compression stop, in that order. Meters shall be located as specified by the public or private water supplier.*

*a. Separate water service for each unit shall be utilized for detached housing where maintenance is the responsibility of the individual homeowner.*

*b. Common water service connections, a cost-efficient design, may be allowed for multifamily housing where there is an entity (such as a homeowners association) responsible for the maintenance of the common water laterals. Where common laterals are utilized, individual water shutoffs shall be provided for each unit.*

*9. In cases where comprehensive water systems are constructed by developers, the meter(s) shall be furnished by the applicant and be of a manufacture and type approved by the municipality. The meter(s) shall read in "gallons" or "cubic feet" (to be determined by local municipality). Where meter feet are paid by the applicant, the meter(s) shall be furnished by the municipality.*

*10.* Pipe Size

*a. Water mains shall be a minimum diameter of six (6) inches unless another size is required for fire flow and other criteria as determined by the Hardy–Cross method or other appropriate procedures.*

*b. House service connection pipe shall be a minimum diameter of three-quarter inch (3/4″) unless otherwise indicated by the Hardy–Cross method or other appropriate procedures.*

*11.* Pipe materials. *Pipe materials used in the construction of water mains shall be cement-lined ductile iron, prestressed concrete cylinder pipe, or PVC pipe. All pipe and appurtenances shall comply with the latest applicable American Water Works Association (AWWA) standards.*

*a. Ductile iron pipe, appurtenances, and fittings shall comply with AWWA C1100 (fittings), C111 (gasket joints), C115 (flanged joints), and C151 (pipe). Thickness shall be designed in accordance with AWWA C150 and be a minimum of Class 52. They shall be cement mortar-lined in accordance with AWWA C104. Joints shall conform to AWWA C111 and be equal to TYTON. In aggressive soils, ductile iron pipe wrapped in polyethylene according to AWWA C105-72 shall be used if it is a suitable system to prevent corrosion. The developer's engineer shall certify the ability of whatever pipe materials are chosen to resist all degradation caused by soil conditions. The exterior of the ductile iron pipe shall be covered with a coal-tar, epoxy-type coating where such protection is necessary (i.e., in acidic soil conditions).*

b. Pre-stressed concrete cylinder pipe *with rubber and steel joints shall conform to AWWA C301.*

c. PVC pipe, *appurtenances, and fittings shall conform to AWWA C900 for pipe sizes 4″ to 15″ and joints shall be elastometric-gasket couplings of a corresponding size. Laboratory performance requirements as specified in ASTM D 3139 shall be met. Solvent-cement couplings shall not be permitted. The utilization of PVC pipe shall be encouraged.*

d. Suitable adapters to flanged fittings shall be furnished where required.

e. Valves. *Gate valves shall be cast-iron body with double disc gates, bronze-mounted. Valves shall be full size, and those on 16-inch mains or larger shall be geared and have suitable bypasses. Valve boxes shall be of the adjustable type, with the cover marked "water" and direction of valve operation indicated.*

f. House service connection pipe *shall be type K copper.*

12. Fire Hydrants

a. Size, type, and installation of *hydrants shall be in accordance with local practice, or shall conform to the American Water Works Association standard for Dry Barrel Fire Hydrants (AWWA C502). Hydrants shall have at least three (3) outlets: one outlet shall be a pumper outlet and the other outlets shall be at least two and one-half inch (2-1/2″) nominal size. Street main connections should be not less than six (6) inches in diameter. Hose threads on outlets shall conform to National Standard dimensions. A valve shall be provided on connections between hydrants and street mains. All pipe, fittings, and appurtenances supplying fire hydrants shall be AWWA- or ASTM-approved.*

b. All fire hydrants shall conform to the color-code system as shown in Exhibit A-9.

## EXHIBIT A-9

## COLOR CODE SYSTEM FOR FIRE HYDRANTS

CLASS "A"
1,000 gpm or greater and water mains of 10" and greater —
*green caps and bonnets*

CLASS "B"
Greater than 500 gpm but less than 1,000 gpm, and water mains of at least 8" but less than 10" —
*orange caps and bonnets*

CLASS "C"
500 gpm or less and water mains of at least 6" but less than 8" —
*red caps and bonnets*

BARRELS
All fire hydrants shall be of *chrome yellow or equivalent,* and all yellow paint shall be of *"traffic yellow"*

## E. Sanitary Sewers: System Design and Placement

1. Plans for sanitary systems shall reflect applicable state and other prevailing regulations.

2. The most desirable location for sanitary sewer mains shall be within the municipal right-of-way at or near the center line of the paved cartway.

3. Curved sewers shall be approved only under special conditions. The minimum diameter shall be 8-inch; the minimum radius of curvature shall be 100 feet; and manhole spacing shall not exceed 300 feet. Approval shall be limited to areas where curved streets comprise the general layout, or where the use of curved sewers would permit substantial savings in cost, or avoid very deep cuts, rock, or obstructions of a serious nature.

4. Easements, which shall be in a form approved by the municipal engineer and attorney, shall be required for all sanitary sewer lines which are not within a public right-of-way. Easements shall be a minimum of 20 feet wide for sanitary sewers up to 15 feet deep; for sewers more than 15 feet deep, easements shall be 30 feet wide. (Depth of sewer shall be measured from the design invert of the pipe to the surface of the proposed final grading.)

5. As with water lines, common sanitary sewer service—a cost-efficient design—may be permitted for multifamily housing where there is an entity, such as a homeowners association, responsible for the maintenance of the common laterals.

6. Minimum Slope

a. All sewers shall be designed to meet minimum slope standards as shown in Exhibit A-10.

b. All sewers shall be designed to flow with a minimum velocity of two (2) feet per second and a maximum velocity of ten (10) feet per second at full flow based on Manning's formula with $n = 0.013$. When PVC pipe is used, an n factor of 0.010 may be used. Inverted siphons shall be designed for minimum velocity of six (6) feet per second.

c. All sanitary sewers, including outfalls, shall be designed to carry at least twice the estimated design flow when flowing half full. (This factor is not constant throughout the range of system sizes; for larger systems, consult state and industry guidelines.)

## EXHIBIT A–10

### MINIMUM SLOPES FOR SEWER SIZE BY PIPE DIAMETER

| Pipe Diameter | Fall in Feet Per 100 Feet of Sewer |
|---|---|
| 8" | 40 |
| 10" | 29 |
| 12" | 22 |
| 14" | 17 |
| 15" | 16 |
| 16" | 14 |
| 18" | 12 |
| 20" | 10 |
| 21" | .095 |
| 24" | .080 |
| 27" | .067 |
| 30" | .058 |
| 36" | .046 |

7. Pipe Materials

a. The applicant shall submit for approval details of the planned pipes, joints, fittings, etc. Specifications referred to below, such as ASA, ASTM, AWWA, etc., shall be the latest revision.

b. Materials used in the construction of sewers, force mains, and outfalls shall be as follows: Gravity sewers shall be constructed of reinforced concrete, ductile iron, polyvinyl chloride (PVC), or acrylonitrile-butadiene-styrene (ABS) plastic pipe. Reinforced concrete pipe shall be used only in sizes 24″ and larger. Inverted siphons, force mains, and outfalls shall be constructed of ductile iron pipe unless otherwise permitted by the municipality. Inverted siphons shall consist of two pipes with provisions for flushing. Flow control gates shall be provided in the chambers.

c. Any sewer within 100 feet of a water supply well or a below-grade reservoir shall be of steel, reinforced concrete, cast iron, or other suitable material; shall be properly protected by completely watertight construction; and shall be tested for watertightness after installation.

d. Reinforced concrete pipe shall meet all the requirements of ASTM C 76. All pipe should be Class IV strength except where stronger pipe is required.

1) For depths less than three (3) feet measured from the top of the pipe, installed under traffic areas, Marston Class V pipe shall be required.

2) The trench depths shown in Exhibit A-11 shall be maximum for the pipe classes noted, installed when site conditions allow with Class C, Ordinary Bedding.

## EXHIBIT A–11

### MAXIMUM TRENCH DEPTHS: PIPE CLASS REQUIREMENTS FOR REINFORCED CONCRETE PIPE

| Pipe Diameter (Inches) | Maximum Width of Trench At Top of Pipe | Depth — Feet Pipe Class IV | V |
|---|---|---|---|
| 12" | 3' — 0" | 6.5 | 18.0 |
| 15" | 3' — 8" | 6.0 | 14.0 |
| 18" | 4' — 0" | 7.0 | 16.0 |
| 21" | 4' — 3" | 8.5 | 17.5 |
| 24" | 4' — 6" | 9.0 | 20.0 |
| 30" | 5' — 0" | 10.5 | 22.5 |
| 36" | 5' — 8" | 11.0 | 22.0 |

3) The existence of clay soils and other unusual loading conditions should be given special consideration.

e. Polyvinyl chloride sewer pipe (PVC) shall have bell and spigot ends and O-ring rubber gasketed joints. PVC pipe and fittings shall conform to ASTM D 3034, with a wall thickness designation of SDR 35 (minimum).

1) The plastic material from which the pipe and fittings are extruded shall be impact types of PVC, unplasticized, having high mechanical strength and maximum chemical resistance conforming to Type I, Grade 1, of the specification for rigid polyvinyl chloride compounds, ASTM D 1784.

2) Pipe shall be free from defects, bubbles, and other imperfections in accordance with accepted commercial practice. The adequacy of the pipe shall be demonstrated, if required, by a test at the manufacturing plant in accordance with ASTM D 2444 for impact and ASTM C 2412 for Deflection and Pipe Stiffness, latest revisions.

3) Joints shall conform to ASTM D 3212. Rubber ring gaskets shall conform to ASTM F 477. The gasket shall be the sole element depended upon to make the joint watertight.

4) The pipe shall be installed as specified in ASTM D 2321, latest revision. In no case shall less than a Class III material be used for bedding and haunching material unless approved in writing by the engineer. Particular attention shall be given to the special requirements for installing pipe in unstable soil or excessive ground water. Any additional cost for materials used under these trench conditions shall be borne by the applicant.

5) Plastic riser pipe for cleanouts shall be polyvinyl chloride sewer pipe (PVC) as above specified, or acrylonitrile-butadiene-styrene (ABS). All joints shall have flexible elastometric seals.

f. Ductile iron pipe shall be centrifugally cast in metal or sand-lined molds to AWWA C151. The joint shall be of a type that employs a single elongated grooved gasket to effect the joint seal, such as United States Cast Iron Pipe Company's Tyton Joint, James B. Clow and Sons, Inc., "Bell-Tite," or approved equal. Pipe should be furnished with flanges where connections to flange fittings are required. Pipe shall be Class 52 (minimum). The outside of the pipe shall be coated with a uniform thickness of hot applied coal-tar coating and the inside lined with cement in accordance with AWWA C104. Ductile iron pipe shall be installed with Class C, Ordinary Bedding, when site conditions allow.

g. Acrylonitrile-butadiene-styrene (ABS) pipe and fittings shall conform to ASTM D 2751 and be installed in accordance with ASTM D 2321 as herein modified. All joints shall be made in accordance with ASTM D 3212 using flexible rubber gaskets conforming to ASTM F 477.

8. Pipe Bedding

a. Pipe bedding shall be provided as specified in Design and Construction of Sanitary and Storm Sewers, ASCE Manuals and Reports on Engineering Practice No. 37, prepared by A Joint Committee of the American Society of Civil Engineers and the Water Pollution Control Federation, New York, 1969.

9. Manholes

a. Manholes shall be provided at ends of sewer lines, at intersections, and at changes of grade or alignment.

b. Spacing intervals between manholes shall not exceed 400 feet for sewers 15 inches or less, and 500 feet for sewers 18 inches to 30 inches, or 600 feet where adequate modern cleaning equipment for such spacing is provided.

c. Where sewers enter manholes and the difference in crown elevation between the incoming and outgoing pipes is equal to or greater than two feet, drop pipes shall be provided and drop manholes should be built.

d. Manholes shall be precast concrete, brick or concrete block coated with two coats of portland cement mortar and a seal coating of an acceptable waterproofing tar, asphalt or polyplastic alloy, with enough time allowed for proper bond between seal coats.

e. If precast manhole barrels and cones are used, they shall conform to ASTM C 478, with round rubber gasketed joints, conforming to ASTM C 923. Maximum absorption shall be 9 percent in accordance with ASTM C 478, method A. The entire outside surface of the manhole shall be coated with a bituminous waterproofing material acceptable to the municipal engineer. Cracked manholes shall not be used. The top riser section of precast manholes shall terminate less than 1 foot below the finished grade to provide for proper adjustment.

f. Manhole frames and covers shall be of cast iron conforming to specification ASTM A 48 Class 30 and be suitable for H 20 loading capacity. All manhole covers in rights-of-way or in remote areas shall be provided with a locking device. In order to allow the municipality to plan better for system management, the name of the municipality, the year, and the word "SEWER" shall be cast integrally in the cover.

g. Watertight and low-profile frames and covers shall be utilized where applicable and should conform to the pertinent ASTM specifications.

h. Manholes shall be supplied

with suitable adapters (inserts or gaskets) for the various pipe materials used.

10. Laterals/Cleanouts

a. The house connection or lateral from the street main to the cleanout shall be considered an integral part of the sanitary sewer system. The type of material used for the house connection shall be the material used for the main line sewer construction and may be as follows:

4" Cast Iron Soil Pipe, Extra Heavy
4" PVC Plastic Pipe, Schedule 40
4" ABS Plastic Pipe, SDR 35

b. Unless connection is made to an existing sewer main utilizing a saddle, wye connections shall be the same as the material used at the junction of the house connection and the sewer main.

c. Bends in house connection lines shall be made using standard fittings. A riser with a cleanout at grade shall be used at the point terminating municipal jurisdiction. This inspection cleanout or observation tee shall be fitted with a metallic cap placed two (2) feet from the outside face of the curb between the curb and sidewalk if installed. If curbs are not required, the cleanout shall be placed one (1) foot beyond the property line in the municipal right-of-way.

d. Connections beyond the cleanout are under the jurisdiction of the Board of Health through its Plumbing Inspector and the pipe size and specifications shall be under the regulations and requirements of the Board of Health.

## F. Storm Water Management: System Demand, Strategy, and Design

1. STORM WATER MANAGEMENT: SYSTEM DEMAND

a. Watershed storm water management requires the determination of two runoff parameters: runoff peak rate of discharge and runoff volume. Both parameters shall be used in the comparison of pre-development and post-development conditions.

b. Peak rate of discharge calculations shall be used to determine the configurations and sizes of pipes, channels, and other routing or flow control structures. Runoff volume calculations shall be used to determine the necessity for, and sizing of, detention and retention facilities.

c. Runoff Peak Rate of Discharge Calculation. The peak rate of runoff for areas of up to one-half of a square mile shall be calculated by the Rational Method or derivatives. The equation for the Rational Method is:

$$Q_p = CIA$$

where

$Q_p$ = the peak runoff rate in cubic feet per second (CFS)
$C$ = the runoff coefficient
$I$ = the average rainfall intensity in inches per hour (in./hr.), occurring at the time of concentration $t_c$ (minutes)
$t_c$ = the time of concentration in minutes (min.)
$A$ = the size of the drainage area

1) Typical C values for storms of 5 to 10 years between periods are provided in Exhibit A-12. Runoff coefficients from the following sources may also be used: U.S. Department of Commerce, Bureau of Public Roads, May 1965, Design of Roadside Channels—Hydraulic Design Series No. 4 as supplemented or amended; and Department of Transportation, Federal Aviation Administration, July 1970, AC1505320-5B, Airport Drainage as supplemented or amended.

2) The time of concentration ($t_c$) shall be estimated from Exhibit A-13. The analysis shall also consider the procedure outlined in section 3.12 (c) of Technical Release (TR) No. 55, Urban Hydrology for Small Watersheds, U.S. Department of Agriculture, Soil Conservation Service, as supplemented and amended (SCS method).

3) Rainfall intensity as a function of duration and storm recurrence frequency shall be based upon geographically appropriate data as depicted in the plates in technical paper No. 25, Rainfall Intensity Duration–Frequency Curves, U.S. Department of Commerce, Weather Bureau, as supplemented and amended. Rainfall intensity values may also be estimated from Exhibit A-14. Intensity curves may be based on local rainfall frequency data, where available. In all instances, a minimum time of concentration of 5 minutes should be used. For storm sewer design, a ten-year storm frequency should be considered as a minimum unless special circumstances are involved, such as evidence of local flooding, inadequate downstream storm water facilities, and technical ambiguities.

4) The size of the drainage area shall include on-site and off-site lands contributing to the design point.

5) Computer software adaptations of the Rational Method calculations are acceptable provided that their data and graphic printout allow review and evaluation.

6) The peak rate of runoff for areas greater than one-half square mile shall be calculated by the hydrograph analysis method as outlined in TR No. 55 (SCS method), as supplemented and amended.

d. Runoff Volume Calculation

1) Runoff volume shall be calcu-

EXHIBIT A-12

RUNOFF COEFFICIENTS
— AMC II —

| Land Use Description | Hydrological Soil Group | | | |
|---|---|---|---|---|
| | A | B | C | D |
| Cultivated land:    without conservation treatment | .49 | .67 | .81 | .88 |
| with conservation treatment | .27 | .43 | .61 | .67 |
| Pasture or range land: poor condition | .38 | .63 | .78 | .84 |
| good condition | — | .25 | .51 | .65 |
| Meadow: good condition | — | — | .44 | .61 |
| Wood or forest land: thin stand, poor cover, no mulch | — | — | .59 | .79 |
| good cover | — | — | .45 | .59 |
| Open spaces, lawns, parks, golf courses, cemeteries | | | | |
| good condition : grass cover on 75% or more of the area | — | .25 | .51 | .65 |
| fair condition   : grass cover on 50% to 75% of the area | — | .45 | .63 | .74 |
| Commercial and business areas (85% impervious) | .84 | .90 | .93 | .96 |
| Industrial districts (72% impervious) | .67 | .81 | .88 | .92 |
| Residential: | | | | |
| Average lot size—Average % Impervious | | | | |
| 1/8 acre or less                    65 | .59 | .76 | .86 | .90 |
| 1/4 acre                            38 | .25 | .55 | .70 | .80 |
| 1/3 acre                            30 | — | .49 | .67 | .78 |
| 1/2 acre                            25 | — | .45 | .65 | .76 |
| 1 acre                              20 | — | .41 | .63 | .74 |
| Paved parking lots, roofs, driveways, etc. | .99 | .99 | .99 | .99 |
| Streets and roads: | | | | |
| paved with curbs and storm sewers | .99 | .99 | .99 | .99 |
| gravel | .57 | .76 | .84 | .88 |
| dirt | .49 | .69 | .80 | .84 |

*Source:* New Jersey Department of Environmental Protection, *Technical Manual for Stream Encroachment* (Trenton, New Jersey: Department of Environmental Protection, 1984), p. 51.

## EXHIBIT A-13

## NOMOGRAPH FOR THE DETERMINATION OF TIME OF CONCENTRATION

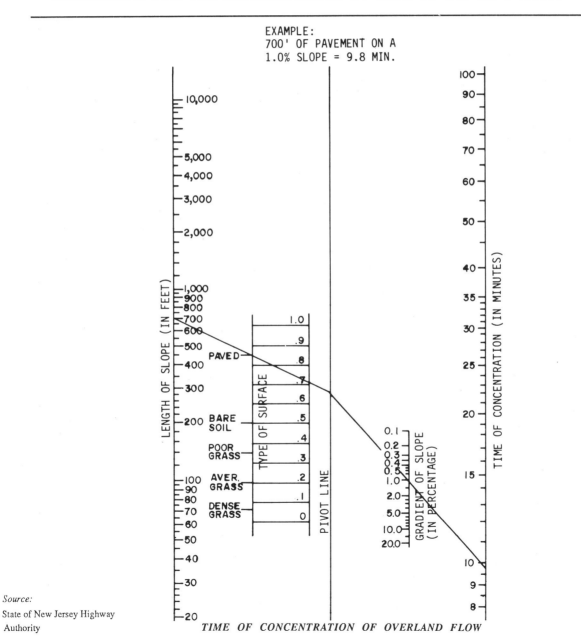

EXAMPLE:
700' OF PAVEMENT ON A
1.0% SLOPE = 9.8 MIN.

*TIME OF CONCENTRATION OF OVERLAND FLOW*

*Source:*
State of New Jersey Highway
Authority

## EXHIBIT A-14

## RAINFALL INTENSITY CURVES (SAMPLE)

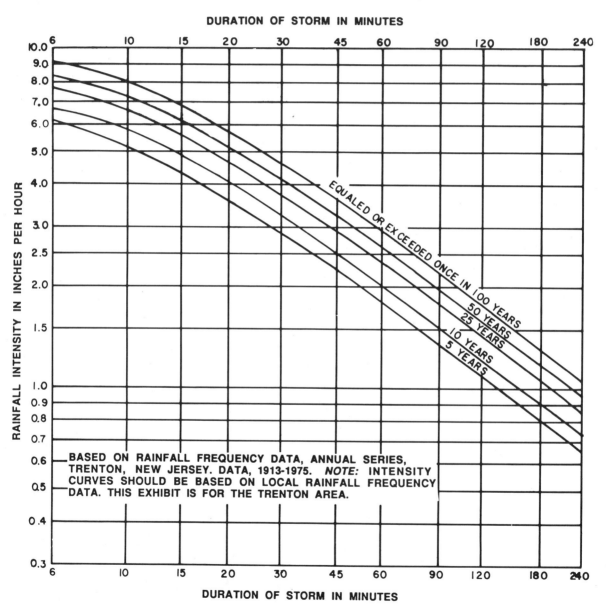

BASED ON RAINFALL FREQUENCY DATA, ANNUAL SERIES, TRENTON, NEW JERSEY. DATA, 1913-1975. *NOTE:* INTENSITY CURVES SHOULD BE BASED ON LOCAL RAINFALL FREQUENCY DATA. THIS EXHIBIT IS FOR THE TRENTON AREA.

*Source:* State of New Jersey, Department of Environmental Protection, Division of Water Resources, *Flood Plain Management* (Trenton, NJ: Department of Environmental Protection, 1976).

lated by the hydrograph analysis method as outlined in TR No. 55 (SCS method). This method shall be used for watersheds with drainage areas of less than 5 square miles. For drainage areas of less than 5 acres, the Rational Method triangular hydrography approximation may be used as an alternative.

2) Runoff volume for drainage areas of greater than 5 square miles shall be calculated by the Stankowski Method.

3) Computer software adaptions of these runoff value calculations are acceptable provided that their data and graphic printout allow review and evaluation.

2. STORM WATER MANAGEMENT: SYSTEM STRATEGY

a. A system emphasizing a natural as opposed to an engineered drainage strategy shall be encouraged.

b. The applicability of a natural approach depends on such factors as site storage capacity, open channel hydraulic capacity, and maintenance needs and resources.

c. Hydraulic capacity for open channel or closed conduit flow shall be determined by the Manning Equation. The hydraulic capacity is termed Q and is expressed as discharge in cubic feet per second. The Manning Equation is as follows:

$$Q = \frac{1.486}{n} A R^{2/3} S^{1/2}$$

where

$n$ = Manning's roughness coefficient
$A$ = Cross-sectional area of flow in square feet
$R$ = Hydraulic radius in feet ($R = A/P$, where P is equal to the Wetted Perimeter)
$S$ = Slope of conduit in feet per foot

The Manning roughness coefficients to be utilized are shown in Exhibit A-15.

d. Velocities in open channels at design flow shall not be less than five-tenths foot per second and not greater than that velocity which will begin to cause erosion or scouring of the channel. Permissible velocities for swales, open channels and ditches are shown in Exhibit A-16.

e. Velocities in closed conduits at design flow shall be at least two feet per second but not more than the velocity which will cause erosion damage to the conduit.

3. STORM WATER MANAGEMENT: SYSTEM DESIGN—PIPE CAPACITY, MATERIALS, AND PLACEMENT

a. Pipe size shall be dictated by design runoff and hydraulic capacity.

b. Hydraulic capacity shall be determined by the Manning Equation.

c. In general, no pipe size in the storm drainage system shall be less than 15-inch diameter. A 12-inch diameter pipe will be permitted as a cross-drain to a single inlet.

d. All discharge pipes shall terminate with a precast concrete or corrugated metal end section or a cast-in-place concrete headwall with or without wingwalls as conditions require.

e. Materials used in the construction of storm sewers shall be constructed of reinforced concrete, ductile iron, corrugated aluminum, or corrugated steel. The least expensive materials shall be permitted unless site and other conditions dictate otherwise. Specifications referred to, such as AASHTO, ASTM, AWWA, etc., should be the latest revision.

1) Reinforced concrete pipe:

a) Circular reinforced concrete pipe and fittings shall meet the requirements of ASTM C 76.

b) Elliptical reinforced concrete pipe shall meet the requirements of ASTM C 507.

c) Joint design and joint material for circular pipe shall conform to ASTM C 443.

d) Joints for elliptical pipe shall be bell-and-spigot or tongue-and-groove sealed with butyl, rubber tape, or external sealing bands conforming to ASTM C 877.

e) All pipe shall be Class III unless a stronger pipe (i.e., higher class) is indicated to be necessary.

f) The minimum depth of cover over the concrete pipe shall be as designated by the American Concrete Pipe Association, as follows:

| Pipe Diameter (inches) | ASTM Class Pipe | Minimum Cover (Surface to top of pipe) |
|---|---|---|
| 12" | III | 17" |
|  | IV | 12" |
|  | V | 7" |
| 15" | III | 16" |
|  | IV | 11" |
|  | V | 7" |
| 18" | III | 16" |
|  | IV | 10" |
|  | V | 6" |
| 24" | III | 15" |
|  | IV | 6" |
|  | V | 6" |
| 30" | III | 10" |
|  | IV | 6" |
|  | V | 6" |
| 36" & above | III | 6" |
|  | IV | 6" |

## EXHIBIT A–15

## MANNING'S ROUGHNESS COEFFICIENTS

| Type of Channel | Minimum | Normal | Maximum |
|---|---|---|---|
| A. *CLOSED CONDUITS FLOWING PARTLY FULL* | | | |
| A–1. *Metal* | | | |
| a. Brass, smooth | 0.009 | 0.010 | 0.013 |
| b. Steel | | | |
| 1. Lockbar and welded | 0.010 | 0.012 | 0.014 |
| 2. Riveted and spiral | 0.013 | 0.016 | 0.017 |
| c. Cast iron | | | |
| 1. Coated | 0.010 | 0.013 | 0.014 |
| 2. Uncoated | 0.011 | 0.014 | 0.016 |
| d. Wrought iron | | | |
| 1. Black | 0.012 | 0.014 | 0.015 |
| 2. Galvanized | 0.013 | 0.016 | 0.017 |
| e. Corrugated metal | | | |
| 1. Subdrain | 0.017 | 0.019 | 0.021 |
| 2. Storm drain | 0.021 | 0.024 | 0.030 |
| A–2. *Nonmetal* | | | |
| a. Lucite | 0.008 | 0.009 | 0.010 |
| b. Glass | 0.009 | 0.010 | 0.013 |
| c. Cement | | | |
| 1. Neat, surface | 0.010 | 0.011 | 0.013 |
| 2. Mortar | 0.011 | 0.013 | 0.015 |
| d. Concrete | | | |
| 1. Culvert, straight and free of debris | 0.010 | 0.011 | 0.013 |
| 2. Culvert with bends, connections, and some debris | 0.011 | 0.013 | 0.014 |
| 3. Finished | 0.011 | 0.012 | 0.014 |
| 4. Sewer with manholes, inlet, etc., straight | 0.013 | 0.015 | 0.017 |
| 5. Unfinished, steel form | 0.012 | 0.013 | 0.014 |
| 6. Unfinished, smooth wood form | 0.012 | 0.014 | 0.016 |
| 7. Unfinished, rough wood form | 0.015 | 0.017 | 0.020 |
| e. Wood | | | |
| 1. Stave | 0.010 | 0.012 | 0.014 |
| 2. Laminated, treated | 0.015 | 0.017 | 0.020 |
| f. Clay | | | |
| 1. Common drainage tile | 0.011 | 0.013 | 0.017 |
| 2. Vitrified sewer | 0.011 | 0.014 | 0.017 |
| 3. Vitrified sewer with manholes, inlet, etc. | 0.013 | 0.015 | 0.017 |
| 4. Vitrified subdrain with open joint | 0.014 | 0.016 | 0.018 |
| g. Brickwork | | | |
| 1. Glazed | 0.011 | 0.013 | 0.015 |
| 2. Lined with cement mortar | 0.012 | 0.015 | 0.017 |

## EXHIBIT A–15 (continued)

| Type of Channel | Minimum | Normal | Maximum |
|---|---|---|---|
| h. Sanitary sewers coated with sewage slimes, with bends and connections | 0.012 | 0.013 | 0.016 |
| i. Paved invert, sewer, smooth bottom | 0.016 | 0.019 | 0.020 |
| j. Rubble masonry, cemented | 0.018 | 0.025 | 0.030 |
| **B. LINED OR BUILT-UP CHANNELS** | | | |
| *B–1. Metal* | | | |
| a. Smooth steel surface | | | |
|     1. Unpainted | 0.011 | 0.012 | 0.014 |
|     2. Painted | 0.012 | 0.013 | 0.017 |
| b. Corrugated | 0.021 | 0.025 | 0.030 |
| *B–2. Nonmetal* | | | |
| a. Cement | | | |
|     1. Neat, surface | 0.010 | 0.011 | 0.013 |
|     2. Mortar | 0.011 | 0.013 | 0.015 |
| b. Wood | | | |
|     1. Planed, untreated | 0.010 | 0.012 | 0.014 |
|     2. Planed, creosoted | 0.011 | 0.012 | 0.015 |
|     3. Unplaned | 0.011 | 0.013 | 0.015 |
|     4. Plank with battens | 0.012 | 0.015 | 0.018 |
|     5. Lined with roofing paper | 0.010 | 0.014 | 0.017 |
| c. Concrete | | | |
|     1. Trowel finish | 0.011 | 0.013 | 0.015 |
|     2. Float finish | 0.013 | 0.015 | 0.016 |
|     3. Finished, with gravel on bottom | 0.015 | 0.017 | 0.020 |
|     4. Unfinished | 0.014 | 0.017 | 0.020 |
|     5. Gunite, good section | 0.016 | 0.019 | 0.023 |
|     6. Gunite, wavy section | 0.018 | 0.022 | 0.025 |
|     7. On good excavated rock | 0.017 | 0.020 | |
|     8. On irregular excavated rock | 0.022 | 0.027 | |
| d. Concrete bottom float finished with sides of | | | |
|     1. Dressed stone in mortar | 0.015 | 0.017 | 0.020 |
|     2. Random stone in mortar | 0.017 | 0.020 | 0.024 |
|     3. Cement rubble masonry, plastered | 0.016 | 0.020 | 0.024 |
|     4. Cement rubble masonry | 0.020 | 0.025 | 0.030 |
|     5. Dry rubble or riprap | 0.020 | 0.030 | 0.035 |
| e. Gravel bottom with sides of | | | |
|     1. Formed concrete | 0.017 | 0.020 | 0.025 |
|     2. Random stone in mortar | 0.020 | 0.023 | 0.026 |
|     3. Dry rubble or riprap | 0.023 | 0.033 | 0.036 |
| f. Brick | | | |
|     1. Glazed | 0.011 | 0.013 | 0.015 |
|     2. In cement mortar | 0.012 | 0.015 | 0.018 |

## EXHIBIT A–15 (continued)

| Type of Channel | Minimum | Normal | Maximum |
|---|---|---|---|
| g. Masonry | | | |
|    1.  Cemented rubble | 0.017 | 0.025 | 0.030 |
|    2.  Dry rubble | 0.023 | 0.032 | 0.035 |
| h. Dressed ashlar | 0.013 | 0.015 | 0.017 |
| i. Asphalt | | | |
|    1.  Smooth | 0.013 | 0.013 | |
|    2.  Rough | 0.016 | 0.016 | |
| j. Vegetal lining | 0.030 | .... | 0.500 |
| **C. EXCAVATED OR DREDGED** | | | |
| a. Earth, straight and uniform | | | |
|    1.  Clean, recently completed | 0.016 | 0.018 | 0.020 |
|    2.  Clean, after weathering | 0.018 | 0.022 | 0.025 |
|    3.  Gravel, uniform section, clean | 0.022 | 0.025 | 0.030 |
|    4.  With short grass, few weeds | 0.022 | 0.027 | 0.033 |
| b. Earth, winding and sluggish | | | |
|    1.  No vegetation | 0.023 | 0.025 | 0.030 |
|    2.  Grass, some weeds | 0.025 | 0.030 | 0.033 |
|    3.  Dense weeds or aquatic plants in deep channels | 0.030 | 0.035 | 0.040 |
|    4.  Earth bottom and rubble sides | 0.028 | 0.030 | 0.035 |
|    5.  Stony bottom and weedy banks | 0.025 | 0.035 | 0.040 |
|    6.  Cobble bottom and clean sides | 0.030 | 0.040 | 0.050 |
| c. Dragline-excavated or dredged | | | |
|    1.  No vegetation | 0.025 | 0.028 | 0.033 |
|    2.  Light brush on banks | 0.035 | 0.050 | 0.060 |
| d. Rock cuts | | | |
|    1.  Smooth and uniform | 0.025 | 0.035 | 0.040 |
|    2.  Jagged and irregular | 0.035 | 0.040 | 0.050 |
| e. Channels not maintained, weeds and brush uncut | | | |
|    1.  Dense weeds, high as flow depth | 0.050 | 0.080 | 0.120 |
|    2.  Clean bottom, brush on sides | 0.040 | 0.050 | 0.080 |
|    3.  Same, highest stage of flow | 0.045 | 0.070 | 0.110 |
|    4.  Dense brush, high stage | 0.080 | 0.100 | 0.140 |
| **D. NATURAL STREAMS** | | | |
| *D–1. Minor streams (top width at flood stage 100 ft.)* | | | |
| a. Streams on plain | | | |
|    1.  Clean, straight, full stage, no rift or deep pools | 0.025 | 0.030 | 0.033 |
|    2.  Same as above, but more stones and weeds | 0.030 | 0.035 | 0.040 |

## EXHIBIT A–15 (continued)

| Type of Channel | Minimum | Normal | Maximum |
|---|---|---|---|
| 3. Clean, winding, some pools and shoals | 0.033 | 0.040 | 0.045 |
| 4. Same as above, but some weeds and stones | 0.035 | 0.045 | 0.050 |
| 5. Same as above, lower stages, more ineffective slopes and sections | 0.040 | 0.048 | 0.055 |
| 6. Same as 4, but more stones | 0.045 | 0.050 | 0.060 |
| 7. Sluggish reaches, weedy, deep pools | 0.050 | 0.070 | 0.080 |
| 8. Very weedy reaches, deep pools, or floodways with heavy stand of timber and underbrush | 0.075 | 0.100 | 0.150 |
| b. Mountain streams, no vegetation in channel, banks usually steep, trees and brush along banks submerged at high stages | | | |
| 1. Bottom: gravels, cobbles, and few boulders | 0.030 | 0.040 | 0.050 |
| 2. Bottom: cobbles with large boulders | 0.040 | 0.050 | 0.070 |
| D–2. Flood plains | | | |
| a. Pasture, no brush | | | |
| 1. Short grass | 0.025 | 0.030 | 0.035 |
| 2. High grass | 0.030 | 0.035 | 0.050 |
| b. Cultivated areas | | | |
| 1. No crop | 0.020 | 0.030 | 0.040 |
| 2. Mature row crops | 0.025 | 0.035 | 0.045 |
| 3. Mature field crops | 0.030 | 0.040 | 0.050 |
| c. Brush | | | |
| 1. Scattered brush, heavy weeds | 0.035 | 0.050 | 0.070 |
| 2. Light brush and trees, in winter | 0.035 | 0.050 | 0.060 |
| 3. Light brush and trees, in summer | 0.040 | 0.060 | 0.080 |
| 4. Medium to dense brush, in winter | 0.045 | 0.070 | 0.110 |
| 5. Medium to dense brush, in summer | 0.070 | 0.100 | 0.160 |
| d. Trees | | | |
| 1. Dense willows, summer, straight | 0.110 | 0.150 | 0.200 |
| 2. Cleared land with tree stumps, no sprouts | 0.030 | 0.040 | 0.050 |
| 3. Same as above, but with heavy growth of sprouts | 0.050 | 0.060 | 0.080 |
| 4. Heavy stand of timber, a few down trees, little undergrowth, flood stage below branches | 0.080 | 0.100 | 0.120 |
| 5. Same as above, but with flood stage reaching branches | 0.100 | 0.120 | 0.160 |
| D–3. Major streams (top width at flood stage 100 ft.) The n value is less than that for minor streams of similar description, because banks offer less effective resistance. | | | |
| a. Regular section with no boulders or brush | 0.025 | .... | 0.060 |
| b. Irregular and rough sections | 0.035 | .... | 0.100 |

Source: State of New Jersey, Department of Environmental Protection, Technical Manual for Stream Encroachment (Trenton, New Jersey, 1984), Table 3.2–11 (A–1).

EXHIBIT A-16

**PERMISSIBLE VELOCITIES FOR SWALES, OPEN CHANNELS, AND DITCHES WITH
UNIFORM STANDS OF VARIOUS WELL-MAINTAINED GRASS COVERS**

| Ground Cover | Slope Range (Percent) | Permissible Velocity on: | |
| --- | --- | --- | --- |
| | | Erosion-Resistant Soils (fps) | Easily Eroded Soils (fps) |
| Bermudagrass | 0–5 | 8 | 6 |
| | 5–10 | 7 | 5 |
| | Over 10 | 6 | 4 |
| Buffalograss | 0–5 | 7 | 5 |
| Kentucky bluegrass | 5–1 | 6 | 4 |
| Smooth brome | Over 10 | 5 | 3 |
| Grass mixture | 0–5 | 5 | 4 |
| | 5–10 | 4 | 3 |
| Lespedeza Weeping lovegrass Yellow bluestem Kudzu Alfalfa Crabgrass | 0–5 | 3.5 | 2.5 |
| Common lespedeza Sundangrass | 0–5 | 3.5 | 2.5 |

*Note:* fps = feet per second

*Source:* Soil Conservation Service, U.S. Department of Agriculture (Washington, D.C.: Government Printing Office, 1959). Cited in ULI–ASCE–NAHB, *Residential Storm Water Management* (Washington, D.C.: Government Printing Office, 1975).

2) Ductile iron pipe *shall be centrifugally cast in metal or sand-lined molds to ANSI A21.51-1976 (AWWA C151-76). The joints shall conform to AWWA C111.* Pipe shall be furnished with flanges where connections to flange fittings are required. Pipe should be Class 50 (minimum). The outside of the pipe should be coated with a uniform thickness of hot applied coal tar coating and the inside lined cement in accordance with AWWA C104. Ductile iron pipe shall be installed with Class C, Ordinary Bedding.

3) Corrugated Aluminum Pipe. *Within the public right-of-way and where severe topographic conditions or the desire to minimize the destruction of trees and vegetation exist, corrugated aluminum pipe, pipe arch or helical corrugated pipe may be used. The material used shall comply with the Standard Specifications for Corrugated Aluminum Alloy Culvert and Under Drains AASHTO M-196 or the Standard Specification for Aluminum Alloy Helical Pipe AASHTO designation M-211. The minimum thickness of the aluminum pipe to be used shall be as follows:* less than twenty-four-inch diameter or equivalent, *seventy-five thousandths (0.75) inch (fourteen-gauge);* twenty-four-inch diameter and less than forty-eight-inch diameter or equivalent, *one hundred and five thousandths (.105) inch (twelve gauge);* forty-eight inch but less than seventy-two-inch diameter or equivalent, *one hundred thirty-five thousandths (.135) inch (ten-gauge);* and seventy-two-inch diameter or equivalent and larger, *one hundred sixty-four thousandths (.164) inch (eight-gauge).*

4) Corrugated Steel Pipe *may be used in place of corrugated aluminum and shall meet the requirements of AASHTO M-36. Coupling bands and special sections shall also conform to AASHTO M-36. All corrugated steel pipe shall be bituminous coated in accordance with AASHTO M-190, Type A minimum.*

f. Pipe bedding shall be provided as specified in Design and Construction of Sanitary and Storm Sewers, *ASCE Manuals and Reports on Engineering Practice No. 37, prepared by A Joint Committee of the Society of Civil Engineers and the Water Pollution Control Federation, New York, 1969.*

g. Maintenance easements shall be provided around storm water facilities where such facilities are located outside of the public right-of-way. The size of the easement shall be dictated by working needs. In general, the easement shall be 20 feet in width for one utility and five additional feet, if practicable, for each additional utility located in the same easement.

## 4. STORM WATER MANAGEMENT: SYSTEM DESIGN—INLETS, CATCH BASINS, AND MANHOLES

a. Inlets, catch basins and manholes shall be designed in accordance with relevant state highway department standard plans and specifications. Frames and grates shall be Campbell Foundry Company Pattern No. 2617 Bicycle Grates with stream-flowing grating, or equal.

b. Manhole spacing shall be increased with pipe size.

| Pipe Size | Manhole Spacing |
|---|---|
| 15″ or less | 500′ |
| 18″ - 36″ | 600′ |
| 42″ - 60″ | 700′ |
| 60″+ | 700′+ |

c. Manholes shall be precast concrete, brick or concrete block coated with two coats of portland cement mortar.

d. If precast manhole barrels and cones are used, they shall conform to ASTM C 478 with round rubber gasketed joints, conforming to ASTM C 923. Maximum absorption shall be 9 percent in accordance with ASTM C 478, method A.

e. If precast manholes are utilized, the top riser section shall terminate less than 1 foot below the finished grade and the manhole cover shall be flush with the finished grade.

f. Manhole frames and covers shall be of cast iron conforming to specification ASTM A 48 Class 30 and be suitable for H 20 loading capacity. All manhole covers in rights-of-way or in remote areas shall be provided with a locking device. In order to allow the municipality to plan better for system management, the name of the municipality, the year, and the words "STORM SEWER" shall be cast integrally in the cover.

## 5. STORM WATER MANAGEMENT: SYSTEM DESIGN—DETENTION FACILITIES

a. Development shall use the best available technology to accommodate storm water management by natural drainage strategies as indicated in Article Five, Section I.1.b. of this ordinance.

b. Non-structural management practices, such as cluster land use development, open space acquisition, stream encroachment and flood hazard controls shall be coordinated with detention requirements. Changes in land use can often reduce the scope and cost of detention provisions required by means of appropriate changes in runoff coefficients.

c. Detention and all other storm water management facilities shall conform to applicable state standards.

d. Where detention facilities are deemed necessary, they shall accommodate site runoff generated from 2-year,

10-year, and 100-year storms considered individually, unless the detention basin is classified as a dam, in which case the facility must also comply with prevailing dam safety standards. These design storms shall be defined as either a 24-hour storm, using the rainfall distribution recommended by the U.S. Soil Conservation Service using U.S. Soil Conservation Service procedures (such as U.S. Soil Conservation Service, Urban Hydrology for Small Watersheds, *Technical Release No. 55*), or as the estimated maximum rainfall for the estimated time of concentration of runoff at the site, using a design method such as the Rational Method. Runoff greater than that occurring from the 100-year, 24-hour storm will be passed over an emergency spillway. Detention will be provided such that after development the peak rate of flow from the site will not exceed the corresponding flow which would have been created by similar storms prior to development. For purposes of computing runoff, lands in the site shall be assumed, prior to development, to be in good condition (if the lands are pastures, lawns or parks), with good cover (if the lands are woods), or with conservation treatment (if the land is cultivated), regardless of conditions existing at the time of computation.

e. In calculating the site runoff to be accommodated by a detention facility, the method to be used is a tabular hydrograph method as presented in TR No. 55 (SCS method) as supplemented and amended.

f. Detention facilities shall be located as far horizontally from surface water and as far vertically from groundwater as is practicable.

g. Detention facilities shall not intercept the post-development groundwater table, where practicable.

h. The following list of general structural criteria shall be used to design storm water detention basins. Due to the uniqueness of each storm water detention basin and the variability of soil and other site conditions, these criteria may be modified or appended at the discretion of the reviewing engineer if reasons for the variance are indicated in writing.

1) Detention Components: Principal Outlets (Quantity Control)

a) To minimize the chance of clogging and to facilitate cleaning, outlet pipes shall be at least 6 inches in diameter. Similarly, riser pipes, if utilized, shall be at least 8 inches in diameter. All pipe joints are to be watertight, reinforced concrete pipe. In addition, trash racks and/or anti-vortex devices shall be required where necessary.

b) Eight (8)-inch-thick anti-seep collars are to be installed along outlet pipes. Reinforcement steel shall be No. 5 bars at 12 inches both ways with 2 inches of cover on both faces (minimum).

c) Where necessary, a concrete cradle shall be provided for outlet pipes.

d) All principal outlet structures shall be concrete block or reinforced concrete. All construction joints are to be watertight.

e) Suitable lining shall be placed upstream and downstream of principal outlets as necessary to prevent scour and erosion. Such lining shall conform to the criteria contained in *Hydraulic Engineering Circular No. 15—Design of Stable Channels with Flexible Linings*, published by the Federal Highway Administration of the U.S. Department of Transportation, or *National Handbook of Conservation Practices*, published by the U.S. Department of Agriculture/Soil Conservation Service.

2) Detention Components: Principal Outlets (Quality Control)

a) Based upon the requirement limiting the size of the outlet to a minimum of 6 inches in diameter, water quality control shall be maintained by providing an amount of storage equal to the total amount of runoff which will be produced by the one-year frequency SCS Type III 24-hour storm, or a 1.25-inch 2-hour rainfall at the bottom of the proposed detention basin along with a minimum 3-inch diameter outlet.

b) The invert(s) of the principal outlet(s) used to control the larger storms for flood control purposes would then be located at the resultant water surface elevation required to produce this storage volume. Therefore, the principal outlets would be utilized for storms only in excess of the 1.25-inch, 2-hour event which, in turn, would be completely controlled by the lower, 3-inch outlet. If the above requirements would result in a pipe smaller than 3 inches in diameter, the period of retention shall be waived so that 3 inches will be the minimum pipe size used. It should be remembered that, in all cases, the basin should be considered initially empty (i.e., the storage provided for the quality requirements and the discharge capacity of its outlet should be utilized during the routing of the larger flood control storms).

3) Detention Components: Emergency Spillways

a) Vegetated emergency spillways shall have side slopes not exceeding 3 horizontal to 1 vertical.

b) Emergency spillways not excavated from non-compacted soil, shall be suitably lined and shall comply with criteria contained in Hydraulic Circular No. 15 or National Handbook of Conservation Practices.

c) Maximum velocities in emergency spillways shall be checked based on the velocity of the peak flow in the spillway resulting from the routed Emergency Spillway Hydrography. Where maximum velocities exceed those contained in Exhibit A-16, suitable lining shall be provided.

4) Detention Components: Dams and Embankments

a) The minimum top widths of all dams and embankments are listed below. These values have been adopted from National Handbook of Conservation Practices.

MINIMUM TOP WIDTHS

| Height (feet) | Top Width (feet) |
| --- | --- |
| 0-15 | 10 |
| 15-20 | 12 |
| 20-25 | 14 |

b) The design top elevation of all dams and embankments after all settlement has taken place shall be equal to, or greater than, the maximum water surface elevation in the basin resulting from the routed Freeboard Hydrograph. Therefore, the design height of the dam or embankment, defined as the vertical distance from the top down to the bottom of the deepest cut, shall be increased by the amount needed to ensure that the design top elevation will be maintained following all settlement. This increase shall not be less than 5 percent. Where necessary, the engineer shall require consolidation tests of the undisturbed foundation soil to more accurately determine the necessary increase.

c) Maximum side slopes for all dams and embankments are 3 horizontal to 1 vertical.

d) All earth fill shall be free from brush, roots, and other organic material subject to decomposition.

e) Cutoff trenches are to be excavated along the dam or embankment centerline to impervious subsoil or bedrock.

f) Safety ledges shall be constructed on the side slopes of all detention basins having a permanent pool of water. The ledges shall be 4 to 6 feet in width and located approximately 2 ½ to 3 feet below and 1 to 1 ½ feet above the permanent water surface.

g) The fill material in all earth dams and embankments shall be compacted to at least 95 percent of the maximum density obtained from compaction tests performed by the appropriate method in ASTM D 698.

5) Detention Facilities in Flood Hazard Areas

a) There will be no detention basins in the floodway except for those on-stream.

b) Whenever practicable, developments and their storm water detention facilities should be beyond the extent of the flood hazard area of a stream. When that is not feasible and detention facilities are proposed to be located partially or wholly within the flood hazard area or other areas which are frequently flooded, some storm conditions will make the facility ineffective at providing retention of site runoff. This will happen if the stream is already overflowing its banks and the detention basin, causing the basin to be filled prior to the time it is needed. In such cases, the standards established in these regulations will be modified in order to give only partial credit to detention capacities located within a flood hazard area. The credit will vary in a ratio intended to reflect the probability that storage in a detention basin will be available at the time a storm occurs at the site.

c) In addition, detention facilities must be in compliance with all applicable regulations.

d) Detention storage provided below the elevation of the edge of the flood hazard area will be credited as effective storage at a reduced proportion as indicated in the table below:

SIZE OF STORAGE AREA*

| Elevation | Less Than 5 Miles | 5-100 Miles | Greater Than 100 Miles |
| --- | --- | --- | --- |
| Less than 2' below edge | 40% | 65% | 90% |
| Between 2' and 4' below edge | 25% | 50% | 75% |
| Over 4' below edge | 10% | 25% | 50% |

*Area contributing floodwaters to the flood hazard area at the site in question. This effective detention storage will be required to provide for drainage of the developed land in accordance with the criteria already established in these regulations. However, the gross storage considered for crediting will not exceed that which would be filled by runoff of a 100-year storm from the site.

e) As an alternative to the approach outlined in section b) above, if the developer can demonstrate that the detention provided would be effective during runoff from the 100-year, 24-hour Type II storm, peaking simultaneously at the site and on the flood hazard area, the developer's plan will be accepted as complying with the provisions of section b) above.

f) In making computations under sections b) or e) above, the volume of net fill added to the flood hazard area portion of the project's site will be subtracted from the capacity of effective detention storage provided. Net fill is defined as the total amount of fill created by the project less the amount of material excavated during the construction of the project, both measured below the elevation of the 100-year flood but above the elevation of low water in the stream.

g) Where detention basins are proposed to be located in areas which are frequently flooded but have not been mapped as flood hazard areas, the provisions of either sections b) or e) will be applied substituting the elevation of a computed 100-year flood for the elevation of the flood hazard area in section b).

6) Detention Facilities: Maintenance and Repair

a) Responsibility for operation and maintenance of detention facilities, including periodic removal and disposal of accumulated particulate material and debris, shall remain with the owner or owners of the property with permanent arrangements that such responsibility shall pass to any successive owner, unless assumed by a government agency. If portions of the land are to be sold, legally binding arrangements shall be made to pass the basic responsibility to successors in title.

b) Prior to granting approval to any project subject to review under this ordinance, the applicant shall enter into an agreement with the municipality (or county) to ensure the continued operation and maintenance of the detention facility. This agreement shall be in a form satisfactory to the municipal attorney, and may include, but may not necessarily be limited to, personal guarantees, deed restrictions, covenants, and bonds. In cases where property is subdivided and sold separately, a homeowners association or similar permanent entity should be established as the responsible entity, absent an agreement by a governmental agency to assume responsibility.

c) In the event that the detention facility becomes a danger to public safety or public health, or if it is in need of maintenance, the municipality shall so notify in writing the responsible person. From that notice, the responsible person shall have fourteen (14) days to effect such maintenance and repair of the facility in a manner that is approved by the municipal engineer or his designee. If the responsible person fails or refuses to perform such maintenance and repair, the municipality may immediately proceed to do so and shall bill the cost thereof to the responsible person.

## 6. STORM WATER MANAGEMENT: SYSTEM DESIGN—PROTECTING WATER QUALITY

a. In addition to addressing water quantity generated by development, a storm water management system shall also enhance the water quality of storm water runoff.

b. In order to enhance water quality of storm water runoff, storm water management shall provide for the control of a water quality design storm. The water quality design storm shall be defined as the one-year frequency SCS Type III 24-hour storm or a 1.25-inch two-hour rainfall.

c. The water quality design storm shall be controlled by best management practices. These include but are not limited to the following:

1) In "dry" detention basins, provisions shall be made to ensure that the runoff from the water quality design storm is retained such that not more than 90 percent will be evacuated prior to 36 hours for all non-residential projects. The retention time shall be considered a brim-drawdown time, and therefore shall begin at the time of peak storage. The retention time shall be reduced in any case which would require an outlet size diameter of 3" or less. Therefore, 3"- diameter orifices shall be the minimum allowed.

2) In permanent ponds or "wet" basins, the water quality requirements of this ordinance shall be satisfied where the volume of permanent water is at least three times the volume of runoff produced by the water quality design storm.

3) Infiltration practices such as dry wells, infiltration basins, infiltration trenches, buffer strips, etc., may be used to satisfy this requirement provided they produce zero runoff from the water quality design storm and allow for complete infiltration within 72 hours.

4) Other suitable best management practices, as described in relevant state manuals, shall be consulted.

# Part II

# Reference

# INTRODUCTION:
# REFERENCE SECTION

During the process of drafting the Rutgers model ordinance, the authors examined a wealth of material on all aspects of subdivision and site plan development. Some of this material was incorporated in the commentary to the ordinance, explaining why and how the standards were derived. Yet, there was much valuable information that was not included. The reference section of the *Handbook* brings together this material and provides the opportunity to discuss in greater detail the issues involved in determining reasonable standards.

The reference section points to the continuous process of reflection that is necessary to ensure that subdivision and site plan standards are appropriate. It is important to guard against rule-of-thumb ratios and dimensions which become enshrined by common application. For example, many communities require that rights-of-way measure fifty to sixty feet, without actually examining how wide a right-of-way should be given its function. Similarly, open space standards are all too often established by a set percentage—again, without considering the particular needs of the residents or the specific site in question. Changing technology is also a factor. As new construction materials and methods become available, communities should reconsider their subdivision and site plan requirements for piping, manhole spacing, and the like.

In short, the reference section provides the background for the many issues to be considered in deriving subdivision standards. In addition, it presents a framework to guide what should be an ongoing process of review of subdivision and site plan requirements. The reference section encompasses the following:

Chapter 1    Background: Evolution of
             Subdivision Regulation
Chapter 2    Procedure
Chapter 3    Site Design
Chapter 4    Improvement Standards

*Chapter 1*

# BACKGROUND: EVOLUTION OF SUBDIVISION REGULATION

Subdivision regulation has been an integral part of American land-use planning for over a half-century. To understand why a model ordinance has been formulated, it is important to first describe what subdivision controls encompass, how they have evolved, and the current state of practice.

## Subdivision Regulation: Description and Importance

Subdivision regulation is the control by a public body of the platting and conversion of undeveloped land into building lots. A city can control the subdivision of real estate by requiring a developer to meet certain conditions in exchange for the privilege of recording a plat. While imposing conditions restricts the use of private property, the cumulative effect of land subdivision on a community is so great as to justify public control of the process. Local governments can point to the following reasons, among others, for their interest in land subdivision: 1) once tracts of land are broken up into lots and blocks and streets are laid out, development patterns are set; 2) the design of the street system will have a long-time effect on neighborhood quality and traffic congestion; 3) the width and configuration of the streets must meet the requirements of emergency vehicles; 4) there must be an adequate supply of water, and provision for sewage disposal; 5) to prevent downstream flooding, storm water runoff after development cannot exceed the amount of runoff prior to development; 6) each lot must be defined in order to avoid boundary disputes and title defects; and 7) the balance between the costs of services and the revenue derived from the new residents will have an impact on the tax rate paid by all residents.

The importance of regulating land development and the consequences of inadequate regulation have been underscored by writers of urban policy:

*When vacant lands are unimproved, the municipality has its best, and sometimes its only, opportunity to obtain the pattern of land development with which it must live in the future. The amount of money which many cities are compelled to spend annually for street widening, redesign, relocation of utility lines, slum clearance, and redevelopment is grim evidence of the cost of failure to develop property in a proper manner.*[1]

It is through the regulations set forth in subdivision ordinances that community interest is expressed and protected.[2] Subdivision ordinances establish the standards and procedures under which the landowner or developer may divide land. Ordinances generally include requirements for the construction of public improvements, such as streets, sidewalks, and utilities, and they often require the developer to provide these improvements before lots can be sold.[3]

On its most basic level, then, subdivision regulation prevents substandard developments. Yet it offers an opportunity to do more:

*(T)he true measures of success are the creation of sound neighborhood patterns; integration of residential development with other land uses; acquisition of sites for public parks, schools, and other facilities; and the continuation of the transportation network, among others.*[4]

In its broadest application as a tool to guide land-use development, subdivision regulation should be part of a planning process that emerges from a studied consideration of community problems and goals. It is one element of land-use controls that include zoning regulations and a master plan detailing land uses extending to undeveloped as well as developed land. Subdivision regulation in accordance with a master plan helps avoid ad hoc growth and irresponsible planning decisions.

This comprehensive view of subdivision control is a fairly recent development in the history of land use regulation—at least as evidenced in field-level practice. The effect of rampant land speculation and uncontrolled subdivision in the 1920s caused Americans to modify somewhat their traditional antipathy to placing restrictions on private ownership and use of land, which led to the "first generation" of subdivision controls.[5] The strain on public resources arising from rapid development in the 1950s and the environmental concerns of the 1960s and 1970s made people aware of more extensive needs in regulating development; subdivision regulations consequently became more detailed, exacting, and discretionary. In the 1980s, a counter-movement could be observed, based on the perspective that some communities had enacted excessive and arbitrary regulations. The cycles in the evolution of land-use controls are the historical background to *The Subdivision and Site Plan Handbook.*

## Subdivision Regulation: The Beginning

### *HISTORICAL ANTECEDENTS*

The subdivision of land, in the sense of the orderly division of land into parcels, is "as old as written records."[6] The Egyptians and the Greeks maintained a system for the division of land and the development of communities, and laws regulating the width of streets appeared as early as the fourth century B.C. The Romans used a grid plan for laying out towns—a pattern borrowed from earlier cultures and later adopted by other European towns. There was also a concern for the health, safety, and welfare of the inhabitants, which in town planning took the form of careful orientation of buildings to capture breezes, provision for sanitary sewers, making sure a good water supply was available, and designation of recreational areas—principles of city planning that are endorsed today. The early efforts to control land use can be characterized by the need to regulate problems that affected urban societies as a unit and with which as a unit it had to deal. This experience of collective attempts to address matters of public concern was drawn on during the colonizing of America.

*TOWN PLANNING IN THE COLONIES*

The process of land division in what is now the United States began with the arrival of first settlers. Very few early towns arose spontaneously—contrary to popular belief, almost all were planned communities. "Some individual, corporate group, or governmental body conceived of a pattern of streets, dwelling sites, and locations for public or institutional activities and stamped this design on the virgin land."[7] Most towns were laid out using patterns and arrangements brought over from the motherland.

The Spanish, more than any other of the colonizing powers, followed a system of land settlement and town planning that was formalized in written rules and regulations.[8] In the early 1500s, leaders of expeditions were given instructions to seek dry land for siting settlements and to divide the land into plots according to a definite arrangement and town pattern, "for towns newly founded may be established according to plan without difficulty. If not started with form, they will never attain it."[9]

As the Spanish extended their settlements, uniform standards for planning towns became necessary. These were codified and promulgated by Philip II in 1573 in the Laws of the Indies, which have been called America's first planning legislation.[10] The Laws consisted of specific regulations governing all aspects of town planning. Site-selection criteria were outlined first: towns were to be sited on land possessing an ample water supply, with fuel and timber nearby, and surrounded by good farming land. The town was to be constructed following a plan, so that development could be orderly. Detailed regulations specified the orientation and dimensions of the main plaza: its four corners were to point to the north, south, east, and west, and 600 by 400 feet was the size recommended for a well-proportioned medium size plaza. The placement of principal and minor roads, the location of important buildings in town, the siting of houses and their construction details, and the layout of the common and the outlying agricultural lands were also specified in the Laws. Even the appearance of the community was covered in one regulation: "Settlers are to endeavor, as far as possible, to make all structures uniform, for the sake of the beauty of the town."[11] Hundreds of towns were planned in conformity with these Laws during the period of Spanish rule in the Western Hemisphere.

In the Virginia and Maryland Tidewater area colonized by English settlers, the Crown sponsored a series of Town Acts that designated sites for towns and detailed the layout and disposition of lots. The plan for Tappahannock, Virginia, for example, provided for a street hierarchy, with the widest streets flanking the public square and measuring 82½ feet in width, three other major streets each 66 feet wide, and narrower "lanes" measuring 49½ feet wide.[12] Colonists were ordered to send all shipments through the towns promoted by the general town acts, but topography, the plantation economy, and opposition from farmers largely defeated these urbanizing efforts, and few towns developed into urban centers.

Even though widescale urbanization did not occur, the planning of individual towns continued in both Tidewater colonies. The 1699 law establishing a new capital of Virginia, Williamsburg, was the most detailed town planning law adopted to that time in the English colonies. It specified the amount of land required and even spelled out the form and dimensions of the capitol building, complete with elevations showing the roof pitch and the number of windows. Other provisions covered lot size, setback specifications, and such details as the type of fencing each homeowner was required to construct within six months after completion of the dwelling.[13] Noteworthy in the plan of Williamsburg and contributing to the appeal of its design was its three-dimensional quality, which was partly due to planning some of the major buildings at the same time as the ground plan was laid out.

The New England land pattern was distinguished by public control over land use and land distribution.[14] Town centers contained shops, public buildings, churches and homes, and the fields beyond were divided into long strips and allotted to settlers for cultivation. Although strips of fields were owned by individuals, in some townships, the proprietors decided what crops would be grown and when they would be harvested. After the harvest and before spring sowing, the fields were used in common. Pasture lands and woodlands were also controlled by the community, with use by individual citizens subject to town regulations. The claim can also be made that the New England system of land use was the first example of regional planning in the colonies since both urban and rural land were subject to planned development and community controls.

Among the early large cities founded in the new world, Philadelphia, planned by William Penn to be the capital of a new colony settled by the Quakers, stands out. Philadelphia is distinguished as the first large American city to be laid out in a grid-iron pattern and is usually credited with being the inspiration for

**Photo 1–1.** *The North Common. Chelsea, Vermont.*

rectangular town planning in the nineteenth century. Unfortunately, later plans applied the Philadelphia pattern mechanistically, without regard to topography and eliminating some of the elements that made Philadelphia unusual for its time—namely, the squares set aside as public space and the exceptionally wide streets. A large central square and four smaller squares reserved for recreational use in Philadelphia constituted America's first designated public parks,[15] and the two principal streets measuring 100 feet in width and the other streets measuring 50 feet in width were exceedingly generous. In addition, Penn made sure that no encroachments on public road rights-of-way would be permitted by planning the roads leading to the agricultural lands outside the town center before the lands were subdivided. Philadelphia can

**Illustration 1–1.** *Plan of Philadelphia, Pennsylvania, 1683.*

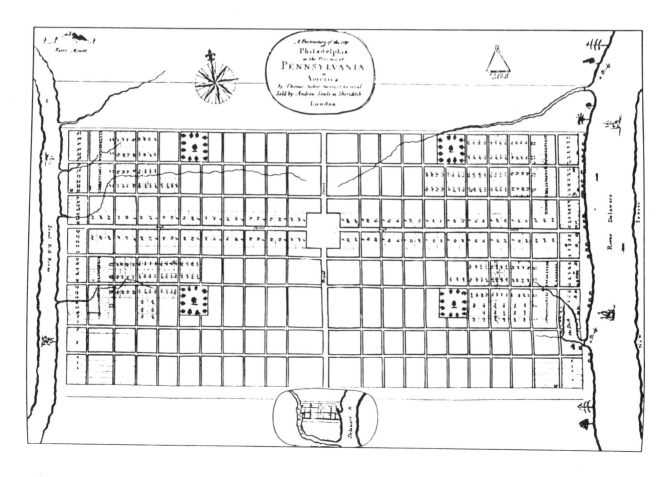

**Illustration 1–2.** *Oklahoma City, Oklahoma, 1889.*

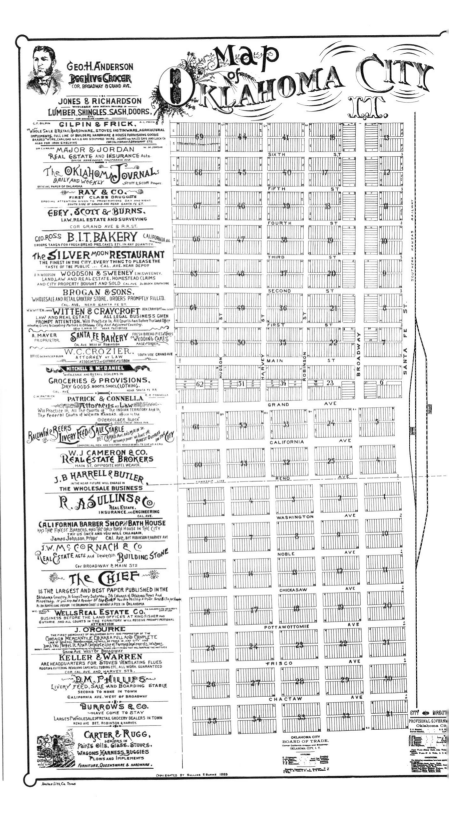

thus be pointed to as an early example in American planning history of the acceptance of at least some degree of public control over land use and development.

Town planning during the colonial era was marked by an awareness of the importance of providing an attractive urban environment with public amenities such as parks and spacious streets. As the number of settlements increased in the New World, the control of land subdivision was largely taken over by private property owners.[16] "Land came to be regarded as a commodity for personal enrichment rather than a resource to be managed wisely by the citizens and their governmental institutions."[17] This change set the stage for the rampant land speculation that characterized the subdivision of land in the late eighteenth, nineteenth, and twentieth centuries.

*PREMATURE SUBDIVISION: THE "GREAT AMERICAN LAND BUBBLE"*[18]

After the Revolutionary War, the Continental Congress enacted the Land Ordinance of 1785, which made land in the public domain available for sale. The ordinance contained regulations to guide the surveying and disposition of lands in the western territories. It established a rectangular system to survey townships and sections—a method still used today, except in some eastern parts of the United States and portions of California and Texas.[19] Parcels were in the form of townships of 36 square miles or sections of 640 acres, but groups of investors soon petitioned Congress to buy much larger tracts.

Although not all groups promoting new settlements were unscrupulous speculators, many were and saw the land sale as an opportunity for high profits at little risk. The early land schemes counted on a quick turnover, not long-term investment. Large tracts of land were eagerly subdivided into thousands of smaller parcels for sale to investors—back East. Land development in the sense of making improvements or investing capital to make the tract more valuable was not the practice. Purchasers traded parcels of land like pieces of merchandise, often without surveys or adequate descriptions. Deeds were often not filed and titles remained unclaimed. When taxes became a burden, the land reverted to the state or municipality for non-payment.[20]

By the turn of the nineteenth century, however, the wild land mania had subsided somewhat. Land dispersal slowed down, and efforts turned to retailing the lands bought from the original speculators. Offices were set up and parcels were offered to individuals or small groups for settlement, with extravagant claims snaring the unwary. Speculators would lay out entire towns in small lots of about 50 by 100 feet, and advertise the sale of the lots to unwary purchasers in the eastern cities. Writers of the time called this the "era of imaginary villages." Some even claimed to have seen surveyors laying out such a town on ice.[21]

**Illustration 1–3.** *Nineteenth century western land subdivision: caveat emptor.*

MARTIN CHUZZLEWIT SELECTS HIS LOT IN THE THRIVING CITY OF EDEN

Some towns, like Cleveland and Cincinnati, to name two examples, were the result of careful site selection and town planning, but as a rule, selling lots was the force motivating town founders. "Gain! Gain! Gain!" exclaimed Morris Birkbeck, an Illinois pioneer, while journeying through the Northwest in 1817. "Gain is the beginning, the middle, and the end, the alpha and omega of the founders of American towns, who, after all, are bad calculators, when they omit the important element of salubrity in their choice of situations."[22]

Not only were inappropriate sites selected for new settlements, wildcat town founding left numerous other problems in its

THE THRIVING CITY OF EDEN "IN FACT"

wake: gullible purchasers lost life savings, governments lost revenue due to the large number of foreclosures, and towns were left with the job and expense of providing basic improvements. A traveler in Pennsylvania noted that such was the haste to build one "embryo city, that there was no time to remove the stumps of the trees that covered the spot ... you make your way from one house to another by leaping over the prostrate trunks and winding round the standing stumps."[23] Even when stumps were removed, roads were rarely paved and often became quagmires during heavy rains. This condition gave rise to the story often told in the nineteenth century of the citizen who offers to help a man stuck up to his neck in a mud hole on a local thoroughfare. "No need to worry," replies the unfortunate... "I have a horse underneath me."[24]

If anything, the excesses of nineteenth-century speculation were exceeded in the early twentieth century when some of the most notorious land speculation activities took place. By 1939, two million vacant lots had been subdivided in Chicago, or "enough to accommodate 15 million people, or triple the city's population at that time."[25] Wholesale subdivision in Florida was even more ambitious: enough land was subdivided there to house the population of the entire United States. Nor was the Northeast immune: newspapers distributed 20-foot lots in New York and New

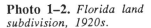

**Photo 1–2.** *Florida land subdivision, 1920s.*

MAKING MORE LAND IN FLORIDA TO MEET THE DEMAND OF SPECULATORS

Jersey to new subscribers as free gifts. Perhaps the most outrageous stunt of all was giving away deeds as premiums with boxes of soap.[26] "The result was that vast quantities of land on the outskirts of every large town and city were roughly hewn up for development with jerry-built homes and without proper roads, water, schools, and other city services."[27]

There is no question that some overnight boom towns did become thriving population centers and that speculation helped spread development across the nation. However, speculative periods historically were followed by price collapse. In fact, many of America's biggest panics and depressions were touched off by overspeculation in land and a bust in land prices, carrying down hundreds of banks and other lending institutions.[28] Tax delinquency and foreclosure rates were staggering, and the wastage of land appalling. Unsuitable land was developed, poor locations were selected, lots were too small to be built on, and the cost of installing utilities to scattered subdivisions added to the financial troubles of many municipalities. These abuses finally resulted in a change in American attitudes: "It took a gigantic boom and bust to alert Americans to the many dangers of unrestricted development and to establish a sympathetic climate for land subdivision controls. . . ."[29]

**Photo 1–3.** *Contemporary land speculation, 1984.*

## Stages of Subdivision Controls

*STAGE I: 1928—WORLD WAR II.*
*ENABLING LEGISLATION AND EARLY ORDINANCES*

Subdivision regulation in the sense that it existed prior to 1928 was not a tool to control and guide development. The land recording system set up after the Revolution dealt only with the mechanical and legal details of survey methods and the registering of deeds. Its purpose was to establish uniformity in survey methods and in boundary and monument descriptions. Gradually the specification of street widths and other layout details was introduced, "(b)ut subdivision controls were not thought of as a means of limiting the amount of development until the vast land speculations of the 1920s showed the folly and ruinous expense to local governments of unrestricted subdivision."[30]

Realizing the inadequacies of existing legislation, professional planners lobbied for model planning laws. In 1928, the federal government published the Standard City Planning Enabling Act. This act, which served as the basis for much state enabling legislation, shifted the concept of subdivision regulation from its limited role as a device for recording plats to "one of providing a means to shape community growth. Emphasis was placed on requiring internal improvements for the subdivision, in addition to providing a convenient method of transferring lots by plat reference."[31] Provisions were included, for example, that dealt with the layout of streets to ensure they were planned in relation to existing and proposed streets and were adequate to handle traffic and emergency vehicles. Congestion of population was another concern, as were the minimum width and area of lots.

The first stage of subdivision controls, then, consisted of securing the legal framework for expanding the role of subdivision controls. During this period, the states enacted subdivision enabling laws, delegating to municipalities the authority to impose subdivision controls. The enabling statutes vary widely among the states, but for the most part they were modeled after the 1928 Standard City Planning Enabling Act, and "they are quite similar in their fundamental patterns."[32] The basic function of subdivision control—the authority to approve or disapprove subdivision plats—is usually vested in a planning board or the legislative body of the municipality. The enabling statutes authorize the municipal legislative bodies to delegate plat approval powers to the planning board. They also specify the nature of that power and the standards and procedure that must be followed by the boards. With the adoption of subdivision ordinances by numerous towns and cities throughout the country, subdivision regulation became a tool with the potential for shaping the growth and development of a community.

This gestation period for subdivision controls saw the publication of numerous studies advocating subdivision regulations that would be rationally formulated and would foster good design. For instance, the 1929 Regional Plan of New York recommended that "one of the prime purposes of platting control should be the conservation of natural beauty to the fullest extent consistent with use for residential purpose."[33] The Regional Plan contended that proper subdivision—following a "neighborhood plan"—would be better designed and more economical than subdivision according to the "standard layout" (Exhibit 1–1). In the landmark 1932 report of the President's Conference on Home Building and Home Ownership, Harland Bartholomew summarized key subdivision design principles, specified subdivision standards such as street width based on functional need, and attempted to integrate the principles of sound design with economical subdivision improvements (Exhibit 1–2).[34] For example, he demonstrated that lot improvement costs would be lower in a subdivision developed on a "model neighborhood basis" compared with the more common gridiron (Exhibit 1–3).

These themes were echoed in other prescient publications of the era, such as the Harvard City Planning Studies *The Design of Residential Areas*[35] (1934; see Exhibit 1–4 for the street design it proposed based on functional need); *Model Laws for Planning Cities, Counties, and States* (1935);[36] The National Resources Committee, *Urban Planning and Land Policies* (1939);[37] and the Public Administration Service, *Subdivision Regulations* (1941).[38] The 1930s also witnessed extensive street, sidewalk, and other subdivision improvements provided by the Depression-era Work Projects Administration (WPA).

The reality of subdivision control/improvements in the 1920s and 1930s was a far cry from what was espoused in this literature or administered by the WPA. Many jurisdictions had no regula-

# EXHIBIT 1–1

## AMERICAN SUBDIVISION COSTS (ACTUAL AND RECOMMENDED) OVER A FIFTY-YEAR PERIOD: TWO CASE-STUDY EXAMPLES

1929 *Subdivision Costs*[1] Per Unit Under Recommended ("Neighborhood Plan") and "Standard" Subdivision Practices (Case Example)

| COST COMPONENTS | SUBDIVISION COSTS PER UNIT | | | |
| --- | --- | --- | --- | --- |
| | Neighborhood Plan | | Standard Layout | |
| | $ | % | $ | % |
| Raw land | $380 | 46% | $400 | 34% |
| Sewers | 99 | 12% | 150 | 13% |
| Utilities | 85 | 10% | 111 | 9% |
| Streets | 124 | 15% | 287 | 24% |
| Curbing and Gutters | 25 | 3% | 74 | 6% |
| Sidewalks | 63 | 8% | 104 | 9% |
| Landscaping/grading | 44 | 5% | 53 | 4% |
| **TOTAL** | $820 | 100% | $1,179 | 100% |

1984 *Subdivision Costs*[2] Per Unit Under Recommended ("Demonstration") and Standard ("Comparison") Subdivision Practice (Case Example)

| COST COMPONENTS | SUBDIVISION COSTS PER UNIT | | | |
| --- | --- | --- | --- | --- |
| | Demonstration | | Comparison | |
| | $ | % | $ | % |
| Raw land/earthwork | $2,897 | 28% | $3,733 | 26% |
| Sewers | 1,338 | 13% | 1,718 | 12% |
| Utilities | 2,750 | 27% | 3,472 | 24% |
| Streets | 1,288 | 12% | 2,009 | 14% |
| Curbing and Gutters | 864 | 8% | 1,342 | 9% |
| Sidewalks/lights | 263 | 3% | 505 | 4% |
| Landscaping/grading | 957 | 9% | 1,424 | 10% |
| **TOTAL** | $10,357 | 100% | $14,203 | 100% |

*Note:* The two geographical areas shown (New York and Sante Fe) are quite distinct in terms of land development costs.

*Sources:*

1. Robert Whitten, "The Economics of Land Subdivision" in Committee on Regional Plan of New York and Its Environs, *Neighborhood and Community Planning,* Vol. VII (New York: Regional Plan, 1929), pp. 352-353.

2. NAHB Research Foundation, Inc., *The Affordable Housing Demonstration* (Santa Fe, New Mexico) (Washington, D.C.: Government Printing Office, 1984), p. 28. Research conducted for the U.S. Department of Housing and Urban Development, Joint Venture for Affordable Housing.

EXHIBIT 1–2

## RECOMMENDED SUBDIVISION DESIGN PRINCIPLES
### (1932)

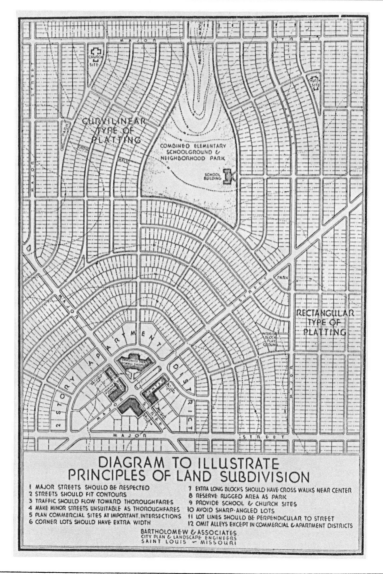

*Source:* Harland Bartholomew, Chairman, "Subdivision Layout," in President's Conference on Home Building and Home Ownership, *Planning for Residential Districts* (Washington, D.C.: National Capital Press, 1932), p. 46.

EXHIBIT 1-3

THE ECONOMICS OF LAND ACQUISITION AND IMPROVEMENTS
UNDER DIFFERENT PLANNING AND SUBDIVISION PRACTICES
(1932)

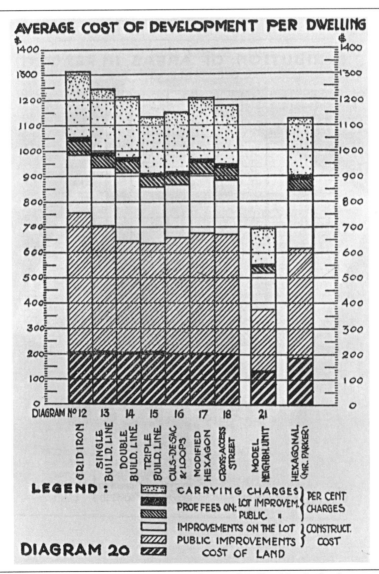

Source: Harland Bartholomew, Chairman, "Subdivision Layout," in President's Conference on Home Building and Home Ownership, *Planning for Residential Districts* (Washington, D.C.: National Capital Press, 1932), p. 108.

EXHIBIT 1–4

EARLY RECOMMENDED STREET STANDARDS BASED ON FUNCTION
(1934)

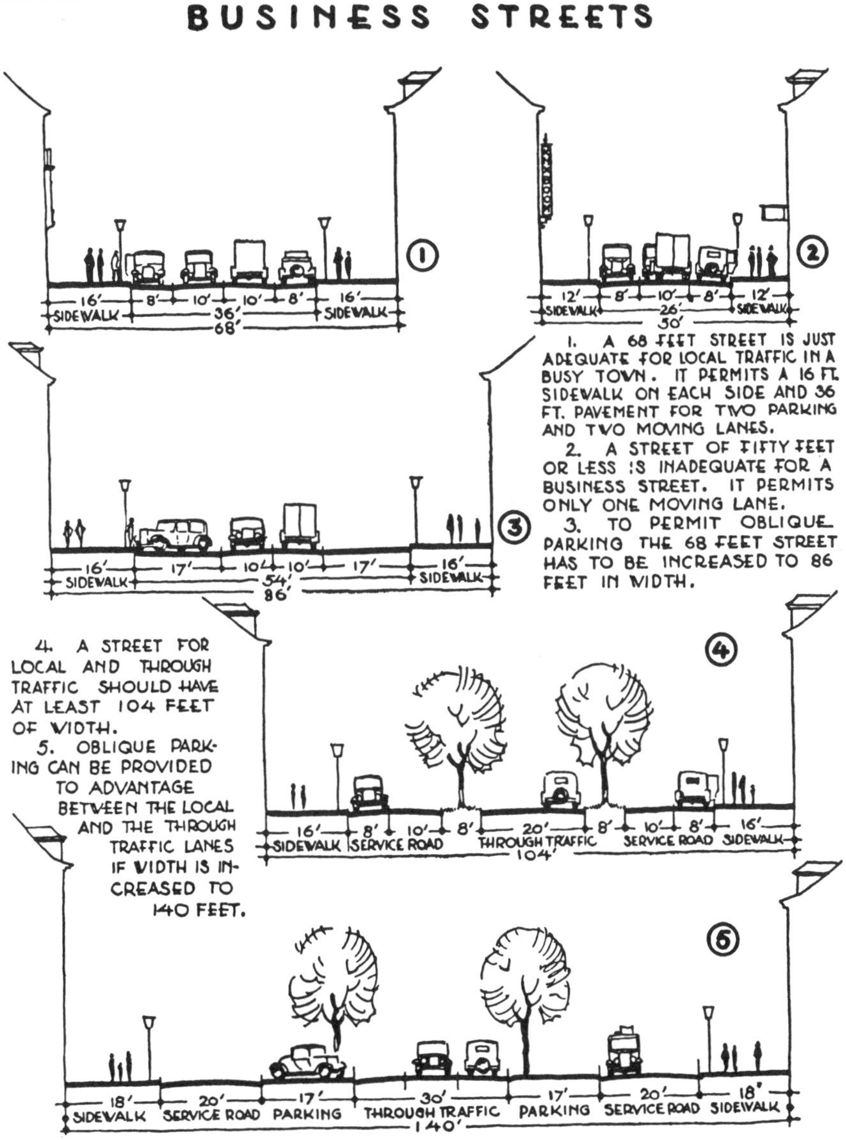

Source: Thomas Adams, *The Design of Residential Areas* (Cambridge, MA: Harvard University Press, 1934), p. 149.

WPA Projects

Part of a 36,000-foot concrete curb project, Huntington, Pa.,

Some of the 900 workers who placed 64 miles of curb, Decatur, Ill.

Placing section of 60-inch concrete sewer pipe on 3-mile project, West Hempstead, L.I., N.Y.

Concrete sidewalk improvements, Monmouth, Ill.

Concrete tennis courts, Glencoe, Ill.

Building 3 miles of concrete paving at Tahlequah, Okla.

**Photo 1–4.** *Work Projects Administration (WPA) public works improvements in American cities, 1930s.*

**Photo 1–5.** *Example of inadequate paving standards: macadam surface worn down to base course, New Jersey, 1920s.*

tions; where controls were adopted, they often were limited to recording issues such as the monumentation to be provided. The physical improvements which were made were often inadequate: it was not uncommon for roads to be scoured to their base from automobile usage, and road widths were often too narrow. More encompassing statutes were commonly harmful in their own right—a rigid gridiron pattern was often required, and excessive pavement widths were typically mandated. In sum, subdivision practice was primitive, leading the Regional Plan of New York to declare that "defective land subdivisions are the rule in all parts of the region."[39]

**Photo 1–6.** *Examples of poor subdivision planning, 1920s.*
*Top: Steep grades resulting from rigid adherence to a rectangular street plan. Mount Pleasant, New York.*
*Bottom: Excessive width of pavement in a local street serving a small-house development. Dumont, New Jersey.*

## STAGE II: POST-WORLD WAR II. PROVISION OF MUNICIPAL INFRASTRUCTURE THROUGH SUBDIVISION CONTROLS

After World War II, the demand for housing led to a suburban building boom that strained municipal facilities and services. In response, planning agencies advocated and many communities adopted subdivision regulations.[40] (Even in wartime, community planning and controls were recommended to guide the anticipated post-war development boom.) The growth of such controls is evident from the results of two surveys. The first was conducted by the Public Administration Service (PAS) in 1941;[41] the second by the Indiana Law Journal a decade later in 1952.[42] The PAS survey, conducted when subdivision ordinances were still a rarity, cited the individual communities with such controls. In fact, the

**Photo 1–7.** *Example of inadequate street width. Wayne County, Michigan, 1927.*

**Photo 1–8.** *Post-World War II suburban development. Levittown, Pennsylvania.*

PAS survey revealed that as of 1941 more than a dozen states had not even enacted enabling legislation. By contrast, the 1952 *Indiana Law Journal* survey found that all states, with the exception of Vermont, had adopted enabling legislation, and that a multitude of communities throughout the nation had enacted subdivision ordinances.

In addition to the growing incidence of subdivision regulations, in the post-war period more was required of developers. In the 1941 PAS survey, only 4 percent of the localities required

## EXHIBIT 1–5

### SUBDIVISION AND SITE PLAN IMPROVEMENT REQUIREMENTS (1941 SURVEY)

| Improvements and Guarantees | Number of Cases | Cases Per Improvement to Total Cases Requiring Improvements Before Plat Approval (in percent) |
|---|---|---|
| *Total Cases Requiring Improvements* | | |
| Before Plat | 215 | 100% |
| *Improvements Required:* | | |
| Monuments | 186 | 87% |
| Street Grading | 123 | 57% |
| Roadway Surfacing | 42 | 20% |
| Roadway Paving | 9 | 4% |
| Curbs | 19 | 9% |
| Sidewalks | 40 | 19% |
| Street Trees | 34 | 16% |
| Storm Sewers and Drainage | 75 | 35% |
| Gutters | 13 | 6% |
| Culverts and Bridges | 33 | 15% |
| Sanitary Sewers and Facilities | 52 | 24% |
| Water Supply | 47 | 22% |
| Street Signs | 7 | 3% |
| *Guarantee Alternatives* | | |
| Security Bond | 89 | 41% |
| Deposit or Certified Check | 18 | 8% |
| Assessment Petition | 13 | 6% |

*Source:* Harold W. Lautner, *Subdivision Regulations: An Analysis of Land Subdivision Control Practices* (Chicago, IL: Public Administration Service, 1941), p. 246. Reprinted with permission of Public Administration Service, McLean, Virginia.

roadway paving, and only about one-fifth mandated water and sanitary sewer facilities (Exhibit 1–5). While precise figures on requirements are not available from the 1952 *Indiana Law Journal* study, we can surmise from the discussion that road and utility requirements were now commonly being included in local subdivision ordinances. (A 1950 survey by the Urban Land Institute dramatically confirmed the growing prevalence of street and utility improvements in local subdivision ordinances.[43] See Exhibit 1–6 and compare its findings to those of Exhibit 1–5.)

## EXHIBIT 1–6

### SUBDIVISION AND SITE PLAN IMPROVEMENT REQUIREMENTS (1950 SURVEY)

| | DEVELOPER RESPONSIBILITY* | | | |
| --- | --- | --- | --- | --- |
| | *All* | *Partial* | *None* | *Total Respondents* |
| Does developer pay for improvements? | | | | |
| Street grading | 89% | 0% | 11% | 100% |
| Street paving | 71% | 10% | 19% | 100% |
| Curbing and Gutters | 75% | 7% | 18% | 100% |
| Sidewalks | 75% | 4% | 21% | 100% |
| Water mains | 40% | 13% | 47% | 100% |
| Sanitary sewer | 71% | 9% | 20% | 100% |
| Storm sewer | 60% | 9% | 31% | 100% |
| | *DEVELOPER RESPONSIBILITY* | | | |
| | *Yes* | *No* | | *Total* |
| Is the developer reimbursed for cost of one or more of items above? | 16% | 84% | | 100% |
| | *DEVELOPER RESPONSIBILITY* | | | |
| Does developer pay all or part of cost of streets or utilities larger than required | *All* | *Part* | *None* | *Total* |
| for his development alone? * | 35% | 19% | 46% | 100% |

All   =   Developer pays for 100 percent of the improvement cost.     *For cities 50,000–100,000 in size.
Partial =   Developer pays for share of the improvement cost.

*Source:* The Urban Land Institute, Technical Bulletin No. 13 (Washington, D.C.: ULI, 1950). Reprinted with permission of The Urban Land Institute.

The scope of improvements to be required also expanded in the post-war period. In addition to streets and utilities, numerous communities added provisions to their subdivision regulations requiring mandatory dedication of schools and parks.[44] In cases where a park or school was not designated in the master plan to be located on land within the subdivision, developers were required to make a monetary payment in lieu of land dedication, which would provide the means for the municipality to build the facility.

A number of influences fostered these changes in subdivision controls. The post-war construction boom was unprecedented, and communities responded with more encompassing land-use controls, both zoning and subdivision. The nature of the land development industry also changed; historically, the subdivider dealt with land alone and carved out smaller parcels from larger tracts. In the post-war period, however, the subdivider typically sold a lot and a house. It was much harder to sell the latter in the absence of improvements in place—utilities, roads, parks, and schools. Finally, there was the influence of the Federal Housing Administration (FHA). Starting in the 1930s, the FHA published Land Planning Bulletins which described "proper subdivision improvements."[45] In the post-war period, many developers relied on FHA insurance, and in order to qualify, they had to satisfy this agency's subdivision recommendations. The FHA was also active in educating the developers with respect to improved design. To this end, its Land Planning Division distributed graphic illustrations of recommended subdivision layouts (see Exhibit 1–7).

While the early post-war period witnessed improvements in the subdivision state of the art, many flaws remained. As discussed in the 1952 *Indiana Law Journal* survey:

1. Numerous jurisdictions lacked requirements or did not relate "the quality of improvements to the actual needs of the subdivision."[46]
2. The statutes typically lacked sufficient guarantees to ensure that improvements were actually provided.
3. Existing controls did not stop premature or excessive subdivision activity.

**Illustration 1–4.** *(opposite page) Sketches showing the need for planning and subdivision controls. Prepared and distributed by the National Committee on Housing, New York, 1944.*

# Your Stake in Community Planning

N' one, remembering the building boom that followed World War I, wants a repetition of the evils, social and fiscal, generated in that dizzy epoch. Shoddy construction, wild-cat finance, and haphazard planning, must be definitely ruled out of the coming Era of Construction. Not for "idealistic" reasons, either. It will be more profitable if we do the job the "planned" way. In fact, it can't be done profitably any other way.

The magnitude of the problem calls for the combined operations of all members of the community. Banker and builder, architect and landlord, homeowner and municipal official, must all join forces in long-range, over-all community planning. Without such planning, we shall slip back disastrously into the hit-or-miss construction of wasteful and unattractive neighborhoods, doomed to premature blight.
—From "Your Stake in Community Planning."

TWENTIETH century planning, if it is to have validity, must increasingly become an expression of democratic needs and the techniques of the power age!

In contrast to the "no plan" method of city growth with its lack of regard for individual and community stability, "Your Stake in Community Planning," a 28-page pamphlet just issued by the National Committee on Housing, recommends as criteria for planning liveable communities the following essential considerations: (1) How large should a neighborhood be? (2) Income range, (3) Range of dwelling types, (4) Means of livelihood, (5) Business and shopping, (6) Recreation, (7) Community center, (8) Education, health and child-care, (9) Appearance.

*What are the steps to be taken in making a master-plan?* Concise and authoritative answers are given in the closing page of this attractive pamphlet.

### REPRODUCE THESE SKETCHES

#### If You Wish, for Local Use

The National Committee on Housing, 512 Fifth Avenue, New York 18, N. Y., has authorized THE AMERICAN CITY to tell its readers that they may feel free to reproduce these sketches, or any others in the pamphlet, "Your Stake in Community Planning," for local use, without charge.

## EXHIBIT 1–7

## EXAMPLE OF FHA DESIGN RECOMMENDATIONS

### REDESIGNING A GRIDIRON PLAN

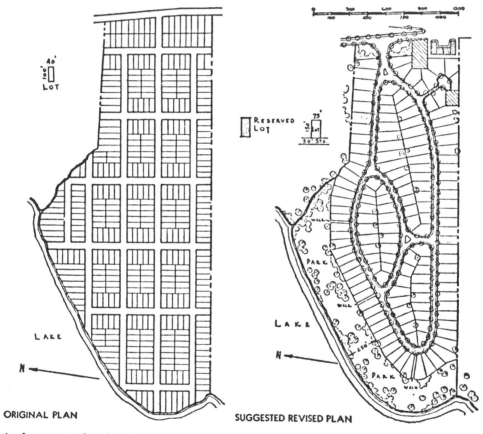

ORIGINAL PLAN    SUGGESTED REVISED PLAN

A glance at what has been accomplished by redesigning the subdivision shown above indicates its entire desirability. A group of shallow oblong lots have been converted into lots that are ample for home sites. An attractive park area has been created and the movement of traffic throughout has been enhanced.

*Source:* Federal Housing Administration. Land Planning Division. Cited in Stanley L. McMichael, *Real Estate Subdivisions* (New York, NY: Prentice-Hall, 1949), p. 128. Copyright 1949 by Stanley L. McMichael.

4. Statutes frequently were limited in jurisdiction; for instance, the state enabling laws did not allow for subdivision control in unincorporated areas.

In the 1960s and 1970s, efforts were made to address these deficiencies.

*STAGE III: 1960s AND 1970s. SUBDIVISION*
*REGULATIONS AS GROWTH CONTROLS*
*AND PROTECTORS OF THE ENVIRONMENT*

During the 1960s and 1970s, increasing numbers of communities adopted subdivision controls. In addition, the regulations became more sophisticated—and demanding. A survey conducted for the Douglas Commission in 1968 revealed that about half of the governmental units contacted had subdivision regulations.[47] The specific incidence varied by geographic location, type of government, and community size. For example, whereas only 40 percent of municipalities located outside Standard Metropolitan Statistical Areas (SMSAs) had subdivision ordinances, this figure rose to near 70 percent for municipalities located in SMSAs. Subdivision regulation was predominantly local; only about one-quarter of counties imposed subdivision controls compared to almost three-quarters of the municipalities surveyed. Community size was an additional factor. Over 95 percent of municipalities with 5,000 or more population had a subdivision ordinance compared to only half the communities with a population under 5,000. Thus, by the 1960s, subdivision controls—while not universal—had been adopted by almost all larger local jurisdictions in metropolitan areas. Other surveys confirmed that subdivision regulations had entered the mainstream of American land-use controls.[48]

The ordinances of the 1960s and 1970s were more demanding than their predecessors. This change is depicted in a national survey conducted by Rutgers University in the late 1970s (Exhibit 1–8). It revealed that developers were almost universally required to install on-site improvements such as streets (paving and right-of-way), and sewerage and water lines. To illustrate, the 1941 survey by the Public Administration Service indicated that "water supply" was a developer's responsibility in only 22 percent of the ordinances surveyed (Exhibit 1–5). By the time of the 1950 Urban Land Institute survey, "water mains" were a developer responsibil-

EXHIBIT 1–8

SUBDIVISION AND SITE PLAN IMPROVEMENT REQUIREMENTS
(1979 SURVEY)

| | Required of Developer | |
| | Developed Communities | Developing/Growing Communities |
| --- | --- | --- |
| *Streets* | | |
| On-Site Street Improvements | 98.1% | 99.4% |
| Off-Site Street Improvements | 34.3% | 68.3% |
| *Streetscape* | | |
| Street Signs | 75.8% | 69.0% |
| Street Lighting | 73.5% | 51.4% |
| Shade Trees | 63.6% | 54.1% |
| Off-Street Parking | 100.0% | 94.9% |
| *Street Hardware* | | |
| Curbs and Gutters | 67.6% | 55.0% |
| Sidewalks (Required both sides of street) | 81.8% | 57.1% |
| *Sewerage Facilities* | | |
| On-Site Sewerage Facilities | 99.1% | 99.3% |
| Off-Site Sewerage Facilities | 39.4% | 67.5% |
| *Drainage/Storm Sewers* | | |
| Storm Drainage Facilities | 97.1% | 97.6% |
| Off-Site Storm Drainage Improvements | 38.2% | 52.5% |
| *Water Facilities* | | |
| Water Mains | 91.4% | 100.0% |
| Water Laterals | 94.3% | 88.1% |
| Fire Hydrants | 97.1% | 92.9% |
| Off-Site Water Facilities (Water main extensions, water treatment plants) | 44.1% | 61.5% |
| *Public Utilities* | | |
| Underground Installations (Mandatory in more than 50% of instances) | 62.9% | 71.4% |
| *Land Dedication* | | |
| For Open Space/Recreation (Mandatory requirement) | 17.6% | 14.3% |
| For Schools (Mandatory requirement) | 0.0% | 35.9% |
| For Government Facilities (Mandatory requirement) | 9.7% | 9.1% |
| *Improvement Guarantees* | | |
| Surety Bonds (Percent required as principal mode of improvement security) | 82.9% | 92.9% |
| Escrow Account (Percent required as principal mode) | 68.8% | 71.4% |

*Source:* Robert W. Burchell and David Listokin. "Design Standards in Developing Areas" (New Brunswick: Rutgers University, Center for Urban Policy Research, 1979).

ity in 40 percent of the communities contacted (Exhibit 1–6). In contrast, by the 1979 Rutgers analysis, on-site "water mains" had to be installed by builders in almost all cases (Exhibit 1–8). In a similar vein, the Rutgers study found that builders were additionally being asked to provide off-site improvements in addition to the on-site infrastructure.

The scope of subdivision controls in the 1960s and 1970s broadened as well. Environmental protection became a more prominent concern. For the first time, some statutes attempted to address the historical problem of premature development by regulating development timing.[49] Perhaps the best-known measure designed to regulate the timing of development was the zoning ordinance passed by the town of Ramapo, New York. This ordinance prohibited developers from subdividing and developing their land for periods up to 18 years until scheduled improvements that would serve the new subdivision could be completed by the town.[50] Petaluma, California, was another example of a community that "developed a system of saying no to developments which are premature."[51]

Subdivision regulations during this period were also marked by a growing imperative to protect the environment. Ordinances typically contained provisions prohibiting development in wetlands or over aquifers, requiring that the amount of runoff after development not exceed the amount occurring prior to development, specifying that the natural vegetation of a site be retained wherever possible, requiring that cutting and filling be minimized, and protecting the natural habitats of endangered species, as well as other measures to protect the environment. Landscaping and screening standards were also often included, indicative of an interest in improving development design and creating projects that would be an asset to the community.

Subdivision control in the 1960s and 1970s thus became much more encompasssing. Certain measures, such as growth controls, added a new dimension to American land use. Yet, there were lingering inadequacies in both statutes and practice. For every well-designed subdivision, there were scores that were poorly planned. Physical inadequacies abounded; there were numerous cases of developments with cracked roadways, buckled sidewalks, and flooded basements. While some communities attempted to protect themselves by enacting stricter standards, more demanding requirements added costs—pricing out many would-be housing consumers. A host of government reports decried "the wasteful and inefficient utilization of the land with its attendant problems of large lot zoning, increased utility and municipal capital and service costs, rising tax rates, environmental degradation, poor quality of services, and racial and socioeconomic exclusion."[52]

*STAGE IV: A SEARCH FOR BALANCE*

The latest period of subdivision controls has been marked by a reaction against subdivision regulations seen as excessive, cost-inflating, and arbitrary—and a search for reasonable and balanced standards. The growth-control techniques that some municipalities had adopted were criticized for giving local authorities too much control. Developments had to meet numerous conditions before approvals were granted, and the approval process had become quite lengthy. In addition, the rising cost of housing during the late 1970s and early 1980s focused attention on outmoded requirements that added unnecessary costs to housing.[53]

Submission requirements and standards governing street widths, sidewalks, parking, off-tract improvements, drainage, and water systems were thought to have contributed to severely limiting the housing industry's ability to deliver affordable housing. These standards were increasingly being questioned and their revision proposed to help remedy the situation.[54] In response, some municipalities modified their infrastructure specifications. Some, for example, reduced street pavement widths, eliminated sidewalks and curbs in large-lot developments, and allowed a developer a choice of materials in the construction of some improvements.

Eliminating unnecessary requirements has also taken the form of relating standards to the function to be served. Instead of enacting inflexible requirements to cover all situations, these standards, using a performance approach, present a range of alternatives whose application depends on the specific situation or need. Establishing a street hierarchy is a familiar example, with street width, pavement specifications, sidewalks, and curbing requirements dependent on the function served by each street in the street hierarchy. A road whose function is to provide access to a limited number of homes on large lots would have different requirements from a collector street whose function is to serve as a link between a number of local streets and arterials. Collectors should have thicker pavement sections to avoid deterioration under heavier volumes of traffic, and curbs would generally be required to delineate and protect the pavement edge.

Thus, subdivision regulation in the 1980s reflects both acceptance and reevaluation. A half-century after the publication of the Standard City Planning Enabling Act, there is widespread acceptance that subdivision controls are needed and near universal adoption by municipalities of subdivision ordinances. Yet, at the same time, there is a growing reexamination of prevailing regulations. Are they adequate? Do they go too far? Do they reflect—and respect—the interests of both the property owner and the community at large?

## Subdivision Controls:
## Legal Basis and Reexamination

Underlying the current reexamination of what constitutes proper subdivision controls is a search to specify those regulations needed to protect the public health, safety, and welfare. This is the legal raison d'être of applying the police power to enact a subdivision ordinance.

*The imposition of subdivision controls is an excercise of the police power, and it seeks to accomplish the orthodox ends of the police power by serving the health, safety, morals, and general welfare of the community.*[55]

The courts have generally upheld the constitutionality of subdivision control as a valid exercise of the police power.[56] As stated by one court:

*A comprehensive scheme of physical development is requisite to community efficiency and progress. To particularize, the public health, safety, order, and prosperity are dependent upon the proper regulation of municipal life. The free flow of traffic with a minimum of hazard of necessity depends upon the number, location, and width of streets, and their relation to one another, and the location of building lines; and these considerations likewise enter into the growth of trade, commerce, and industry.... To challenge the power to give proper direction to community growth and development in the particulars mentioned is to deny the vitality of a principle that has brought men together in organized society for their mutual advantage.*[57]

In sum, subdivision controls have been accepted in American land-use jurisprudence as a generally valid exercise of the police power.[58] In this respect, it is analogous to zoning when in the half-century since the 1926 *Euclid v. Ambler*[59] decision, there has been little legal challenge to the American practice of zoning.

The legal status quo may be changing, however, for both zoning and subdivision controls as a result of two recent United States Supreme Court decisions: *First Evangelical Lutheran Church v. County of Los Angeles*[60] and *Nollan v. California Coastal Commission.*[61] In the former, the court ruled that a zoning authority must compensate a landowner when it is found to have illegally prevented the owner from using his land, even temporarily.[62] In the latter, the court ruled that putting conditions on land development that are unrelated to the impact of development amounted to an illegal taking of property.[63]

While the *Evangelical Lutheran* and *Nollan* decisions may not portend a legal revolution in land-use controls, especially given the "extreme" facts of both cases,[64] "the two decisions, considered together, direct attention to the potentially serious consequences to local governments that adopt overly restrictive land-use regulations."[65] For a half-century, American land-use controls operated under the presumption—both in a legal and practical sense—that regulations acted to further the public welfare. The Supreme Court decisions reawaken the need to examine the nexus between a public regulation and an acceptable and stated public purpose.

For example, in Chapel Hill, North Carolina, a small-scale developer challenged a city exaction requiring the donation of land for a new highway in exchange for permission to subdivide.[66] The developer's suit cited the *Nollan* decision. In the initial legal skirmish, the developer received a court order exempting her from the exactions; the town is appealing the ruling, however. A new era of litigation involving subdivision controls has begun.

Developers are increasingly turning to the courts because of spiraling subdivision costs. This inflation is reflected in the figures shown in Exhibit 1–1. In the late 1920s, land and improvement costs totaled about $1,000 per single-family detached home, according to one study. By the 1980s, land and subdivision expenditures had risen to about $14,000 per unit—even in a low-cost area. In constant dollars, land and subdivision costs increased by almost 70 percent during this period. Municipalities need to weigh the trade-offs between increased amenities and increased homeownership costs. This continuing search for balancing interests in subdivision regulations and practice prompts the Rutgers *Subdivision and Site Plan Handbook*.

## Model Subdivision Ordinances:
## A Long Legacy

From the onset of subdivision controls in the 1920s, model ordinances have played an important role in influencing local legislation and practice. The landmark 1928 Standard City Planning Enabling Act and 1935 Harvard City Planning Studies have already been discussed. There were other early efforts at models and state-prepared guides. In 1929, the New York Bureau of Municipal Information published "Model Subdivision Regulation."[67] This was followed by a 1939 model released by the New York State Division on State Planning entitled "Suggested Subdivision Regulation for City Planning Boards."[68] New York was not alone. In 1938, the Massachusetts State Planning Board published a guide with the timorous title of "Subdivision Regulations Suggested As A Basis for Adoption by Planning Boards—Under Massachusetts Laws."[69]

Professional and regional organizations have also prepared model ordinances. Examples include "Subdivision Regulations,"[70] prepared by the Committee on Subdivision Control of the American City Planning Institute in 1937 (but not officially accepted by the Institute); the "Land Subdivision Manual,"[71] published by the American Society of Civil Engineers (1938); and the Chicago Regional Plan Association's "Proposed Ordinance Regulating the Subdivision of Land"[72] (1938). Local professional chapters also recommended model subdivision practices.

In the post-war period, the publication of subdivision models continued, and in the 1970s, the federal government sponsored

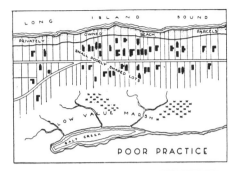

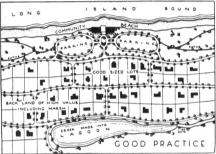

**Illustration 1–5.** *"Poor" versus "good" subdivision practice. Fairfield County, Connecticut (1937).*

**Illustration 1–6.** *National Housing Agency: description of subdivision controls.*

# Subdivision Problems Discussed In Community Action Bulletin

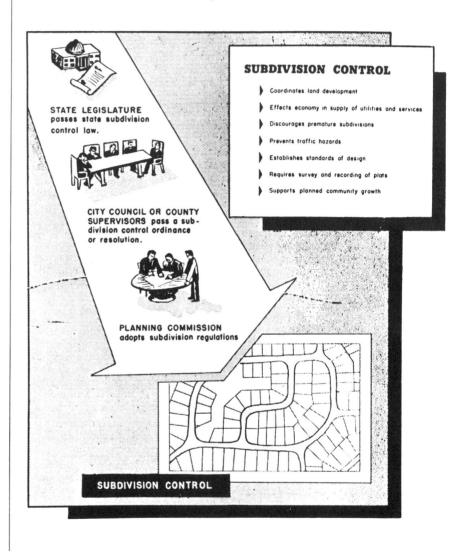

research on cost-efficient development procedures and land-use controls, including subdivision regulations.[73] The Joint Venture for Affordable Housing at the U.S. Department of Housing and Urban Development, and other organizations analyzed cost-saving subdivision and construction techniques. These approaches were field-tested in developments throughout the United States. The "demonstration" subdivision techniques resulted in dramatic cost savings (see Exhibit 1-1).

State government, as the enabling authority for local land-use controls, has also played an important role in developing subdivision models. New Jersey,[74] Indiana,[75] Oregon,[76] and Pennsylvania,[77] to cite just a few examples, published subdivision guides in the 1970s and 1980s. County and regional planning agencies, in an effort to improve local practices, also recommended model subdivision standards.[78] Most notable in this latter regard was *Performance Streets*, written by the Bucks County Planning Commission in 1980.[79] This publication was an important contribution in formulating street standards functionally: a street hierarchy was defined, and separate standards were determined for the different classes of roadways.

As in earlier periods, professional and trade associations also were active in suggesting model standards. Significant efforts in this regard include Robert H. Freilich and Peter S. Levi's *Model Subdivision Regulations*,[80] published by the American Society of Planning Officials in 1975, and Michael Brough's *A Unified Development Ordinance*,[81] published by the American Planning Association a decade later. The Urban Land Institute, National Association of Home Builders, and the Institute of Transportation Engineers, among other groups, also were active in developing model standards.[82]

The Rutgers *Subdivision and Site Plan Handbook* follows and builds upon this rich literature. It also reflects the experience of developing a model ordinance for the state of New Jersey.[83] The goals, process of development, and emphasis of *The Handbook* are described in detail in the introduction to the ordinance section of *The Handbook*. In brief, the study attempts to improve the current subdivision state of the art, particularly in terms of fostering cost-efficient standards and enhanced design. To this end, regulations are developed in a functional fashion, performance standards are established, and fundamental design principles and the integration of design with proper engineering are stressed.

Historically, this effort parallels many prior attempts to develop model subdivision standards. *The Handbook's* design of the street right-of-way according to need, for example, is reminiscent of the approach followed by the Harvard City Planning Studies a half-century ago. (Compare Exhibit 1–4 in this chapter to Exhibit 5 in the model ordinance.) Similarly, *The Handbook's* design sections parallel the emphasis on design underscored by Bartholomew and others in the earliest commentaries on American subdivision controls.[84]

In sum, *The Subdivision and Site Plan Handbook* continues a half-century effort to improve the American subdivision state of the art.

## Notes

1. Webster, *Urban Planning and Municipal Public Policy* (New York: Harper & Brothers, 1958), p. 437; quoted in Yearwood, *Urban Planning*, p. 21.

2. Yearwood, Richard M., *Land Subdivision Regulation* (New York: Praeger, 1971), p. 20.

3. Yearwood, *Land Subdivision Regulation*, p. 22, and Leonard M. Nelson, "The Master Plan and Subdivision Control," *Maine Law Review 16*, 1964, p. 112.

4. International City Managers Association, *Local Planning Administration*, 3rd edition (Chicago: International City Managers Association, 1959), p. 345; quoted in Yearwood, *Land Subdivision Regulation*, p. 24.

5. See Michael B. Brough, *A Unified Development Ordinance* (Chicago: American Planning Association, 1985), who has classified ordinances into "generations" of subdivision controls, pp. xvi-xvii.

6. Robert M. Anderson, *American Law of Zoning: Zoning, Planning, Subdivision Control*, Vol. 3 (Rochester, NY: The Lawyers Co-operative Publishing Company; and San Francisco, CA: The Bancroft–Whitney Company, 1968), p. 377.

7. John Reps, *Tidewater Towns: City Planning in Colonial Virginia and Maryland* (Williamsburg, VA: The Colonial Williamsburg Foundation, 1972), p. 1.

8. John Reps, *Town Planning in Frontier America* (Columbia, MO: University of Missouri Press, 1981), p. 24.

9. Dan Stanislawski, "Early Spanish Town Planning in the New World," *Geographical Review*, Vol. 37 (January 1947), p. 95; quoted in Reps, *Town Planning in Frontier America*, p. 27.

10. Reps, *Town Planning in Frontier America*, p. 27.

11. Ibid., p. 29.

12. Reps, *Town Planning in Frontier America*, p. 81.

13. Ibid., p. 96.

14. Ibid., p. 101-105.

15. Ibid., p. 147.

16. Stanley L. McMichael, *Real Estate Subdivisions* (New York: Prentice Hall, 1949), p. 9.

17. Reps, *Town Planning in Frontier America*, p. 209.

18. See A.M. Sakolski, *The Great American Land Bubble* (New York: Harper & Brothers Publishers, 1932), which describes a century and a half of American land speculation.

19. Syd Smith, *Subdivision Guidelines for the Jackson (MS) Metropolitan Area* (Springfield, VA: NTIS, 1973), p. 12.

20. A.M. Sakolski, *The Great American Land Bubble* (New York: Harper & Brothers Publishers, 1932), p. 69. See also pp. 47, 73-74.

21. Smith, *Subdivision Guidelines*, p. 12. This story is evidently taken from "Commercial Delusions—Speculations," *The American Review*, Vol. II (October 1945), pp. 341-57, reprinted in Charles N. Glaab, *The American City: A Documentary History* (Homewood, IL: The Dorsey Press, Inc., 1963), pp. 147-48. The site for the town laid out on ice was a swamp in the summer, which could be traversed only by boats.

22. Morris Birkbeck, *Notes of a Journey in America* (Dublin Edition, 1818), p. 71; quoted in Sakolski, *Land Bubble*, p. 174.

23. Michael Chevalier, *Society, Manners and Politics in the United States* (Boston, 1839), pp. 172-74; reprinted in Glaab, *The American City*, pp. 148-49.

24. Glaab, *The American City*, p. 115.

25. Yearwood, p. 33.

26. Yearwood, p. 35.

27. John Delafons, *Land-Use Controls in the United States* (Cambridge, MA: The M.I.T. Press, 1969), p. 28.

28. "How to Get Better Land for Less," *House and Home*, August 1960, p. 135; quoted in Yearwood, *Land Subdivision Regulation*, p. 32.

29. Yearwood, *Land Subdivision Regulation*, p. 34.

30. Delafons, *Land-Use Controls*, pp. 28-29.

31. Robert H. Freilich and Peter S. Levi, *Model Subdivision Regulations: Text and Commentary* (Chicago, IL: American Society of Planning Officials, 1975), p. 2.

32. Robert M. Anderson, *American Law of Zoning: Zoning, Planning, Subdivision Control*, Vol. 3 (Rochester, NY: The Lawyers Co-operative Publishing Co.; and San Francisco, CA: The Bancroft–Whitney Co., 1968), p. 393.

33. Regional Plan of New York and Its Environs, *Neighborhood and Community Planning* (New York: Regional Plan, 1929), p. 19.

34. Harland Bartholomew, Chairman, "Subdivision Layout" in the President's Conference on Home Building and Home Ownership, *Planning for Residential Districts* (Washington, D.C.: National Capital Press, 1932), p. 47.

35. Thomas Adams, *The Design of Residential Areas* (Cambridge, MA: Harvard University Press, 1934), Harvard City Planning Studies, Volume VI.

36. Edward M. Bassett, Frank B. Williams, Alfred Bettman and Robert Whitten, *Model Laws for Planning Cities, Counties, and States* (Cambridge, MA: Harvard University Press, 1935), Harvard City Planning Studies, Vol. VII.

37. National Resources Committee, *Urban Planning and Land Policies* (Washington, D.C.: Government Printing Office, 1939), Vol. II of the Supplementary Report of the Urbanism Committee to the National Resources Committee.

38. Harold W. Lautner, *Subdivision Regulations: An Analysis of Land Subdivision Control Practices* (Chicago, IL: Public Administration Service, 1941).

39. Regional Plan of New York and Its Environs, *Neighborhood and Community Planning*, p. 245.

40. See, for instance, G.E. Varenhorst, "How We Control Our Subdivisions," *The American City* (July 1960), p. 161.

41. See note 38.

42. "An Analysis of Subdivision Control Legislation," *Indiana Law Journal*, Vol. 28 (1952), pp. 544-586.

43. See also American Society of Planning Officials, *Installation of Physical Improvements As Required in Subdivision Regulations* (Chicago, IL: ASPO, 1952), Planning Advisory Service Information Report, No. 38.

44. Yearwood, *Land Subdivision Regulation*, p. 144.

45. Stanley L. McMichael, *Real Estate Subdivisions* (New York: Prentice Hall, 1949).

46. Ibid., "An Analysis of Subdivision Control Legislation," p. 570.

47. Allen D. Manvel, "Local Land and Building Regulation," Commission Report No. 6. Cited in National Commission on Urban Problems, *Building the American City* (Washington, D.C.: Government Printing Office, 1969), p. 209.

48. See, for instance, Robert M. Anderson and Bruce B. Roswig, *Planning, Zoning, and Subdivision: A Summary of Statutory Law in the 50 States* (Syracuse, NY: July 1965).

49. William Lamont, Jr., "Subdivision Regulation and Land Conversion," in Frank S. So (ed.), *The Practice of Local Government Planning*, p. 399.

50. *Golden v. Planning Board of Town of Ramapo*, 30 N.Y. 2d 359, 285 N.E. 291 (1972) appeal dismissed, 409 U.S. 1003 (1972).

51. Lamont, "Subdivision Regulation and Land Conversion," p. 399.

52. Freilich and Levi, *Model Subdivision Regulations*, p. 4. The following reports are cited: National Commission on Urban

Problems (Douglas Commission), *Alternatives to Urban Sprawl* 45, Research Report No. 15 (1968); National Commission on Urban Problems (Douglas Commission), *Building the American City* 245 (1968); The Regional Plan Association, *Second Region Plan for Greater New York*, 90 *Regional Plan News* 9 (1969); J. Noble, *A Proposed System for Regulating Land Use in Urbanizing Counties* 16 (American Society of Planning Officials, 1967); and Advisory Committee on Intergovernmental Relations, *Urban and Rural America: Policies for Future Growth* 12 (Document A-32, 1968).

53. For some of the "classical" exclusionary zoning studies, see: Norman Williams, Jr., and Edward Wacks, "Segregation of Residential Areas Along Economic Lines: Lionshead Lake Revisited," *Wisconsin Law Review*, Vol. 1969, pp. 838-839; Richard Babcock and Fred Bosselman, "Suburban Zoning and the Apartment Boom," *University of Pennsylvania Law Review*, Vol. III, 1963, p. 1060; Mary Brooks, *Exclusionary Zoning* (ASPO Planning Advisory Service), No. 254. February 1970; Lawrence Sager, "Tight Little Islands: Exclusionary Zoning, Equal Protection and the Indigent," *Stanford Law Review*, Vol. 21, No. 4 (April 1970), p. 767; Anthony Downs, *Opening Up the Suburbs: An Urban Strategy for America* (New Haven: Yale University Press, 1973).

54. See note 52.

55. Robert M. Anderson, *American Law of Zoning*, p. 392.

56. Freilich and Levi, *Model Subdivision Regulations*, p. 14.

57. *Mansfield & Swett, Inc. v. Town of West Orange*, 120 N.J.L. 148, 198 A. 235 (1938), p. 229. Cited in Freilich and Levi, *Model Subdivision Regulations*, p. 15.

58. See Norman Williams, *American Land Planning Law: Land Use and the Police Power* (Wilmette, IL: Callaghan, 1985), Vol. 5, p. 344.

59. *Euclid v. Ambler Realty*, 272 U.S. 365 (1926).

60. 482 U.S. 304, 107 S.Ct. 2378, 96 L. Ed. 2d. 250, 55 U.S.L.W. 4781 (1987).

61. 483 U.S. 825, 107 S. Ct. 3141, 97 L.Ed. 2d. 677, 55 U.S.L.W. 51454 (June 26, 1987).

62. Iver Peterson, "Builders Battle Takings of Property," *The New York Times*, February 28, 1988, Section 8, p. 1.

63. Ibid.

64. Charles L. Siemeon and Wendy V. Larsen, "Exactions and Takings After *Nollan*," *Land Use Law* (September 1987), p. 3.

65. Jerome G. Rose, "A Revolution in Land Use Regulations," *Journal of the American Planning Association* (Winter 1988), p. 109.

66. Peterson, "Builders Battle Takings of Property," p. 20.

67. New York Bureau of Municipal Information, "Model Subdivision Regulation." Report No. 397, January 1, 1929.

68. New York Division of State Planning, "Suggested Subdivision Regulation for City Planning Boards" (February 1939), and "Suggested Regulations for Town Planning Boards" (January 1939).

69. Massachusetts State Planning Board, "Subdivision Regulations Suggested as a Basis for Adoption by Planning Boards—Under Massachusetts Laws" (April 20, 1938).

70. Committee on Subdivision Control, American City Planning Institute. "Subdivision Regulations" (May 1937).

71. American Society of Civil Engineers, "Land Subdivision Manual." Prepared by the Committee of the City Planning Division on Land Subdivision Manual. September 1938.

72. Chicago Regional Planning Association, "Proposed Ordinance Regulating the Subdivision of Land" (1938).

73. See, for instance, U.S. Department of Housing and Urban Development, Office of Policy Development and Research, *Reducing the Development Costs of Housing: Actions for States and Local Governments* (Washington, D.C.: HUD, 1979); U.S. Department of Housing and Urban Development,

*Streamlining Land Use Regulation: A Guidebook for Local Governments* (Washington, D.C.: U.S. Department of Housing and Urban Development, November 1980); U.S. Department of Housing and Urban Development and NAHB Research Foundation, *Building Affordable Homes: A Cost Savings Guide for Builders/Developers* (Washington, D.C.: HUD and NAHB Research Foundation, 1982); U.S. Department of Housing and Urban Development, *Innovative Site Utility Installation* (Washington, D.C.: HUD, 1983).

74. See, for instance, William Queale et al., *Subdivision Guide.* Study prepared for the New Jersey Department of Community Affairs (Trenton, N.J.: 1975); Harvey Moskowitz and Carl Lindbloom, *A Guide for Residential Design Review* (Trenton, N.J.: New Jersey Department of Community Affairs, 1976).

75. William R. Patterson, *Model County Subdivision Regulations* (Indiana: Purdue University & HERPICC Publication, July 1983), Publication No. 4-83-4.

76. University of Oregon, Bureau of Governmental Research, *A Model Land Subdivision Ordinance Format* (Eugene, OR: University of Oregon, Bureau of Governmental Research, 1979).

77. Pennsylvania, Department of Transportation, *Guidelines for Design of Local Roads and Streets* (Harrisburg, PA: Pennsylvania Department of Transportation, 1972), PDT Publication 190.

78. See, for instance, East Central Florida Regional Planning Council, *Subdivision Guide* (Springfield, VA: NTIS, 1968); Escambia-Santa Rosa (Florida) Regional Planning Council, *Model Subdivision Regulations* (Springfield, VA: NTIS, 1971); Saginaw County (Michigan) Metropolitan Planning Commission, *Model Subdivision Regulation Ordinance* (Springfield, VA: NTIS, 1972); William Queale, William Miller, Robert McEldowney, and Carl Lindbloom, *Model Subdivision Ordinance.* Study prepared for Hunterdon County, N.J. and the New Jersey Department of Community Affairs Local Planning Assistance Unit (September 1975).

79. Bucks County Planning Commission, *Performance Streets: A Concept and Model Standards for Residential Streets* (Doylestown, PA: Bucks County Planning Commission, 1980).

80. Robert H. Freilich and Peter S. Levi, *Model Subdivision Regulations* (Chicago, IL: American Society of Planning Officials, 1975).

81. Michael B. Brough, *A Unified Development Ordinance* (Washington, D.C.: American Planning Association, 1985).

82. Urban Land Institute, American Society of Civil Engineers and National Association of Home Builders, *Storm Water Management: Objectives, Principles and Design Considerations* (Washington, D.C.: ULI, ASCE, NAHB, 1975); Urban Land Institute, National Association of Home Builders, and American Society of Civil Engineers, *Residential Streets: Objectives, Principles, and Design Considerations* (Washington, D.C.: ULI, 1976); National Association of Home Builders, *Subdivision Regulation Handbook: NAHB Land Development Series* (Washington, D.C.: National Association of Home Builders, 1978); Institute of Transportation Engineers, *Recommended Guidelines for Subdivision Streets* (Washington, D.C.: ITE, 1984).

83. David Listokin and Carole W. Baker, *Model Subdivision and Site Plan Ordinance.* Prepared for the New Jersey Department of Community Affairs, January 1987.

84. See notes 33 through 37.

*Chapter 2*

# PROCEDURE

## Introduction

Article Four of the model ordinance specifies the procedure to be followed in seeking approval for land development. This chapter presents the background for the procedural provisions included in the ordinance. A review of the literature shows that the approval process as presently structured has become a problem with far-reaching consequences. After defining and illustrating the problem of processing, the chapter explores various avenues of relief. The national literature recommending procedural and substantive changes to expedite the subdivision and site plan application and review process is highlighted, and field-level experience in initiating procedural reforms is reviewed. With this as background, specific recommendations incorporated in the model subdivision and site plan ordinance are listed and explained.

## Land Use Approval Procedure: The Problem Defined

*INTRODUCTION*

The last decade has witnessed growing interest in the provision of affordable housing. While much attention has been paid to standards related to the physical character of housing and the changes needed in these standards to provide for affordable-cost dwellings,[1] there is growing recognition that reform in just this one area is inadequate. Shelter costs are influenced by not only the physical standards to which housing must be built, but also by the approval process through which development must proceed. Given the highly leveraged nature of most development ventures, coupled with steep financing charges, the time elapsed in securing development approval can increase housing costs significantly. Higher density lot size, efficient construction techniques, and other frequently turned-to remedies for reducing housing costs will not suffice in the face of a protracted development process.

The issue of process has begun to receive the recognition it deserves. A HUD Task Force on Housing Costs observed that "the American developer is confronted with a bewildering and time-consuming proliferation of development approval regulations at virtually every level of government. These costs are passed through to the consumer in the form of higher housing costs."[2] Builders associations have also voiced their concern. A 1980 statement by the Urban Land Institute declared that "local and state governments should simplify and clarify the development review and permitting process in order to reduce the delays, uncertainty, and risk to which the housing production process is exposed."[3] The travails of securing development approval were graphically summarized in a recent California study concerning the delivery of affordable housing:

*From the builder's point of view, obtaining permission to build is like traveling along a toll road. They must make the journey or they cannot build. Stops along the turnpike are frequent, the tolls are high, especially for bridges over water or for those near the sea, toll collectors are exacting and demanding for right change, and the road is poorly maintained.*[4]

*NATIONAL RECOMMENDATIONS AND ACTIONS*

The growing complexity of land-use development procedures has induced calls for reform. The following recommendation from an Urban Land Institute task force is reflective of such concern:

*American developers of housing must deal with an expanding array of regulations at every level of government. Unreasonable regulations on development inevitably inflate paperwork required for a project and intensify the complexity of data, analysis, and review procedures for both public and private sectors. Ultimately, the delay caused by the regulatory maze produces higher cost housing through holding costs, increased expenses due to risk, uncertainty, overhead, and inflated costs of labor and materials, and other more hidden costs. Actions to improve the predictability and continuity of requirements and procedures can reduce these costs. . . .*[5]

Numerous task forces and studies have examined specific avenues of land-use processing reform. Some notable examples include *Streamlining Local Regulations: A Handbook for Reducing Housing/Development Costs* (International City Management Association),[6] *Affordable Housing: How Local Regulatory Improvements Can Help* (HUD),[7] *Streamlining Your Local Development Process* (National League of Cities),[8] and *Streamlining Land Use Regulation—A Guidebook for Local Governments* (American Planning Association).[9]

These task forces and studies have recommended numerous changes to expedite and, in other ways, improve development application review. Such recommendations include:[10]

- *Codify/simplify local land-use regulations.* Many communities are overdue for such revision, as their land-use regulations are dispersed, vague, and sometimes contradictory.
- *Prepare a permit register or checklist.* This may consist of a directory or checklist of all permits required, information about departments and regulations, and/or a manual or instruction sheet(s) on steps for obtaining approvals.
- *Standardize application forms.* Good forms are tools for increasing efficiency.
- *Allow preliminary informal conference/general concept approval.* Pre-application meetings provide an opportunity to iron out difficulties with the planning or other staffs before the developer has prepared expensive technical, engineering, and other submission materials. Allowing for

general concept or development plan approval has a similar beneficial effect.

- *Consolidate or abbreviate commission review.* If the professional staff has done its homework, expedited review by planning and other boards should suffice.
- *Appoint a review subcommittee.* A subcommittee appointed by the planning or other review board may be given responsibility for routine development applications. The full board would consider the most significant and controversial applications.
- *Classify development by level of significance* (i.e. "minor" versus "major"). Such a strategy separates projects with minor impacts and processes them through an abbreviated approval routine.
- *Allow simultaneous permit processing.* When applications require review by multiple boards (i.e., planning and zoning), allow simultaneous rather than sequential consideration. The review process would be further expedited if, in certain cases, one board could be authorized to consider numerous issues (i.e., planning, zoning, variances, etc.).
- *Provide processing deadlines.* Many phases of the approval process are legislatively mandated, some at the state level. However, time overruns are common. One widespread practice, frequently an abuse, is for communities to ask developers to waive adherence to deadlines. Realistic deadlines should be given and adhered to in practice.
- *Improve public hearing procedures.* Much time at public hearings is lost in wrangling over misunderstandings and non-substantive procedural questions. This could be avoided by adopting fair and consistent rules about who is to be heard, when and for how long, and how decisions are to be made.
- *Improve the scheduling cycle.* Infrequent board meetings in communities with a high volume of development result in delays just in getting onto the agenda. The obvious solution is to hold more frequent meetings.
- *Provide "one-stop" permitting,* such as a centralized department or office which accepts and processes applications and maintains central files.

- *Appoint an individual or agency to be responsible for orderly and expeditious processing of development applications.*

The model subdivision ordinances referred to in this study incorporate similar recommendations to improve processing. Freilich and Levi classify development as either major or minor and provide accelerated review and abbreviated submission requirements for the latter.[11] In addition, they recommend that the developer participate in informal discussions and review the proposed development with the community before submitting detailed plans in order to secure "an agreement... as the best design for the subdivision."[12] Following the initial general discussion, the developer proceeds to preliminary and the final plat review with more detailed submission requirements at each stage.

The Indiana *Model County Subdivision Regulations* incorporate similar provisions. Development is classified into major and minor categories, and review proceeds from an initial sketch plat submission to detailed final plans.[13] The Oregon *Model Land Development Ordinance* classifies development applications into three "types" depending on how "objective the issues are that they raise" and how "minimal their effect is on others."[14] Applications which are deemed the most "objective" and with "minimal" impact (Type I procedures) are reviewed summarily by the technical planning staff; conversely, applications involving complex and subjective decisions with considerable impact on others (Type III procedures) are reviewed at length with extensive public hearings. In all instances, the Oregon ordinance encourages initial pre-application meetings between the developer and municipality:

*A pre-application conference allows the applicant to become acquainted with the procedures and requirements for submitting and processing the application and, at the same time, provides the staff with notice of the applicant's intentions. The summary provided to the applicant establishes a record of the permit application requirements and ensures that the applicant has been informed of the various requirements that need completion before the application may be accepted for consideration.*[15]

Numerous jurisdictions across the country have enacted many of the substantive and procedural changes discussed above to expedite development processing. A brief sampling follows:

- *Breckenridge* (Colorado) has received national attention for its land-use innovations.[16] These include pre-application conferences between the developer and municipal planning staff, the reduction of notification requirements, and expedited hearing procedures.
- *Dade County* (Florida) has a development impact committee which brings together departments of planning, public works, parks, recreation, etc., to consider development applications jointly.[17]
- *Fairfax County* (Virginia) provides one-stop land-use "shopping." Under this system, an applicant files all permit applications with the building department, which in turn circulates the application to other departments for approval. Pre-application conferences are stressed and different review procedures are stipulated for different categories of development (minor versus major).[18]
- *Los Angeles County* (California) created a Land Development Coordinating Center where builders' applications are considered and reviewed on a one-stop basis.[19]
- *Montgomery and Arundel Counties* (Maryland) have established the position of a zoning/hearing officer. The officer first reviews the evidence presented by affected parties in land-use matters and then submits a written recommendation to the planning agency or local legislative body.[20]
- *Orange County* (California) has provided numerous avenues to expedite lower-cost housing under its inclusionary provisions:

*The county has taken several steps to reduce processing time: the general plan land-use element has been modified to eliminate unnecessary amendments which can now be handled at the zone change level; revisions in the site plan approval process now allow many subdivisions to be approved administratively rather than by the planning commission; and tentative map approval authority has been transferred from the planning commission to a subdivision committee, an act which reduces processing time by three weeks.*[21]

A similar spirit of rational and expeditious review of subdivision and site plan applications is incorporated in Michael Brough's *A Unified Development Ordinance.*[22] Brough's ordinance differentiates applications into "minor" and "major" categories: the former category requires only a one-step approval process; the latter, a two-step procedure. The *Unified Development Ordinance* also explicitly calls for expeditious processing:

*Recognizing that inordinate delays in acting upon appeals or applications may impose unnecessary costs on the appellant or applicant, the city shall make every reasonable effort to process appeals and permit applications as expeditiously as possible, consistent with the need to ensure that all development conforms to the requirements of this chapter.*[23]

## Recommendations and Actions to Expedite Development Processing: Rutgers Model Ordinance

The subdivision and site plan processing procedures in the model ordinance (Article Four—Procedure) incorporate many national recommendations and actions to expedite review. Examples include:

1. *Informal plan review between the applicant and municipality/other review jurisdiction.* The model ordinance encompasses pre-application, application, and review steps as outlined in Exhibit 2-1. The pre-application stage is designed to "expedite applications and reduce design and development costs." To this end, it provides (at the request of the applicant) for both a pre-application conference and a concept plan review. The former is envisioned as a forum for both the developer's and the municipality's technical staffs to meet informally; the latter is a forum for informal presentation to the planning board (or subdivision and site plan committee).

## EXHIBIT 2–1

## MODEL ORDINANCE SUBDIVISION AND SITE PLAN APPROVAL PROCEDURE

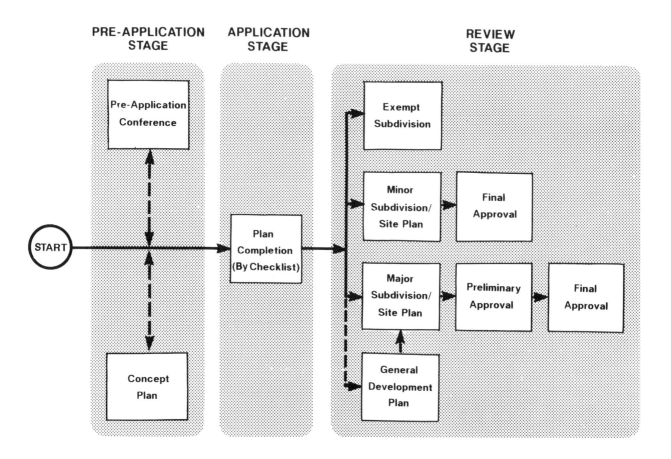

Graphic by Carl Lindbloom, P.P., A.I.C.P.

2. *Subdivision and Site Plan Committee.* The model ordinance provides for establishment of this committee. Its purpose is to assist the planning board in performing its subdivision and site plan deliberative functions. Such committees have effectively served this role in many localities. It is important, however, that this committee not add an extra, non-functional step to the regulatory process. For instance, under the model ordinance, the committee is empowered to approve, under certain conditions, minor subdivision and site plan applications—freeing the full board to focus on major applications.

3. *Administrative officer.* The model ordinance also provides for the position of an administrative officer assigned numerous administrative functions (i.e., to receive applications, issue a certificate if a board does not act within prescribed time limits, etc.). The administrative officer or other individual appointed by the mayor and governing body is given the further responsibility "for ensuring orderly and expeditious processing of subdivision and site plan applications." This provision is prompted by the belief that such an appointment will focus continued attention and the search for means to improve the subdivision and site plan approval process.

4. *Differentiation of development applications.* Development applications are divided into "minor" and "major" categories. (Certain applications are also exempt from review.) A more expedited single-stage procedure is provided for the former, while the latter is reviewed in a two-stage process—"preliminary" and then "final." This provision allows developers of "major" applications to proceed in a step-by-step fashion. First, they obtain "preliminary" approval. Only when this approval is secured are they required to post bonds and to take other action to secure "final" approval.

5. *General Development Plan.* The model ordinance provides for General Development Plan (GDP) approval for large developments (i.e., PUDs above a stipulated size). It is extremely costly to prepare the full engineering work for large developments which would ordinarily be required at the first part of the formal review stage—the preliminary review stage (see Exhibit 2–1). The GDP is introduced as a stage before preliminary subdivision or site plan review. It is designed to permit the developer of a large-scale

project to go before the planning board with a description, but not full engineering details, of the development, and secure formal approval of basic development parameters, such as the total number of residential units and major circulation patterns. Once having secured such approval—an agreement which cannot be obtained in a binding manner at the informal or pre-application stage—the developer proceeds with full engineering plans to be considered at length at the preliminary subdivision and site plan review stage.

6. *Time limits for public response.* A time limit of 45 days is set for declaring a submission "complete." To make this provision more effective, municipalities must specify a "checklist" of items to be submitted for an application to be considered "complete." Following submission of a "complete" application, further time limits of 45 to 90 days are established depending on the nature of the application (i.e., the longer 90-day period applies for submissions involving a variance or encompassing a larger number of units).

7. *Protection of applicants.* Applicants are protected by giving them a reasonable period to proceed during which they are safeguarded from zoning changes which may affect development economics. For example, a multi-year protection period is granted following final approval of a major subdivision or site plan.

8. *Single review body jurisdiction.* This is permitted to minimize the necessity for applicants to go before multiple boards. For example, the zoning board is empowered in certain instances (i.e., on applications involving a request for variances) to grant, to the same extent and subject to the same restrictions as the planning board, subdivision and site plan approval. This provision obviates the need for an applicant to go before both the planning board and the zoning board.

In sum, the model ordinance administrative and procedural provisions encompass many of the innovative procedures recommended in the national literature and industry studies and already successfully adopted in numerous jurisdictions throughout the country.

## Notes

1. National Association of Home Builders, *Building Affordable Homes;* Douglas R. Porter and Susan Cole, *Affordable Housing: Twenty Examples From the Private Sector* (Washington, D.C.: The Urban Land Institute, 1982); National Association of Home Builders and the U.S. Department of Housing and Urban Development, *An Approach for the '80s: Affordable Housing Demonstration* (Washington, D.C.: NAHB and HUD, no date); U.S. Department of Housing and Urban Development, *Approach 80* (Washington, D.C.: U.S. Government Printing Office, December 1980); U.S. Department of Housing and Urban Development, *Housing Cost Reduction Demonstration* (Washington, D.C.: U.S. Government Printing Office, no date); National Association of Home Builders Research Foundation, Inc., *The Affordable Housing Demonstration Case Study—Lincoln, Nebraska* (Washington, D.C.: U.S. Government Printing Office, October 1982); Center for Community Development and Preservation, *Reducing Housing Development Costs: Strategies for Affordable Housing* (White Plains, New York: Center for Community Development and Preservation, 1980); U.S. Department of Housing and Urban Development, *Homebuilding Cost Cuts* (Washington, D.C.: U.S. Government Printing Office, 1983). See also U.S. Department of Housing and Urban Development and the National Home Builders Association, *Energy-Efficient Residence;* National Association of Homebuilders, *Productivity Improvement Manual;* U.S. Department of Housing and Urban Development, *Building Value Into Housing: 1980 Awards;* U.S. Department of Housing and Urban Development, *Design for Affordable Housing: Cost-Effective/Energy-Conserving Homes.*

2. U.S. Department of Housing and Urban Development, *Final Report of the Task Force on Housing Costs* (Washington, D.C.: HUD, 1978), p. 28.

3. Urban Land Institute, "Statement/Proposed Actions to Reduce Housing Costs Through Regulatory Reform," *Urban Land* (June 1980), p. 14.

4. California Office of Appropriate Technology, *The Affordable Housing Book* (Sacramento, CA: Office of Appropriate Technology, 1982).

5. Urban Land Institute, "Statement/Proposed Actions to Reduce Housing Costs Through Regulatory Reform," *Urban Land* (June 1980), p. 14.

6. International City Management Association, *Streamlining Local Regulations: A Handbook for Reducing Housing and Development Costs* (Washington, D.C.: ICMA, 1983), Management Information Services Special Report, May 1983, No. 11. Report prepared by Stuart S. Hershey and Carolyn Garmise.

7. U.S. Department of Housing and Urban Development, *Affordable Housing: How Local Regulatory Improvements Can Help* (Washington, D.C.: U.S. Government Printing Office, 1982).

8. National League of Cities, *Streamlining Your Local Development Process* (Washington, D.C.: National League of Cities, Technical Bulletin Number 10, 1981).

9. John Vranicar, Wilford Sanders, and David Mosena, *Streamlining Land Use Regulation—A Guidebook for Local Governments* (Washington, D.C.: U.S. Government Printing Office, November 1980). Report prepared by the American Planning Association, with the assistance of the Urban Land Institute, for the U.S. Department of Housing and Urban Development. See also Council of State Community Affairs Agencies, *State Actions for Affordable Housing* (Washington, D.C.: Council of State Community Affairs Agencies, July 1982). Report prepared by Marvin Tick and John Sidor of the Council of State Community Affairs Agencies for the U.S. Department of Housing and Urban Development; New Jersey Department of Community Affairs, Division of Housing and Planning; and the Tri-State Regional Planning Commission, *The Affordable Housing Handbook* (Trenton, New Jersey: New Jersey Department of Community Affairs, 1972); Urban Land Institute, *Reducing the Development Costs of Housing: Actions for State and Local Governments—Proceedings of the*

*HUD National Conference on Housing Costs* (Washington, D.C.: U.S. Government Printing Office, October 1979). Frank S. So, "Tips on Cutting the Delays of Regulation," *Planning* (October 1978), p. 26; Gregory Longhini, "Streamlined Permitting Procedures," *PAS Review*, Sept. 1978, p. 1.

10. Most of the recommendations in this section are cited from Urban Land Institute, *Reducing the Development Costs of Housing: Actions for State and Local Governments* (Washington, D.C.: Government Printing Office, 1979)—Proceedings of the HUD National Conference on Housing Costs.

11. Robert H. Freilich and Peter S. Levi, *Model Subdivision Regulations* (Chicago, IL: American Society of Planning Officials, 1975), Section 2.

12. Ibid., p. 44.

13. T. William Patterson, *Model County Subdivision Regulations* (Publication H-83-4, July 1983).

14. Bureau of Governmental Research Service, *Procedure for Making Land Development Decisions—A Supplement to the Model Land Development Ordinance* (Eugene, OR: Bureau of Government Research and Service, February 1983).

15. Ibid., p. 6.

16. Kirk Wickersham, Jr., "Breckenridge, Colorado: An Experiment in Regulatory Simplification," in Annette Kolis (ed.), *Thirteen Perspectives on Regulatory Simplification* (Washington, D.C.: The Urban Land Institute, 1979), U.L.I. Research Report No. 29, p. 85.

17. Frank S. So, "Regulatory Simplification: Can the Local Administrative Process Be Improved?", in Annette Kolis (ed.), *Thirteen Perspectives on Regulatory Simplification* (Washington, D.C.: The Urban Land Institute, 1979), U.L.I. Research Report No. 29, p. 107.

18. Ibid.

19. California Office of Appropriate Technology, *The Affordable Housing Book* (Sacramento, CA: Office of Appropriate Technology, 1982).

20. Duane L. Searles and Sharon M. Canavan, "Land Use Planning, Zoning, and the Development Process," in Annette Kolis (ed.), *Thirteen Perspectives on Regulatory Simplification* (Washington, D.C.: The Urban Land Institute, 1979), U.L.I. Research Report, No. 29, p. 97.

21. Seymour I. Schwartz and Robert A. Johnston, *Local Government Initiatives for Affordable Housing: An Evaluation of Inclusionary Housing Programs in California* (Davis, CA: Institute of Governmental Affairs and Institute of Ecology, December 1981), p. 24.

22. Michael B. Brough, *A Unified Development Ordinance* (Washington, D.C.: American Planning Association, 1985).

23. Ibid., p. 44.

*Chapter 3*

# SITE DESIGN

## The Design Process

The dismal quality of the built environment is a common refrain often sounded by writers on urban design. While acknowledging that many developments are attractive in themselves, they point to chaotic patterns of development and jarring or inappropriate design.[1] Incompatible land uses, through traffic disrupting residential areas and unsightly highway commercial strips, are all too familiar. Clearly, a problem exists: a solution has proved elusive. "You can't legislate good design" may be a truism, but is also an abdication of responsibility. Better design and improvement regulations, such as those presented in the model ordinance, are an essential ingredient in the design process. Yet, "no set of rules can anticipate all the situations and conflicts that will eventually surface."[2] More is required.

**Photo 3–1.** *Sprawling housing developments encroaching on farmland.*

# Frequent Subdivison Problems

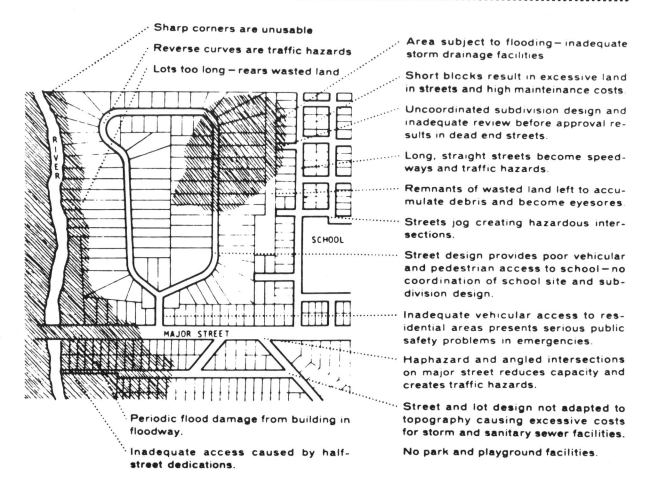

Sharp corners are unusable

Reverse curves are traffic hazards

Lots too long — rears wasted land

Area subject to flooding — inadequate storm drainage facilities

Short blocks result in excessive land in streets and high mainteinance costs.

Uncoordinated subdivision design and inadequate review before approval results in dead end streets.

Long, straight streets become speedways and traffic hazards.

Remnants of wasted land left to accumulate debris and become eyesores.

Streets jog creating hazardous intersections.

Street design provides poor vehicular and pedestrian access to school — no coordination of school site and subdivision design.

Inadequate vehicular access to residential areas presents serious public safety problems in emergencies.

Haphazard and angled intersections on major street reduces capacity and creates traffic hazards.

Street and lot design not adapted to topography causing excessive costs for storm and sanitary sewer facilities.

No park and playground facilities.

Periodic flood damage from building in floodway.

Inadequate access caused by half-street dedications.

SCHOOL

MAJOR STREET

RIVER

**Illustration 3–1.** *Some frequent problems caused by poor subdivision design that are unfortunately sometimes still encountered are pointed out in a 1964 planning guide.*

It cannot be stressed too strongly that good design is a process that involves the active participation of municipalities and developers working together. Developers have an obvious stake in delivering a well-designed product. Public sector concerns are equally legitimate, and there is ample historical precedent for involvement. As urban historian John Reps has pointed out,

*The examples of Annapolis, Williamsburg, Savannah, Washington, and many of the 19th-century planned state capital cities remind us that public initiative and investment for the planning of cities once served to create an urban environment superior in quality to that of the present. . . . If American urban history has anything to contribute to the modern world . . . it is that good cities—beautiful, as well as safe and efficient—will arise only when it is the city itself that assumes the obligation for its own destiny.[3]*

The legal authority to impose design standards and review site plans is found in state enabling statutes authorizing zoning and subdivision ordinances. The New Jersey Municipal Land Use Law, for example, permits municipalities to adopt regulations that will "promote a desirable visual environment through creative development techniques and good civic design and arrangements."[4] The law allows municipalities through their planning boards to regulate various aspects of site design, such as site topography, vegetation, landscaping, drainage facilities, utility services, signs, lighting, and screening devices.[5]

Municipal planning bodies, however, are sometimes reluctant to press for design changes. The standards themselves may be unclear, or there may be no standards at all. Lay boards may feel uneasy about questioning development proposals because they lack professional training,[6] or they may bow to pressure against making changes in the plans submitted to them if such changes are alleged to threaten a project's economic viability.[7] In other cases, planning bodies may take the opposite tack, exacting unreasonable conditions in return for development approval.

The design review process is an opportunity for municipalities and developers to work together to ensure that a development meets both the design goals of the community and the requirements of the developer. For the process to work well, however, there are a number of prerequisites:

- interaction between municipality and developer should begin at the outset, during the planning stages of a project
- the municipality should have clearly defined design standards, with board members or review staff in general

agreement on design goals

- application of design standards should be consistent
- reasons for exceptions should be open to public examination.[8]

The discussion that follows first defines site design, raising the issues that should be addressed during the site review process. It then examines each element of development design in more detail.

## Site Design Defined

The dictionary definition of site design—"the arrangement of buildings, structures, lot lines, roads, utilities and plantings on a particular piece of property"[9]—while technically correct, essentially limits site design to the layout of the functional systems, or to two-dimensional space. In reality, the total environment of a development consists not only of built and natural forms, but also of the spaces around them: buildings, streets, and landscaping exist in three-dimensional space.

Consideration of the three-dimensional aspect of site design, however, has largely been absent from American urban planning. There have been exceptions, of course, the most notable in Reps's view being Williamsburg. "Here was a town in which the plan of streets and building sites was developed as part of a larger vision of the future which included the location, size, and elevational treatment of its major structures. This approach to total urban design is the great lesson which Williamsburg has to teach...."[10] Reps concludes, "the third dimension of architecture is a vital ingredient of urban planning."[11] Site design, then, should be concerned with three-dimensional spatial arrangements: the location and placement of buildings, infrastructure, roads and walkways, landscaping, and other design elements within their surroundings.

Implicit in such a definition of site design is the importance of relating design to the contextual setting. Design, however, tends to be very much a creature of fashion, varying and changing with the times. What seems like good design during one period may be rejected during the next. Not so long ago, for example, the combination of rapid stylistic change and—according to Hedman—a self-centered design approach, were turning our cities into what

Hedman calls "architectural zoos."[12] He regards the recent interest in contextualism a "ray of hope."[13] Other commentators would disagree, preferring a more eclectic approach to design and finding "harmonious" design constricting—or boring at best. This raises the issue of the "subjectivity" of design and the very legitimate concern that it is impossible to propose design requirements that reflect the desires and meet the needs of all communities. In response, we would argue that there are certain fundamental principles of design and steps to be followed that can be universally applied in planning and laying out developments. These have been enumerated in the site design standards of the Rutgers model ordinance (Article Five) and will be described in further detail in this section. But communities need to think about their own design objectives and make the necessary additions or deletions to the standards presented.

## Planning the Development

*SITE ANALYSIS*

Successful developments are marked by a sense of internal cohesiveness and compatibility with their surroundings. To achieve this requires a thorough understanding of the nature of the development site and its setting.[14] The first step, then, in designing a development is to gather and evaluate information about the site and surrounding area. The alternative is cookie-cutter developments that bear no relationship to their surroundings.

A systematic data search should include certain basic types of information about a site. The checklist presented in Exhibit 3-1 contains a list of categories that can be used as a guide to site analysis.[15] A word of warning, however, is in order when using the checklist. It is not meant to be followed mindlessly, but rather, should be used with the awareness that each site and each development are unique and that the data collected will therefore vary, depending on factors such as the nature of the site, the purpose and design of the development, and available resources.

Once the data gathering is complete, the information is sometimes depicted on a base map with a number of overlays, one for each different category of information.[16] Together the maps graphically illustrate the three-dimensional form of the development site and its surrounding area. For a simple development or

EXHIBIT 3–1

SITE ANALYSIS CHECKLIST

GENERAL SITE CONTEXT
- Adjacent land-use patterns; circulation systems
- Population characteristics
- Ecological and hydrographic systems of region
- Area economy; nearby projects and their effects on the site

PHYSICAL DATA OF SITE AND ADJACENT LAND
- *Geology and Soil*—underlying geology, rock character, soil types and depth, areas of fill or ledge, aquifer recharge areas
- *Water*—water bodies, drainage pattern, water table, water supply, flood plains
- *Topography*—pattern of land forms, unique features, slope
- *Climate*—regional patterns of temperature, humidity, precipitation, sun angles, cloudiness, wind direction and speed; site microclimate; snowfall and snow drifting patterns; ambient air quality; sound levels
- *Ecology*—plant and animal communities; pattern of plant cover, wooded areas, specimen trees
- *Man-made Structures*—existing buildings; road and path networks; location and condition of utilities, fences, walls, and other structures
- *Sensory Qualities*—character and relationship of visual spaces; viewpoints, vistas, focal points; quality and variation of light, sound, smell

CULTURAL DATA, SITE AND ADJACENT LAND
- *Resident Population*—number, composition; social structures; economic status; organization, political participation
- *Use of Site*—nature, location, participants
- *Site Values and Restrictions*—ownerships, easements; zoning, subdivision, and other regulations; economic value; political jurisdictions
- *Past and Future*—history of site; plans for future use of site, if any
- *Site Character and Images*—feelings that groups or individuals have about the site

CORRELATION OF DATA
- Areas of consistent structure and areas where site can be subdivided—character, problems
- Identification of key points, views, areas best left undeveloped, areas best developed
- Ongoing changes of site—its dynamic aspects
- Areas where present uses to be preserved
- Summary of significant problems and potentials; key positive and negative impacts of development proposal

*Source:* Adapted from Kevin Lynch and Gary Hack, *Site Planning*, 3rd edition (Cambridge, MA: The MIT Press, 1984), pp. 420-425.

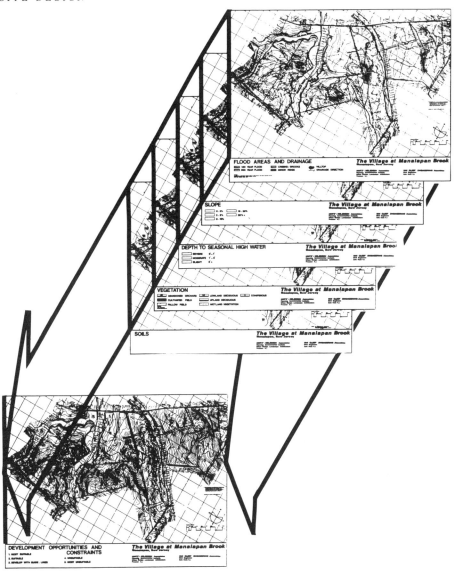

site, data collection may be much more brief and the information summarized in a concise graphic and written statement describing the essential nature of the site—its major constraints and potentialities and its suitability for development. For a larger development or site, a much more comprehensive analysis is warranted. In all cases, the process of data gathering and site analysis is not static. As the design unfolds and the development is laid out, more visits to the development site may be needed, for analysis continues as long as the design is being created.

**Illustration 3–2.** *Overlay technique resulting in development suitability maps.*

**Photo 3–2.** *By designing this development in accordance with the natural features of the site, a forested area was preserved, adding much to project attractiveness.*

*SITE LAYOUT*

The second step in designing a development involves laying it out, with the site analysis serving as the basis for the design. The layout of a development should respond to the site, emphasizing its strong points, such as views, stands of trees, or unusual rock formations, and building up its potential. Land unsuitable for development or environmentally fragile should be protected. Often, clustering offers the best opportunity to preserve special site characteristics.

Open space and scenic areas can be planned for portions of the site that are unsuitable for development, yet usable for recreational purposes. These portions would include water courses, wetlands, areas with seasonal high water, flood zones, hilltops forming natural landmarks, areas of mature stands of trees, or historic structures and sites. Where possible, open space should be located near natural drainageways, since water fosters temperature control, sound control, and clean air.

**Photo 3–3.** *Homes can be built on steep slopes if erosion control measures are taken during construction. Salt Lake City, Utah.*

Buildings and roads can then be fitted into the natural pattern of the landscape. This approach protects the environment, economizes on construction, and minimizes clearing, grading, and the removal of trees. As a general rule, clearing and grading are best limited to those areas to be built on. Wooded hillcrests, in particular, should be maintained in their natural state to preserve their aesthetic quality and to prevent erosion. Sites with steep slopes can provide dramatic views and unique opportunities for development, however, as long as proper construction techniques are followed.

Storm drainage facilities should be planned as an integral part of the development, with systems designed to minimize the possibility of soil erosion, siltation, and flooding. Lots should be situated so that, through the natural topography, drainage is away from buildings. There should be no increase in the rate of water runoff or velocity after development. Flood-prone areas should be identified and kept free from development, and setback distances established along all waterways.

Neighborhood compatibility is another consideration in laying out developments. New developments should not dominate or interfere with the development and use of neighboring property.

**Photo 3–4.** *Low-lying and frequently inundated acreage offered for sale as residential lots. Some other use would be more appropriate. Brownfield, Texas.*

In practice, this means that lots, roads, and buildings should be located to avoid adverse effects of shadow, noise, and traffic on site residents or nearby properties.

Finally, all proposed lots must meet a number of criteria. First of all, they must be developable. While this may seem obvious, it has been pointed out that "in an effort to maximize lot configurations, an applicant may try and squeeze in some questionable lot configurations. While the lot requirements of the zoning ordinance are met, the design standards of the subdivision ordinance may not be met."[17] If for any reason a lot is not suitable for development (such as in flood fringe areas, over aquifer recharge areas, or where there are unstable soil conditions), the planning board and developer should work out alternative designs that preserve the environment while allowing the development to go forward. In general, lots and blocks should be laid out so that there will be no unreasonable difficulties due to topography, flooding, high water table, sewage disposal, or inadequate access, and residential lots should front on lower order streets because they have less traffic.

**Photo 3–5.** *Proper construction techniques could have avoided the loss of these buildings to a land slip after heavy rains. Marin County, California.*

**Photo 3–6.** *Natural drainage pattern was altered in this development without provision of adequate storm drainage facilities. Missoula, Montana.*

## Residential Development Design

*ORGANIZING CONCEPTS*

In planning residential developments, buildings are not simply scattered about a development site without purpose, but are arranged according to some organizing concept. Two concepts that have influenced the layout of subdivisions are the neighborhood unit and clustering.

**Illustration 3–3.** *Prototypical neighborhood unit.*

### Neighborhood Unit

The neighborhood unit is a concept of residential organization that is based on a presumed optimum size and arrangement

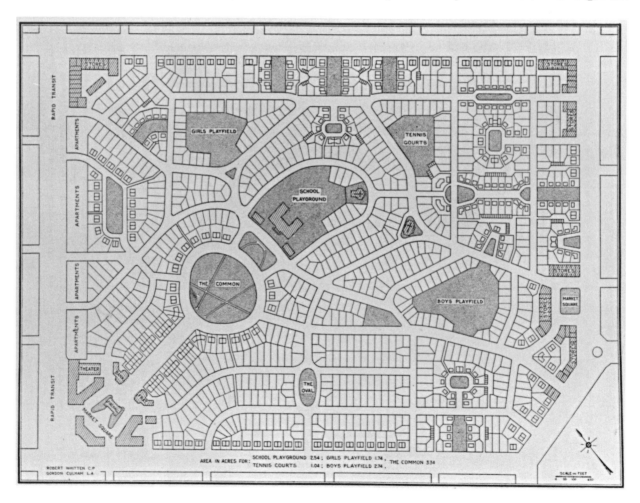

of social organization.[18] It calls for grouping housing into "neighborhoods" of between 2,000 and 10,000 people, bound by arterial roads, contained in terms of community facilities and shopping, often centered around an elementary school, with open space preserved, and motor and foot traffic separated. In very large developments, the concept expands to include superblocks composed of a number of neighborhood units.

The neighborhood unit concept served as a blueprint for the development of post-World War II suburbs and was influential in new town planning. It still holds relevance for planning today:

*The idea worth saving is that local facilities should be distributed to be easily accessible to dwellings ... it is important to keep speeding vehicles out of residential streets and to see that small children do not have to cross busy streets on their way to school. ... It may be desirable to group dwellings to encourage the formation of true neighborhoods, that is, into areas within which people are on friendly terms because they live close to one another.*[19]

Other reasons often given for arranging housing in neighborhood units is to provide a sense of belonging and "territory" that will encourage social relationships, permit surveillance by neighbors, and reduce crime.[20]

## Clustering

Clustering closely resembles the neighborhood unit concept, but allows a builder to develop smaller lots and to site buildings closer together. Overall densities, however, remain the same as permitted under conventional zoning regulations for subdivisions, and the remaining land is preserved as open space.

The cluster form of development has been described as "the most fundamental and enduring form of human settlement."[21] It dates to the practice by early cultures of grouping dwelling units together to form a community area and to create a defensible enclosure. The concept has flourished throughout history in many countries and has gained favor from time to time in the United States: it appeared in the plan for Radburn, New Jersey, for example, in the late 1920s and was the basic site design concept in the

**Illustration 3–4.** *These drawings show graphically the difference in the layouts of conventional and cluster subdivisions.*

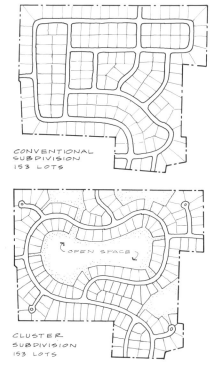

CONVENTIONAL
SUBDIVISION
153 LOTS

CLUSTER
SUBDIVISION
153 LOTS

**Illustration 3–5.** *Clustering development offers numerous advantages.*

Residential collector road

Clustering allows a better mixture of unit types and densities; single family detached and attached units

Increased safety — no cars backing onto through residential streets

Residential loop road

Effectiveness of cluster layout in creating usable open space

Provision of open space means less environmental disturbance, more existing natural resources especially when trees are left in place

Natural drainage system can be retained

More compact development reduces clearing and grading and saves on the infrastructure needed to service the residential units

Clustering concentrates houses, streets and utilities on the most buildable parts of a site

new towns of Reston, Virginia, and Columbia, Maryland.

Although clustering has not replaced the conventional subdivision as the most dominant form of development, its advantages have caused it to grow in popularity. Clustering is an excellent design arrangement for a number of reasons:

1. Clustering enables a developer to concentrate units on the most buildable portion of the site, preserving natural drainage systems, open space, and environmentally sensitive areas.
2. Development is more economical: only the portion of the site being developed needs to be cleared, and streets and utility lines are shorter.
3. Maintenance costs are reduced because infrastructure is more compact.

4. Clustering reduces impervious surfaces, thereby promoting aquifer recharge.

Whether the organizing concept is the neighborhood unit or clustering, authorities recommend limiting the number of buildings in each neighborhood unit or cluster. Lynch and Hack give a rather wide range of 10 to 40 families to a cluster.[22] Untermann and Small suggest that clusters should be composed of between 4 and 20 units.[23]

Multifamily buildings can be arranged in a number of combinations: two buildings containing six units each—either townhouse

**Photo 3–7.** *Aerial view of Lake Anne, Reston, Virginia, showing cluster development and a variety of housing types.*

## ZERO LOT LINE DWELLINGS

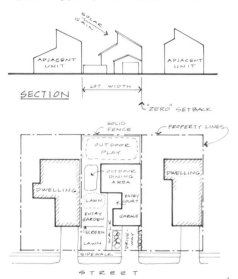

**Illustration 3–6.** *Zero lot line arrangement allows consolidation of outdoor space.*

or garden apartment units—are typical. (Higher densities are, of course, permissible, especially to provide for affordable housing.) "Zero lot line" and conventional single-family detached units can be grouped in neighborhood clusters. For all residential types, access to open space is desirable.

*PLACEMENT OF UNITS*

Building placement for all types of residential developments should be based on topography, privacy, building height, orientation, daylight needs, drainage, and aesthetics. The conventional wisdom has been that spacing between buildings varies depending on building type. For example, apartment complexes would not be placed next to single-family units without some kind of buffering. Arranging units in self-contained clusters is not the only approach, however, and some municipalities may prefer different arrangements. Mixing different housing types without buffers or transition areas when done carefully can result in significant benefits in terms of promoting the concept of community.

For those communities preferring separation between housing types, the spacing distances shown in Exhibit 3-2 can be used as general guidelines. These recommendations apply to spacing between residential buildings that are similar in design, with adjustments depending on the specific site.[24] When residential buildings are different in design, some sources recommend providing an area of transition between them.[25]

*SUMMARY OF RESIDENTIAL
DESIGN PRINCIPLES*

1. As a general practice, buildings should be clustered in groups; alternative designs may, however, be considered if consistent with community design goals.

2. Layout design should be guided by such factors as the topography of the site, privacy, building height, orientation, daylight needs, drainage, and views. Environmentally sensitive areas should not be developed.

3. Spacing between buildings that are similar in design can be closer than spacing between buildings that are different types.

4. A transition area, consisting of a natural feature, a park, a landscaped buffer, or a gradual density change, can be provided, if desired, between residential units that are different types.

**EXHIBIT 3–2**

## RESIDENTIAL BUILDING SPACING GUIDELINES

| | | |
|---|---|---|
| Windowless wall to windowless wall | 20 | feet |
| Window wall to windowless wall | 30 | feet |
| Window wall to window wall | | |
|     Front to front | 75 | feet |
|     Rear to rear | 50 | feet |
|     End to end | 30 | feet |
| Any building face to right-of-way | 25 | feet |
| Any building face to residential access street curb | 30 | feet |
| Any building face to subcollector street curb | 35 | feet |
| Any building face to collector street curb | 40 | feet |
| Any building face to common parking area | 12 | feet |

*Source:* Harvey S. Moskowitz, P.P., AICP

5.  Each unit should, if possible, have a private outdoor area and access to the open-space network.

## Circulation System Design

The circulation system is the pedestrian and vehicle movement pattern through a town or development. Streets and sidewalks or paths form the circulation system, with streets being the most important element. The layout of the circulation system is basic to the design of a new subdivision and to the arrangement of buildings on a development site.

Circulation systems should work efficiently, safely, and aesthetically. This is no small task: public roadways cover some 30 percent of our total metropolitan land, and cars dominate the landscape. Standards regulating the circulation system are designed primarily to serve auto efficiency.[26] Roads are wide and straight to speed traffic along, and houses must be set back in order to minimize the intrusion of automobiles. For those hardy

**Photo 3–8.** *Two common circulation patterns: the grid of the older development in the foreground and the curvilinear layout and cul-de-sacs of the new development above.*

pedestrians who venture out, routes are circuitous or unpleasantly redolent of exhaust fumes. There is a place for roads designed to move traffic quickly, but not in residential developments. Circulation system design should consider the needs of the residents for safety, peace, and quiet. Besides, land is at a premium and should not be used extensively to buffer the adverse effects of automobiles.

*CIRCULATION PRINCIPLES*

The problems associated with traffic in residential neighborhoods have caused planners and urban designers to take a closer look at circulation patterns. Patterns may take a number of forms:

grid, radial, linear, or several of these in combination. The pattern is extremely important, as faulty designs may cause later development or traffic problems. The grid pattern is a case in point and will be used as an example to demonstrate the kinds of problems that can arise from street design. In its purest form, this pattern consists of streets laid at right angles and all streets treated as if they were of equal importance. While the grid pattern offers many advantages in terms of logic and order, it can result in monotonous development, excessive cutting and filling, and traffic problems in residential neighborhoods. Some of these drawbacks were noted in an appraisal on the design of subdivisions: "...the uniformity of street widths has induced a random use of any and all the streets by inviting vehicles to attempt to avoid traffic, thus creating hazards at all the intersections."[27]

However, as Lynch and Hack point out, the problems cited above are not inherent in the grid pattern:

*Heavy or through traffic can be directed onto particular lines of the grid, and monotony can be avoided by varying the building and landscape pattern. The grid can be curved to fit topography. The essence of a grid system is its regularity of interconnection. It need not be composed of geometrically straight lines, nor must it enclose blocks of equal size and shape.*[28]

Traffic flow through the grid can also be modified: streets can be made one-way; movement can be directed clockwise and counterclockwise around adjacent blocks, making through travel exceedingly inconvenient; or occasional interruptions in the grid can block traffic.

Another way of improving the grid pattern is to use the Woonerf (or "living yard") concept to discourage through and fast traffic on residential streets.[29] This concept was developed in Holland and consists of using physical design elements to control traffic speeds. The street space is shared by vehicles and pedestrians, there are no continuous curbs, and several different patterns and textures of pavement are used. The driver is forced to follow a winding route around planters, parking places, trees, and play areas.

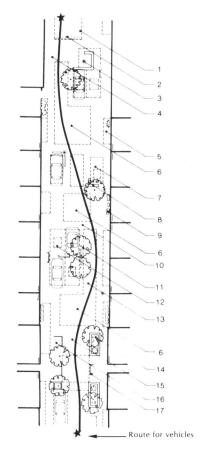

1. no continuous curb
2. private access
3. bench around low lighting column
4. use of varied paving materials
5. private footway
6. bend in the roadway
7. empty parking lot place to sit or play in
8. bench/play object
9. on request plot with plants in front of façade
10. no continuous roadway marking on the pavement
11. tree
12. clearly marked parking lots
13. bottleneck
14. plant tub
15. space for playing from façade to façade
16. parking prevented by obstacles
17. fence for parking bicycles, etc.

**Illustration 3–7.** *Dutch woonerf, which uses design elements to slow down traffic.*

*Working examples demonstrate that it works.... The appearance of the right-of-way is more that of a meandering private driveway than a typical street.... Everything about the design says that this is a street for people, and in the process the recreational value of the street space is enriched.*[30]

Not only is the design of the circulation system important to avoid later traffic problems, but because of the characteristics of the lots formed, the road layout also has a decisive effect on the development potential of the land. The streets are usually designed so that the lots formed are as regular as possible—the more nearly lots approximate squares or rectangles with right-angle corners, the easier they are to develop. Generally, streets should be depressed in relation to lots in order to take the drainage from the lots and to set the housing units off to their best advantage.

### SUMMARY OF CIRCULATION SYSTEM DESIGN PRINCIPLES

1. The design of the circulation system should be appropriate for the site. It should take into consideration physical factors, such as topograpy, grade, and drainage, and aesthetic factors, such as the visual organization of the street pattern and the highlighting of special site features. Designing streets to follow the contours of a site has a number of advantages: lots are more level with each other, the need for retaining walls is lessened, drainage problems are minimized, the costs of cutting and filling are also minimized, and site amenities can be preserved.

2. The design of the circulation system should meet the functional needs of the residents, drivers, and pedestrians. The needs of the residents are put first, because too many site plans are dominated by what is most appropriate and convenient for the car. The street design should protect residents and pedestrians from the noise and hazards of through traffic. For this reason, streets should be designed according to a hierarchy of functions. Roads that provide access to housing units should be designed for that function: they can be shorter, narrower, and curving. Loops or cul-de-sacs are appropriate designs for residential access roads. Roads carrying through traffic going at higher speeds should be designed accordingly, and no housing units should front on them.

**Illustration 3–8.** *The Radburn plan, consisting of cul-de-sacs grouped in a super-block around a central park.*

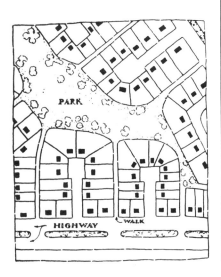

3. Sidewalks should be placed where needed. In some developments, walks are completely separate from streets, often meandering through the open space behind the units. Experience has shown, however, that sidewalks are needed in front of units as well, expecially in high-density developments. These sidewalks are used by younger children for play, and they serve as a social focus for the neighborhood. There is less need for branch walks giving access to the rear of individual units, unless the design calls for it.[31]

**Photo 3–9.** *Aerial view, Radburn, New Jersey.*

## Landscape Design

Landscape design is based on three considerations: 1) landscaping serves multiple functions; 2) landscape design should be consistent with general design principles; and 3) the landscape design plan must be sensitive to the characteristics and maintenance requirements of the most common landscaping material—namely plants.

*LANDSCAPE FUNCTIONS*

The landscape design should recognize and make use of the various functions served by landscaping:[32]

**Photo 3–10.** *Landscaping softens the surface of the retaining wall on this steep slope.*

1. *Aesthetic function*—the most familiar function of landscaping. Through the use of plantings and other landscaping elements, a site may be made more attractive, or undesirable views may be hidden. Landscaping can help unify the parts of a site, blend inharmonious land uses, and buffer incompatible uses. Landscaping can complement the design of a building, add color to the built environment, or soften spaces and surfaces that appear cold or unwelcoming.

2. *Architectural function*—the use of landscaping to articulate and define space by forming walls, canopies, and floors. Plants and other landscaping materials conceal, reveal, modulate, direct, contain, and complete space—all architectural functions. "Lines of tall trees, visible from a distance, mark the major axes of the plan, plant masses define the major spaces, particular textures indicate the important areas."[33]

3. *Engineering function*—the use of landscaping to control soil erosion, reduce harsh, unpleasant sounds, remove pollutants from the air, control glare and reflection, and slow the effects of erosive winds.

4. *Climatological function*—the use of landscaping materials, such as shade trees, windbreaks, and snow fences, to help control climate. Plants increase human comfort by shading the

sun's rays and intercepting solar radiation. A vine-covered wall is cooler than a bare one; and in general, through transpiration plants release water into the air and reduce soil evaporation, resulting in a cooler, more humid, more stable microclimate.[34] In addition, plants filter pollutants, helping to purify the air. Landscaping materials can also block and divert winds, or channel them through narrow openings. With careful placement of plantings and buildings, a summer breeze can be captured and winter winds diverted when the prevailing wind direction shifts with the season. Long, thin walls are the most effective windbreak, particularly if they are not completely impenetrable.[35]

## OVERALL APPROACH TO LANDSCAPE DESIGN

Landscape design should also be guided by general design principles. As in site design, the initial concern in landscape design is with the overall pattern and total effect. Using plantings as an example, landscape design begins with the arrangement of groups of plants; then individual specimens are used as accents. "Trees are the backbone; they form the structure of the plan, while the occasional specimen tree may be used for particular effect.... The shrubs, man-height, are the effective space formers. They are privacy screens and barriers to movement."[36] In the overall landscape design, there should be a "visual fit" between the landscaping and the site—tall trees should be concentrated in groups at the ends of buildings to break up long vistas; smaller trees are usually more appropriate in scale for narrow streets; and flowering plantings should be related to the colors of the built environment.

## PLANT MATERIALS

Since plants are the most common—and most complex—landscaping material, landscape design must be sensitive to their special characteristics and requirements. Plants assume a variety of forms depending on their environment and their age. The designer must consider growth rate, eventual size, color, life span, scent, and seasonal effect. Species must be chosen that are hardy for the climate and soil conditions and that are resistant to disease and insects. Those planted near roadways must be able to tolerate the expected traffic.

**Illustration 3–9.** *Landscaping used to help control climate.*

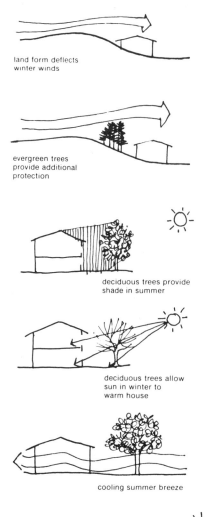

land form deflects winter winds

evergreen trees provide additional protection

deciduous trees provide shade in summer

deciduous trees allow sun in winter to warm house

cooling summer breeze

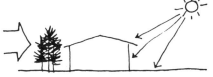

winter wind

The designer must also consider maintenance requirements. For example, the specific tree variety must be chosen with care: some species clog drains and sewers, others are brittle and break easily in storms. Where heavy foot traffic is expected, paving or dense turf might be appropriate choices. Areas requiring mowing should be large, simple, and accessible to machines. Where maintenance costs must be kept to a minimum, leaving areas in a natural state could be the best design option.

## Building Design Guidelines

Planning boards are often unwilling to make decisions on the appearance of buildings: "For some reason we mandate the type of buffer planting to be required on a site plan in excruciating detail—but are reluctant to tell an applicant that his jazzy stone and plastic store front is unacceptable in our brick and wood façade."[37] Yet, architectural styles are key in defining the character and in setting the atmosphere or tone of a development. Buildings, when seen together, produce a total effect that characterizes a community. In addition, appearance influences the economic health of a community.

Concern with appearance has led a growing number of towns to take tentative steps toward regulating building design.[38] After formulating their own design goals, some communities give bonuses for good design; others offer design awards; still others have adopted appearance codes and set up design review boards empowered to deny an application if it does not meet the established standards. While not usually considered within the purview of subdivision and site plan regulation, building design guidelines have been included in this chapter because they raise many issues relevant to site design.

*APPEARANCE CODES*

Appearance codes generally regulate the exterior design features of commercial, multifamily, or industrial buildings, although in some communities single-family housing is also subject to design standards. Generally, requirements apply to both new construction and buildings undergoing renovations. Most codes include criteria specifying the scale and proportion required for harmony and compatibility with existing buildings, and many

**Photo 3–11.** *A city street before the adoption of a unified design code. New Brunswick, New Jersey.*

**Photo 3–12.** *The same street after implementation of a design code.*

include more prosaic directives such as requiring the screening of mechanical equipment.[39] Regulations vary depending on the differing design goals of communities. Communities wishing to preserve their present appearance, for example, would require new development to conform to existing design. Regulations in these communities might prohibit excessive dissimilarity in building size, floor area, height or form, materials, or design quality. By contrast, communities preferring more diversity in design would require new development to avoid excessive similarity with existing design. Regulations might prohibit identical façades, doors, windows, porticos, or other elements. These categories are not mutually exclusive, however. Another community might wish to encourage innovative design, but within certain boundaries in order to preserve neighborhood harmony. It might require that structures conform in terms of building materials, mass and scale, or other details.

## LEGAL ISSUES IN REGULATING
## BUILDING DESIGN

For any community adopting building design requirements, the issue of legality presents itself, usually boiling down to the question: How far can a community go in regulating aesthetics? The Planning Advisory Service (PAS) Report on appearance codes summarizes the case law on the legitimacy of regulating aesthetics and concludes, "...its legitimacy is not yet fully recognized in many states, although there has been a tremendous change in judicial attitudes toward aesthetic regulation during the last half century."[40]

There are basically three arguments in defense of standards that regulate appearance: 1) the traditional argument based on health and safety grounds—frowned upon "where (these grounds) are flimsy excuses for the real concern, which is aesthetic," but still accepted when linked to traffic safety; 2) the argument that aesthetic control is necessary for economic reasons—accepted by the courts as a reasonable justification; and 3) the argument that aesthetics is a legitimate community concern under the police power—confirmed by the Supreme Court in *Berman v. Parker*, but only slowly being accepted by state courts.[41]

Most of the litigation dealing with aesthetics has been concerned with uses such as junkyards and billboards—"the 'lowest common denominators,' (which) do not raise the real problem of defining what is ugly and what is not."[42] But legitimate questions arise when attempting to legislate what is fundamentally a subjective decision. "Who can say what is beautiful? And isn't beauty, after all, in the eye of the beholder?"[43] What may look like an unsightly clutter of benches, vending machines, lighting fixtures, and trash cans along a street to one person, may be perceived as a sign of vitality and life to another. Officials in communities surveyed for a Planning Advisory Service study agreed that because appearance code standards are subjective, "it is necessary that someone with design experience guide the commission in its deliberations; otherwise judgments are likely to be capricious and unreasonable or at least may be viewed as such."[44] However, designers and architects have widely divergent styles and preferences; their design choices may be considered unreasonable by those who have different opinions. The best solution may be for a community to seek the advice of an expert whose taste is compatible with the design goals the community has set for itself.

Another issue usually raised in regulating community appearance is the possibility that such efforts will result in monotonous design, conformity, and the squelching of individual creativity. Communities with appearance codes are aware of the danger: one administrator in the PAS study raised the issue as a potential (though, he felt, not serious) problem; and there is language in most codes that stresses the desire for creative design.[45] Nevertheless, architects and designers may be tempted to "play it safe" and conform strictly to the regulations. But this is, after all, the intent of many of the design guidelines: to establish a sense of order and organization in the built environment instead of what otherwise might be—and often has been in the past—disjointed and haphazard development.

In sum, there is a tension in regulating design between wanting an improved appearance and not stifling creativity. There is no easy answer to this problem, but communities can be aware of it when formulating and administering design guidelines and standards.

*EXAMPLES OF BUILDING DESIGN CRITERIA*

The following pages outline a representative, but by no means exhaustive, list of criteria included in appearance codes, design plans, and ordinances. The Sample Building Design Criteria are offered as a guide to communities electing to incorporate building design standards in their municipal ordinances. In adopting design guidelines, municipalities should, however, consider both legal issues and the issue of stifling creativity, invention, and innovation.

## SAMPLE BUILDING DESIGN CRITERIA

HARMONY OF DESIGN

a. To preserve the design character of the existing development, to protect the visual pattern of the community, and to promote harmony in the visual relationships and transitions between new and older buildings, new buildings should be made sympathetic to the scale, form, and proportion of existing development. This can be done by repeating building lines and surface treatment and by requiring some uniformity of detail, scale, proportion, textures, materials, color, and building form.

b. The use of unusual shapes, color, and other characteristics that cause new buildings to call excessive attention to themselves and create a jarring disharmony shall be avoided, or reserved for structures of broad public significance.

c. New buildings should strengthen site-specific or community design attributes by framing views, enclosing open spaces, or continuing particular design features or statements.

d. The height and bulk of new buildings shall be related to the prevailing scale of development to avoid overwhelming or dominating existing development.

e. The existing building line at the streetline should be maintained unless a proposed setback conforms to the municipal design plan or is part of a larger development plan.

f. The rhythm of structural mass to voids (i.e. windows) of a front façade shall relate to rhythms established in adjacent buildings.

g. If several storefronts are located in one building, they should be unified in design treatment of windows, door openings, materials, and color. All storefronts shall include display windows with a sill height not more than two feet from grade.

h. Building additions should be designed to reflect existing buildings in scale, materials, window treatment, and color. A change in scale may require a transitional design element between the addition and the existing building. Façade renovations should include as few different materials as possible.

i. Adjacent buildings of different architectural styles shall be made compatible by such means as materials, repetition of certain plant varieties, screens, and sight breaks.

CREATIVITY AND DIVERSITY OF DESIGN

a. These criteria are not intended to restrict imagination, innovation, or variety, but rather to help focus on design principles that will result in creative solutions.

b. Monotony of design in single or multiple building projects shall be avoided. Variation of detail, form, and siting shall be used to provide visual interest.

c. Architectural design is not restricted. Evaluation of the appearance of a project shall be based on the quality of its design and relationship to surroundings.

## SAMPLE BUILDING DESIGN CRITERIA

BUILDING DESIGN

a.  Where large structures are required, mass should be broken up through the use of setbacks and other design techniques. Buildings with excessive blank walls are discouraged. *(Note: Some ordinances contain more specific language, such as the following:* No building shall measure longer than 150 feet on any plane. Building offsets shall be provided along each building to relieve the visual effect of a single long wall. Roof lines shall also be varied. An individual building shall use a combination of story heights to provide further visual relief. The development should incorporate masonry chimneys, cupolas, dormers, skylights, or belvederes.)

b.  Buildings should be designed so that the roofs are visually less dominant than the walls.

c.  The orientation of buildings to provide access through rear entrances from parking lots is encouraged, with the rear façade receiving appropriate design treatment.

d.  New buildings shall be oriented or designed with setbacks to minimize shadows falling on public or semi-public spaces.

BUILDING DETAILS

a.  A human scale should be achieved at ground level, at entryways, and along street frontages through the use of such elements as windows, doors, columns, and canopies.

b.  Mechanical equipment or other utility hardware on roofs, the ground, or on the building itself shall be screened from public view with materials harmonious with the building; or it shall be so located as not to be visible from any public way.

c.  Building components, such as windows, doors, eaves, and parapets, shall be in proportion to one another.

d.  The structural lines of a building and its material should be retained at the storefront level—for instance, brick piers and columns should be carried down to street level.

e.  Roof shape (flat, hip, mansard, or gable) and material should be architecturally compatible with the rest of the building and reflect the area pattern.

f.  Materials shall be selected that are suitable for the type and design of building. Buildings shall use the same materials, or ones that are architecturally harmonious, on all building walls and other exterior building components visible from public ways. Materials shall be of durable quality. *(Note: Some ordinances contain more explicit criteria, such as the following:* Primary building material shall be brick and shall be used on all exterior wall surfaces; *or,* the recommended standard is brick with white wood trim; *or,* no bare metal is permitted—metal may be bronzed or painted with the recommended colors; *or,* aluminum siding, metal panels, and mirrored glass surfaces are discouraged.)

# SAMPLE BUILDING DESIGN CRITERIA

BUILDING DETAILS (continued)

g.    Colors shall be harmonious, and only compatible accents shall be used. *(Note the more explicit criteria in some ordinances:* Building colors shall be earth tones—browns, beiges, grays, soft greens. Accent or complementary colors, harmonizing with the main color, may be used for trim or awnings.)

h.    No metal awnings may be installed. Awnings should be solid or striped canvas in colors recommended for exterior paints.

i.    Façade renovations should not destroy or cover original details on a building. These details are often vital to the proper proportion of the façade.

j.    In renovations, natural, unpainted brick should be retained. Already painted brick, if weathered and losing its paint finish, can be stripped using chemical solutions. In many cases, painted brick should remain painted to protect the older, softer brick.

k.    Brick and stone façades should not be covered with artificial siding or panels. Generally, no material will look more appropriate on a façade than the one originally used.

l.    Retain, repair, replace, or add roof cornices; they cap or terminate a building. When replacing windows on a façade, use a window of the same trim size and character as the original.

SIGNS AND LIGHTING

a.    Signs should complement the architectural style and scale of the building and should be designed as an integral architectural element of the building and site to which it principally relates. As an architectural element, the sign should reflect the period of architecture and be in harmony with building character and use. It must not interfere with architectural lines and details. Each sign shall be compatible with signs on adjoining premises and shall not compete for attention. The number of graphic elements on a sign shall be held to the minimum needed to convey the sign's major message and shall be in proportion to the area of the sign face. Identification signs of a prototype design and corporation logos shall conform to the criteria for all other signs.

b.    Lighting fixtures shall be of a design and size compatible with the building and adjacent areas. Lighting shall be restrained in design and excessive brightness avoided.

MAINTENANCE

a.    Continued good appearance depends on the extent and quality of maintenance. Materials and finishes shall be selected for their durability and wear, as well as for their beauty. Proper measures shall be taken for protection against weather, neglect, damage, and abuse.

b.    Provision for washing and cleaning buildings and structures, and control of dirt and refuse, shall be included in the design. Configurations that tend to catch and accumulate leaves, dirt, and trash shall be avoided.

# Open Space and Recreation

## Introduction

Open space is an essential community asset and an important component of development design. Among its many critical functions, open space:

- Preserves ecologically important natural environments
- Provides attractive views and visual relief from developed areas
- Provides sunlight and air
- Buffers other land uses

**Photo 3–13.** *Locating a golf course next to residential units serves a recreational purpose, provides open space, and acts as a buffer.*

- Separates areas and controls densities
- Functions as a drainage detention area
- Serves as a wildlife preserve
- Provides opportunities for recreational activities
- Increases project amenity
- Helps create quality developments with lasting value

The importance of open space and recreation has been recognized for thousands of years. In the past, the ceremonial functions and the architectural value of open space and parks were emphasized. During the nineteenth century, however, unhealthy conditions in crowded industrial cities and the growth of democratic values "dramatically changed perceptions of the values of urban parks and of the role of governments in providing for the recreation needs of citizens."[46]

Since the 1850s, there have been two main influences on the development of park and recreation facilities in the United States. One, related to the conservation movement, has been to protect unique and natural resources from unsuitable development; the other, rooted in democratic and humanistic motives, has been to provide parks within cities in an effort to improve social conditions and to make cities healthier and more livable. By the early 1900s, most large American cities had parks which provided sanctuaries from urban blight and congestion and places for relaxation. Organizations such as the National Park Association—later the National Recreation and Park Association (NRPA)—were founded that promoted the benefits of parks and recreational areas. These organizations developed and published standards for the amount of parkland and the number of facilities required to serve different population figures. These standards were widely promoted as community goals, and municipalities adopted the notion of open space as a component of subdivision development.

Today, subdivision ordinances typically contain open space standards to ensure the benefits of this key community asset, and increasingly, the private sector is being called upon to provide recreation space in new developments.[47] There must be proper statutory authorization, however, before local governments can require developers to provide recreational areas.

## Open Space Defined

Open space is essentially unimproved land or water, or land that is relatively free of buildings or other physical structures, except for outdoor recreational facilities.[48] In practice, this means that open space does not have streets, drives, parking lots, or pipeline or power easements on it, nor do walkways, schools, clubhouses, and indoor recreational facilities count as open space. Private spaces, such as rear yards or patios not available for general use, are not included in the definition either.[49]

Open space is usually classified as either developed or undeveloped. Developed open space is designed for recreational uses, both active and passive, whereas undeveloped open space preserves a site's natural amenities. The terms "open space" and "recreation land" are sometimes used interchangeably and distinctions between the two blurred. Where recreation on open land or water is involved, the terms can be used interchangeably, but the term "recreation land" also applies to areas with recreation facilities, such as city playgrounds, swimming pools, and recreation centers.[50]

In sum, open space consists of both developed and undeveloped land, and municipalities are concerned with the provision of both types. For purposes of measurement, open space is defined as land that is essentially unimproved except for outdoor recreational facilities. Some ordinances make a distinction between land and water surfaces in calculating open space amounts. The amount permitted for water surfaces is sometimes specified ("water bodies may account for not more than 10 percent of the open space requirements," for example), or left up to the discretion of the reviewing authority. Similarly, because excessive slope can limit use of open space, measurement standards relating to grade are sometimes specified ("slopes over 15 percent may account for only 10 percent of open space requirements").

## Minimum Requirements

Minimum open space requirements usually include specifications in a number of categories. The most important, clearly, is the total amount of land to be set aside as open space. The size of individual open space parcels is also sometimes specified, as well as their location in the development. In addition, some ordinances distinguish between developed and undeveloped open space and contain language specifying the amount of land that should be left in its natural state. Many communities base their open space requirements on national recommendations, despite the fact that the national standards may be inappropriate depending on the specific case. The issues and problems surrounding the adoption of standards in each open space category are discussed in the following sections.

## Total Land Area Required

*RATIOS AND NATIONAL RECOMMENDATIONS*

Over the years, standards often consisting of ratios for different types of recreational activity and the amount of space required depending on population served have been developed.[51] These ratios, which are listed in various sources,[52] can be converted into land requirements and used by communities to calculate open space requirements. The National Recreation and Park Association (NRPA), for example, recommends a total of 6.25 to 10.50 acres of open space per 1,000 population, to be divided in a system of municipal parks of varying sizes and distances from residences (see Exhibit 3-3). NRPA also recommends standards for various recreational facilities (Exhibit 3-4).

To determine community-wide open space needs, planners generally use a combination of methodologies: the population ratio (number of acres of parks per 1,000 people, number of tennis courts per 1,000 people, etc.); a specified percentage of land area to be devoted to open space; user characteristics or demand projections; and/or carrying capacity of land. As an alternative method, NRPA has developed a model which surveys the service area population to determine demand for different activities. Demand is then converted to facilities needs and then to land requirements.[53]

## EXHIBIT 3-3

## NRPA RECOMMENDED STANDARDS FOR LOCAL DEVELOPED OPEN SPACE

This classification system is intended to serve as a *guide* to planning—not as an absolute blueprint. Sometimes more than one component may occur within the same site (but not on the same parcel of land), particularly with respect to special uses within a regional park. Planners of park and recreation systems should be careful to provide adequate land for each functional component when this occurs.

NRPA suggests that a park system, at a minimum, be composed of a "core" system of parklands, with a total of 6.25 to 10.5 acres of developed open space per 1,000 population. The size and amount of "adjunct" parklands will vary from community to community, but *must* be taken into account when considering a total, well-rounded system of parks and recreation areas.

| Component | Use | Service Area | Desirable Size | Acres/1,000 Population | Desirable Site Characteristics |
|---|---|---|---|---|---|
| | | LOCAL/CLOSE-TO-HOME SPACE | | | |
| MINI-PARK | Specialized facilities that serve a concentrated or limited population or specific group such as tots or senior citizens. | Less than 1/4 mile radius | 1 acre or less | 0.25 to 0.5A | Within neighborhoods and in close proximity to apartment complexes, townhouse developments, or housing for the elderly. |
| NEIGHBORHOOD PARK/ PLAYGROUND | Area for intense recreational activities, such as field games, crafts, playground apparatus area, skating, picnicking, wading pools, etc. | 1/4 to 1/2 mile radius to serve a population up to 5,000 (a neighborhood). | 15+ acres | 1.0 to 2.0A | Suited for intense development. Easily accessible to neighborhood population—geographically centered with safe walking and bike access. May be developed as a school-park facility. |
| COMMUNITY PARK | Area of diverse environmental quality. May include areas suited for intense recreational facilities, such as athletic complexes, large swimming pools. May be an area of natural quality for outdoor recreation, such as walking, viewing, sitting, picnicking. May be any combination of the above, depending upon site suitability and community need. | Several neighborhoods. 1 to 2 mile radius. | 25+ acres | 5.0 to 8.0A | May include natural features, such as water bodies, and areas suited for intense development. Easily accessible to neighborhood served. |

TOTAL CLOSE-TO-HOME SPACE = 6.25-10.5 A/1,000

*Source:* National Recreation and Park Association, *Recreation, Park and Open Space Standards and Guidelines,* p. 56. Copyright © 1983 by the National Recreation and Park Association, 3101 Park Center Drive, Alexandria, Virginia 22302.

# EXHIBIT 3–4

## NRPA SUGGESTED FACILITY DEVELOPMENT STANDARDS

| ACTIVITY/ FACILITY | RECOMMENDED SPACE REQUIREMENTS | RECOMMENDED SIZE AND DIMENSIONS | RECOMMENDED ORIENTATION | NO. OF UNITS PER POPULATION | SERVICE RADIUS | LOCATION NOTES |
|---|---|---|---|---|---|---|
| Badminton | 1620 sq. ft. | Singles — 17' x 44' Doubles — 20' x 44' with 5' unobstructed area on all sides | Long axis north-south | 1 per 5000 | ¼-½ mile | Usually in school, recreation center, or church facility. Safe walking or bike access. |
| Basketball 1. Youth 2. High School 3. Collegiate | 2400-3036 sq. ft. 5040-7280 sq. ft. 5600-7980 sq. ft. | 46'-50' x 84' 50' x 84' 50 x 94' with 5' unobstructed space on all sides | Long axis north-south | 1 per 5000 | ¼-½ mile | Same as badminton. Outdoor courts in neighborhood and community parks, plus active recreation areas in other park settings. |
| Handball (3-4 wall) | 800 sq. ft. for 4-wall, 1000 for 3-wall | 20' x 40' — Minimum of 10' to rear of 3-wall court. Minimum 20' overhead clearance. | Long axis north-south. Front wall at north end. | 1 per 20,000 | 15-30 minute travel time | 4-wall usually indoor as part of multi-purpose facility. 3-wall usually outdoor in park or school setting. |
| Ice Hockey | 22,000 sq. ft. including support area. | Rink 85' x 200' (minimum 85' x 185'). Additional 5000 sq. ft. support area. | Long axis north-south if outdoor | Indoor—1 per 100,000. Outdoor—depends on climate. | ½-1 hour travel time | Climate important consideration affecting no. of units. Best as part of multi-purpose facility. |
| Tennis | Minimum of 7,200 sq. ft. single court. (2 acres for complex.) | 36' x 78'. 12' clearance on both sides; 21' clearance on both ends. | Long axis north-south. | 1 court per 2000. | ¼-½ mile | Best in batteries of 2-4. Located in neighborhood/community park or adjacent to school site. |
| Volleyball | Minimum of 4,000 sq. ft. | 30' x 60'. Minimum 6' clearance on all sides. | Long axis north-south | 1 court per 5000. | ¼-½ mile | Same as other court activities (e.g., badminton, basketball, etc.) |
| Baseball 1. Official 2. Little League | 3.0-3.85 A minimum 1.2 A minimum | • Baselines—90' Pitching distance— 60 ½' Foul lines—min. 320' Center field—400'+ • Baselines—60' Pitching distance—46' Foul lines—200' Center field—200'-250' | Locate home plate so pitcher throwing across sun and batter not facing it. Line from home plate through pitcher's mound run east-north-east. | 1 per 5000 Lighted—1 per 30,000 | ¼-½ mile | Part of neighborhood complex. Lighted fields part of community complex. |
| Field Hockey | Minimum 1.5A | 180' x 300' with a minimum of 10' clearance on all sides. | Fall season—long axis northwest to southeast. For longer periods, north to south. | 1 per 20,000 | 15-30 minutes travel time | Usually part of baseball, football, soccer complex in community park or adjacent to high school. |

## EXHIBIT 3–4 (continued)

## NRPA SUGGESTED FACILITY DEVELOPMENT STANDARDS

| ACTIVITY/ FACILITY | RECOMMENDED SPACE REQUIREMENTS | RECOMMENDED SIZE AND DIMENSIONS | RECOMMENDED ORIENTATION | NO. OF UNITS PER POPULATION | SERVICE RADIUS | LOCATION NOTES |
|---|---|---|---|---|---|---|
| Football | Minimum 1.5A | 160' x 360' with a minimum of 6' clearance on all sides. | Same as field hockey. | 1 per 20,000 | 15-30 minutes travel time | Same as field hockey. |
| Soccer | 1.7 to 2.1A | 195' to 225' x 330' to 360' with a 10' minimum clearance on all sides. | Same as field hockey. | 1 per 10,000 | 1-2 miles | Number of units depends on popularity. Youth soccer on smaller fields adjacent to schools or neighborhood parks. |
| Golf—Driving Range | 13.5A for minimum of 25 tees | 900' x 690' wide. Add 12' width for each additional tee. | Long axis south-west-northeast with golfer driving toward north-east. | 1 per 50,000 | 30 minutes travel time | Part of golf course complex. As a separate unit, may be privately operated. |
| ¼-Mile Running Track | 4.3A | Overall width—276' length—600.02' Track width for 8 to 4 lanes is 32'. | Long axis in sector from north to south to north-west-south-east with finish line at northerly end. | 1 per 20,000 | 15-30 minutes travel time | Usually part of high school, or in community park complex in combination with football, soccer, etc. |
| Softball | 1.5 to 2.0A | Baselines—60' Pitching distance—46' min. 40'—women. Fast pitch field radius from plate—225' between foul lines. Slow pitch—275' (men) 250' (women) | Same as baseball. | 1 per 5,000 (if also used for youth baseball) | ¼-½ mile | Slight difference in dimensions for 16" slow pitch. May also be used for youth baseball. |
| Multiple Recreation Court (basketball, volleyball, tennis) | 9,840 sq. ft. | 120' x 80' | Long axis of courts with *primary* use is north-south. | 1 per 10,000 | 1-2 miles. | |
| Trails | N/A | Well defined head maximum 10' width, maximum average grade 5% not to exceed 15%. Capacity rural trails—40 hikers/day/mile. Urban trails--90 hikers/day/mile. | N/A | 1 system per region | N/A | |
| Archery Range | Minimum 0.65A | 300' length x minimum 10' wide between targets. Roped clear space on sides of range minimum of 30', clear space behind targets minimum of 90' x 45' with bunker. | Archer facing north + or - 45°. | 1 per 50,000 | 30 minutes travel time | Part of a regional/metro park complex. |

## EXHIBIT 3–4 (continued)

## NRPA SUGGESTED FACILITY DEVELOPMENT STANDARDS

| ACTIVITY/ FACILITY | RECOMMENDED SPACE REQUIREMENTS | RECOMMENDED SIZE AND DIMENSIONS | RECOMMENDED ORIENTATION | NO.OF UNITS PER POPULATION | SERVICE RADIUS | LOCATION NOTES |
|---|---|---|---|---|---|---|
| Combination Skeet and Trap Field (8 station) | Minimum 30A | All walks and structures occur within an area approximately 130' wide by 115' deep. Minimum cleared area is contained within two superimposed segments with 100-yard radii (4 acres). Shot-fall danger zone is contained within two superimposed segments with 300-yard radii (36 acres). | Center line of length runs northeast-south-west with shooter facing northeast. | 1 per 50,000 | 30 minutes travel time | Part of a regional/ metro park complex. |
| Golf 1. Par 3 (18-Hole) 2. 9-hole standard 3. 18-hole standard | • 50-60A • Minimum 50A • Minimum 110A | • Average length-vary 600-2700 yards • Average length—2250 yards • Average length—6500 yards | Majority of holes on north-south axis. | • 1/25,000 • 1/50,000 | ½ to 1 hour travel time | • 9-hole course can accommodate 350 people/day. • 18-hole course can accommodate 500-550 people a day. Course may be located in community or district park, but should not be over 20 miles from population center. |
| Swimming Pools | Varies on size of pool and amenities. Usually ½ to 2A site. | Teaching—minimum of 25 yards x 45' even depth of 3 to 4 feet. Competitive—minimum of 25m x 16m. Minimum of 27 square feet of water surface per swimmer. Ratios of 2:1 deck vs. water. | None—although care must be taken in siting of lifeguard stations in relation to afternoon sun. | 1 per 20,000 (Pools should accommodate 3 to 5% of total population at a time.) | 15 to 30 minutes travel time | Pools for general community use should be planned for teaching, competitive, and recreational purposes with enough depth (3.4m) to accommodate 1m and 3m diving boards. Located in community park or school site. |
| Beach Areas | N/A | Beach area should have 50 sq. ft. of land and 50 sq. ft. of water per user. Turnover rate is 3. There should be 3-4A supporting land per A of beach. | N/A | N/A | N/A | Should have sand bottom with slope a maximum of 5% (flat preferable). Boating areas completely segregated from swimming areas. |

*Source:* National Recreation and Park Association, *Recreation, Park and Open Space Standards and Guidelines.* Copyright © 1983 by the National Recreation and Park Association, 3101 Park Center Drive, Alexandria, Virginia 22302

On a subdivision level, sources recommend the following standards (summarized in Exhibit 3-5):

*NRPA:* a total of 1.25–2.5 acres per 1,000 population (mini-park or subdivision level added to neighborhood-subdivision level)

*Brough:* 2.5 acres recreational space per 1,000 population expected to reside in the development. If 5 percent or more of the residents are children under 12, at least 15 percent of the open space must be in "tot lots." In addition to recreational space, 5 percent of the total area of the development is required as usable open space, either left undisturbed or landscaped for ball fields or picnic areas.[54]

To calculate the number of persons expected to reside in a development, Brough's model ordinance specifies using one of the two following formulas:

### Method 1

| Dwelling Unit (DU) Size | Persons per DU |
|---|---|
| 1 BR | 1.4 |
| 2 BR | 2.2 |
| 3 BR | 3.2 |
| 4 or more BR | 4.0 |

### Method 2

| Lot Size | Persons per DU |
|---|---|
| Each lot large enough for 1 DU | 3.2 |
| Each lot large enough for more than 1 DU | 2.2 |

Despite the existence of ratios and recommendations, there are wide variations of open space requirements among communities. A national review of standards showed, for example, that the amount of neighborhood recreation land required by communities

## EXHIBIT 3–5

## OPEN SPACE REQUIREMENTS: A SUMMARY OF RECOMMENDATIONS

| MUNICIPAL OPEN SPACE SYSTEM | OPEN SPACE CATEGORY | | | |
|---|---|---|---|---|
| | DEVELOPED OPEN SPACE | | | UNDEVELOPED |
| | Amount of Land Area Required | Size of Parcels | Area Served by Open Space | Amount of Land Area Required |
| Mini-Park or Sub-neighborhood Level | 0.25 to .5 acres/ 1,000 population (NRPA) | 1 acre or less (NRPA) | Less than 1/4 mile radius (NRPA) | |
| | | 500 sq. ft to 2 acres (D&K) | From 100 yds. to 1/4 mile radius (D&K) | At least 5% of total area of every residential development in permanent usable open space (Brough) |
| | | Not less than 6,000 sq. ft. (M&L) | | |
| Neighborhood-Subdivision Level | 1.0 to 2.0 acres/1,000 population (NRPA) | 15+ acres (NRPA) | 1/4 to 1/2 mile radius to serve population up to 5,000 (NRPA) | For all other authorities, amount of open space required will vary depending on site conditions |
| | | 4 to 20 acres (D&K) | 1/4 to 1/2 mile radius to serve population up to 5,000 (D&K) | |
| | 2.5 acres/1,000 population expected to reside in development, at least 15% of which must be in tot lots if 5% or more of residents likely to be under 12 (Brough) | Not less than 2,000 sq. ft. nor more than 30,000 sq. ft. (Brough) | | |
| Community Level | 5.0 to 8.0 acres/1,000 population (NRPA) | 25+ acres (NRPA) | Several neighborhoods, 1 to 2 mile radius (NRPA) | |
| | | | Several neighborhoods, 15,000 to 25,000 population (D&K) | |

NRPA : National Recreation and Park Association, *Recreation, Parks and Open Space Standards and Guidelines*, 1983.

D&K : DeChiara and Koppelman, *Time-Saver Standards for Site Planning*, 1984.

Brough : Michael Brough, *A Unified Development Ordinance*, 1985.

M&L : Moskowitz and Lindbloom, *A Guide for Residential Design Review*, 1976.

ranged from a low of 1 acre to a high of 10 acres per 1,000 population.[55] Similar variation is shown when examining open space requirements among municipalities in the same state. In New Jersey, for example, one town may require that a subdivision set aside at least 10 percent of the total land area for recreation and open space, while another will require that 40 percent of the total land area be set aside for the same purposes. These variations suggest that there are a number of issues and problems involved in applying uniform standards.

*APPLYING NATIONAL STANDARDS AT THE*
*LOCAL LEVEL: ISSUES AND PROBLEMS*

Although national standards have been widely promoted as goals, they are not universally accepted.[56] One criticism is that the national standards are excessive and "based on past community desires or expectations."[57] Also, communities differ in terms of resources, preferences, and land costs; standards that are appropriate for one community may not be for another.

Another problem with the national standards is that while they specify the minimum land acreage required to meet needs for recreational facilities, they do not address conservation, preservation, or amenity requirements, nor do they take into account density or size of the specific development or conditions of the terrain. A requirement that 10 to 20 percent of the total area of a subdivision be set aside as open space may not be sufficient in a high-density development, for example, and a 40 to 50 percent requirement is likely to be excessive for a two-acre development. Similarly, standards based on population ratios can be equally inappropriate when applied at the local level. If ten acres of open space are required per 1,000 individuals, this could lead to absurd requirements in high-density developments.[58]

*DETERMINING LOCAL REQUIREMENTS*
*FOR TOTAL LAND AREA REQUIRED*

While it might be tempting for a community to simply adopt the national standards, even the authors of the standards warn against such an approach:

*Ideally, the national standards should stand the test in communities of all sizes. However, the reality often makes it difficult or inadvisable to apply national standards without question in specific locales. The uniqueness of every community, due to differing geographical, cultural, climatic, and socioeconomic characteristics, makes it imperative that every community develop its own standards for recreation, parks, and open space.*[59]

For best results, open space and recreation requirements should be flexible and customized to each community. Lynch and Hack point out that instead of adopting uniform space standards in subdivision ordinances, open space and recreational requirements should be determined by a host of factors, including type of housing occupancy, utilization ratios, terrain conditions, existing facilities, and so on. "As we grow more doubtful about uniform recreational space standards, we will turn to the actual diversity of recreational place and activity and think of providing for this complexity according to the particular people we house."[60]

The Rutgers model ordinance, therefore, does not specify minimum uniform standards for open space. Rather, it suggests that the national standards can be used as guides, but that each municipality should examine its own needs and determine its own standards. A number of local characteristics and site-specific issues should be examined in setting open space requirements. These include socioeconomic conditions, regional recreational preferences, physical and natural features of the site itself, and other factors highlighted below.

1. *Socioeconomic characteristics.* Socioeconomic characteristics are important because where household income is above average, for example, families typically seek out private and nonlocal facilities, thus decreasing the need for public open space. More recreation land should be provided in neighborhoods where household incomes are low, since low-income families tend to confine their outdoor activities to local public areas.[61]

2. *Other demographic characteristics.* Age of population, for example, affects recreation needs: older population groups generally require more passive recreation facilities, whereas families with young children need tot lots and playgrounds.

3. *Population density.* Developments with high population densities require more recreation land than developments with lower population densities. Thus, a cluster development with multifamily units would generally require more open space than one

composed of single-family homes surrounded by private open space.

4. *Economic considerations.* Localities with high population densities are, however, also often characterized by high land prices. Some authorities have suggested that as land prices rise, less land should be provided for recreational purposes. This solution denies the fundamental premise that recreational facilities should be based on population needs. An alternative solution for localities faced with high land prices is to use less land, but to increase the number of facilities per recreational acre. "For example, gardens and sculpture can enhance the pleasures derived from the 'vest pocket' park. Additional playground equipment...can increase the output of a playground while holding its land input constant."[62]

5. *Regional and cultural recreation preferences.* Regional and cultural groups differ in the type of recreation preferred. Such differences will have an impact on open space standards because activities vary in the amount of space they require.

6. *Topographical features of development site.* If a site consists of steep grades, additional space may be required to provide a usable area. A site with a large body of water offers an opportunity for water-based recreational activities.

**Photo 3–15.** *This combination fountain and concrete sculpture is a good example of intensifying recreational pleasures in a high-density area.*

*REQUIREMENTS FOR UNDEVELOPED OPEN SPACE*

A community's open space standards should also require that the natural amenities and unique features of a site be retained and incorporated into the open space system. Natural features add substantially to the attractiveness and harmony of the development, and preservation of fragile areas in their natural state can avoid a number of future problems and potential dangers. Among the areas that should be preserved are flood hazard areas, wetlands, areas containing specimen trees, steep slopes, existing watercourses, ponds, bogs, swamps, and other ecologically sensitive areas. Some recreational uses, of course, are quite compatible with preservation: playing fields and tennis courts are very often located on floodplains.

No general standard can specify the amount of open space that should remain undeveloped: determination will depend on the particular development site. Once the amount of undeveloped open space is resolved, it should be balanced with the amount of developed open space desired to arrive at the total area of open space required.

## Size of Parcels

The dimensions of open space parcels are important in order to ensure that the open space is functional. Specification of size also protects the community from the dedication of numerous useless small parcels of land. A national survey showed that minimum required dimensions ranged from 400 to 6,000 or more square feet.[63] A parcel measuring 6,000 square feet will accommodate one tennis court. Exhibit 3–5 summarizes recommendations from a number of sources.

## Location of Parcels

Open space parcels should be easily accessible by development residents. In smaller developments, one large, centrally located parcel may suffice; but a large development may require several parcels, equitably distributed. Linking open space parcels is a good strategy, because it enlarges the area available for recreation. Parcels containing noise generators, such as basketball courts or playgrounds, should be sited to minimize disturbance to residents.

## Improvement of Parcels

Some level of site preparation requirements is necessary to ensure that the open space will be usable and have value as an amenity. Generally, a developer will want to provide the recreational amenities that will appeal to the target market, anyway. For example, a builder of homes targeted to young families would probably include tot lots or playgrounds; homes targeted to senior citizens might offer golf courses, shuffleboard courts, or walking trails. Tennis courts, swimming pools, jogging trails, putting greens, and racquetball courts are not unusual recreational amenities included in many developments today.

Open space that is otherwise undeveloped may contain areas for hiking or picnicking or may be left in its natural state to provide attractive views for the developed areas. Undeveloped open space may need to have diseased trees removed, vegetation thinned, or areas graded or seeded to prevent erosion.

## Open Space Ownership

In order to assign responsibility for a development's open space, it is important to clarify its ownership at the outset. There are basically three types of open space: private, public, and common.

- *Private* open space is generally located immediately adjacent to a dwelling unit, reserved for the use of its residents, and owned and maintained by them. The private open space in rental developments is owned by the developer and is the responsibility of the developer or of a hired maintenance company.
- *Public* open space is dedicated to a municipality or one of its agencies and is operated and maintained by them.
- *Common* open space is generally reserved for the use of residents of planned unit or cluster developments and is owned and maintained in common by them.

Most concerns about maintenance arise from common ownership. In order to protect themselves against neglected properties, municipalities need to make sure that developments will be maintained and that there are recourses when they are not. The Rutgers model ordinance contains a number of safeguards to ensure continued maintenance of open space.

# Landscaping

Photo 3–16. *Landscaping provides privacy and helps unify site design. Rock ledge blasted from the development site is used to stabilize slopes and to create decorative walls. Manchester, New Hampshire.*

Photo 3–17a. *Landscaping is needed in single-family residential developments . . .*

Photo 3–17b. *. . . and in multifamily developments.*

## Definition and Purpose

Landscaping has been defined as "the organization of outdoor space."[64] Since the development of any site—planning the circulation system, arranging buildings, and so on—involves organizing space, all sites are in a sense "landscaped." However, landscaping should accomplish more: "What we look for is a landscape, technically organized so that its parts work together, but perceptually coherent as well."[65] In practice, however, this goal is often not realized, and landscaping is not made part of the total design. Instead, landscaping "is usually thought to be concerned with the spotting of trees on a plan after buildings and roads have been located."[66] As such, plantings are "the 'extra' in site development, the first item to be cut when the budget pinches."[67] This restricted view of landscaping is no longer acceptable in site design today. Harvey Moskowitz and Carl Lindbloom, in *A Guide for Residential Design Review,* assert that landscaping "is just as important a site design element as are circulation proposals or engineering requirements."[68] ULI's *Residential Development Handbook* affirms the importance of landscaping, defining its role as follows: "Landscaping is the one element which can tie together all other elements of a design. Landscaping more than anything can give an identity to an environment."[69]

The importance of landscaping in relating the elements of a site—the buildings, the spaces between them, and the objects in those spaces—and in giving the site an identity makes landscaping requirements essential components of subdivision ordinances. Landscaping assumes even greater importance in high-density and small-lot developments. In a study evaluating affordable housing developments, the American Planning Association and the Joint Venture for Affordable Housing found that landscaping, fencing, and walls were essential to ensure privacy. Dade County, Florida, for example, required three trees on each lot in its affordable housing developments to screen dwelling units from each other and to provide shade. These requirements were in addition to those for street trees. In Coon Rapids, Minnesota, mature plantings were included in the landscaping plan for the affordable housing project, both for privacy and to give small-lot developments a more "finished" look.[70]

## Landscaping Materials

Plant materials come to mind when discussing landscaping, but as sources point out, "Some great landscapes are treeless, and there are handsome squares that do not include a plant of any description."[71] Landscaping, then, makes use of both natural elements and man-made materials. Natural elements include trees, shrubs, ground cover, rocks, and water. Man-made materials include walls, fences, paving, sculpture, and street furniture. These have also been categorized as "soft surfaces"—trees, shrubs, and ground cover—and "hard surfaces"—paving stones, gravel areas, street furniture, fencing, and sculpture.[72] Street furniture covers a wide range of items: benches, bus shelters, signs, trash cans, kiosks, canopies, lights, plant containers, newsstands, bollards, and notice boards. Street hardware—the mechanical and utility systems, such as traffic signals, utility poles and lines, parking meters, fire plugs, and directional signs—are also part of the landscape. Even though their design is usually regulated by the

**Photo 3–18.** *Walls are used effectively in this landscape design. Princeton, New Jersey.*

state, their presence is important in the overall landscape plan. Nevertheless, plants remain the fundamental landscaping material, and most writing on landscaping concerns plantings and their requirements.

## Landscape Plan

A landscape plan should be required for all site plan applications. It should show existing plantings and natural features such as boulders, rock outcroppings, bodies of water, and vegetation. It should indicate the number, type, and size of trees, shrubs, and ground cover to be planted and their placement. Any other landscaping elements such as walls, fences, or street furniture and their construction details should also be included. If existing vegetation is to remain, the plan should indicate the methods that will be used to protect the existing growth. Protection devices include fences, berms, curbing, and tree wells.

**Photo 3–19.** *Proper grading and the use of soil stabilization techniques during construction prevent sedimentation problems like those shown here.*

## Planting Requirements

*TOPSOIL PRESERVATION*

Site grading should preserve topsoil wherever possible. This is important because topsoil contains humus and the nutrients needed for the growth of healthy plants. In addition, when topsoil is removed and the surrounding ground is disturbed, erosion can become a serious problem, particularly where rainfall is heavy. If topsoil is removed during construction, instead of bringing in new topsoil—which would be prohibitive in cost—the original topsoil should be stockpiled and redistributed on all regraded surfaces. Experts recommend that the layer of topsoil measure from four to six inches.[73] To prevent erosion, the soil should be stabilized by seeding or planting. Plantings are one of the most effective ways to control erosion—they help reduce the impact of rain on the soil, and their roots hold soil particles together, preventing them from washing away.[74]

*PROTECTION OF EXISTING PLANTINGS*

Natural plantings are an asset on a site. When they are saved, the natural beauty of the site is retained, the cost of landscaping and maintenance is reduced, and the structures, paved areas, and other plantings are more attractive. Sound existing trees, substantial clumps, and fine specimens should be carefully protected. Protection is particularly important during construction, because such activity disturbs the microclimate of the plantings: soil is compacted, depriving roots of oxygen; roots can be damaged by equipment or lost if the grade is lowered; the addition of fill changes the moisture content around roots; and roots are often cut during installation of underground utilities. Steps must be taken to protect trees and roots during construction if they are to be saved.

First, to avoid damaging the roots of existing plantings, no soil should be placed around trees that are intolerant of fill and are to be saved. Some varieties of trees can tolerate fill, but others cannot. Dogwoods, birches, and most conifers are intolerant because their roots are near the surface.[75] Oaks and sugar maples will also not tolerate any fill. "Even piling soil temporarily over a root system can kill a tree."[76] Stockpiling of soil should be done only in open areas, and soil should be left undisturbed in a 10-

**Photo 3–20.** *Careful protection measures were taken to preserve this magnificent specimen tree.*

foot radius around any tree to be preserved.[77] Temporary fences erected at the drip line may be necessary to prevent encroachment, soil compaction, and damage from equipment. If a tree has a large spread, a triangular fence may be built instead of a circular fence at the drip line.

If fill soil is required, a dry well can be constructed before the fill is added; it will be too late if done after the tree has shown symptoms of decline. Care should be taken to ensure the tree well is constructed properly.[78]

A point which perhaps should be noted more often is that although mature trees are an asset to the landscape and add value to a development site, any plant system is by its nature growing and declining. Deciding which trees and plantings to preserve should take that dynamic fact into consideration. "It is a mistake to preserve only the large trees, while cutting out the young plants that would have replaced them, and unwise to save large ancient trees long past their prime, whose removal after development will be costly."[79]

**Photo 3–21.** *Uncontrolled erosion due to poor site planning and inadequate construction practices is threatening this new housing development.*

*SLOPE PLANTINGS*

Erosion can be a serious problem on slopes, particularly in areas where rainfall is heavy, in soils which have a low moisture-holding capacity, where slopes are long and steep, and where the soil is bare.[80] Along with mechanical means of controlling erosion—site grading, diversions such as berms and terraces, and drainage systems—developers can use vegetation to stabilize slopes. During construction, temporary cover can be planted to protect slopes from erosion, followed by permanent vegetation for long-term stabilization. If the season is not favorable for planting, straw mulches will protect slopes until they can be seeded. Mulches are also recommended on steep slopes to prevent runoff until the grass or other ground cover has become firmly established. Grass alone is not recommended for steep banks, since most grasses need a lot of maintenance and will give way to weeds if they are not mowed and fertilized regularly. Crown vetch is a good choice of ground cover because it requires little maintenance and works well in many soils.

**Temporary ground covers.** As noted above, temporary covers can be used to control erosion during construction or when cover is needed for a temporary period. Rapidly growing plants are most often used for this purpose. Exhibit 3–7 gives examples.

**Permanent ground covers.** In considering the choice of permanent ground cover, maintenance requirements, climate, soil, and aesthetic values should all be taken into account. Examples of plants that are long-lived and require a minimum of maintenance include servicea lespedeza, crown vetch, and honeysuckle. Indigenous plants are preferred since they will thrive without special care.

## ADDITIONAL LANDSCAPING

In addition to specific requirements for compensatory plantings, shade trees, and buffering, a site design may include additional plantings or other landscaping elements such as walls or fences. For some sites, however, additional plantings will not be necessary because the site may be heavily wooded, or adding plantings will not be appropriate to the design. Sometimes developments are over-landscaped, with buildings lost in a jungle of plantings.

**Photo 3–22.** *Heavily wooded sites need few additional plantings to enhance the units. Reston, Virginia.*

**Photo 3–23.** *The woods were preserved in this development of single-family homes.*

**Photo 3–24.** *Too many shrubs can also distract from buildings.*

Generally, however, the opposite is the case. Municipalities and developers have found, particularly when intensity of land use is high, that additional plantings are necessary. In a study of affordable housing developments, it was found that, "Small-lot development required landscaping, fences, or walls to ensure privacy between dwellings and to minimize the impact of street traffic."[81]

*PLANTING SPECIFICATIONS*

**Balled and burlapped versus bare-root plants.** Balled and burlapped (B&B) and bare root (BR) refer to ways of preparing plants for sale. For B&B plants, the plant is dug with an intact soil ball that contains most of the plant's roots; the ball is then wrapped in burlap to reduce the chance of damaging the soil ball and to facilitate shipping. Balled and burlapped trees are often recommended over bare root trees which have had all soil removed during the digging process in the nursery. B&B trees can be transplanted more easily from the nursery to the development site, and B&B trees are thought to have greater survival and initial growth rates.

Bare root trees, however, have been found to be equally satisfactory in certain situations. "[I]f handled properly during shipment and during the planting process, bare-root plants can be a good investment, particularly if you are going to use a large number of plants."[82] For example, in an experiment conducted at Rutgers University that compared BR and B&B trees planted in a parking lot, the BR trees grew at least as well, if not better, than the B&B trees. BR maples exceeded B&B trees in leaf area, dry weight and height growth, and unfertilized BR green ash generally grew better than corresponding B&B trees.[83] Since B&B trees are more expensive to lift, transport, and plant than BR trees, municipalities might consider allowing the planting of BR trees as long as certain conditions are met. These would include quick planting to minimize root desiccation between the time of receipt of the plants and planting, planting in good quality soil in openings that are an adequate size, and ensuring ample soil moisture.[84]

**Plant size.** It is important to understand how plants are measured because planting specifications refer to plants by size. Shade trees are generally measured by caliper: for small trees (those with trunk diameters of 4 inches or less), the trunk diameter is measured 6 inches above the ground; for large trees (those with diameters of more than 4 inches), the trunk is measured 12 inches above the ground.[85] Bare-root trees, however, are measured by their height from the soil line to the top, up to 8 feet.

Deciduous shrubs are sold on the basis of their height and spread. The overall size of a group of shrubs should be the average of the various sizes of plants. For example, five 3- to 4-foot shrubs should average 3 1/2 feet, and none should be smaller than 3 feet. When shrubs are container-grown, both the plant size and container size are usually included.

Evergreens are sized according to their growth habits. A low-growing evergreen shrub is sized by its spread, based on the measurement of the main part of the plant, not its maximum spread; columnar-type evergreens are measured by height. As with deciduous shrubs, the overall size of a group of shrubs should be an average of the various sizes. Container-grown evergreens are measured the same way as balled and burlapped evergreens, except the size of the container is also often included.

**Recommended planting procedure.** Trees and shrubs should be planted according to the following procedures:[86]

1. Plant materials should be well-formed and healthy nursery-grown stock. The root ball should be inspected to ensure that it is undamaged and of good quality soil, and that it encompasses the entire root system.

2. Planting should take place when trees and shrubs are dormant because transplanting during this period greatly increases the chance of success.

**Photo 3–25.** *Even large trees can be successfully transplanted if proper procedures are followed.*

3.  Planting holes should be dug 2 times as wide and 1½ times as deep as the root ball. Topsoil and subsoil should be mixed thoroughly with sphagnum peat moss according to the recommendations of the county agricultural agent. A layer of 6 to 7 inches of the mix should be placed in the bottom of the hole. Fertilizer should not be added to the soil mix, since it can burn tender new roots, slowing down the growth of the plant or even killing it. The soil in the bottom of the hole should be tamped down without compacting it.

4. Trees and shrubs should be positioned in the planting hole so that trunks are straight and so that the base is at the finished grade of the new location and at the same depth as it was when it was growing. Roots should be spread evenly throughout the hole, and soil added carefully.

5. The backfilled soil should be tamped in place, and the hole filled to the top of the root ball. The added soil should be tamped gently, but not compacted, and a ring of soil 2 to 3 inches high should be formed around the edge of the planting hole to aid in watering.

6. Plantings should be watered with a fertilizer/water solution, the amount of fertilizer depending on an analysis. Watering should be thorough and done slowly and gently to avoid damage to the soil structure.

7. The area within the watering saucer should be filled to a depth of 2 to 3 inches with mulch.

8. Tree trunks should be coated with an insecticide to reduce the chances of attack by borers. The specific insecticide can be recommended by the county agricultural agent. Trunks should be wrapped with tree kraft paper or burlap strips.

9. All newly planted trees and shrubs should be pruned. Balled and burlapped and container-grown plants should be shaped lightly and have broken and damaged branches removed. Bare-root plants require much heavier pruning to reduce the water demand by the top of the plant in order to compensate for the roots lost when the plants were dug up. One-third to one-half of the leaf area should be removed by thinning the branches and reducing their length. Pruning should retain the natural form of the tree or shrub; the central leader, or top, of a newly planted tree should never be removed, since this will destroy its natural growth habit.

10. If properly planted, shrubs will not have to be staked, although oversized shrubs may need some support. Trees should be staked in accordance with good nursery practice.

11. Special planting techniques may be necessary when planting in heavy, poorly drained, or sandy soils. Recommendations of the county agricultural agent should be followed.

12. After planting, the most critical requirement is to supply an adequate and even amount of moisture. Because of the

wide variation in soil types and the different moisture needs of plant species, it is impossible to present specific watering requirements. Plant conditions should be carefully observed, and if the soil is dry 3 to 6 inches beneath the surface, water should be added immediately. The water should be applied slowly so that it soaks in and does not run off. As a general rule, plants in well-drained soils should be watered 1 inch per week, and those in lighter soils, 2 inches per week, except during periods of heavy rainfall.

*PLANT SPECIES*

Plant species vary greatly in their hardiness. A committee of the American Horticultural Society has divided the country into temperature zones based on average minimum winter temperature in order to help define the areas in which different plant species are hardy. These zones have been delineated on a plant hardiness map (see Exhibit 3–6), developed and published by the United States Department of Agriculture. To use the map, first the climatic zone of the development site is located. Then a standard reference book on landscaping can be consulted to determine the minimum temperature at which different species are hardy. If the climatic zone number is within the range of temperatures cited for a particular plant species, the plant should be hardy for that location. To be absolutely certain of success only plants classified as hardy to the zone should be used, and a one-zone safety factor for unusually hard winters should be considered. Exhibit 3–7 lists examples of recommended ground covers, low shrubs, and mid-size shrubs by hardiness zone.

*SHADE TREES*

It is standard practice in subdivisions to plant shade trees along streets for numerous reasons. Besides softening the streetscape, trees help buffer traffic noise, filter pollution, and lower the high temperatures created from heat radiating off pavement. When planted between the street and sidewalk, they also provide a measure of protection for pedestrians, or at least a sense of separation between pedestrian and vehicular traffic.

**Location.** Shade trees should be planted along both sides of a street so that their benefits may be enjoyed on both sides. The choice of whether trees are planted in groups or spaced regularly should be based on site and development requirements. Some

## EXHIBIT 3–6

## PLANT HARDINESS ZONES

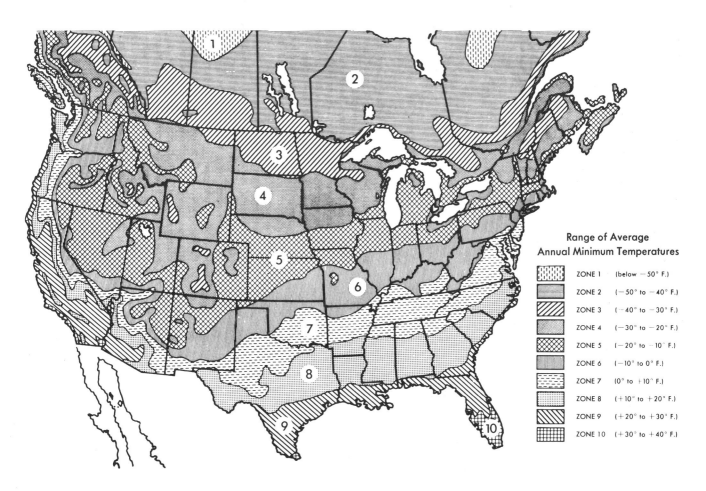

Range of Average
Annual Minimum Temperatures

ZONE 1 (below −50° F.)
ZONE 2 (−50° to −40° F.)
ZONE 3 (−40° to −30° F.)
ZONE 4 (−30° to −20° F.)
ZONE 5 (−20° to −10° F.)
ZONE 6 (−10° to 0° F.)
ZONE 7 (0° to +10° F.)
ZONE 8 (+10° to +20° F.)
ZONE 9 (+20° to +30° F.)
ZONE 10 (+30° to +40° F.)

*Source:* Theodore D. Walker, *Residential Landscaping I* (Mesa, AZ: PDA Publishers Corporation, 1982), p. 99. Reprinted with permission.

## EXHIBIT 3–7

## EXAMPLES OF RECOMMENDED PLANTINGS:
## GROUND COVERS, LOW SHRUBS,
## AND MID-SIZED SHRUBS

| Proper Name | Common Name | Type | Remarks | Hardiness Zone |
|---|---|---|---|---|
| **GROUND COVERS** | | | | |
| *Euonymus fortunei* | Wintercreeper | Semi-evergreen | Spray to prevent scale attack | Zone 5 |
| *Hedera helix "Baltica"* | Baltic ivy | Evergreen | Shade or sun, mows well, good for slopes | Zone 5 |
| *Juniperus spp.* | Ground juniper | Evergreen | Full sun, well-drained soil, tolerates drought, several varieties | Varies; Zones 2-9 |
| *Pachysandra terminalis* | Japanese spurge | Evergreen | Shaded areas only | Zone 5 |
| *Vinca minor* | Periwinkle, myrtle | Evergreen | Sun or partial shade, mows well, purple flowers | Zone 4 |
| **LOW SHRUBS** | | | | |
| *Berberis triacanthophora* | Threespine barberry | Evergreen | (H) May be sheared, thorny, makes low hedge | Zone 5 |
| *Euonymus alatus "compacius"* | Dwarf-winged euonymus | Deciduous | May be sheared | Zone 4 |
| *Ilex crenata* | Japanese holly | Evergreen | Sheared periodically to within this height range, lustrous dark green foliage | Zone 6 |
| *Juniperus horizontalis "plumosa"* | Andorra juniper | Evergreen | Feathery texture, purple in fall, good for slopes | Zone 2 |
| *Taxus baccata "repandens"* | Spreading English yew | Evergreen | Low, flat-topped shrub | Zone 5 |

(H) indicates the shrub can be used for hedges.

**EXHIBIT 3–7 (continued)**

| Proper Name | Common Name | Type | Remarks | Hardiness Zone |
|---|---|---|---|---|
| **MID-SIZED SHRUBS** | | | | |
| *Berberis julianae* | Wintergreen barberry | Evergreen | (H) Thorny, yellow flowers, excellent city plant | Zone 5 |
| *Euonymus alatus* | Winged euonymus | Deciduous | (H) Dense red in autumn | Zone 3 |
| *Forsythia* | Forsythia | Deciduous | (H) Yellow flowers, soil and shade tolerant | Zone 5 |
| *Ilex cornuta Burfordii* | Burford Chinese holly | Evergreen | (H) Berries, spines, glossy dark green foliage, hardy | Zone 6 |
| *Ilex crenata* | Japanese holly | Evergreen | (H) Popular in all types of ornamental plantings | Zone 6 |
| *Ilex crenata microphylla* | Little-leaf Japanese holly | Evergreen | (H) Small leaves, extremely hardy variety | Zone 6 |
| *Ligustrum ibolium* | Ibolium privet | Deciduous | (H) Tolerant of city conditions, excellent hedge | Zone 4 |
| *Prunus laurocerasus schipkaenis* | Cherry laurel | Evergreen | (H) Hardy variety, used as specimen, hedge, and windbreak | Zone 5 |
| *Pyracantha coccinea "lalandei"* | Scarlet firethorn | Semi-evergreen | (H) Thorns, flowering, berries, tolerates city conditions, drought-resistant | Zone 6 |
| *Rhododendron spp. (includes azaleas)* | Rhododendron/ azaleas | Mostly evergreen | Flowers, many varieties, partial shade, moist, acid soil | Varies; Zones 2–8 |
| *Syringa vulgaris* | Common lilac | Deciduous | Flowers, many varieties, soil tolerant | Zone 3 |
| *Taxus cuspidata* | Japanese yew | Evergreen | (H) Soil and shade tolerant, pest free | Zone 4 |
| *Thuja occidentalis* | American arborvitae | Evergreen | (H) Good screen, tall narrow growth | Zone 2 |

**Photo 3–26.** *Informal street tree plantings.*

**Photo 3–26.** *Informal street tree plantings.*

authorities note that regular spacing is monotonous and should be avoided,[87] and, in fact, informal plantings may be more appropriate along short, narrow streets, in situations where one side of a street is higher than the other, or in developments where buildings or housing units are clustered. If costs are a concern, grouping street trees as part of individual lot treatment may be pre-

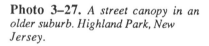

**Photo 3–27.** *A street canopy in an older suburb. Highland Park, New Jersey.*

**Photo 3–28.** *Formal street planting in a southern locale: trees make a strong visual impact. Hollywood, Florida.*

ferred since this method is less expensive than planting in strips.[88]

On the other hand, the strong visual impact of trees planted in evenly spaced intervals along a street may be the effect sought by the designer. Branches from the trees will form a canopy above the road—a high foliage crown which filters the sun, unifies the area, and provides a dominant architectural feature. Although some design sources believe that rows of trees belong only in urban environments,[89] many of the most magnificent tree canopies are in older subdivisions and along country roads. In short, the placement of street trees—in an offset, irregular tree line or at regularly spaced intervals—should be determined by site conditions and development design.

**Tree spacing.** Proper spacing distances depend on the tree type, its growing habits, and whether freestanding specimens or an interlaced canopy is desired. Some sources note that trees are commonly planted too close to each other. One recommends, "A good guide is to space trees so as to exceed somewhat the farthest extent of branch development at maturity."[90] Closer spacing is required, however, if a canopied effect is desired. Another possibility is to plant smaller ornamental trees between the larger trees.

Trees should be located so that they will not interfere with utilities, block sight easements, or obscure street lights. The following spacing distances, recommended by DeChiara and Koppelman, can be used as guidelines:[91]

| Object | Distance |
|---|---|
| parking meter | 6 feet |
| fire hydrant | 8 feet |
| stream line | 20 feet |
| light pole | 25 feet |
| street corner | 40 feet |

**Tree type.** In choosing tree type, the main consideration in terms of design is the overall effect desired. One species may be used throughout a development, species may vary by neighborhood or street, or species may alternate along the streets in a formal or informal fashion. Since disease can obliterate a species, it may be wise to include a variety of tree types. As a general principle, however, it is recommended that in large developments with extensive landscaping, trees be restricted to a few species, both for economy and the power of effect. "[S]elect a theme tree, from three to five supporting secondary trees, and a limited palette of supplementary species for special conditions and effects."[92]

Tree choice should also consider the growth rate and maintenance needs of different species. It is a good idea to choose trees that are indigenous, relatively fast-growing, and require little care. Trees that are relatively impervious to the environmental abuse they are likely to receive from fumes, dirt, soot, salt, and deicing compounds should be selected. Examples of trees that are adaptable to the urban environment include London plane trees, sweet gums, lindens, locusts, Norway maples, zelkovas, and oaks. Among the trees that are tolerant of salt and deicing compounds, the most tolerant are red oaks, white oaks, and red cedars; birches, aspens, ash, and locusts are also tolerant. Certain trees, such as willows, poplars, and silver maples, should not be planted near drains and sewers because they have a tendency to clog them. Other trees that should be avoided are species that are brittle, particularly susceptible to insects and disease, short-lived, and those with shallow root systems that damage pavement. Exhibit 3–8 lists common shade trees and provides comments on each species.

**Planting specifications.** Shade trees should be carefully planted following proper horticultural methods in order to maximize their survival rate. In addition, a regular maintenance program should be followed. Regular watering is particularly essential until the trees are established. One source specifies, "New trees should be watered weekly for two years after transplanting. The more concrete in sight, the more need to watch the tree."[93] Rather than specifying how often trees should be watered, a municipality can require regular maintenance until plantings are established. Making a developer responsible for replacing dying trees during the next planting season acts as an incentive for implementing a regular maintenance program.

## Buffering

*FUNCTIONS*

Buffering, usually consisting of a landscaped open area, berms, or fences, is often required in subdivision developments to minimize adverse impacts. Buffers are used to screen land uses that create nuisances, to create privacy, to divert or soften glare, to filter noise, and to modify climatic conditions.

**Separating land uses.** When land uses create nuisances—such as fumes, traffic, or noise—landscaped buffer areas may be required to separate an undesirable land use from other land uses. Residential and industrial areas, for example, generally require a buffer zone between them. Sometimes commercial development acts as a buffer separating residential from industrial areas. Buffering requirements, however, must take into account local conditions and preferences. For instance, a mix of uses may be desired in urban areas. Buffering should not be done automatically, but only when there is an identified need.

**Creating privacy.** When land-use intensity is high, buffering may be necessary for privacy between dwellings and to minimize the impact of street traffic. For example, residential cluster developments with narrow street frontages and contiguous rear yards need fencing, walls, or landscaping if building design or siting does not ensure outdoor privacy.[94]

**Diverting or softening glare.** Glare can result from numerous sources, such as light standards, car lights, and reflections from large bodies of water. In some cases, it may not be possible to prevent glare, but foliage can be used to alleviate or reduce its impacts. Hedges will screen the glare from headlights, and trees planted upwind from lakes and other bodies of water will produce ripples on water, scattering the reflection.[95]

**Photo 3–29.** *Buffering is needed to screen residential from industrial uses.*

**Photo 3–30.** *These dumpsters present an unsightly view from the road and should be buffered.*

## EXHIBIT 3–8

## SHADE TREES FOR STREET PLANTING

| Species | | Mature Height |
| --- | --- | --- |
| Botanical Name | Common Name | Tall (more than 40')<br>Medium (30'–40')<br>Small (less than 30') |
| *Acer campestre* | Hedge Maple | Small |
| *Acer platanoides* | Norway Maple | Tall |
| *Acer platanoides 'Cleveland'* | Cleveland Norway Maple | Tall |
| *Acer platanoides 'Columnare'* | Columnar Norway Maple | Tall |
| *Acer platanoides 'Crimson King'* | Crimson King Norway Maple | Medium |
| *Acer platanoides 'Erectum'* | Mount Hope Norway Maple | Medium |
| *Acer platanoides 'Globosum'* | Globe Norway Maple | Small |
| *Acer platanoides 'Summer Shade'* | Summershade Norway Maple | Tall |
| *Acer pseudoplatanus* | Sycamore Maple | Tall |
| *Acer pseudoplatanus 'Pyramidale'* | Upright Sycamore Maple | Medium |
| *Acer rubrum* | Red Maple | Tall |
| *Acer rubrum 'Columnare'* | Columnar Red Maple | Tall |
| *Acer rubrum 'October Glory'* | October Glory Red Maple | Tall |
| *Acer rubrum 'Scanlon'* | Scanlon Red Maple | Medium |
| *Acer saccharinum 'Pyramidale'* | Upright Silver Maple | Tall |
| *Acer saccharum* | Sugar Maple | Tall |
| *Acer saccharum 'Columnare'* | Columnar Sugar Maple | Tall |
| *Acer saccharum 'Green Mountain'* | Green Mountain Sugar Maple | Tall |
| *Acer saccharum 'Temple's Upright'* | Temple's Upright Sugar Maple | Tall |
| *Aesculus carnea 'Brioti'* | Ruby Horsechestnut | Medium |
| *Aesculus hippocastanum 'Baumanni'* | Double Flowering Horsechestnut | Tall |
| *Carpinus betulus* | European Hornbeam | Small |
| *Carpinus betulus 'Fastigiata'* | Pyramidal European Hornbeam | Medium |
| *Carpinus caroliniana* | American Hornbeam | Small |
| *Carpinus japonica* | Japanese Hornbeam | Tall |
| *Celtis occidentalis* | Common Hackberry | Tall |
| *Cercidiphyllum japonicum* | Katsura Tree | Tall |
| *Cladrastis lutea* | Yellowwood | Medium |
| *Cornus florida* | Flowering Dogwood | Small |
| *Cornus florida 'Rubra'* | Pink Flowering Dogwood | Small |
| *Fraxinus americana* | White Ash | Tall |

| Recommended Street Use by Street Type | Value as a Street Tree | Comments |
|---|---|---|
| Minor Residential (includes Residential Access and Subcollector) Residential Collector Commercial Collector | | |
| Minor Residential | Moderate | Globe-shaped, urban tolerant |
| Residential Collector | Moderate | Upright oval shape, urban tolerant |
| Commercial Collector | Poor | Broad oval shape, urban tolerant, good for narrow places |
| Minor Residential | Moderate | Columnar, urban tolerant, good for narrow places |
| Residential Collector | Excellent | Globe-shaped, urban tolerant, maroon leaf color |
| Minor Residential | Excellent | Conical shape, urban tolerant |
| Minor Residential | Moderate | Globe-shaped, urban tolerant |
| Commercial Collector | Excellent | Narrow, conical shape, urban tolerant |
| Commercial Collector | Moderate | Broad oval shape, seashore tolerant |
| Residential Collector | Moderate | Columnar, seashore tolerant, good for narrow places |
| Commercial Collector | Excellent | Globe-shaped, wet site tolerant, invasive roots |
| Residential Collector | Moderate | Columnar, wet site tolerant, invasive roots |
| Residential Collector | Excellent | Broad oval shape, wet site tolerant, good fall color |
| Residential Collector | Excellent | Columnar, wet site tolerant, urban intolerant |
| Residential Collector | Poor | Columnar, weak wooded, invasive roots |
| Commercial Collector | Excellent | Broad oval shape, urban intolerant |
| Residential Collector | Excellent | Columnar, urban intolerant |
| Commercial Collector | Excellent | Broad oval shape, urban intolerant |
| Commercial Collector | Moderate | Columnar, urban intolerant |
| Residential Collector | Moderate | Globe-shaped, red flowers, urban tolerant |
| Commercial Collector | Moderate | Narrow conical shape, double white flowers, urban tolerant |
| Minor Residential | Moderate | Broad oval shape, urban tolerant |
| Minor Residential | Moderate | Fastigiate shape, urban tolerant |
| Minor Residential | Moderate | Spreading shape, difficult to transplant |
| Minor Residential | Moderate | Broad oval shape, slow grower |
| Commercial Collector | Moderate | Globe-shaped, wet site, dry site, urban tolerant |
| Commercial Collector | Moderate | Vase-shaped, drought intolerant |
| Residential Collector | Moderate | Globe-shaped, white flowers in early summer |
| Minor Residential | Excellent | Spreading shape, year-round beauty, spray for borers |
| Minor Residential | Excellent | Spreading shape, year-round beauty, spray for borers |
| Commercial Collector | Excellent | Globe-shaped, urban tolerant, spray for borers |

## EXHIBIT 3–8

## SHADE TREES FOR STREET PLANTING

| Species | | Mature Height |
|---|---|---|
| Botanical Name | Common Name | Tall (more than 40') Medium (30'–40') Small (less than 30') |
| *Fraxinus ornus* | Flowering Ash | Tall |
| *Fraxinus pennsylvanica lanceolata* | Green Ash | Tall |
| *F.p. lanceolata 'Marshall's Seedless'* | Marshall's Seedless Green Ash | Tall |
| *Gingko biloba* | Gingko | Tall |
| *Gingko biloba 'Sentry'* | Sentry Gingko | Tall |
| *Gleditsia triacanthos inermis 'Shademaster'* | Shademaster Thornless Honeylocust | Tall |
| *Gleditsia triacanthos inermis 'Skyline'* | Skyline Thornless Honeylocust | Tall |
| *Gymnocladus dioicus* | Kentucky Coffeetree | Tall |
| *Koelreuteria paniculata* | Golden Raintree | Medium |
| *Liquidambar styraciflua* | American Sweet Gum | Tall |
| *Magnolia lebneri 'Merrill'* | Dr. Merrill Magnolia | Small |
| *Magnolia salicifolia* | Anise Magnolia | Medium |
| *Malus baccata 'Manchurian'* | Manchurian Crabapple | Medium |
| *Malus arnoldiana* | Arnold Crabapple | Small |
| *Malus 'Hopa',* | Hopa Red—Flowering Crabapple | Small |
| *Malus 'Katherine'* | Katherine Crabapple | Small |
| *Malus 'Scheideckeri'* | Scheidecker Crabapple | Small |
| *Malus zumi 'Calocarpa'* | Zumi Crabapple | Small |
| *Nyssa sylvatica* | Sour Gum | Medium |
| *Ostrya virginiana* | American Hophornbeam | Medium |
| *Oxydendrum arboreum* | Sorrel Tree | Small |
| *Phellodendron amurense* | Armur Corktree | Medium |
| *Platanus acerifolia* | London Planetree | Tall |
| *Platanus occidentalis* | American Sycamore | Tall |
| *Prunus avium 'plena'* | Mazzard Cherry | Medium |
| *Prunus cerasifera 'Thundercloud'* | Thundercloud Purple-Leafed Plum | Small |

| Recommended Street Use by Street Type | Value as a Street Tree | Comments |
|---|---|---|
| Minor Residential (includes Residential Access and Subcollector) Residential Collector Commercial Collector | | |
| Residential Collector | Excellent | Broad oval shape, white flowers, spray for borers |
| Commercial Collector | Excellent | Spreading, wet site, urban tolerant, spray for borers |
| Commercial Collector | Excellent | Narrow conical, wet site, urban tolerant, spray for borers |
| Commercial Collector | Moderate | Spreading, urban tolerant, avoid female |
| Residential Collector | Moderate | Fastigiate shape, urban tolerant |
| Commercial Collector | Moderate | Broad oval shape, mimosa webworm problem, urban tolerant |
| Commercial Collector | Moderate | Narrow conical shape, mimosa webworm problem, urban tolerant |
| Commercial Collector | Moderate | Broad oval shape, urban tolerant |
| Commercial Collector | Moderate | Globe-shaped, yellow flowers, weak-wooded |
| Residential Collector | Moderate | Broad oval shape, good fall color, wet site tolerant |
| Minor Residential | Moderate | Broad oval shape, white flowers, urban tolerant |
| Residential Collector | Excellent | Narrow conical shape, white flowers |
| Residential Collector | Excellent | Broad oval shape, white flowers, urban tolerant |
| Minor Residential | Excellent | Broad oval shape, pink buds, white flowers, urban tolerant |
| Minor Residential, Residential Collector | Excellent | Broad oval shape, red flowers, urban tolerant |
| Minor Residential | Excellent | Broad oval shape, profuse flowers and fruit |
| Residential Collector | Excellent | Broad oval shape, urban tolerant, pink flowers |
| Minor Residential, Residential Collector | Excellent | Narrow conical shape, urban tolerant, good ornamental fruit |
| Commercial Collector | Moderate | Spreading shape, wet site tolerant |
| Residential Collector | Moderate | Rounded shape, dry site tolerant, intolerant of road salts |
| Minor Residential, Residential Collector | Poor | Pyramidal, red fall color |
| Commercial Collector | Excellent | Vase-shaped, urban tolerant, dry site tolerant |
| Commercial Collector | Moderate | Spreading shape, urban tolerant |
| Commercial Collector | Poor | Spreading shape, wet site tolerant, subject to twig blight |
| Residential Collector | Poor | Broad oval shape, glistening fragrant flowers |
| Minor Residential | Poor | Globe-shaped, purple foliage |

**EXHIBIT 3–8**

**SHADE TREES FOR STREET PLANTING**

| Species | | Mature Height |
|---|---|---|
| Botanical Name | Common Name | Tall (more than 40')<br>Medium (30'–40')<br>Small (less than 30') |
| Prunus sargenti | Sargent Cherry | Medium |
| Prunus sargenti 'Rancho' | Rancho Columnar Sargent Cherry | Medium |
| Prunus serrulata 'Amanogawa' | Amanogawa Cherry | Small |
| Prunus serrulata 'Kwanzan' | Kwanzan Cherry | Small |
| Prunus serrulata 'Shirofugen' | Shirofugen Cherry | Small |
| Prunus subhirtella | Higan Cherry | Medium |
| Prunus subhirtella 'Autumnales' | Autumn Flowering Higan Cherry | Small |
| Prunus yedoensis | Yoshino Cherry | Medium |
| Pyrus calleryana 'Bradford' | Bradford Callery Pear | Medium |
| Quercus coccinea | Scarlet Oak | Tall |
| Quercus palustris | Pin Oak | Tall |
| Quercus phellos | Willow Oak | Tall |
| Quercus rubra | Red Oak | Tall |
| Sophora japonica | Japanese Scholar-Tree | Tall |
| Sophora japonica 'Regent' | Regent Scholar-Tree | Tall |
| Sorbus alnifolia | Korean Mountainash | Tall |
| Sorbus aucuparia | European Mountainash | Small |
| Syringa amurensis 'Japonica' | Japanese Tree Lilac | Small |
| Tilia cordata | Little Leaf Linden | Medium |
| Tilia cordata 'Greenspire' | Greenspire Little Leaf Linden | Medium |
| Tilia tomentosum | Silver Linden | Tall |
| Zelkova serrata | Japanese Zelkova | Tall |
| Zelkova serrata 'Village Green' | Village Green Zelkova | Tall |

*Source:* Hintz/Nelesson Associates, P.C.

| Recommended Street Use by Street Type<br>Minor Residential (includes Residential Access and Subcollector)<br>Residential Collector<br>Commercial Collector | Value as a Street Tree | Comments |
|---|---|---|
| Residential Collector | Poor | Broad oval, dense shade, pink flowers, good fall color |
| Residential Collector | Excellent | Columnar, pink-flowers |
| Minor Residential | Moderate | Fastigiate shape, fragrant, double light pink flowers |
| Minor Residential | Excellent | Vase-shaped, hardy, double pink flowers |
| Minor Residential | Moderate | Spreading shape, pink flowers turning white |
| Residential Collector | Moderate | Globe-shaped, cloud of pink flowers |
| Minor Residential | Moderate | Spreading shape, pink flowers in autumn |
| Residential Collector | Moderate | Spreading shape, white flowers |
| Residential & Commercial Collector | Excellent | Broad oval shape, urban tolerant, white flowers, red fall color |
| Residential Collector | Moderate | Spreading shape, difficult to transplant, dry site tolerant |
| Residential Collector | Moderate | Narrow conical, wet site tolerant, lower branches are a problem |
| Minor Residential, Residential Collector | Moderate | Broad oval shape, wet site tolerant, fine texture |
| Commercial & Residential Collector | Excellent | Spreading shape, urban tolerant |
| Residential Collector | Moderate | Oval shape, urban tolerant, dry site tolerant |
| Residential Collector | Moderate | Oval shape, urban tolerant, dry site tolerant |
| Residential Collector | Moderate | Globe-shaped, susceptible to borers |
| Minor Residential Access, Subcollector | Poor | Globe-shaped, susceptible to many pests |
| Minor Residential Access, Subcollector | Moderate | Spreading shape, creamy white flowers in June |
| Residential Collector | Excellent | Upright oval, urban tolerant |
| Residential Collector | Excellent | Columnar, urban tolerant |
| Residential & Commercial Collector | Moderate | Upright oval shape, urban tolerant, dry site tolerant |
| Residential & Commercial Collector | Moderate | Vase-shaped, resembles elm, dry site tolerant |
| Residential & Commercial Collector | Excellent | Vase-shaped, resembles elm, dry site tolerant |

**Photo 3–31.** *Buffering effectively screens this residential development from the noise and traffic on an adjacent street.*

Filtering noise. Noise, defined as any undesirable sound, can come from a number of sources: linear sources (highways), activity sources (airports), and spot sources (swimming pools), with the method of control dependent on the source.[96] To filter traffic noise (a linear source), for example, a wide buffer area planted with trees and shrubs or an earth berm with vegetation may be required. In many cases, it will not be possible to eliminate noise entirely (especially with landscaping only), but more pleasing sounds, such as trickling water, can be used to mask it.

Modifying climatic conditions. Buffering can be used to reduce the effects of high winds. It will also block strong sunlight during summer months and allow solar access during the winter months. A screen of evergreens planted upwind from buildings and perpendicular to the direction of strong winter winds will act as a wind barrier and help to reduce heating costs in the winter.[97] Similarly, vines and deciduous trees and shrubs can significantly reduce temperatures inside protected buildings during the summer while allowing solar access during the winter, thus reducing both cooling and heating costs.[98]

Other functions. Buffering can also serve other functions, such as snow drift control, enhancement of wildlife habitats, and air purification.

*BUFFERING MATERIALS*

Buffering materials usually consist of densely planted evergreens or other thick foliage, solid or closely woven fences or stone walls, or earth berms planted with shrubs and trees.

*MINIMUM REQUIREMENTS*

1. Buffer zones are often required in subdivision regulations to screen land uses that create nuisances. Dimensions vary between 25 to 30 feet, with 25 feet being more common.[99]

2. Screening around parking lots, garbage areas, and loading areas should consist of at least one row of evergreen shrubs. Sources variously set the dimension of the buffer strip at between 4 and 10 feet.

3. Traffic noise and headlight glare can be a major source of irritation, particularly for residential developments. Residential lots should front lower-order streets both to minimize these nuisances and for safety reasons. For effective screening from traffic noise generated by higher-order streets, sources set the width of buffer strips at between 25 and 35 feet, with vegetation no closer than 20 to 50 feet from the center of the nearest lane.[100] Where residential developments abut interstate highways, a belt 65 to 100 feet wide is suggested, with the near edge of the belt 50 to 80 feet from the center of the nearest traffic lane.[101] Both trees and shrubs are required because neither is sufficient by itself to muffle sounds. It should also be noted that there are other solutions to control noise. A six- to eight-foot berm with dense shrubs planted in front and taller trees behind was used as a noise buffer in Irvine, California, for example, and solid concrete walls with landscaping have been used at other locations.[102]

4. Buffering also helps ensure privacy in developments with high land-use intensities. In addition, requiring fencing or landscaping avoids the jarring effect created when each homeowner in a cluster development comes up with a different design.

*DESIGN*

The model ordinance does not attempt to dictate the exact placement of trees and shrubs in the buffer area. Buffering designs and plant materials can vary substantially, yet still be functional. Plantings should be located, however, to avoid damage to existing plantings and to provide maximum protection to adjacent properties.

**Photo 3–32.** *The preservation of existing trees adds to the landscaping of this parking lot.*

## Parking Lot Landscaping

In all developments, but in residential developments in particular, the location and appearance of parking are critical factors in good design. Design solutions will be affected by the number of off-street spaces required by the type of development, the topography of the site, and cost restrictions. Landscaping can play a significant role in minimizing and moderating many adverse effects of parking lots. It softens the appearance of the lot and screens it from the street and surrounding properties. Well-designed planting strips and islands help guide the circulation of vehicles and pedestrians, creating a safe environment for both.[103] Visual barriers also minimize the hazard of nighttime glare from headlights. Plants moderate the microclimate as well—a tree-shaded surface is 20°F cooler on an 84°F summer day, while landscaping of the appropriate density and height can buffer winter winds.[104] In some cases it may be possible to use the natural topography and existing vegetation in landscaping a parking lot. Unfortunately, no landscaping "can ever completely eliminate the awareness of the presence of cars, it will just make them less noticeable."[105]

Screening for parking lots includes hedges, vegetation, earth berms, walls, fences, and changes in grade. Plant selection should

take into consideration size at maturity, differences in seasonal foliage, and maintenance needs. Maintenance needs include feeding, pruning, spraying, watering, and how often a particular species needs replacement.[106] The varieties selected should be tolerant of exhaust fumes and salt and be able to withstand pavement heat. Varieties that could have an adverse effect (trees with berries, for example, are a nuisance in a parking lot) should be avoided.

*MINIMUM REQUIREMENTS*

There are three different types of landscaping requirements pertaining to parking lots:

1. *Interior landscaping* is intended to improve a lot's appearance, microclimate, and circulation. Moskowitz and

**Photo 3–33.** *Freestanding planters are used as well as trees and shrubs in this attractively landscaped parking area. Chicago, Illinois.*

**Photo 3–34.** *Example of land-scaping in a street frontage strip.*

Lindbloom's recommendation that between five and ten percent of the parking lot area be devoted to landscaping is fairly standard.[107] Requirements can also be expressed in terms of number of trees per parking space; this method is found in ordinances of a number of municipalities. Municipalities should specify requirements in accordance with their own needs and preferences.

2. *Perimeter strips* adjacent to neighboring properties are also usually required. If effective buffers exist or neighboring land uses are insensitive to the parking lot, however, requirements for perimeter strips may be relaxed.[108] On the other hand, if land uses are incompatible, a buffer strip may be required in addition to the perimeter strip. If a buffer is necessary, the trees or shrubs planted should be higher than those on the street frontage strip—usually between 3 and 8 feet.[109]

3. *Street frontage* strips are also sometimes required. Usually the height of street frontage landscaping is limited to 3 feet so that sight lines are not obstructed.[110] Trees may be included if their branches are trimmed at least 6-8 feet from the ground.

A review of typical parking lot landscaping requirements published by *Zoning News* shows the width of frontage strips varying between 5 and 10 feet, with that of perimeter landscaping generally set at 5 feet.[111] To ensure that parking lots have an adequate number of plantings, landscaping requirements should be exclusive of other planting requirements, such as for shade trees.

*LOCATION*

Depending on the layout of the parking lot, as long as the driver's vision is not obstructed, interior landscaping can be located in any number of areas. In parts of the country where snow removal is an issue, however, this should be taken into consideration when designing planting strips and islands.

*PLANT TYPE*

The trees and shrubs used in parking lot landscaping should have low maintenance requirements and be able to withstand fumes and pavement heat. A mixture of flowering, deciduous, and evergreen trees is desirable for screening cars and to provide color and textural interest year-round. On narrow islands, low-spreading plants, such as creeping juniper, English ivy, myrtle, or pachysandra, are appropriate. Where more space is available, yews, juniper, and forsythia can be used.[112]

## Paving Materials, Walls and Fences, and Street Furniture

Landscaping does not refer only to plant materials, although plants are usually the most important element in landscape design. Paving materials, walls and fences, and street furniture are also part of landscaping. Paving materials and walls and fences are key elements of site design: paving covers the base plane—the "floor" of the site; and walls and fences are important vertical elements dividing, containing, and articulating space. Lynch and Hack call surface paving and walls and fences "the most important of the artificial outdoor elements" and deplore that they are often added at the last moment with little thought.[113] Other sources also stress the importance of paving materials and walls and fences.[114] To ensure that these landscape elements receive the attention they deserve, the following sections look at them in detail.

**Photo 3–35.** *Brick is used to pave this courtyard. Alexandria, Virginia.*

*PAVING MATERIALS*

## Definition and Purpose

Paving materials refer to the materials used to cover a ground surface artificially. Paving often consists of man-made materials, but natural materials, such as stones, tanbark, and other materials occurring naturally, are also used to cover surfaces in landscaping.

Surface paving serves a number of functions. *First,* it creates a firm level surface to facilitate passage. Sidewalks, courtyards, and roads are examples of this function. *Second,* by varying materials, textures, and colors, it defines areas. A crosswalk on a street is an example. *Third,* it divides spaces. The change to private residential areas from public sidewalks can be signalled by a change in paving materials, for example. *Fourth,* paving stabilizes the surface by preventing erosion. And *finally,* paving is decorative and provides visual interest.

## Materials

A wide range of paving materials is available. Concrete and asphalt are the most familiar; other materials include stabilized earth, light gravel, tanbark, sand, surface aggregates, wood blocks, decking, bricks, tile, ceramic tile, pebble mosaic, terrazzo, cobblestones, stone blocks, and pavers made of slate, asphalt, cement, and other substances. Pavers and other paving materials can be laid in many decorative patterns or used in combination with concrete or asphalt paved surfaces. Exhibit 3–9 lists and compares some of the more common paving materials.

In choosing a paving material, initial cost and maintenance are two important considerations. Some materials require frequent weeding, cleaning, or replacement. Suitability for the intended function is another important consideration: tanbark might be perfectly appropriate for a jogging trail, but it would be a poor surface where there is heavy pedestrian traffic. Still other considerations that should guide choice of material are weather conditions and the characteristics of people likely to use the surface. For example, some of the decorative pavers are extremely slippery when wet or icy, and their joints can cause people to trip. Their use is not advisable for areas with cold or rainy climates or in cases where the users are likely to be elderly. Other factors to

consider in the selection of paving materials are durability, appearance, glare, heat, drainage, noise, compatibility with surroundings, and availability.

**Photo 3–36.** *A variety of paving materials add visual interest to this city park. Chicago, Illinois.*

## EXHIBIT 3–9

## PAVING MATERIALS

| MATERIAL | COST | COMMENTS |
|----------|------|----------|
| Asphalt | Lowest in construction cost | Resilient, reasonably durable, can be cut and patched as repairs are needed. Requires occasional resurfacing. Aesthetically unappealing and monotonous, looks worse with age, absorbs heat. Can be enclosed with brick, stone, or concrete or topped with peastone. |
| Concrete | Moderate initial cost | Requires little maintenance but can crack if not made properly. Offers a nonchip textured surface. Not very handsome in large expanses but also can be enclosed or varied with other materials. |
| Concrete (Exposed Aggregate Finish) | Usually costs twice as much as ordinary concrete work | Minimal maintenance required. Reasonably long life expectancy. More attractive than plain concrete. |
| Cement Pavers | Cost only slightly higher than ordinary concrete paving | Attractive textured surface. Limited color range. Long useful life expectancy and only minimal maintenance required. |
| Asphalt Pavers | Initial cost somewhat more expensive than concrete but less than brick paving | Attractive with slightly resilient surface, pleasant for walking. Will withstand heavy usage and traffic although edges of asphalt pavers will crumble. Easily maintained. |
| Brick and Brick Pavers | Higher in cost than cement and asphalt pavers | One of the most attractive of outdoor surfaces, comes in wide range of color, can be laid in many interesting patterns, ages gracefully. Must be hard-burned to resist frost damage. Where frosts occur, should be set in asphalt base or on concrete slabs topped with a setting bed of sand. Difficult to clear of snow without chipping or dislodging bricks. Hazardous to pedestrians when they become uneven. |

**EXHIBIT 3–9 (continued)**

**PAVING MATERIALS**

| MATERIAL | COST | COMMENTS |
|---|---|---|
| Brick Grid (in Concrete Paving) | Less expensive than surfaces paved with brick only | Economical and attractive way to incorporate brick into paving surfaces. Effective at entrance plazas or courts, or to mark semi-private spaces. If constructed properly requires minimal maintenance. |
| Wood Decking | Low initial cost | Can be used for special effects, many variations in design. Limited life span, requires constant repair and maintenance, must be carefully installed and treated to resist rotting. Use of end-grain wood blocks as paving has been discontinued because it is dangerously slippery when wet. |
| Cellular Concrete Block | Fairly expensive | Blocks whose interstices are filled with earth and sown with grass. Attractive surface used for extended pedestrian areas or parking of light vehicles. Grass requires watering and mowing. |
| Stone | Most expensive, not only for cost of material, but also because it must be carefully installed | Finest surface material—it is durable, handsome, and comes in an enormous range of color, texture, and character. Availability varies. Granites are most permanent and have strongest character. Bluestone useful, but will not tolerate road salt. Limestone, marble and slate beautiful materials, but they wear down. Stone can be laid in large finished blocks or smaller sets, as rounded cobbles, or in patterns of cobbles and smoother blocks. |

*Sources:* Kevin Lynch and Gary Hack, *Site Planning,* pp. 433-36; and Joseph DeChiara and Lee Koppelman, *Time-Saver Standards for Site Planning,* pp. 313-14.

### Design

The ground surface has more visual importance than many people realize.

*Fine ground textures—moss, monolithic pavement, or close-cropped grass—emphasize the shape and mass of the underlying ground and increase its apparent size. They act as a background for the objects that rise from them. Coarse textures—rough grass, cobbles, bricks, or blocks—work in the opposite way, calling attention to the surface itself rather than to the underlying mass or the objects above it.*[115]

Thus, the design of the paving material is not only a source of interest in itself; it also has a great impact on the perception of the space around it. It can be a harmonious background that unifies the scene, or it can be a dominant feature that sets the pattern of the plan.

Choice of material is integral to the design of surface paving, and the same factors guiding the choice of material (cost, maintenance, suitability for intended function, weather conditions, characteristics of users, compatibility with surroundings, etc.) should guide the design.

*WALLS AND FENCES*

**Photo 3–37.** *Wall used as a privacy screen.*

## Definition and Purpose

Walls and fences are barriers erected to provide screening, create privacy, prevent trespassing, confine animals, or hold back pressure such as water or sliding earth.[116] They are particularly important for privacy in developments with high land-use intensities. In terms of site design, as vertical elements they are powerful space definers. Areas are tightly controlled and enclosed with solid walls, or more loosely defined with transparent walls. Walls and fences direct the eye of the beholder to a focal point,[117] or they can be a link between a building and the landscape. The functions of walls and fences can be summarized as follows:

- Provide enclosure
- Separate areas
- Provide security
- Screen areas from view
- Serve as a backdrop or to focus a view
- Aid in climate control as wind barriers or sun screens and by absorbing heat and radiation
- Retain water or earth

## Placement

Placement of walls and fences depends on their function—if they are to serve as a link between a building and the landscape, they most likely will extend from the building; if they are to act as a windscreen, they will be placed at some distance from the structure; when their function is to direct interest to an object, they will be placed accordingly.

## Materials

Whatever the choice of material, it should be remembered that walls and fences not only serve a function, but often become a dominant spatial feature as well. Therefore, the wall or fence material should work with the site itself.

Walls can be constructed of materials such as brick, stone (rough cut, flagstones, or ledge), or formed concrete; they can be constructed of concrete or blocks and faced with tile, bricks, blocks, precast units, or ashlar; or they can consist of fieldstones laid in a dry wall. "Brick and stone make the finest solid walls, but

**Photo 3–38.** *For a better and more attractive design, all fencing in a development should be constructed of the same materials.*

stone is very costly, and brick not cheap.... Concrete block is a less expensive material and makes a good masonry wall if carefully laid and given a well-designed coping."[118] Concrete block walls, however, require more frequent maintenance than brick or concrete walls, and this should be taken into consideration when making a selection.

Fences can be wooden; picket, basket weave, lattice, split rail, plank, panels, or woven saplings are possibilities. Stained fences require less maintenance than those that are painted, but all wooden fences must be protected where they come in contact with the ground. Cast and wrought iron fences are beautiful and long-lasting, but expensive. Chain-link fences are perhaps the most ubiquitous, but they are ranked low in terms of aesthetics: "Chain-link fences with plastic strips may be fine around an industrial plant, but they do nothing for any house design."[119] Chain link has "... the emotional meaning of barbed wire ... it is one of our less than happy contributions to the beauty of the world. Unfortunately ... it is cheap, durable, and effective."[120] However, even its effectiveness can be questioned: DeChiara and Koppelman assert that not only is chain-link fencing the "least attractive in appearance," it is the "least resistant to vandalism."[121] Using an alternative fencing material is preferable, but if chain link is chosen, it should be dark in color and planted out with bushes or vines to reduce its visibility. For security fences, DeChiara and Koppelman recommend using wrought iron, citing its attractive appearance, moderate maintenance requirements, and the difficulty of vandalizing it. They point out that its high initial cost is offset by a potentially long useful life.

**Design**

Variation in the design and materials of walls and fences is often part of a regional tradition—stone walls conjure up New England, and redwood, California landscapes, for example—but the following principles guiding the design of walls and fencing and choice of material can be applied everywhere:

1. Walls and fences should be functional. If screening is the objective, for instance, the fence or wall should be solid; if the purpose is to provide shade while allowing air circulation, a semi-transparent design should be selected.

2. They should complement the character of the site and the structural type of the building. "A solid structure should have a fence or wall projecting that impression. More contemporary designs may call for lighter, more open types of fences or walls."[122]

3. They should be suited to the nature of the project. The design of fencing for a commercial or industrial development, for example, will differ from that for a residential development.

**Photo 3–39.** *Fencing materials that are the same as those used in the units give this residential development a unified look. Memphis, Tennessee.*

**Photo 3–40.** *Fencing materials complement the buildings.*

**Photo 3–41.** *This urban park combines bollards, planters, and seating in a coordinated design of street furniture. Philadelphia, Pennsylvania.*

*STREET FURNITURE*

## Street Furniture Defined

Street furniture consists of the man-made elements of a streetscape located on the sidewalk, on a plaza, or in another type of pedestrian area. Street furniture elements are generally associated with amenities for pedestrians, and they may be freestanding or fixed. Included are benches or other forms of seating, bollards or posts, kiosks, drinking fountains, planters, bus shelters, information signs, trash receptacles, bike racks, game tables, lighting fixtures, phone booths, and notice boards. Some authorities point to a distinction between street furniture and street hardware. The latter category refers to the utility and mechanical systems located within a street right-of-way and includes fire hydrants, manhole covers, traffic lights and signs, utility poles and lines, and parking meters.[123]

## Placement

Since much street furniture is functional in nature, it should be located where it is needed. Benches should be placed at street corners, in plazas, or where people congregate; bollards should be placed where necessary to prevent vehicle access while still allowing access for pedestrians and cyclists; bus shelters should be required at major intersections or where there is heavy bus usage; bike racks should be located at schools, in shopping areas, and at playgrounds; kiosks, drinking fountains, game tables, and notice boards should be located in public plazas, in parks, or in other recreational areas.

## Design

Street furniture often accumulates without design, creating a sense of clutter and disharmony in a landscape. To overcome this visual chaos, pieces should be coordinated with each other and with their setting. Sources recommend the following guidelines in selecting and designing street furniture:[124]

1.  Items should be functional. For example, benches should have backs, especially where they will be used by the elderly; trash receptacles should have openings large enough for trash to be deposited easily; planters should be wide enough to allow for root growth; etc.

2.  Style of street furniture should be coordinated with the style of the existing or proposed site architecture.

**Photo 3–42.** *Street furniture is more than a design detail—game tables add much to the enjoyment of this city park.*

**Photo 3–43.** *An attractively designed entrance to a housing development. Falmouth, Massachusetts.*

**Photo 3–44.** *Good design can eliminate unsightly views such as this.*

**Photo 3–45.** *Dumpsters are screened in this development, adding to project amenity.*

3. Items should be compatible in form, material, and finish. Street furniture planned for a site should be related in a coordinated family of shapes, materials, and finishes. Strong, simple shapes, native materials, and natural finishes generally work best, with black, grays, and earth tones the basic colors, and bright colors reserved for accent.

4. Items should be durable. Street furniture must be designed to withstand the effects of the elements, including sun, expansion and contraction, wind stress, moisture, and in some cases, salt spray, frost, or ice.

5. In selecting items, long-term cost should be considered: a higher initial expense may be good economics if it buys a longer life with less maintenance.

6. To simplify maintenance, street furniture components such as lighting globes, signposts, bench slats, bolts, and stains and paint colors, should be standardized.

Designers should avoid concentrating too much on the details of street furniture or stressing the wrong ones.[125] The street furniture that people use deserves more attention than other items. For example, pedestrians are more likely to be affected by the texture of pavement, the shape of steps, or the design of a bench because they use them. They will not care or may not even be aware of whether a kiosk is round or octagonal. Thus, following this logic, the designer should focus on making sure benches are comfortable and conveniently located.

In sum, street furniture should be functional and harmonize with the setting, and individual pieces should be coordinated to help define the unique character of the site. As a final caveat, the designer should resist overprettifying a development to the point that it becomes contrived. No matter how real under the surface a development may be, hanging baskets of flowers, cute signs, and quaint displays make it look and feel more like a chunk of Disneyland.[126]

# Design Evaluation Criteria Checklist

Subdivision design covers many areas, including circulation, building arrangement, open space, and landscaping. It is the product of a process that begins with planning a development and continues throughout the construction phase. To be successful, it requires the joint, active participation of both the community and the developer.

To help guide this interactive process, this chapter concludes with a checklist of design criteria. The items on the checklist can be reviewed by the planning or design review board and the developer when formulating and acting on development plans. The checklist should not be used to prolong regulatory review of subdivision and site plans, but rather to improve the quality of the plans submitted and approved.

**Photo 3–46.** *The effect of these mailboxes could be softened through landscaping or screening.*

**Photo 3–47.** *These mailboxes have been incorporated into the overall site design by using the same building materials as for the units.*

## DESIGN EVALUATION CRITERIA CHECKLIST

### SITE ANALYSIS

- Is the project in conformance with municipal and county plans and goals and with relevant state plans?
- Was a site analysis an integral step in the site plan development process?
- Does any part of the development encroach on a critical area, for example, areas of high water table, steep slopes over 20 percent, poor drainage, and major tree stands?
- Are soil conditions suitable for the proposed development?
- Does the project result in adverse environmental effects, such as flooding and sedimentation off-site? Have flood hazard area designations and regulations been complied with, where applicable?
- Have measures been taken to minimize storm water runoff and to detain the increment over the natural rate as close as possible to the point of origin? Have buildings been protected from flooding?
- Is there adequate setback from rivers and streams? Have stream corridors been allowed to remain undeveloped, so they can act as runoff buffers and/or recreation areas?

### SUBDIVISION LAYOUT

RESPECT FOR NATURAL FEATURES/CONSTRAINTS

- Does the project avoid areas unsuitable for development? Does it use existing elements of the landscape, such as views, trees, and natural land contours to advantage?
- Have natural features of the site, such as topography, tree cover, and bodies of water been saved and integrated into the site plan in order to minimize site development costs and provide amenity?
- Have landmarks been incorporated into the site plan?
- Does the placement of the buildings take advantage of sun angles, prevailing winds, tree stands, hills, and other natural conditions to save energy in heating and cooling?
- Are the buildings oriented to site views? Do any proposed structures block views?
- Are the buildings arranged for some apparent purpose (to accommodate site topography, for example), or do they appear scattered about the site for no apparent design purpose?
- Does the design of the residential clusters encourage the creation of neighborhoods and promote a sense of community, while protecting privacy?
- Can the buildings be grouped more compactly to provide more usable open space? And conversely, are the buildings spaced too closely, or is the site too crowded for type of dwelling unit proposed?
- Are safe play, sitting, and walking areas provided, and are they conveniently located?
- Is there some transition provided between different residential building types?

## DESIGN EVALUATION CRITERIA CHECKLIST

SITE AND BUILDING LAYOUT AND DESIGN

- Does the site plan embody a coherent layout that can be easily understood by those who visit and live in the development?
- Do units front on residential access streets and not on major roadways?
- Do the units overlook open space and not parking or road areas or other units?
- Does the layout facilitate leaf and brush collection, snow and trash removal, and other grounds maintenance work?
- Have utilities been placed to make their construction and maintenance economical and efficient?
- Are electric and telephone lines placed underground except under exceptional circumstances?
- Are electric and gas meters, air conditioning units, transformers, and other utilities screened or otherwise out of sight?
- Are garbage storage areas located and covered to avoid spreading odors? Are they screened?
- Has outside storage been provided for bikes, play equipment, lawn furniture, gardening supplies, and barbeque equipment?
- Does each unit entry have some form of weather protection, such as an overhang or a porch, and a place to set packages down before entering the unit?

PRIVACY/SECURITY

- Do residents have adequate privacy? Do the design of the site and individual units promote security?
- Are units screened or located to avoid glare from automobile headlights and direct street lighting?
- Are housing units buffered from traffic to minimize the impact of noise and vibrations?
- Is there a minimal number of vehicular and pedestrian entrances to clusters of houses? Are these entrances well-lit and defined?
- Are parking areas and the walkways from parking to homes well-lit without producing glare?
- Are units clustered in a way that would allow neighbors to observe other homes and aid in crime prevention?
- Is surveillance of public spaces near units possible for security purposes and for watching children at play?
- Does each unit have its own semi-public entrance area, such as a deck, porch, or defined front yard, that must be passed through before entering the unit?
- Does each unit have a private entrance?
- Does each unit have a clearly defined private outdoor area, such as a deck, patio, balcony, or yard, for the exclusive use of its residents? Is it fenced, if necessary, for privacy?

## DESIGN EVALUATION CRITERIA CHECKLIST

### OPEN SPACE

- Is there a network of functional open space integrated into the site plan?
- Does the development's open space relate to the municipal and regional open space network?
- Is the developed open space functional in terms of area, dimensions, and location?
- Are there areas of the site appropriate for designations as undeveloped open space?
- Are open spaces interconnected where desirable?
- Are provisions for maintenance of the common open space adequate?
- Would it be desirable to locate small sitting areas with recreational equipment and benches in each neighborhood?
- Are high-nuisance recreational activities, such as swimming pools or tennis courts with glaring lights, carefully located and buffered to reduce any adverse impact on the surrounding area?
- Are parking areas for recreational facilities screened and buffered from surrounding residences?

### LANDSCAPING

#### GENERAL

- Have existing trees and plants been saved?
- Are the proposed plants appropriate for their intended function?
- If grass is inappropriate for an area, has a textured hard surface material, such as paving stones, or light gravel interspersed with shrubs, been used instead?
- Has topsoil been saved, and has the site been cleared of debris?
- Have slopes and cut-and-fill areas been protected against erosion?

#### SHADE TREES

- Have shade trees been provided in accordance with the requirements of the subdivision ordinance?

#### BUFFERING

- Has buffering been provided around the perimeter of the site where necessary to minimize adverse impacts, such as more intensive land uses, noise, lights, or traffic on higher-order streets?
- Have parking, garbage collection, utility, and loading and unloading areas been provided with buffering?
- Are both trees and shrubs provided in buffer areas?

## DESIGN EVALUATION CRITERIA CHECKLIST

PARKING LOTS

- Has landscaping been provided in parking areas as required by the subdivision ordinance?
- Have plantings been located so as not to obstruct drivers' vision?

WALLS AND FENCES

- Have walls and fences been provided where necessary for privacy, security, screening, climate control, or to highlight a view?
- Does the design and choice of material: 1) serve the function for which the wall or fence is intended, 2) complement the character of the site and the type of building, and 3) facilitate easy and cost-efficient maintenance?

PAVING AND STREET FURNITURE

- Have the various elements of street furniture been provided as necessary and located where needed?
- Has the design of street furniture been coordinated with the character and style of the architecture? Are elements compatible with each other in form, material, and finish?
- Are the items selected durable? What sort of maintenance is required?

### LAYOUT OF THE CIRCULATION SYSTEM

STREETS

- Is the road system designed to meet the projected traffic demand and does the road network consist of a hierarchy of roads designed according to function?
- Does the road network follow the natural topography and preserve natural features of the site as much as possible? Have alignments been planned so that grading requirements are minimized?
- Are entry roads clearly visible from the major arterial roads? Are proper sight distances provided at intersections?
- Is through traffic directed around the development and avoided on minor residential streets?
- Is automobile movement within the site provided without having to use the peripheral road network?
- Does the road system provide adequate access to buildings for residents, visitors, deliveries, and garbage collection?
- Have the edges of the roadways been landscaped? If sidewalks are provided alongside the road, have they been set back sufficiently from the road, and has a landscaped planting strip between the road and the sidewalk been provided?

## DESIGN EVALUATION CRITERIA CHECKLIST

PEDESTRIAN AND BIKE PATHS

- Are pedestrian and bicycle paths clearly separated from traffic?
- Are they located to take advantage of topography, views, and the natural features of the site?
- Does the path system link buildings with parking areas, entrances to the development, open space, and recreational and other community facilities?
- Are paths ramped and graded to facilitate the use of strollers, bicycles, and wheelchairs?

PARKING AREAS

- Is the number of parking spaces sufficient to serve the buildings?
- Is there sufficient distance between the entrance to the parking lot and the parking stalls?
- Are the parking spaces the appropriate size and within convenient walking distance of the buildings they are to serve?
- Are parking spaces and aisles angled and sized for convenient maneuvering?
- Are parking bays provided with turnarounds so that cars can leave if the bay is filled?
- Are the parking lots broken up into smaller areas through the use of trees and landscaped islands?
- Are curbs rather than bumpers used?
- Are sidewalks wide enough so that the car overhang does not block them? Is the overhang area hard-landscaped rather than planted?
- Are the parking lots buffered and screened from view? Are they adequately lighted?

## SIGNS AND LIGHTING

SIGNS

- Are signs easy to understand both by visitors and by those who live in the development?
- Does the design of signs relate to and complement other elements of the overall site design?
- Are signs placed where they are needed?

LIGHTING

- Is the lighting appropriate for the purpose required, such as for safety or security? (For safety purposes, sufficient lighting should be provided at intersections and spaced along walkways. For security purposes, lighting should be provided at entryways and between buildings and parking areas.)
- Is the spacing of the light standards appropriate for their height? (Spacing should be equal to approximately four times the height of the standard.)
- Are the standards suitable in size and style for the surroundings? (The maximum height should not exceed the maximum building height permitted, or 25 feet, whichever is less.)
- Are spotlights, if used, placed on standards pointing toward the buildings without blinding residents, rather than on the buildings and directed outwards which would create dark shadows adjacent to the buildings?

## Notes

1. Richard Hedman with Andrew Jaszewski, *Fundamentals of Urban Design* (Chicago, IL: American Planning Association, 1984), p. 2.

2. Ibid., p. 136.

3. John Reps, *Town Planning in Frontier America* (Columbia, MO: University of Missouri Press, 1981), p. 295.

4. N.J.S.A. 40:55D-2(i).

5. Ibid., 40:55D-7.

6. For more on the problems of decision makers in reviewing site plans and making design decisions, see ibid., p. 7; Harvey Moskowitz and Carl Lindbloom, *A Guide for Residential Design Review* (Trenton, NJ: New Jersey Department of Community Affairs, 1976), pp. 1–4; and Carl Lindbloom, "The Role of Urban Design in the Planning Process," New Jersey American Planning Association *Newsletter*, vol. III, no. 3, Spring 1985.

7. A *New York Times* article describing the controversy surrounding the design of a skyscraper illustrates the issues typical in these cases. The office building was proposed for a site on the edge of Brooklyn Heights, a residential neighborhood of brownstones and small institutional buildings so valued that it was designated the city's first historic district in 1965.

   *The project...points up, perhaps more clearly than any other in New York, the clash of values between economic development and intelligent planning, between the forces of politics and the forces of design.*

   *The problem, put simply, is that the city would like to keep Morgan Stanley's computer operations, and the hundreds of jobs they generate, but to do so requires the kind of building that is impossible to put up within the normal constraints of the zoning laws. Why the zoning laws do not encourage this type of building is not hard to understand—the laws are written with the intention of keeping at least some light and air in most streets. And this building, if erected as now designed, will cast a marked shadow over some of Brooklyn Heights, and will turn narrow Clinton Street into a dark canyon.*

Paul Goldberger, "Plan for Skyscraper in Brooklyn Hts. Pits Livability Against Development." *The New York Times,* October 11, 1985, pp. B1 +.

8. Adapted from Hedman, *Urban Design,* pp. 136–37.

9. Marilyn Spigel Schultz and Vivian Loeb Kasen, *Encyclopedia of Community Planning and Environmental Management* (New York, NY: Facts on File Publications, 1984), p. 362.

10. Reps, *Town Planning in Frontier America,* p. 293.

11. Ibid.

12. Richard Hedman, *Urban Design,* p. 6.

13. Ibid., p. 7.

14. Hedman, *Urban Design,* pp. 9–11; Lindbloom, "The Role of Urban Design," 1985.

15. This list is adapted from Kevin Lynch and Gary Hack, *Site Planning* (Cambridge, MA: The Massachusetts Institute of Technology, 1984), Appendix G, "A Site and Impact Check- list," pp. 420–425. Other sources on site analysis include Harvey Moskowitz and Carl Lindbloom, *A Guide for Residential Design Review* (Trenton, NJ: New Jersey Depart- ment of Community Affairs, 1976), Chapter 3; Joseph DeChiara and Lee E. Koppelman, *Time-Saver Standards for Site Planning* (New York: McGraw-Hill, 1984), pp. 1–14, 159–90; Urban Land Institute, *Residential Development Handbook* (Washington, D.C.: Urban Land Institute, 1978), pp. 148–153; and John Ormsbee Simonds, *Landscape Archi- tecture* (New York: McGraw-Hill, 1983), pp. 94–105.

16. Although the number and content of the overlay sheets will depend on the complexity of the project, the following are usually included: slope, drainage, soils, water resources, vegetation, structures, circulation, utilities, climate, visual analysis, impact assessment, preservation, and conservation. Simonds, *Landscape Architecture,* p. 101.

17. Moskowitz and Lindbloom, *Guide*, p. 41; emphasis in the original.

18. ULI, *Residential Development Handbook*, p. 115. See also, Lynch and Hack, *Site Planning*, pp. 292–94.

19. Lynch and Hack, *Site Planning*, p. 292.

20. Moskowitz and Lindbloom, *Guide*, p. 62. This notion is based on Oscar Newman, *Defensible Space* (New York, NY: MacMillan, 1972).

21. Richard Untermann and Robert Small, *Site Planning for Cluster Housing* (New York, NY: Van Nostrand Reinhold, 1977), p. 1.

22. Lynch and Hack, *Site Planning*, p. 292.

23. Untermann and Small, *Site Planning for Cluster Housing*, p. 151. "Four or five units is about the minimum while twenty is about the maximum number of units able to identify with the cluster. Twenty units provide enough diversity to allow people to meet others with compatible interests while creating a large enough group so individuals may have privacy."

24. Moskowitz and Lindbloom, *Guide*, p. 60.

25. Ibid. The comment in ULI, *Residential Development Handbook*, p. 126, is typical of this viewpoint: "It is good to place a buffer land use such as a park, school, or church between multifamily and single-family housing, but a land use which unites people rather than one which divides them. Well-designed townhouses between the multifamily building and single-family areas also provide good transition."

26. Untermann and Small, *Site Planning for Cluster Housing*, p. 83.

27. Joshua H. Vogel, *Design of Subdivisions* (Seattle, WA: Bureau of Governmental Research and Services, 1965), pp. 28–29.

28. Lynch and Hack, *Site Planning*, p. 185.

29. Ibid., p. 195.

30. Hedman, *Urban Design*, pp. 90–91.

31. Lynch and Hack, *Site Planning*, p. 199, make the point about branch walks.

32. For more discussion on the functions of landscaping, see Moskowitz and Lindbloom, *Guide*, pp. 120–121; ULI, *Residential Development Handbook*, pp. 187–189; Lynch and Hack, *Site Planning*, pp. 153–192; Theodore D. Walker, *Residential Landscaping I* (West Lafayette, IN: DDA Publishers, 1982), pp. 55–99; and Gary O. Robinette, *Plants, People and Environmental Quality* (Washington, D.C.: Department of the Interior, 1972).

33. Lynch and Hack, *Site Planning*, p. 185.

34. Ibid., pp. 54–55.

35. If the wall is impenetrable, air pressure in the lee is lowered so far that it will cause strong turbulence, ibid., p. 55.

36. Ibid., p. 181.

37. Lindbloom, "The Role of Urban Design," 1985, p. 1.

38. Peggy Glassford, *Appearance Codes for Small Communities*, PAS Report 379 (Chicago: American Planning Association, 1983), p. 1. This report summarizes municipal design control measures and focuses on the use of appearance codes in eight suburban communities in the Chicago area.

39. Schultz and Kasen, *Encyclopedia of Community Planning*, p. 24.

40. Glassford, *Appearance Codes*, p. 10.

41. The language of the court in the *Berman* case reads, "The concept of the public welfare is broad and inclusive...the values it represents are spiritual as well as physical, aesthetic as well as monetary. It is within the power of the legislature to determine that the community should be beautiful as well as healthy, spacious as well as clean, well-balanced as well as carefully patrolled." In the period since the *Berman* decision, three states have upheld the use of police power solely for aesthetics: New York, Oregon, and Florida. Ibid., pp. 11–12.

42. Ibid., p. 12. The phrase, "lowest common denominators," is from Norman Williams, *American Land Planning Law: Land Use and the Police Power* (Wilmette, IL: Callaghan and Co.), p. 250.

43. Glassford, *Appearance Codes*, p. 5.

44. Ibid., p. 8.

45. The following is typical: "These criteria are not intended to restrict imagination, innovations, or variety, but rather to assist in focusing on design principles that can result in creative solutions...." Ibid.

46. United States Department of the Interior, *National Urban Recreation Study Executive Report* (Washington, D.C.: U.S. Government Printing Office, 1978), p. 15.

47. Urban Land Institute, *Recreational Development Handbook* (Washington, D.C.: Urban Land Institute, 1981), p. 225.

48. See Schultz and Kasen, *Encyclopedia of Community Planning*, which defines open space as "land that is either under-developed or is relatively free of buildings or other structures," p. 279; and Moskowitz and Lindbloom, *Guide*, which defines it as "space devoid of buildings and other physical structures except for outdoor recreational facilities," p. 134.

49. Moskowitz and Lindbloom, *Guide*, p. 134.

50. Department of the Interior, *Recreation Study Executive Report*, p. 30.

51. In 1906, the Playground Association of America (PAA) was formed and adopted the London requirement of 30 square feet of playground for each schoolchild. This, and a PAA plan that every school district in Washington, D.C., was to have a playground with at least one acre of land for each 2,000 children, were among the earliest recorded recreation space standards. National Recreation and Park Association, *Recreation, Park and Open Space Standards and Guidelines* (Alexandria, VA: NRPA, 1983), p. 15.

52. See, for example, DeChiara and Koppelman, *Time-Saver Standards;* and Robert D. Buechner (ed.), *National Park,*

*Recreation and Open Space Standards* (Arlington, VA: NRPA, 1971).

53. NRPA, *Standards*, pp. 41, 46–49.

54. Michael B. Brough, *A Unified Development Ordinance* (Chicago, IL: American Planning Association, 1985), pp. 109, 111.

55. NRPA, *Standards*, pp. 90–91.

56. Frank S. So et al., *Planned Unit Development Ordinances*, PAS Report No. 291 (Chicago, IL: ASPO, 1973), p. 30.

57. David Jensen, *Community Design Guidelines: Responding to a Changing Market* (Washington, D.C.: National Association of Homebuilders, 1984), p. 48.

58. While admittedly an extreme example, in a study on open space requirements, Henry M. Levin points out that a fixed standard of 10 acres per 1,000 population "would require parkland for Manhattan that would encompass more area than the Borough itself." Levin, *Estimating the Municipal Demand for Recreation Land* (Washington, D.C.: The Brookings Institution, 1966), p. 13.

59. NRPA, *Standards*, p. 37. Emphasis in the original.

60. Lynch and Hack, *Site Planning*, p. 291; and generally, pp. 289–291. See also Gary Hack, "Research Opportunities," *Planning*, October 1984, pp. 20–21.

61. Levin, *Estimating the Municipal Demand for Recreational Land*, pp. 218–219.

62. Ibid., pp. 223–225.

63. So, *PUD Ordinances*, p. 31.

64. Moskowitz and Lindbloom, *Guide*, p. 120; and Lynch and Hack, *Site Planning*, p. 179.

65. Lynch and Hack, *Site Planning*, p. 153. Emphasis in the original.

66. Ibid., p. 179.

67. Ibid., p. 181. Moskowitz and Lindbloom, referring to a recommendation contained in *House and Home,* suggest that developers budget a figure equal to two to three percent of gross project costs on landscaping, *Guide,* p. 122.

68. Moskowitz and Lindbloom, *Guide,* p. 122.

69. ULI, *Residential Development Handbook,* p. 187.

70. American Planning Association and the Joint Venture for Affordable Housing, *Affordable Single-Family Housing: A Review of Development Standards* (Chicago, IL: APA, 1984), p. 18. See also, Jensen, *Community Design Guidelines,* p. 44.

71. Lynch and Hack, *Site Planning,* pp. 179–181.

72. Moskowitz and Lindbloom, *Guide,* p. 120.

73. See Philip L. Carpenter, *Residential Landscaping II* (Mesa, AZ: PDA Publishers Corp., 1983), p. 70. Many municipalities require a six-inch topsoil cover.

74. Walker, *Residential Landscaping I,* p. 96.

75. ULI, *Residential Development Handbook,* p. 189; Simonds, *Landscape Architecture,* p. 68.

76. Carpenter, *Residential Landscaping II,* p. 10.

77. ULI, *Residential Development Handbook,* p. 189.

78. Carpenter, *Residential Landscaping II,* describes the proper method for constructing a dry well, p. 10.

79. Lynch and Hack, *Site Planning,* p. 182.

80. The recommendations made in this section on controlling erosion are drawn primarily from Walker, *Residential Landscaping I,* p. 96; ULI, *Residential Development Handbook,* pp. 196–200; and DeChiara and Koppelman, *Time-Saver Standards,* pp. 52–53.

81. APA and Joint Venture, *Affordable Single-Family Housing,* p. 18. See also pp. 40, 66–67.

82. Carpenter, *Residential Landscaping II*, p. 30.

83. Gordon M. Heisler et al., "Effect of Planting Procedures on Initial Growth of *Acer rubrum L.* and *Fraxinum pennsylanicum L.* in a Parking Lot," U.S. Department of Agriculture, Northeast Forest Experiment Station, Research Paper NE–513, 1982.

84. Heisler, "Effect of Planting Procedures," pp. 2, 6.

85. Carpenter, *Residential Landscaping II*, p. 31; DeChiara and Koppelman, *Time-Saver Standards*, p. 702.

86. Adapted from DeChiara and Koppelman, *Time-Saver Standards*, pp. 310–311; and Carpenter, *Residential Landscaping II*, pp. 35–49.

87. See, for example, ULI, *Residential Development Handbook*, p. 189, and Simonds, *Landscape Architecture*, p. 73.

88. ULI, *Residential Development Handbook*, p. 189.

89. Simonds, *Landscape Architecture*, p. 73.

90. Moskowitz and Lindbloom, *Guide*, p. 124. See also, ULI, *Residential Development Handbook*, p. 189.

91. *Time-Saver Standards*, p. 702.

92. Simonds, *Landscape Architecture*, p. 69. See also Lynch and Hack, *Site Planning*, p. 185.

93. Moskowitz and Lindbloom, *Guide*, p. 125.

94. See APA and Joint Venture, *Affordable Single-Family Housing*, p. 66.

95. ULI, *Residential Development Handbook*, p. 195.

96. Ibid.

97. Gordon M. Heisler, "Planting Design for Wind Control," in E. Gregory McPherson (ed.), *Energy-Conserving Site Design* (Washington, D.C.: The Landscape Architecture Foundation, 1984), p. 183.

98. E. Gregory McPherson, "Planting Design for Solar Control," in McPherson, *Energy-Conserving Site Design*, p. 164.

99. See ULI, *Residential Handbook*, p. 187; and So, *PUD Ordinances*, p. 41.

100. *Residential Development Handbook*, p. 195.

101. "Noise Control," *Journal of Conservation*, cited in ULI, *Residential Development Handbook*, p. 195.

102. ULI, *Residential Development Handbook*, p. 195.

103. M.A. Corwin, *Parking Lot Landscaping*, PAS Report No. 335 (Chicago, IL: ASPO, 1978), p. 3.

104. Ibid., p. 4.

105. ULI, *Residential Development Handbook*, p. 178.

106. ULI, ASCE, NAHB, *Residential Streets: Objectives, Principles and Design Considerations* (Washington, D.C.: Urban Land Institute, 1976), p. 21; and ULI, *Residential Development Handbook*, p. 178.

107. Moskowitz and Lindbloom, *Guide*, p. 126.

108. "Illustrated Guide to Parking Lot Landscaping," *Zoning News*, APA, March 1984.

109. Corwin, *Parking Lot Landscaping*, p. 9, Table 2.

110. Ibid., Table 3.

111. "Illustrated Guide," *Zoning News*, pp. 1–2.

112. Moskowitz and Lindbloom, *Guide*, p. 127.

113. Lynch and Hack, *Site Planning*, p. 185.

114. See for example, Moskowitz and Lindbloom, *Guide*, pp. 131–140.

115. Lynch and Hack, *Site Planning*, p. 170.

116. Simonds, *Landscape Architecture*, p. 158. See also, Lynch and Hack, *Site Planning*, p. 157.

117. Lynch and Hack, *Site Planning*, p. 161; and Moskowitz and Lindbloom, *Guide*, p. 130.

118. Lynch and Hack, *Site Planning*, p. 186.

119. Moskowitz and Lindbloom, *Guide,* p. 131.

120. Lynch and Hack, *Site Planning,* p. 185.

121. DeChiara and Koppelman, *Time-Saver Standards,* p. 312.

122. Moskowitz and Lindbloom, *Guide,* p. 131.

123. Harvey S. Moskowitz and Carl G. Lindbloom, *The Illustrated Book of Development Definitions* (New Brunswick, NJ: Center for Urban Policy Research, 1981), p. 186.

124. These recommendations are drawn primarily from Simonds, *Landscape Architecture,* p. 131; and Schultz and Kasen, *Encyclopedia of Planning,* p. 386.

125. Lynch and Hack, *Site Planning,* p. 187.

126. Hedman, *Fundamentals of Urban Design,* p. 95.

*Chapter 4*

# IMPROVEMENT STANDARDS

## Streets

### The Case for Reducing Standards

Numerous authorities have criticized subdivision and site plan ordinances as requiring unnecessary improvements that result in costly overbuilding.[1] Nowhere has this issue been more acute than in the debate over setting appropriate street standards. Generally, authorities and communities have approached the regulation of residential streets in one of two ways: 1) they have adopted the traditional standards usually patterned after state highway design, or 2) more recently, they have advocated an approach embodying the concept that residential streets should be designed to serve neighborhood needs.[2] According to this latter perspective, street standards adapted from highway design result in roads that are unnecessarily wide, costly, and unsafe. By contrast, building streets to serve residents (as opposed to through traffic) results in a safe, convenient, quiet neighborhood, while still providing for necessary movement of automobiles, ample parking, and access by emergency vehicles. Another influence challenging traditional standards was the growing acceptance in the 1970s of more innovative suburban design, such as cluster or planned-unit development, which led some authorities to question a perceived overdesign of residential streets in conventional subdivisions.

This position was articulated in a number of publications, including *Recommendations of the National Committee for Traffic Safety;* Bucks County, Pennsylvania, Planning Commission's *Performance Streets* and *Residential Streets,* the latter a joint publication by the Urban Land Institute (ULI), the American Society of Civil Engineers (ASCE), and the National Association of Home Builders (NAHB).[3] These publications all called into question subdivision regulations for residential streets and urged a reevaluation of prevailing standards. *Residential Streets,* for example, was published in 1974 after extensive research and a national survey of street design and construction practices. Its authors were strongly motivated to assure quality standards, yet eliminate unnecessary improvement costs. They recommended flexible regulations and design standards specifically oriented to residential as opposed to commercial or industrial streets. This effort was followed in 1978 by NAHB's *Subdivision Regulation Handbook,* which reiterated many of the same principles for street standards, but also included other areas of subdivision control.

Bucks County's *Performance Streets* was a model ordinance of street standards. Like *Residential Streets,* it advocated that all standards be premised on the concept that residential streets support neighborhood activities, properly serving their needs and no other. It also pointed to a number of problems in residential subdivisions caused by designing streets to meet highway standards:

a. Excessively wide residential streets are costly to install and to maintain. Initial costs are passed on to the homebuyer in the cost of housing; maintenance costs are passed on to residents in the form of higher taxes.

b. Overdesign may result in undesirable environmental effects—more cut and fill, more runoff, diminished groundwater supply, and higher potential for erosion.

c. Overdesigned and excessively wide streets tend to move traffic rather than control it, encouraging speeding and creating hazards. Narrower, curved streets discourage speeding.

d. Planning and design of residential streets should clearly indicate their function as local streets.

In designing streets to serve neighborhood needs, *Performance Streets* recommended basing street standards on the following considerations:

a. Street width should be based on the number of cars expected to use it, the need for on-street parking, and the choice of curbing or shoulders.
b. Engineering standards (sight distances, horizontal curves, etc.) should be based on the requirements for safe control of traffic.
c. Street arrangement should encourage short, quiet residential streets that create recognizable neighborhoods and discourage through traffic.

Tailoring the design of each street to its specific purpose is known as a performance approach to street design. The Bucks County model ordinance used this approach in setting street standards. It created a street hierarchy classification system with requirements for each street based on function and intensity of development as measured by lot size.

Recent publications by highway engineers have now also embraced the performance approach and the principle that residential streets should be designed to serve local neighborhood needs. *Recommended Guidelines for Subdivision Streets*, published by the Institute of Transportation Engineers (ITE), specifically warns against overdesign and overbuilding of local streets: "These streets should have an appearance commensurate with their function as local streets."[4]

ITE's recommended standards, which are intended for adoption within local subdivision ordinances, are similar to Bucks County's in that they establish a street hierarchy and vary with development intensity. In addition, ITE's standards vary according to terrain (i.e., flat versus rolling). A similar performance-based approach is used by Michael B. Brough in *A Unified Development Ordinance*.[5]

In sum, in the last few years, there has been a growing recog-

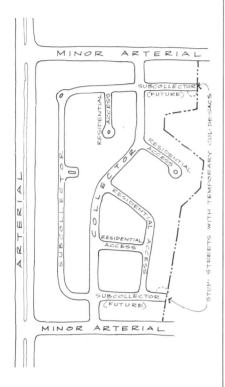

**Illustration 4–1.** *Residential street hierarchy.*

nition that street standards should support residential needs and be based on variations in usage, density, the need for parking, and choice of curbs or shoulders. Streets can thus be thought of in terms of different members of the street hierarchy having different requirements.

## The Street Hierarchy

All residential streets can be defined in terms of relative movement of through traffic and property access. Some streets, for example, may serve five or six houses—traffic is light and moves slowly. Other streets are much busier, acting as collectors for traffic from a number of streets and serving dozens of homes. These different functions allow streets to be classified in a street hierarchy system with design tailored to function. Such a system offers numerous advantages:

1. *Safety*—fast traffic is kept out of neighborhoods.
2. *Municipal efficiency*—priorities can be assigned by municipal officials to maintenance operations and routing of snow plows and buses.
3. *Residential quality*—traffic restricted on roads immediately serving residences promotes quieter, safer, more pleasant neighborhoods.
4. *Land-use efficiency*—overbuilding of roads is avoided, thus lowering maintenance costs, housing costs, and adverse impact on the environment.

### AVERAGE DAILY TRAFFIC (ADT)

The street hierarchy system is defined by road function as measured by average daily traffic (ADT). The ADT of a proposed development can be estimated by calculating number of trips by housing or other land-use category. A "trip" is a single or one way vehicle movement either to or from a property or study area. "Trips" can be added together to calculate the total number of trips entering and leaving a specific land use, site, or street over a designated period of time.

Various references can be used in projecting total trips. These references list number of trips that can be expected from, or "generated" by, different land uses. One source is the National Cooperative Highway Research Program Report Number 187—*Quick Response Urban Travel Estimation Techniques and Transferable Parameters*. Report Number 187 gives trip generation information by land-use category (residential, retail, manufacturing, etc.), urbanized area population (50,000-100,000; 100,000-250,000; 250,000-750,000, etc.), and other parameters. Other sources on trip generation include Arizona Department of Transportation, *Trip Generation Intensity Factors*, Phoenix, AZ, 1976; Federal Highway Administration, *National Personal Transportation Study*, 1983-84, and various reports in 1985 and 1986; and J. Mehra and C.R. Keller, *Development and Application of Trip Generation Rates*, Federal Highway Administration, 1985 (FHWA/PL/85/003).

For *local* trip generation, many analysts use a report published by the Institute of Transportation Engineers (ITE) entitled *Trip Generation*, although trip generation rates from other sources may be used if they better reflect local conditions.[6]

The ITE trip data are differentiated by major land-use categories—residential, office buildings, industrial, lodging, retail, etc. These major groupings are further broken down by specific type of use. For example, within the residential category, trip generation information is broken down by housing type—single-family detached, apartment, mobile homes, recreation homes, etc. ITE's figures are shown in Exhibit 1 of the model ordinance, which also contains trip generation figures for numerous nonresidential land-use categories.

The total trip generation for a street constitutes its ADT, which, in conjunction with street function, differentiates streets so that they can be placed in a street hierarchy. At the lower end of the hierarchy are *residential access streets*—streets with relatively low ADTs designed for local traffic. They are followed in ascending order by *residential subcollectors* and *residential collectors*, each with higher ADT counts and designed to accommodate increasing volumes of traffic. Each member of the hierarchy as well as *special purpose streets* (rural residential lanes, alleys, cul-de-sacs, marginal access streets, divided streets, and stub streets), are defined in Exhibit 2 of the model ordinance and described in further detail below.

## Street Types

### RESIDENTIAL ACCESS STREETS

Residential access streets are lowest-order streets in the street hierarchy. They provide access to residential lots and carry only traffic generated on the street itself. The elimination of through traffic promotes safety and a quieter, more pleasant neighborhood environment. Typically, residential access streets are short loops, cul-de-sacs, or courts. Residential subdivisions should be designed so that all housing units, or the maximum number possible, front on this type of street.

Residential access streets should be designed for a maximum ADT of 250; in the case of loop streets, each half may be classified as a single residential access street, but the total traffic volume on the loop street should not exceed 500 ADT, nor should it exceed 250 ADT at any point of traffic concentration. This restriction effectively limits the number of single-family homes served by a residential access loop to 50 (50 units × 10 trips per unit), or the number of townhouses served to 85 (85 units × 5.9 trips per unit).

### RESIDENTIAL SUBCOLLECTORS

Like residential access streets, residential subcollectors also provide frontage and access to residential lots, but differ in that they are designed to carry somewhat higher traffic volumes. This traffic, however, should be limited to that collected from intersecting residential access streets and the small amount generated on the street itself. Ideally, all homes should front on residential access streets, but in cases where this proves unworkable, frontage on a subcollector may be the only, although less desirable, alternative. In any case, subcollectors are not intended to interconnect adjoining neighborhoods or subdivisions, and should be designed to discourage shortcutting by through traffic. This can be achieved by laying out subcollectors as loops or in patterns that are unappealing as shortcuts.

Residential subcollectors should be designed for a maximum ADT of 500; in the case of a loop, each half may be classified as a single subcollector street, but the total traffic volume on the loop street should not exceed 1,000 ADT, nor should it exceed 500 ADT at any point of traffic concentration. The volume of traffic may be determined by adding the trips generated by the total number of units taking access from the street to the trips generated by the tributary residential access streets. The 1,000 ADT is thus equivalent to the amount of traffic generated by 100 single-family homes or approximately 150 townhouses.[7]

## RESIDENTIAL COLLECTORS

The function of residential subcollectors is to carry and distribute traffic between lower-order streets—residential access streets and residential subcollectors—and higher-order streets—arterials and expressways. Because their purpose is to promote free traffic flow, collectors should not be used for parking, deliveries, or trash pickup, nor should they provide access to residential lots. These activities interrupt the flow of traffic and properly belong on frontage streets (residential access streets). Although collectors are designed to conduct traffic quickly and efficiently, residential subdivisions should not be burdened with external traffic. Therefore, collectors should be laid out to discourage their use by through traffic as shortcuts from one municipality to another.

Residential collectors should be designed for a maximum ADT of 3,000.[8] Not all developments, however, will need collectors. Need is related to development size, and some developments will simply be too small to require collectors. As a rule of thumb, once a development reaches the size of 150 dwelling units, collectors may be required.[9] In some cases, minor retail or other commercial establishments may be present along a collector, especially if they pre-date the development. Municipalities may find it necessary to plat new streets to relieve congestion and convey traffic.

## ARTERIALS

The function of arterials is to convey traffic between municipalities and other activity centers and to provide connections with major state and interstate roadways. Significant community, retail, commercial, and industrial facilities may be located on arterials. Arterials have high ADT levels and their inclusion is not appropriate in the residential street hierarchy.

## SPECIAL PURPOSE STREETS

This street category includes rural residential lanes, alleys, cul-de-sacs, marginal access streets, divided streets, and stub streets.

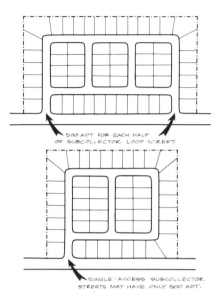

**Illustration 4–2.** *ADT volume for subcollectors.*

**Photo 4–1.** *Access to rear parking provided by alley.*

## Rural Residential Lanes

Rural residential lanes serve very low-density areas with a minimum of two-acre zoning. A maximum ADT level of 200 limits the number of single-family homes on this road to 20.

## Alleys

Alleys are service roads whose function is to provide a secondary means of public access to abutting property. Alleys are not intended for general traffic circulation, and they are classified on the same level in the street hierarchy as residential access streets.

The use of alleys has fallen into disfavor in subdivision design, but as density increases and lot sizes narrow, alleys offer an alternative to numerous curb cuts along the frontage street. Among their advantages, alleys provide access to rear-lot parking. They also afford maintenance access to rear-line overhead utilities and provide a secondary means of access for emergency vehicles and service trucks. Their disadvantages, however, include the cost of constructing and maintaining additional pavement, the loss of revenue of land removed from the tax rolls, and added costs of street lighting. The trend toward clustered design, the integration of various housing types in one development, the pressure for more open space, and the attempts to separate vehicular and pedestrian traffic all suggest that alleys will play a limited role in the construction of future residential subdivisions.

If alleys are permitted by a municipality, they are generally limited to high-density situations (lot frontage widths of less than 40 feet) as a means of providing secondary access to a lot. By definition, alleys may not provide the exclusive means of frontage to a lot. Should they do so, they are governed by the standards of the appropriate category of streets in the classification system. Because narrow cartways are specified for alleys (see section on cartway width), parking should not be permitted in the alley itself, and through traffic discouraged. The amount of activity on alleys should be minimized: they should be laid out to discourage their use as shortcuts, and they should serve only a limited number of units.

The model ordinance suggests that alleys provide rear access to no more than 85 townhouse units—a number derived from the ADT levels specified for residential access loops (500 ADT divided by 5.9 trips per unit). This figure may seem high, and municipalities might wish to use a lower figure. It was selected so that the residential access street and alley would serve a development in a reciprocal manner.

Although alleys should connect to a street at both ends, when this is not possible, alleys may be designed as cul-de-sacs, with a turnaround large enough to accommodate garbage trucks. Standards for alley cul-de-sacs are the same as for other cul-de-sacs.

## Cul-de-sacs

Cul-de-sacs are streets with a single means of entry and exit. They have two parts: the stem and the turnaround. The configuration of the turnaround may vary—all are acceptable as long as they provide the proper turning radius, but a round turnaround is the most efficient in terms of turning requirements for vehicles. Cul-de-sacs are valued in residential developments because their design promotes a sense of neighborhood identity, and their low traffic volumes allow for safer, quieter living conditions.

**Illustration 4–3.** *Arranging units around courts or cul-de-sacs reduces overall street length.*

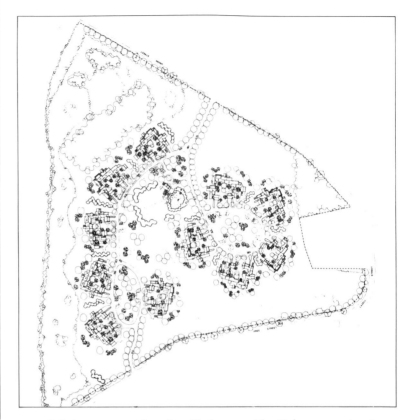

Cul-de-sacs may be classified as residential access streets or subcollectors, depending on estimated ADT: residential access cul-de-sacs are designed for an ADT of 250 and subcollectors for 500. Cul-de-sacs may also be classified as alleys, depending on function. Given their unique physical characteristics, all cul-de-sac classifications are treated together here.

**Length.** Some sources recommended setting a maximum cul-de-sac length for the following reasons: 1) to minimize inconvenience and back-up time for service vehicles, such as delivery vehicles and garbage trucks; 2) to minimize the likelihood that a motorist drawn in by mistake will pull into a private driveway instead of using the turnaround at the end of the street; and 3) to control speeding.[10] Many sources set the maximum length of a cul-de-sac at 400 to 600 feet,[11] although some relate maximum length to density or location, allowing longer maximum lengths in low-density developments or rural areas.[12] ITE, for example, recommends a 700-foot maximum length, but permits cul-de-sacs to be 1,000 feet long in low-density developments.

Instead of specifying a maximum length limit for all cul-de-sacs, however, the Rutgers model ordinance proposes that cul-de-sacs be classified by ADT level with different standards depending on classification. Both the ITE and Bucks County ordinances use ADT levels to set standards for cul-de-sacs. ITE's maximum length limit (1,000 feet) is based on an ADT level of 200, considered the maximum for any cul-de-sac. Thus, if each single-family home generates 10 trips a day, a 200 ADT is equivalent to a 20-home generation. A 100-foot lot width for each of the 20 homes gives a cul-de-sac length of 1,000 feet (ten homes on each side of the street).[13]

Bucks County makes a distinction in the classification of cul-de-sacs, recommending an ADT limitation of 200 for cul-de-sacs classified as residential access streets. For this low volume of traffic, Bucks County argues that a maximum length standard is unnecessary, but recommends turning circles at 500-foot intervals.[14] Once the ADT level exceeds the level established for residential access streets (200), the cul-de-sac is classified as a sub-collector (ADT level between 200 and 500) and is restricted to a 1,000-foot maximum length. The Bucks County ordinance imposes this restriction on the grounds that as traffic increases, more people will be inconvenienced by long cul-de-sacs: visitors, emergency vehicles, lost motorists, and delivery men and trash haulers must backtrack after making deliveries or pickups.[15]

The Rutgers model ordinance, finding the Bucks County argument persuasive, also classifies cul-de-sacs into two street categories: residential access streets with an ADT maximum of 250, and subcollectors with an ADT maximum of 500 and a length limit of 1,000 feet, with design standards conforming to the appropriate classification.

## Marginal Access Streets

Marginal access streets are service streets that run parallel and adjacent to a freeway or expressway. They are designed to provide access to abutting properties and separation from through traffic. Like cul-de-sacs, marginal access streets may be designed at the level of a residential access street or a residential subcollector depending on anticipated traffic volumes.

**Photo 4–2.** *Example of a divided street.*

### Divided Streets

Divided streets are permitted in subdivisions as long as design standards of the street class are met for widths and other dimensions. Divided streets may be used advantageously as a design feature and to protect environmental features—rock outcroppings or specimen trees, for example—or to accommodate grade changes.

### Stub Streets

Stub streets are portions of streets for which extensions have been proposed and approved. They may be permitted when construction is phased over a period of time, but only if the street in its entirety has been approved in the preliminary plan. Otherwise, there is a risk that dead-end streets will be created—an undesirable practice that should be prohibited.

### Cartway Width

The cartway is the area of the street within which vehicles are permitted. It includes moving lanes and parking areas, but does not include shoulders, curbs, sidewalks, or swales. A minimum cartway width must allow safe passage of moving traffic exclusive of other interferences.

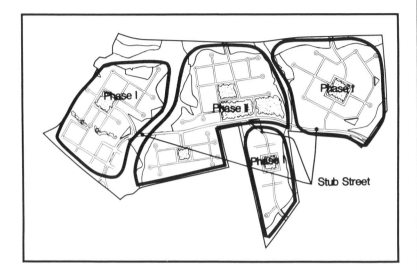

**Illustration 4–4.** *Example of stub streets in a phased development.*

*DETERMINING CARTWAY WIDTH*

The calculations for determining cartway width at first glance seem quite straightforward: cartway width for each street in the street hierarchy is computed by adding up the number and widths of moving traffic and parking lanes required. In carrying out the calculations, however, two issues arise: 1) how wide parking and moving lanes should be for each street in the street hierarchy; and 2) how many parking and moving lanes should be required for each street in the street hierarchy.

## Lane Width

**Parking lanes.** Parking lanes must be wide enough to accommodate vehicles, allow room for maneuvering, and permit the opening of doors without impeding traffic flow. In most residential subdivisions, on-street parking consists of parallel parking. Lane width for on-street parallel parking generally is given as 8 feet.[16]

**Moving lanes.** The dimensions of moving lanes differ according to the function of the road and its place within the street hierarchy. For roads with less traffic, narrower lane widths are adequate, but as traffic and speeds increase, wider moving lanes are required for safety. For *residential access streets*, Lynch and Hack set the standard at 10 feet wide,[17] whereas Bucks County's model code finds 9 feet generally adequate for the low traffic volume and speed.[18] However, Bucks County also recommends a minimum 10-foot lane for residential access streets where the moving lane is bounded by a curb or where parking lanes are located on both sides of the moving lane. (In very low-density subdivisions, Bucks County reduces the dimension of the moving lane to 8 feet.) For *subcollectors*, Bucks County recommends 10-foot-wide moving lanes, with an additional foot if bounded by a curb.

Recommended moving lane widths for *collectors* vary from 10 to 12 feet, with width increasing as a function of truck traffic and volume.[19] Highway design standards call for 12-foot lanes in order to accommodate trucks which are typically 2 feet wider than most passenger cars. Bucks County's model code suggests that residential collector streets designed for automobile use may thus be reduced in width by 2 feet without affecting road performance. Narrower widths for residential collectors may also be preferred in order to reduce traffic speed.

In sum, parallel parking lanes are 8 feet wide, and moving lanes are typically from 9 feet to 12 feet wide depending on curbing, density, and traffic volume.

**Number of Lanes**

In addition to the width of parking and moving lanes, another consideration in determining cartway width is the number of parking and moving lanes required. Number of lanes is a function of amount of development and traffic volume. In general, fewer lanes are required for streets that serve areas with limited development and low traffic volumes; more lanes are required for streets that serve areas with more development and a greater volume of traffic.

This general rule, however, must be qualified. It is not only the number of units that has a bearing on cartway width: how they are arranged is also important and will affect both number of lanes and lane width. A short street with high development intensity will have different requirements from a long street with the same number of units spread out. High development intensity means activities are concentrated—parking lanes may be required to handle cars and wider moving lanes may be necessary. At low development intensities, since activities are diffuse, there is room for cars to park on the side of the road and moving lanes can be narrower without endangering safety.

**Measuring intensity of development.** Development intensities can be expressed in terms of lot frontage. A suggested gradation, appropriate for the state of New Jersey, is shown below. The frontage dimensions and the number of categories can be adjusted within reason to correspond to regional and local patterns.

## INTENSITY OF DEVELOPMENT

|  | *Low* | *Medium* | *High* |
|---|---|---|---|
| Lot | more | 75 | less |
| Frontage | than | to | than |
| (in feet): | 150 | 150 | 75 |

*PERFORMANCE APPROACH*

Given the number of factors influencing cartway width, it is not surprising to find in a search of the literature a considerable variety in recommendations (see Exhibit 4-1). In general, national sources and model codes allow a range of dimensions, with the determination of cartway width made on a case-by-case basis. This performance approach is recommended in a study of standards published by the Planning Advisory Service of the American Planning Association: "Expected average daily traffic, the design and layout of dwelling units, whether on-street parking will be provided, and other factors related to street design should be taken into account."[20] Thus, cartway dimensions will vary for each street in the street hierarchy, and often within each street category as well.

*RESIDENTIAL ACCESS STREETS*

Widths recommended for residential access streets are a good example of the range of alternatives, depending on need and function. By using the performance approach, the determination of cartway width can be made on a case-by-case basis. Bucks County's model ordinance, for example, specifies widths from 16 to 26 feet for residential access streets depending on the situation.

Cartway widths of 16 feet (two 8-foot moving lanes) are proposed for subdivisions with lots five acres or larger and where no on-street parking is required; 18 feet (two 9-foot moving lanes) for

## EXHIBIT 4–1

### COMPARISON OF CARTWAY AND RIGHT-OF-WAY
### RESIDENTIAL STREET STANDARDS FROM NATIONAL SOURCES,
### MODEL ORDINANCES, AND LOCAL ORDINANCES
(in feet)

| SUBDIVISION AND SITE PLAN LITERATURE | RESIDENTIAL ACCESS STREETS | | SUBCOLLECTORS | | COLLECTORS | |
|---|---|---|---|---|---|---|
| | Cartway | Right-of-Way | Cartway | Right-of-Way | Cartway | Right-of-Way |
| **National Sources** (Selected) | | | | | | |
| DeChiara & Koppelman | 36 | 50 | 44 | 64 | 60 | 80 |
| HUD Affordable* | 32 | 50 | NA | NA | 36 | 50 |
| ITE | 22–36[a] | 50–60 | NA | NA | 36–40 | 70 |
| Moskowitz & Lindbloom | 28–30 | 50 | NA | NA | 40 | 60 |
| NAHB | 20 | b | 26 | b | 36 | b |
| National Bureau of Standards** | 20–26 | NA | 26–32 | NA | 28–36 | NA |
| ULI, ASCE, NAHB | 20 | NA | 26 | NA | 36 | NA |
| **Model Ordinances** (Selected) | | | | | | |
| Brough | 20–24[c] | 40 | 26 | 50 | 34 | 50 |
| Bucks Co. | 16–26[d] | 50 | 20–36[d] | 50 | 20–24[d] | 60 |
| Freilich & Levi | 20–32[e] | 50–60[f] | 22–32[e] | 50–70[f] | 24–44[e] | 60–80[f] |
| Indiana | 18[g] | 40–50[h] | 26[g] | 50–60[h] | 33[g] | 60–65[h] |
| Oregon | 28 | 50 | 36 | 60 | 36–48 | 60–80 |
| Jackson, MS | 20–27[i] | 50 | 20–30[i] | 50 | 22–36[i] | 60 |
| **Local Ordinances** (Selected) | | | | | | |
| Dover, NJ | 22–34[j] | 50 | 34–42 | 60 | 50 | 70 |
| Berkeley, NJ | 30 | 50 | 30 | 50 | 30 | 60 |
| Hamilton, NJ | 34 | 50 | 40 | 60 | 44 | 70 |
| Montgomery, NJ | 30 | 50 | 36 | 56 | 54 | 66 |
| South Brunswick, NJ | 30–36 | 50–60 | 40 | 66 | 52 | 72 |
| Wall, NJ | 36 | 60 | 36 | 60 | 40 | 70 |
| Keene, NH | 24 | 50 | 24 | 54 | 30 | 60 |
| Dade Co., FL | NA | 45–50 | NA | 50–60 | NA | 70 |
| Beaumont, TX | 26 | 50 | 36 | 60 | 36–60 | 60–90 |

## EXHIBIT 4-1 (continued)

NA = Not Available

\* Reduced standards in Riverside County, California, designed to facilitate construction of affordable housing, used as an example.

\*\* Standards represent a synthesis of those commonly recommended by NAHB, ITE, AASHTO, and HUD.

  a) Range in cartway widths based on such factors as development density and terrain classification, with narrowest widths specified for low development density on level land and widest widths specified for high development density on hilly land.

  b) NAHB recommends that rights-of-way should be established at pavement edge and include 2 feet on either side and sidewalks and drainage swales where applicable.

  c) Narrower width is for a minor road serving not more than 9 dwelling units and up to 75 trips per day; wider width is for a local street serving at least 10 but not more than 25 dwelling units and between 75 and 200 trips per day. Brough's ordinance also allows an 18-foot cartway with a 45-foot right-of-way for residential access streets constructed with 6-foot wide shoulders and drainage swales.

  d) Differences in cartway widths based on density of development and whether parking is permitted on street. The lower the density of development, the narrower the paved surface. On-street parking necessitates wider roadways.

  e) Cartway width based on density of development. Higher density areas require wider paved surface. Addition of curbs as opposed to shoulders adds to cartway width.

  f) Right-of-way based on density of development. High-density areas require wider rights-of-way than low-density areas.

  g) Cartway width does not include curb and gutter. In urban areas combined 2-foot minimum required on each side.

  h) Right-of-way based on location in urban or rural areas. Rights-of-way in rural areas are wider.

  i) Cartway width based on location in urban or rural areas. Cartway widths in urban, higher-density areas are wider.

  j) 22 feet is the standard for one-way street; 34 feet is the standard for a two-way street.

*Sources:*

NATIONAL SOURCES: NAHB, *Subdivision Regulation Handbook,* 1978; DeChiara and Koppelman, *Urban Planning and Design Criteria,* 1982; National Bureau of Standards, *A Review of Standards and Common Practices in Building Site Regulation,* 1981; ULI, ASCE, NAHB, *Residential Streets,* 1976; ITE, *Recommended Guidelines for Subdivision Streets,* 1984; HUD, *Affordable Housing,* 1982; HUD and NAHB Research Foundation, *Building Affordable Homes: A Cost-Savings Guide for Builder/Developers,* 1982; Moskowitz and Lindbloom, *A Guide for Residential Design Review,* 1976.

MODEL ORDINANCES: Brough, *A Unified Development Ordinance,* 1985; Bucks Co., *Performance Streets,* 1980; Freilich and Levi, *Model Subdivision Regulations,* 1975; Indiana: William R. Patterson, *Model County Subdivision Regulations,* 1983; Oregon: University of Oregon, *A Model Land Subdivision Format,* 1979; Jackson, MS: S. Smith, *Subdivision Guidelines for the Jackson Metropolitan Area,* 1973.

LOCAL ORDINANCES: Dover, NJ: *Land Use and Development Regulations,* 1980; Berkeley, NJ: *Land Subdivision Ordinance,* 1977; Hamilton, NJ: *Land Development Ordinance,* 1980; Montgomery, NJ: *Land Subdivision Ordinance,* 1976; South Brunswick, NJ: *Municipal Land Use Ordinance,* 1979; Wall, NJ: *Land Subdivision Ordinance,* 1979; Keene, NH: *Planning Board Regulations Concerning the Subdivision of Land,* 1982; Dade Co., FL: *Chapter 28 Subdivision Code,* 1983; Beaumont, TX: *Subdivision Regulations,* 1983. (See bibliography for complete citation.)

lot widths of 100 feet or greater and no parking; and 26 feet (two 8-foot parking lanes and one 10-foot moving lane) for lot widths less than 100 feet.[21] Similarly, ITE recommends cartway widths ranging from 22 to 36 feet for residential access streets depending on density, with wider widths required for higher-density developments. ITE adds another variable as well in calculating cartway width: classification of terrain into "level," "rolling," and "hilly" categories. As terrain becomes more difficult, curves increase and wider cartway areas are recommended. Thus, a residential access street serving a low-density development in a hilly terrain would require a wider pavement surface than one serving the same development on level ground.[22]

**Rutgers model ordinance.** As discussed in the commentary, the Rutgers model ordinance also uses the performance approach in specifying cartway widths for residential access streets, with widths varying from 20 to 28 feet according to development intensity and parking and curb requirements.

### RESIDENTIAL SUBCOLLECTORS AND COLLECTORS

Like cartway width recommendations for residential access streets, those for subcollectors and collectors vary. Typically, a range of dimensions is specified allowing a choice of appropriate cartway width depending on intensity of development and on-street parking requirements. For subcollectors, recommended widths range from 20 feet to 44 feet; for collectors, they range from 20 feet to 60 feet (see Exhibit 4-1).

**Rutgers model ordinance.** For subcollectors, cartway width standards range from 20 feet, situations where there is low development intensity, to 36 feet, where development intensity is high and parking is permitted on both sides of the street. For collectors, the Rutgers ordinance requires a cartway width of 24 feet, allowing for two 12-foot lanes. No parking is permitted on collectors, which are designed to facilitate traffic flow.

### SPECIAL PURPOSE STREETS

Cartway width recommendations from the national sources for some categories of special purpose streets also vary, although some do not. *Rural residential lanes,* for example, will have very

little traffic—sources agree that narrow cartways are adequate for this street category. The Rutgers ordinance specifies 18-foot cartway widths for rural residential lanes.

Recommended cartway widths for *alleys*, however, do vary— from a low of 12 feet in Bucks County's ordinance to 20 feet in Freilich and Levi's ordinance. The Rutgers ordinance assumes two nine-foot lanes for a cartway width of 18 feet. If the alley is a one-way loop, however, a narrower cartway is permissible.

Cartway widths for *cul-de-sac* stems depend on their classification in the street hierarchy. Residential access cul-de-sacs will be narrower than those classified as subcollectors. For the *cul-de-sac turnaround,* cartway width depends on the radius, with sources recommending it be no larger than necessary to permit the free turning of the largest vehicles regularly servicing the neighborhood. Larger paved areas are unsightly and will cost the municipality more to maintain. A general recommendation is that the radius be a few feet larger than the turning radius of a typical garbage truck or fire engine—or from 28½ feet to 35 feet. The

**Photo 4–3.** *Excessive cul-de-sac cartway widths result in an unsightly paved expanse.*

**Photo 4–4.** *An island improving the appearance of a cul-de-sac.*

turnaround diameter should therefore be no less than 70 feet for a complete turn without backing up. Larger diameters do allow more space for maneuvering, but diameters in excess of 80 feet are wasteful.

A review of the literature shows that most references recommend a cartway radius for round turnarounds of 40 feet (ITE; DeChiara and Koppelman; Jackson, MS; and Oregon), although others recommend less (Freilich and Levi require a minimum radius of 25 to 30 feet; Bucks County recommends 38 feet; and AASHTO recommends 30 feet for a turnaround in residential areas).[23]

The T-type or hammerhead cul-de-sac uses less land area than the standard cul-de-sac, but sources warn that this configuration should be used only in very low traffic situations because of hazardous backing movements required for turning.[24]

The Rutgers model ordinance stipulates a 40-foot turnaround. This minimum requirement should, however, also be regarded as a maximum requirement.

Cartway widths for *marginal access streets* will depend on classification. However, because lot frontage is restricted on one side of the street, there will be less demand for on-street parking, and cartway width can be reduced. For *divided streets*, cartway width also depends on classification and should be applied to the aggregate dimensions of the street segments. For *stub streets*, the cartway width will also depend on classification in the street hierarchy. If the stub street is likely to remain unconnected for a lengthy period, a municipality could require that stub streets with five or more houses be provided with temporary turnarounds paved to an outside radius of 35 feet.

## Curbs and Gutters

Curbs and gutters serve a number of important functions. However, because curbing is expensive and can aggravate storm

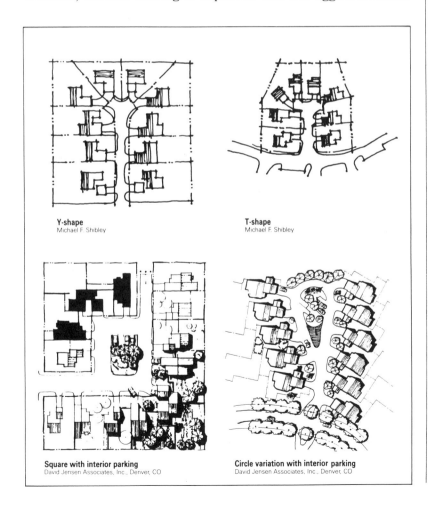

**Y-shape**
Michael F. Shibley

**T-shape**
Michael F. Shibley

**Square with interior parking**
David Jensen Associates, Inc., Denver, CO

**Circle variation with interior parking**
David Jensen Associates, Inc., Denver, CO

**Illustration 4–5.** *Cul-de-sac design options.*

water runoff problems, many sources recommend using alternatives. The various functions of curbs and gutters and alternatives to using curbs are discussed in the sections below.[25]

*FUNCTIONS*

**Drainage control.** Curbs are often used as channels for storm water as part of a development's storm water management system. Since storm water runoff increases with impervious cover, high-density developments, in particular, use curbs and gutters as part of a closed, or piped, system of storm water management. Since curbing also intensifies runoff, however, every opportunity for a natural drainage system should be encouraged.

**Delineation of pavement edge.** Curbs serve to delineate the vehicular from pedestrian area. Particularly for asphalt surfaces at night, roadways without curbing are poorly defined. Curbs encourage vehicles to stay within the cartway width and help direct vehicles around curves. Curbs also delineate the pavement edge within which parking is allowed. They cannot, however, be justified as a safety barrier to protect pedestrians, because in most cases vehicles striking curbs will mount them out of control.[26] Alternatives to curbs for the purpose of delineating pavement edge include railings, bollards, wheel stops, and edge plantings.

**Protection of pavement edge.** Because curbs limit encroachment of vehicles on the pavement edge, cartway erosion is minimized and unraveling of the pavement edge is reduced—particularly where an asphalt surface is used. However, instead of using curbs to reduce unraveling of the cartway edge, unraveling can be avoided by extending the base course at least 18 to 24 inches beyond the top layer of asphalt.

*MINIMUM REQUIREMENTS*

There is a debate in the literature about curb and gutter requirements, with some studies recommending minimizing the use of curbs and gutters.[27] In residential subdivisions with very large lots, curbs may not be necessary. In fact, where a specific site permits a natural, open drainage system of swales and recharge and/or retention basins, curbing is not only unnecessary—it may actually be a hindrance to the storm water management system.

Other studies, however, point out disadvantages to the complete elimination of curbs and gutters.[28] These drawbacks include pavement unraveling, poorly defined roadways causing hazardous conditions, and lack of drainage control, etc. Curbs and gutters are especially important in intensive development where "heavy use may erode the planted area at the edge of the pavement."[29] They also protect the pavement from unraveling along parking lanes. Curbing is also recommended on higher order streets. The higher traffic levels and increased speed on collector streets make the clear delineation of the pavement edge necessary for safe movement of traffic. Consequently, most municipalities will require curbs except for large-lot developments.

The Rutgers ordinance bases its curb standards on a performance approach, to be determined on a case-by-case basis. Curbs are, however, required where necessary for drainage control and at medium and high development intensities when there is on-street parking.

*CURB TYPE*

The curb most commonly required by municipalities is a 6″ × 8″ × 18″ solid line (vertical) concrete curb. However, some ordinances require integral curb and gutter, and others require, or offer as an option, granite or Belgian block curb. The rolled or mountable curb, a variation of the integral curb and gutter, has been advocated as cost-effective. However, the rolled or mountable curb is criticized for certain characteristics: its drainage handling capacity is poor compared to that of a vertical curb, especially when used in areas of moderate-to-severe slopes.[30] In addition, there is dispute concerning the cost efficiency of the rolled or mountable curbs. While some sources suggest that construction costs of the different curb types are comparable,[31] others maintain that the rolled curb is somewhat less costly.[32] When vertical curbs are installed, however, if any changes are made such as in driveway locations or from one-car to two-car driveways, the vertical curb must be removed. When mountable curbs are used, location and width of driveways are not important. (See Exhibit A-1 in the model ordinance for examples of curb types.)

As long as the curb type accommodates the system of drainage proposed, there should be flexibility in the choice of curbing. Communities should allow the most economical curb

**Illustration 4–6.** *Types of curb— vertical and mountable.*

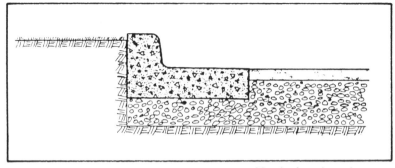

Vertical curb and gutter

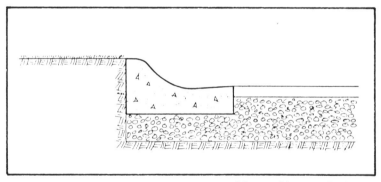

Mountable or rolled curb

**Photo 4–5.** *Deteriorated asphalt curbing.*

types, but asphalt curbing is not recommended as it quickly disintegrates. Developers should also be permitted to install more costly alternatives (i.e., to install Belgian block for marketing purposes) provided drainage constraints are satisfied.

All concrete used in any subdivision or site improvement for curb purposes should be prepared in accordance with the requirements of the Standard Specifications by class of concrete.

## Shoulders

*SHOULDERS DEFINED*

When present, a shoulder is that portion of the roadway contiguous with the traveled way that can be used to accommodate stopped vehicles, for emergency use, and for lateral support of the pavement. It also provides an additional width of pavement, allowing a driver meeting or passing other vehicles to drive on the edge

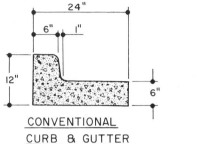

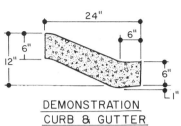

CONVENTIONAL
CURB & GUTTER

DEMONSTRATION
CURB & GUTTER

**Illustration 4–7.** *Specifications and cost savings of "conventional" versus innovative ("demonstration") curbs and gutters.*

```
Curb Cost Comparison

                        As Built   Comparison   Savings

2 ft. vertical curb,
   6 in. high           $------     $46,656     $46,656
2 ft. roll curb          36,288      ------     (36,288)
5 ft. wide valley gutter  4,350       4,350       ------

      TOTAL            $40,638     $51,006     $10,368

      COST PER UNIT   $   865*    $ 1,342**   $    477

 *47 Units
**38 Units
```

of the roadway without leaving the surface. Shoulders also provide space for pedestrians and bicycle riders in areas where there are no sidewalks.[33] In addition, shoulders may be required for storm water management or road stabilization.[34]

### MINIMUM REQUIREMENTS

The national literature points out that shoulders may vary in width from 4 feet or more on minor roads, where the shoulder is not surfaced or the surfacing is applied along the entire road bed, to about 12 feet on major roads, where the entire shoulder may be stabilized or paved. Shoulders may be surfaced in whole or in part to provide a better all-weather load support.

A vehicle stopped on the shoulder should clear the pavement edge by at least one foot. Accordingly, this has led to the adoption of 10 feet as the standard shoulder width that should be provided along roadways, such as arterials, which carry substantial traffic

**Photo 4–6.** *Angled Belgian block curbing.*

**Photo 4–7.** *Rolled curbing, Levittown, Pennsylvania.*

volume. In difficult terrain and on low-volume streets, sources note that shoulders of this width may not be feasible or desirable. The minimum usable shoulder width that should be considered for lower-order streets is four feet.

Although, ideally, shoulders should be wide enough for a vehicle to be driven completely off the traveled way, sources recommend that narrow shoulders are better than none at all. Where narrow shoulders are provided, even though a vehicle making an emergency stop may occupy 1 to 4 feet of the cartway, the width of the remaining pavement should be adequate to allow vehicles safe passage.

*MATERIALS*

Materials used to surface shoulders include gravel, crushed stone, bituminous treatments, and other forms of pavement. Bucks

Photo 4-8. *The absence of curbing complements a natural appearance.*

County, citing AASHO, recommends stabilized turf shoulders where shoulders are required:

*Turf has the advantage of requiring little maintenance other than mowing, has a pleasing appearance, does not invite use as a moving lane, and maintains the narrow appearance of the street which in turn tends to discourage speeding.*[35]

## Sidewalks and Graded Areas

*SIDEWALKS DEFINED*

Sidewalks are surfaced or leveled areas, usually parallel to and separate from the street, used as pedestrian walkways. The primary function of sidewalks is to provide for safe pedestrian movement.[36] In the typical subdivision, pedestrians consist of chil-

**Photo 4–9.** *Sidewalks can provide an important benefit to pedestrians. Highland Park, New Jersey.*

dren walking to and from school and neighborhood activities, and adults walking to and from neighborhood shopping and transit stops. Sidewalks are also used by children as play areas—one of the most important and sometimes overlooked of sidewalk functions.

*MINIMUM REQUIREMENTS*

Increasingly in the national literature there has been a tendency to view sidewalks as an expensive luxury, and their inclusion in subdivisions is no longer as automatic as it once was. Critics point to sidewalks as raising development costs and increasing impervious area. Some would eliminate sidewalks under almost all circumstances; some, like NAHB, would require sidewalks only within ¼ mile of major pedestrian generators.[37]

This is, perhaps, the extreme view. Other sources point to the benefits of sidewalks, and conclude they should be required components of any development:

*Apart from the need for sidewalks for circulation and safety, sidewalks can be an important element in the recreational system of a community. They serve as walking and hiking trails for all age groups . . . and are also the primary informal and unsupervised recreational system for preschoolers. . . . [S]idewalks should be required as part of any large-scale residential development.*[38]

Lynch and Hack concur, especially on the importance of sidewalks as play areas: "Sidewalks are a more important recreational facility than playgrounds."[39]

These divergent views on the need for sidewalks suggest that the best approach—and the one followed by the Rutgers model ordinance—is a performance approach, with the need for sidewalks determined on a case-by-case basis, depending on street classification, development intensity, probable volume of pedestrian traffic, the proximity of schools and shopping, school bus stops, and relation to population areas. As densities increase, more pedestrian movement is to be expected, and sidewalks should be required. Similarly, as traffic volume and speeds increase up the street hierarchy, there is more need for a separate pedestrian way. Additional factors such as the existing sidewalk system and probable future development should also be con-

**Photo 4–10.** *Example of a narrower (twenty-four foot) cartway with sidewalk on one side of the street.*

sidered in determining whether a specific development requires sidewalks. If sidewalks are not required in the initial construction of a subdivision, a possible course of action would be for a municipality to reserve right-of-way space to build them in the future.

*LOCATION*

In general, sidewalks are located in the street right-of-way, on one or both sides, parallel to the street. This alignment should be allowed to vary in order to preserve topographic and natural features or to provide visual interest.[40] The sidewalk edge closest to the curb is usually separated by a planting area of some specified width. Along cul-de-sac streets, sidewalks sometimes abut the curb in order to reduce right-of-way dimensions.

In cluster subdivisions, the traditional placement of sidewalks in the street right-of-way has been replaced by a flexible pedestrian circulation system connecting individual dwelling units with other units, off-street parking, the open space system, and recreational facilities. There are numerous advantages to this layout: 1) it conforms better to topographical features; 2) because it is separated from traffic, it is safer and more pleasant; 3) pedestrian access from origin to destination may be more direct; 4) there is less site disturbance and impervious cover; and 5) costs are reduced. Additional sidewalks along subdivision streets, however, may also be necessary in cluster developments for access to schools, bus stops, shopping, or other facilities.

**Illustration 4–8.** *Illustration of a path system.*

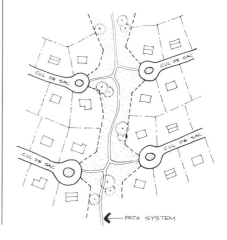

**Illustration 4–9.** *Innovative walkway system, town of Seaside, Florida. Walks on both sides of every street and footpaths through mid-blocks make walking more convenient than driving. Public squares and a boardwalk along the beach complete the pedestrian areas.*

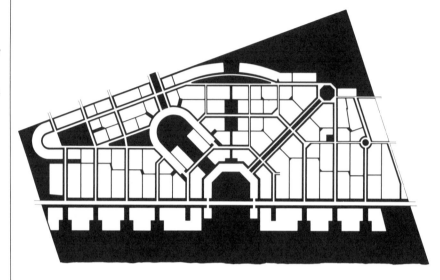

Increasingly, planners and others are recommending that more flexible sidewalk requirements should be considered in conventional subdivision development, as in cluster developments, to encourage the construction of a more functional and usable comprehensive system. For example, where sidewalks are required, the sidewalk system could be permitted to meander through the development within prescribed sidewalk easements. In cases where there are long blocks, pedestrian ways should be provided midway through the block. In rural or low-density areas, sidewalks, if required at all, could be restricted to one side of the street only.

### SIDEWALK CONSTRUCTION

Sources generally require that sidewalks in residential areas be 4 feet wide—a width adequate to provide two pedestrian lanes or one pedestrian and one bicycle lane[41]—and 4 inches thick, except at driveway crossings where the thickness is increased to 6 inches. At vehicular crossings, sidewalks should be reinforced with welded wire fabric mesh or an equivalent.[42] Handicap ramps are usually required at intersections in accordance with local or state regulations.

Other widths may be considered, however, depending on the circumstances. Narrower sidewalks may be adequate in low-density

**Photo 4–11.** *"Natural" path system.*

areas; wider sidewalks may be warranted along collector and arterial streets or near pedestrian generators, schools, employment centers, or where parked cars overhang the sidewalk.

Finally, the literature points to the variety of paving materials available for sidewalk surfaces. Pedestrian ways may be constructed with bituminous concrete, porous paving material, gravel, crushed stone, or other suitable surface.

**Photo 4–12.** *Pedestrian walkway.*

## Bikeways

### BIKEWAYS DEFINED

A bikeway can be defined as a pathway designed to be used by bikers.[43] Although ideally bikeways are separated from streets and sidewalks, they can take one of the following forms: 1) *bicycle paths* designed specifically to satisfy the physical requirements of bicycling; 2) *bicycle lanes* at the edge of streets reserved and marked for the exclusive use of bicycles; and 3) *shared or bicycle-compatible roadways* designed to accommodate the shared use of the roadway by bicycles and motor vehicles.[44] Essentially, a bicycle-compatible roadway is either a roadway with low traffic volume, a roadway with moderate volume and speed and having a 15-foot-wide lane width in each direction, or a roadway with high traffic volume and speed and having a paved shoulder. Bikeways can also share sidewalks with pedestrians, but this practice is recommended only where pedestrian traffic is light.

### MINIMUM REQUIREMENTS

National sources recommend that separate bicycle paths should be required only when they have been specified as part of a municipality's adopted master plan. Most sources recognize that high land and construction costs make bicycle lanes and shared roadways a more feasible alternative than separate bike paths. Residential streets are usually satisfactory as bikeways because of low traffic volumes.[45] Designated bike lanes are recommended where the flow of cyclists is likely to be heavy, such as near schools, commercial areas, employment centers, or railroad stations. Many cluster developments include combination bicycle/ jogging paths as part of an amenities package aimed at attracting buyers.

**Photo 4–13.** *Bicycle path along C&O Canal. Washington, Maryland.*

*LOCATION*

The location of bikeways depends to some extent on their purpose. In planning for bicycling commuting, for example, reasonably direct routes should be provided. Recreational bike trails, on the other hand, often follow scenic routes through parks, along canals, or along the right-of-way of utility easements or abandoned railroads. In most cases, however, bikeways will be part of the road system. When a bicycle path uses the street right-of-way and parallels the roadway, it should be located as far from the traveled way as possible to minimize possible conflicts. Minimum distances of 20 feet, and preferably 30 feet, between the path and cartway are recommended, unless a natural barrier, such as a ditch or earth berm, is present.[46] When the minimum distance requirements are insufficient, hedges, fences, or guardrails can be installed to provide some protection for the cyclist, although, realistically speaking, costs make such wide right-of-way and improvements unlikely.

Bicycle lanes are typically located in the outside lane of a roadway, adjacent to the curb or shoulder. When on-street parking is permitted, however, two placements are possible: 1) the bicycle lane may be immediately adjacent to the curb beyond the parking lane; or 2) the bicycle lane may be located between the parking lane and the outer lane of moving vehicles. In the first placement, some type of curb should be provided between the parking lane and bicycle lane to prevent encroachment. This arrangement may, however, pose a possible conflict between bicyclist and pedestrians wishing to reach parked vehicles. The preferred arrangement when on-street parking is permitted is to place the bicycle lane between the parking lane and the outer lane of moving vehicles.[47] Bicyclists, however, should be alert to the hazard of opening car doors.

Bicycle lanes along roadways can be delineated by a number of pavement markings: striping, full-width pavement coloring or painting, pavement markers (dots), or reflectorized raised pavement markings.[48] Raised reflectors, however, are not recommended because they are a surface irregularity that can be hazardous to bicycle traffic.[49] Curbs, which are sometimes used as a means of controlling vehicle encroachment, are not recommended either, also for safety reasons and because they obstruct maintenance operations.

Although separate bicycle lanes have a number of advantages for areas with heavy bicycle traffic—they improve traffic flow and minimize bicycle–vehicle conflicts, for example—experienced cyclists often prefer riding in outside traffic lanes to riding in separate bicycle lanes.[50] This is because cars sweep the cartway free of debris—sand, gravel, glass—which is particularly hazardous to cyclists and causes bicycle accidents.

*CONSTRUCTION DETAILS*

## Bicycle Paths

Dimensions and construction specifications of bicycle paths should be based on the following considerations: 1) number and type of users, and 2) location and purpose of the bicycle path. Specific recommendations in the literature often vary. For example, recommendations for the pavement width of a two-way bike path range from 6.5 feet (DeChiara and Koppelman) to 12 feet (Lynch and Hack). AASHTO's *Guide for the Development of New Bicycle Facilities* recommends a minimum 8-foot paved width for two-way bike traffic, plus a 2-foot shoulder adjacent to each side, graded and clear of obstructions.

Bicycle path construction specifications, such as for surface and sub-base paving materials, grade, and turning radii, can be found in numerous references, including AASHTO's *Guide for the Development of New Bicycle Facilities*, NJDOT's *Bicycle Compatible Roadways*, Moskowitz and Lindbloom's *A Guide for Residential Design Review*, and DeChiara and Koppelman's *Urban Planning and Design Criteria*.[51]

## Bicycle Lanes

Bicycle lanes for exclusive or preferential use by bicyclists are usually on the outside edge of the roadway. Dimensions should be sufficient to allow for the safe movement of bicycle traffic— AASHTO suggests a 4-foot width for one-way travel. Pavement surface is generally constructed to the same specifications as for the entire pavement. For additional design standards, AASHTO's *Guide* can be used as a reference.

## Bicycle-Compatible Roadways

In the design of bicycle-compatible roadways, dimensions of cartway moving lanes are important because they must be wide enough to accommodate both vehicular and bicycle traffic. Although 12-foot lanes are assumed, the cartway width of lower-order residential streets (residential access and subcollector streets) should be adequate for shared use of the road by bicycles and vehicles because of low traffic volumes.[52] At the collector-street level, 15 feet of paved surface in the outside lane (cartway lane alone or usable shoulder included) is required for shared use of the roadway.

Extremely important in the construction of bicycle-compatible roadways is the installation of "bicycle-safe" drainage grates rather than stream-flow drainage grates which can trap the front wheel of a bicycle. This type of grate should be required on all residential streets.

## Utility and Shade Tree Areas

In addition to curbs, shoulders, and sidewalks, there are two other components of the right-of-way: 1) utility areas, and 2) shade tree areas. Utility areas (or strips) contain underground utilities, such as sewers, water, and telephone, electric, and cable lines. Although some utility companies require that utility lines be placed under the cartway, it is usually better to place them under a planted rather than under a paved area. This location facilitates maintenance and replacement of aging utility systems. If there is a graded area provided along the roadway, the utilities may be placed there, making separate utility areas unnecessary. Utility areas are located within the right-of-way on both sides and parallel to the street.

Shade tree areas provide space for the planting of street trees. They are usually located within the right-of-way of both sides and parallel to the street. An alternative placement for shade trees is outside the public right-of-way.

Separate areas should be provided for the utility and shade tree strips because problems arise when they occupy the same space: tree roots can damage utility lines, and utility line maintenance can kill trees. While separate areas must be provided, the specific location of each can vary. For example, the tree strip may be located immediately adjacent to the curb between the curb and sidewalk, or it may be beyond the sidewalk at the far edge of the right-of-way or on private property. The exact location is a matter of municipal preferences and local practice. Trees planted in a strip next to the street ultimately provide a tree canopy shading the street, yet depending on the tree species, when the trees mature their roots can buckle the sidewalk. Trees planted on private property can save a municipality on maintenance, but forcing an uncooperative homeowner to care for the trees can sometimes be a problem. Whatever the placement, both utility and shade trees strips should be planted with grass or covered with suitable ground cover.

**Photo 4–14.** *Mature tree buckling a sidewalk. Highland Park, New Jersey.*

## Street Right-of-Way

*STREET RIGHT-OF-WAY DEFINED*

The right-of-way is the total public strip of land within which there is public control and common right of passage and within which all pavement and utility lines are located. Rights-of-way must be wide enough to contain: 1) cartway; 2) curbing; 3) shoulders; 4) sidewalks; 5) utility strip; and 6) shade tree strip. Some of the elements may not be present or required in all cases. Utilities, for example, may be placed in utility easements located through a development, instead of along the street alignment. Sidewalks and bicycle paths may meander through a site, independent of the road system. Usually, however, the right-of-way is designed to provide for the elements enumerated above, unless separate areas are provided.

*MINIMUM REQUIREMENTS*

A review of the national literature shows that rights-of-way vary according to street hierarchy, with the following minimum rights-of-way recommended most often: 16 to 20 feet for alleys, 50 to 60 feet for residential access streets and subcollectors, and 60 to 70 feet for collectors.[53] For cul-de-sac turnarounds, sources recommend minimum rights-of-way radii of 45 feet (DeChiara and Koppelman) and 50 feet (ITE and Oregon).

Besides street hierarchy, other variables may also be included when determining right-of-way. For example, ITE and Freilich and Levi both include development intensity as a factor in right-of-way width,[54] and in Indiana's model ordinance, a road's classification as urban or rural helps determine its right-of-way. In line with its performance approach, in Bucks County's model ordinance, the required right-of-way may be reduced or increased on a case-by-case basis.

The right-of-way requirements in the Rutgers model ordinance vary according to the street hierarchy, with the narrowest width usually prescribed for residential access streets, and the widest specification for higher-order streets. Intensity of development is another factor that is considered in determining right-of-way dimensions—at higher development intensities, on-street parking is required, which in turn necessitates wider rights-of-way of connecting streets must correspond across subdivisions. These right-of-way dimensions are summarized in Exhibit 4-2.

**EXHIBIT 4–2**

**RIGHT-OF-WAY COMPONENTS AND DIMENSIONS**

| Street Category [a] | Cartway Width | Curb (0') or Shoulder* | Other Right-of-Way Components (Sidewalk or Graded Area and Utility and Shade Tree Areas*) | Sum of Dimensions of Right-of-Way Components* | Total Right-of-Way Width* |
|---|---|---|---|---|---|
| **RESIDENTIAL ACCESS** | | | | | |
| Low intensity | 20' | Not Req. (0') | 12' | 32' | 40' |
| Medium intensity | 28' | Curb (0') | 12' | 40' | 40' |
| High intensity | | | | | |
|   On-street parking | 28' | Curb (0') | 20' | 48' | 50' |
|   Off-street parking | 20' | Not Req. (0') | 20' | 40' | 40' |
| **RESIDENTIAL SUBCOLLECTOR** | | | | | |
| Low intensity | 20' | Not Req. (0') | 12' | 32' | 40' |
| Medium intensity | 28' | Curb (0') | 20' | 48' | 50' |
| High intensity | | | | | |
|   One-side parking | 28' | Curb (0') | 20' | 48' | 50' |
|   Two-side parking | 36' | Curb (0') | 20' | 56' | 60' |
|   Off-street parking | 22' | Curb (0') or | 20' | 42' | 40' |
| | | Shoulder (8') | 24' | 46' | 50' |
| **RESIDENTIAL COLLECTOR** | | | | | |
| Low intensity | 24' | Not Req. (0') | 12' | 36' | 40' |
| Medium intensity | 24' | Curb (0') or | 20' | 44' | 50' |
| | | Shoulder (8') | 24' | 48' | 50' |
| High intensity | 24' | Curb (0') or | 20' | 44' | 50' |
| | | Shoulder (8') | 24' | 48' | 50' |
| **SPECIAL PURPOSE** | | | | | |
| Rural residential lane | 18' | Not Req. (0') | 8' | 26' | 40' |
| Alley | 18' | Not Req. (0') | 4' | 22' | 22' |
| Cul-de-sac [b] | | | | | |
| Marginal access [c] | | | | | |
| Divided street [d] | | | | | |
| Stub street [e] | | | | | |

Not Req. = Not Required (curb or shoulder)

\* See Exhibit 5 in the Rutgers model ordinance for details

a–e See Exhibit 4 in the Rutgers model ordinance

## Other Street Dimensions

Other street standards typically specified in a subdivision and site plan ordinance include street grade, specifications for intersections, pavement section standards, and other engineering critiera.

*STREET GRADE*

Street grade standards are often expressed as a range of minimum and maximum allowable grades. The minimum grade usually permitted in ordinances is 0.5 percent, which is the minimum grade at which water drains off a road.[55] Topographical conditions in some locations make 0.5 percent the only practicable grade that can be used. However, because ponding occurs as grades become flatter, roads should be constructed at grades in excess of 0.5 percent where topographical conditions permit. If streets must be constructed at this grade, they should be closely monitored and construction techniques used to avoid ponding.

Recommendations for the maximum grade are generally based on road classification, with flatter grades required for roads with higher traffic volumes and speeds.[56] Maximum road-grade requirements must also reflect winter conditions. Severe icing, for example, may limit the maximum allowable street grade to 8 to 10 percent.[57] Terrain can also be a factor in determining grade. As ITE points out: "The maximum permissible grade represents a compromise between construction costs and road safety. This allowable grade must increase as difficulty of terrain increases."[58]

In the Rutgers model ordinance, street grade requirements depend on street hierarchy, with 0.5 percent the minimum allowed. However, at this grade, curbs and gutters may be advisable. The maximum street grade also varies depending on road classification, speed, winter conditions, and terrain characteristics.

*INTERSECTIONS*

### Minimum Intersection Angle

Streets should be laid out to intersect as nearly as possible at right angles, and multi-leg intersections (over four) should be avoided. Studies have shown that skewed intersections generally have higher accident rates than those intersecting at 90 degrees.[59] Multi-leg intersections are also undesirable for traffic control and safety reasons. The model ordinance prohibits angles less than 75°.

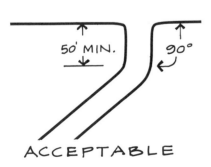

**Illustration 4–10.** *Intersection angles.*

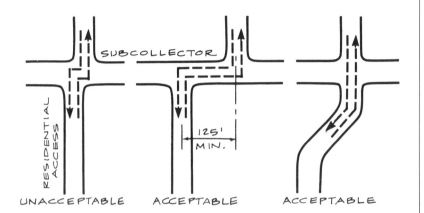

**Illustration 4–11.** *Intersection spacing on a subcollector.*

## Minimum Centerline Offset of Adjacent Intersections

To avoid dangerous jogs, proposed streets that intersect another street should be laid out to intersect directly opposite each other or to be offset by a minimum distance. As long as an adequate offset between adjacent intersections is provided, T-type intersections are highly recommended in residential subdivisions, because they are far safer than cross-type intersections.[60] ITE and numerous other sources recommend offsets of at least 125 feet between centerlines for residential access streets, with increased offsets recommended for higher-order streets.[61] The model ordinance incorporates these recommendations in its regulations.

## Minimum Curb Radius

Minimum curb radius standards must strike a balance between overly generous and substandard curb radii. The former encourage higher turning speeds, increase paving costs, and increase the area required for pedestrians to traverse; the latter result in unnecessary lane encroachment and higher accident potential.[62] Bucks County's model ordinance recommends a curb radius between 5 and 15 feet, depending on classification of the street. These standards are less than those recommended by other sources, and would appear to be inadequate, particularly in view of the narrow cartway widths recommended by Bucks County. ITE recommends radii of 20 to 30 feet depending on road classification. A 20-foot radius, for two residential access streets, allows a car to turn without lane encroachment on a "typical width street" (cartway width recommended by ITE for streets in this classification is 28-34 feet); it will also allow a garbage truck or moving van to turn with wide swings.[63] With narrower cartway width, increased curb radii are necessary. The Rutgers model ordinance uses a performance approach in setting curb radii requirements which range from 20 to 35 feet depending on street hierarchy.

## Grade

Intersections should be designed with a flat grade, but in hilly areas this may not be feasible. In cases where terrain makes it necessary, the allowable grade may be increased. The approach grade within 50 feet of an intersection should also be specified—4 percent is the maximum recommended by ITE, and only in hilly terrain.[64]

## Sight Triangles

Intersections of local streets should be designed to operate without control devices wherever possible. The best way to achieve this is through proper sight distance and sight triangles. Anything that would create a traffic hazard by limiting visibility, such as embankments, buildings, parked cars, shrubbery, fences, or low-growing trees, should be removed or lowered.

In addition to right-of-way requirements, sight triangle easements may also be required on the corners of street intersections. Such easements should include restrictions and provisions to relocate structures higher than 30 inches that obstruct visibility.

## Pavement Section

The thickness of the pavement section depends on three factors: 1) level of usage; 2) the strength properties of the subgrade supporting the paved surface; and 3) type of pavement.

1. *Usage* varies by the street hierarchy. A minor residential street, for example, experiences less intense usage than a collector, and pavement thickness requirements should be less. As usage increases, thickness should also increase.

2. *Subgrade properties* are generally classified into three categories: "very good" (or "excellent"), "good" (or "medium"), or

"poor," depending on the strength of the soil as well as the soil classification. Soil strength is derived from CBR (California Bearing Ratio) testing, and soil classification depends on whether the soil is gravel or clay. Exhibit A-6 in the model ordinance summarizes "very good," "good," and "poor" soil categories.

3. *Pavement thickness* also varies by the *pavement type*. Two common types are full-depth or all asphalt, and asphalt surface or combination. Full-depth asphalt consists of an asphalt concrete surface—often referred to as the top surface, or FABC—and an asphalt concrete base—often referred to as a stabilized base. An asphalt surface or combination pavement application consists of three levels: a top surface, a stabilized base, and a granular base. For a given level of usage and soil classification, a thicker pavement section is required for an asphalt surface than for a full-depth asphalt application (see Exhibits A-4 and A-5 in the model ordinance). As in other areas of subdivision requirements, the Rutgers model ordinance uses a performance approach to pavement section requirements, with standards based on the factors discussed above.

## Street Hardware

Street hardware includes such street details as lighting and signs. While some subdivision ordinances establish detailed and definitive standards with respect to street hardware, other ordinances leave this responsibility to the municipal or planning board engineer or to the board itself. The type, location, and size of the required street hardware also vary from municipality to municipality—some towns have very detailed and specific regulations, while others have more flexible regulations. For example, street lights are often mandated every two hundred feet, when more interspersed lighting, which is permitted by some towns, might be more appropriate for low-density developments. Requirements for street hardware should bear a direct relationship to lot frontage, density, ADT, street hierarchy, and other factors. The influence of these variables on street hardware standards is discussed below.

*LIGHTING*

## Function

The principal purpose of fixed lighting is to create a night-time environment that provides quick, accurate, and comfortable vision for both drivers and pedestrians.

## Minimum Requirements

Many local ordinances require that street lights of a certain intensity be placed every 200 feet within a development regardless of density.[65] However, some local governing bodies and planning boards have begun to question such uniform standards and to recommend that requirements be tailored to the needs of the specific development. One reason for this change is because after a developer installs street lights in a subdivision and the surety guarantees are released, the street lights and their operating and maintenance costs often become the responsibility of the municipality. Recent increases in the cost of providing electrical services have thus prompted municipalities to review more carefully the lighting plans submitted by developers.

The Rutgers model ordinance requires that street lights be sensitive to the street hierarchy and to the character of the area. Roads that carry greater traffic volumes and have wider rights-of-way and cartways need better lighting. The type of area also has an impact on lighting requirements. For example, streets in commercial locations—areas that often attract a relatively heavy volume of nighttime vehicular and pedestrian traffic—require more lighting than streets in residential locations.

The placement of wiring—overhead or underground—varies among communities, with many local ordinances requiring new developments to place wiring underground. Overhead wiring could be allowed as an exception by a municipality seeking to lower development costs to provide affordable housing.

*SIGNS*

Residential subdivision and site plan review is concerned with three types of signs: 1) traffic control signs (for example, stop signs, yield signs, one-way signs, no-parking signs); 2) street name signs; and 3) information signs in cluster developments. Although traffic and street sign standards may be included in subdivision and site plan ordinances, many communities have enacted separate ordinances to regulate signs.[66] The design and placement of information signs are, however, usually part of subdivision and site plan review.

**Traffic Control Signs**

Traffic control signs are required to ensure efficient vehicular and pedestrian movement within a subdivision. They are provided at the developer's expense, and their design, construction, and placement are usually in accordance with state standards and criteria. As part of the preliminary subdivision and site plan approval process, traffic signs are often reviewed by a local traffic control officer, a representative of the municipal police department, and/or the planning board. To ensure uniformity of traffic signs throughout a community and to facilitate their replacement, subdivision and site plan ordinances should either specify minimum standards or adopt applicable state standards regulating traffic signs.

**Street Name Signs**

Street name signs are needed to locate places within the subdivision. Continuations of existing streets should bear the same name, and new streets should be given names that are different from other streets in the community.[67] Street name signs are often designed according to a theme used throughout the development. A design theme would include, for example, style of lettering, construction, materials, size, and lighting.[68] The materials used to construct street signs are often of special concern to municipalities because after installation, maintenance and replacement of street signs become a public responsibility.

At least two street name signs should be placed at each four-way street intersection and one at each "T" intersection, and then be installed under light standards. The design of street name signs should be consistent with others in the community.

**Information Signs**

Information signs are used in cluster developments to indicate parking areas, delivery areas, fire zones, and building names. These signs often follow a design theme throughout the development which should be related to other elements of the overall site design—the buildings, lighting, and landscaping, for example.[69] Their maintenance is often assumed by a homeowners association.

**Illustration 4–12.** *(opposite page)* *"Shared" parking resources should be considered.*

## Off-Street Parking

Off-street parking includes garages, driveways, and parking lots. Its purpose in residential developments is to provide safe, adequate, and convenient parking for residents and their visitors. Given this function, off-street parking should be located within a reasonable distance of the population it is intended to serve.

Many local ordinances, especially those which permit only conventional subdivision development with single-family detached homes, do not contain off-street parking standards. With the increasing variety of choice of housing types, many communities have developed parking standards specifying number of spaces, size of spaces, and sometimes location of parking spaces in cluster, townhouse, and other multifamily residential configurations. However, even in municipalities where the number of off-street parking spaces per unit or unit type is specified, the number varies from municipality to municipality. Parking-stall size also varies.

As in the other areas of subdivision and site plan control, the need for a particular improvement, its location, and its dimensions should depend on demand and good planning and design considerations. These factors are discussed below.

*NUMBER OF SPACES*

### Residential Developments

Residential off-street parking should provide enough spaces to accommodate residents' cars and those of their visitors. Calculations determining the number of off-street parking spaces required should take into account demand (based on type of dwelling unit, household characteristics, and availability of mass transit) and number of existing parking spaces, such as on-street parking or, possibly, nearby nonresidential parking that can be shared.

The number of parking spaces required is usually expressed in terms of type of dwelling unit (single family, townhouse or multifamily), based on the presumption that each type of unit has different parking demands: "[s]ingle-family detached housing will generally be larger, have more family members and therefore be more susceptible to visitors and parties. This situation will be least prevalent in the apartment class of dwelling units. Twins and townhouses are expected to fall somewhere between the two."[70] Most sources in the literature recommend as a general standard

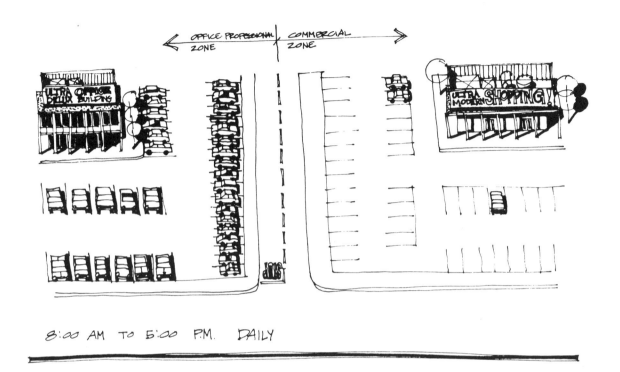

8:00 AM TO 5:00 P.M. DAILY

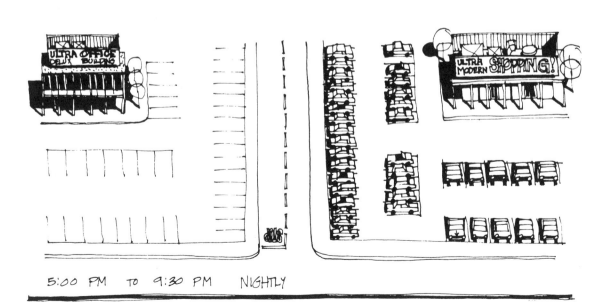

5:00 PM TO 9:30 PM NIGHTLY

**Photo 4–15.** *The automobile often dominates residential development. Riverside, California.*

two off-street parking spaces per single-family dwelling unit.[71] Other factors, however, should be considered when calculating number of parking spaces required. Two spaces per unit may be insufficient under certain circumstances, while too stringent under others. Consequently, more targeted standards may be justified.

Household characteristics, for example, can be a key determinant of off-street parking demand. If a development is oriented toward senior citizens, fewer spaces are required than in developments with a wider occupant age distribution. Some sources find household income, as reflected in house price, the most important indicator of number of parking spaces required per household: higher-priced houses generally indicate higher income, which in turn indicates a greater likelihood of car ownership.[72]

Unit size may be another factor affecting parking demand. In setting standards for parking, some communities have revised their old standards, which based the number of required parking spaces on number of units. Instead, the new standards tie the number of required spaces to the number of bedrooms per unit. Independence, Missouri's old ordinance, for example, required two parking spaces per dwelling unit; its new one specifies two spaces for units with 2 or more bedrooms and 1.5 spaces for units with one or fewer bedrooms.[73] Brough's *A Unified Development Ordi-*

*nance* also relates parking demand to unit bedroom count.[74]

Census data indirectly indicate the relationship between housing type (single-family, townhouse, and garden apartment) and housing size (number of bedrooms) with parking demand—the latter as measured by vehicle ownership per housing unit. For example, Exhibit 4-3, the basis for Exhibit 6 in the model ordinance, shows variations in vehicle ownership in the state of New Jersey. Vehicle ownership varies by housing type and size. Charts like this can be prepared and used for calculating the number of spaces required to meet the parking needs of different types of housing units. To that figure, visitor parking is added to determine the total number of off-street parking spaces needed.

Availability or absence of adequate mass transit facilities is another factor affecting parking demand. In areas where these facilities are lacking, each adult household member may need a car, increasing parking requirements.

Other factors affecting parking requirements include parking resources, such as on-street parking, driveways, and garages. When on-street parking is available, demand for off-street parking is reduced. If, however, streets are designed to avoid excessive pavement, and cartway width is reduced, on-street parking may be excluded or limited to one side of the street. Off-street parking needs would increase under these circumstances. Inclusion of driveways and garages in subdivision developments reduces the need for off-street parking; however, calculations of the number of off-street parking spaces should take into consideration that garages and driveways may not be fully utilized for parking. Garages are often used as storage areas, and residents will park on-street or in parking areas instead.

## Nonresidential Developments

Nonresidential off-street parking demand varies considerably among uses. The model ordinance presents guidelines for parking standards for various commercial, retail, and industrial uses based on studies conducted by the Institute of Transportation Engineers, the Eno Foundation, and The Urban Land Institute, as well as experience in New Jersey. The guidelines are shown in Exhibit 7 of the model ordinance.

Because number of parking spaces for residential and non-residential land uses may vary considerably, the Rutgers ordinance

EXHIBIT 4–3

## OFF-STREET PARKING REQUIREMENTS FOR
## RESIDENTIAL LAND USES: DETAILED
(As Indicated by Number of Vehicles by Type and Size of Housing Unit—
State of New Jersey)

| Housing Unit Type/Size | Off-Street Parking Requirements | | |
| --- | --- | --- | --- |
| | Resident Parking Need (as indicated by number of vehicles per unit) | Guest Parking (.5 per multi-family unit) | Total Parking Requirement* |
| *Single-Family Detached* | | | |
| 2 Bedroom | 1.4 | NA | 1.5 |
| 3 Bedroom | 1.9 | NA | 2.0 |
| 4 Bedroom | 2.0 | NA | 2.5 |
| 5 Bedroom | 2.3 | NA | 3.0 |
| *Garden Apartment* | | | |
| 1 Bedroom | 1.3 | .5 | 1.8 |
| 2 Bedroom | 1.5 | .5 | 2.0 |
| 3 Bedroom | 1.6 | .5 | 2.1 |
| *Townhouse* | | | |
| 1 Bedroom | 1.3 | .5 | 1.8 |
| 2 Bedroom | 1.8 | .5 | 2.3 |
| 3 Bedroom | 1.9 | .5 | 2.4 |
| *High-Rise* | | | |
| Studio | .3 | .5 | .8 |
| 1 Bedroom | .8 | .5 | 1.3 |
| 2 Bedroom | 1.4 | .5 | 1.9 |
| *Mobile Home* | | | |
| 1 Bedroom | 1.3 | .5 | 1.8 |
| 2 Bedroom | 1.5 | .5 | 2.0 |

NA = not applicable

*Parking requirements for single-family detached units have been adjusted to reflect perceived requirement.

*Source:* U.S. Department of Commerce, Bureau of the Census, Public Use File—New Jersey (cross-tabulation of vehicles by housing unit for units constructed 1975 to 1980).

allows applicants the option of presenting local studies and other data to modify the requirements shown in ordinance Exhibits 6 and 7.

### LOCATION

Off-street parking areas should be located within a reasonable distance of the buildings they are designed to serve. Some sources recommend a 300-foot maximum distance between parking spaces for residents and their units, and 400 feet between parking for visitors and the units.[75] HUD recommends closer placement: 200 feet between parking spaces for residents and their units and a 300-foot distance for guest parking spaces.[76] DeChiara and Koppelman agree that a 200-foot walk is maximum, adding that tradespeople are generally willing to walk only 150 to 200 feet from their vehicles.[77] Parking areas for shoppers and employees can be located at greater distances—between 500 and 800 feet for shoppers and up to 1,000 feet for employees.

### SIZE OF SPACES

The standard parking stall size has traditionally been 10 feet by 20 feet, or 200 square feet. However, as some sources note, residential parking is considered long-term parking, and narrower widths are adequate. Nine-foot widths are not uncommon.[78] In addition, if curbs are used as bumpers, up to two feet of the vehicle will overhang the curb and stalls need only be 18 feet deep.

The growing number of smaller cars has led some communities to reduce parking stall size requirements. In Newark, Delaware, and Seattle, Washington, for example, the minimum stall size requirement is 8 × 16 feet; in Keene, New Hampshire, the size is 8 × 18 feet; and in Dade County, Florida, it is 7½ × 15 feet. These communities and others are specifying that parking lots should contain areas that have smaller parking spaces for subcompact cars.[79] Other sources do not believe the shift to compact cars should have a significant impact on the dimensions of parking spaces, and that as a general policy, parking lots should be designed for the dimensions of full-size cars.[80] Separate areas for subcompact cars have often not proved successful where attempted. Making sure that car owners comply with restrictions is the major problem.[81]

**Photo 4–16.** *Parking spaces must be properly sized.*

*PARKING LOT DESIGN*

Parking lot design is affected by a number of factors, including municipal requirements, site topography, and cost considerations. Since the design of parking lots varies, the town engineer should approve all plans. Entrances and exits should be designed so as not to impede the free flow of traffic, causing congestion or traffic hazards. To avoid potential conflict, access from collector streets to parking lots may be prohibited and access drives required. There should be sufficient maneuvering room for vehicles to enter and leave the lot and individual spaces without endangering themselves, vehicles traveling the roadway system, or pedestrians. Minimum recommended aisle width for 90-degree, right-angle parking, if permitted, is 24 feet. Landscaping and berms can greatly improve the appearance of parking areas.

# Water Supply System

Provision of clean water has been a responsibility of municipal governments since at least Roman times.[82] Today it is estimated that public water utilities in the United States deliver more than 30 billion gallons of water daily of which approximately 19 billion gallons are used for residential purposes.[83] Residential uses of water include washing, transporting wastes, drinking, food preparation, heating and cooling, and watering lawns.

Because clean water is a basic public requirement, public interest in governing water quality has been strong, and standards governing the water system—once the responsibility of the local community or individual property owner—have become a matter of broader social concern subject to more encompassing governmental regulations (see also "Storm Water Management").

In many jurisdictions, standards for potable water supply systems are determined by the state and regulated through such agencies as the state department of environmental protection. Municipal water systems must conform to the design and construction standards detailed in state statutes. In addition, regional utility authorities and municipal water departments may impose stricter standards necessitated by particular conditions unique to a community or general region. Characteristics such as topography, soil type and properties, depth to ground water, and available

**Photo 4–17.** *Laying water utility lines. Guttenberg, Iowa.*

capacity and pressure vary across the states and account in part for the range of construction practices among municipalities.

A review of the subdivision literature and ordinances with reference to water supply shows concern for such issues as *system demand*—specifying water supply needs; *system strategy*—determining the delivery strategy for meeting that need (i.e., through public systems or individual wells); and *system design*—defining the character and dimensions of the water supply system. The latter, concerning itself with such matters as pipe size, materials, placement, etc., should be guided by the specified system demand and determined system strategy.

## System Demand

Several factors have an impact on determining consumption of water and required system capacity. First, municipal water supplies more than the drinking and washing needs of residents: industrial, commercial, institutional, agricultural, and other users share in the demand for water. Second, requirements for fire protection must be added to system demand. A third factor affecting the water supply system is the peaked nature of water use, particularly among residential users. The unevenness of demand requires that sufficient quantities of water be available to the system at periods of high demand. Each of these factors is addressed below.

*RESIDENTIAL AND NONRESIDENTIAL NEED*

In order to determine the system demand of a new development, water consumption must be estimated. One method for doing this is to multiply a per capita consumption rate by the anticipated development's population. Another method is to project water consumption for each component of the development—residential, industrial, and commercial—and sum them.

A review of the literature shows that residential water demand has been estimated by some sources at 100 gallons per day per capita for single-family dwellings and 75 gallons per day per capita for apartments,[84] although other sources put the figure higher, at 100 to 125 gallons per capita per day.[85] Residential water demand can also be estimated by the Linnaweaver method which uses a regression equation in which demand is related to income, size of plot, type of waste disposal, type of housing, whether the water is to be metered, and climate.[86] Residential water demand can also be related to the anticipated population calculated according to the type and size of housing units.

Sources note that *industrial* and *commercial* water use can also be derived in a functional manner. An example of this approach is the use of coefficients such as those derived by Hittman Associates. These coefficients, which are broken down by SIC code, estimate water usage in terms of number of gallons per day per employee.[87] A Hittman coefficient can also be used to calculate institutional and unaccounted-for demand (20.0 gallons per capita daily.)[88]

To summarize, average daily water requirements can be related to numerous residential and nonresidential parameters—housing unit, persons, employees, and square footage.[89] In the model ordinance, *residential* water demand is calculated according to household size with household size differing by type and size of housing unit. Nonresidential water demand is linked to different nonresidential uses with anticipated usage indicated per employee (see Exhibits 8 and 9 in the model ordinance).

*FIRE PROTECTION*

A second factor affecting the required capacity of the water supply is the fire flow required for fire protection by the American Insurance Association and the National Board of Fire Underwriters.[90] The Board's recommendations of minimum fire flows by the size of the population served are incorporated as standards in the model ordinance. (See Exhibit 10 in the model ordinance.)

For reasons of safety and welfare, fire protection should be furnished for any development numbering 50 or more dwelling units and for any development connected to the municipal water supply system. The minimum fire flows should be provided in addition to the daily per capita consumption requirements.

*PEAK NEED CONSIDERATIONS*

The third factor affecting the water supply system is the peaked nature of water use, with the result that the peak demand for water is considerably greater than the hourly average. In order to ensure that sufficient quantities are available to meet peak demand, local reservoirs generally contain roughly one full day's capacity to maintain both pressure and quantity during peak periods.[91] The water system should be designed to carry peak-hour flows and be capable of delivering the peak hourly demand. These factors are incorporated in Exhibit 11 of the model ordinance.

To summarize, the Rutgers model ordinance calculates water system demand for new developments by estimating consumption by each component of the development. To this figure is added fire flow requirements recommended by the American Insurance Association and the National Board of Fire Underwriters. Finally, the water supply system is designed to meet peak demands.

## System Strategy

Once having determined the water demand, the means of satisfying that demand should be considered. Adequate potable water—which must be supplied to every new subdivision—may be provided in one of the following ways: 1) connection to the existing public water supply system; 2) construction of a privately operated system; or 3) individual, on-lot wells.[92] Sometimes in the latter case, in order to save the future installation cost, construction of a capped system which will service lots once service is extended, may be required.

A review of the literature shows that most sources recommend that all new subdivisions be connected to an existing public water supply system. In some cases, however, a public system may not be in place or its extension may not be feasible, and individual wells may be necessary to provide the water supply. The issue is to determine when connection to an existing system is feasible. Among the national sources, NAHB recommends that when an adequate public water supply system exists within 1,000 feet of a new development, the system should be extended to the new development—if "normal" engineering methods can be used. Where such a system is not in place or cannot be extended, the developer may provide individual wells or develop a private community water system.[93] NAHB also recommends that in situations where the local government has "binding" plans to extend the public water supply system to the area of the development during a 5-year capital improvement program, the developer should install capped water lines between the street right-of-way and the structures in preparation for the time when public water service becomes available.[94]

The model codes considered in the literature search (see bibliography) contain similar recommendations. Freilich and Levi, in *Model Subdivision Regulations*, require subdivision developers to extend or create a water supply system; or developers are required to "make arrangements" for future water service if a connection to the public system may eventually be provided.[95] The state of Connecticut recommends extension of the public water supply system if it is located within 1,000 feet of the development and can be made available by "normal" engineering methods; otherwise a privately operated system may be required, or private wells permitted with installation of a capped system required if the local government has binding plans to extend the public system.[96]

The Rutgers model ordinance incorporates similar provisions with respect to connection to a public water system. Such connection is called for in those instances where it is economically feasible, i.e., sufficient units are being built to amortize the cost of the water connection. Similarly, a capped system is limited to instances where future public water supply is indicated in the municipal water master plan and other official documents.

## System Design

Good land-use design helps foster an enhanced utilities plan. For instance, water and sewer installation costs are reduced in a cluster-lot arrangement.

More specifically, there are numerous technical considerations which must be satisfied. For instance, the maintenance of continuous pressure is a primary concern in the design of water supply systems. In order to maintain pressure, water systems should be laid out in the form of a loop rather than dead-ending. The Rutgers model ordinance requires that the Hardy Cross or an equivalent method be used to balance loops in a design.

Other critical considerations in designing the water supply system include various pipe specifications, such as size, materials, and placement. Hydrant spacing and other characteristics are also issues in designing water supply systems.

Pipe size. Pipes should be large enough to provide an adequate quantity and pressure of water. The most commonly recommended size for water-main pipes is six inches in diameter;[97] this specification is adopted in the model ordinance.

Pipe materials. Ductile iron is the most common material used in water mains, although plastic, steel, and asbestos cement are also used.[98] (The use of asbestos cement pipe is discouraged, however, for health reasons. It is on the list of asbestos product categories that the Environmental Protection Agency has proposed to ban.) Among national authorities examined in the literature search, HUD recommends the use of plastic instead of copper or ductile iron pipe, citing cost savings and ease of installation as advantages. A review of local ordinances shows that some municipalities require ductile iron pipe for their water system while oth-

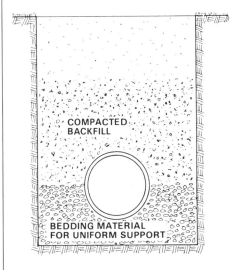

**Illustration 4–13.** *Ditch cross section for PVC pipe.*

COMPACTED BACKFILL

BEDDING MATERIAL FOR UNIFORM SUPPORT

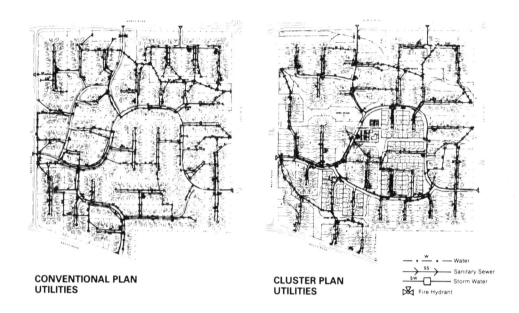

**CONVENTIONAL PLAN
UTILITIES**

**CLUSTER PLAN
UTILITIES**

| | | Water |
|---|---|---|
| | SS | Sanitary Sewer |
| | SW | Storm Water |
| | | Fire Hydrant |

### SUMMARY OF SITE DEVELOPMENT COSTS *

| | CONVENTIONAL | | CLUSTER | |
|---|---|---|---|---|
| | Total Costs | Costs/DU | Total Costs | Costs/DU |
| Street Pavement | $ 862,165 | $ 1,827 | $ 540,569 | $1,145 |
| Curbs and Gutters | 433,872 | 919 | — | — |
| Street Trees | 412,496 | 874 | 374,640 | 794 |
| Driveways | 743,400 | 1,575 | 527,715 | 1,213 |
| Storm Drainage | 696,464 | 1,476 | 278,295 | 590 |
| Water Distribution | 746,044 | 1,581 | 492,792 | 1,044 |
| Sanitary Sewer | 1,142,647 | 2,421 | 1,009,601 | 2,139 |
| Grading | 332,044 | 703 | 220,755 | 468 |
| Clearing/Grubbing | 156,915 | 332 | 109,785 | 233 |
| Sidewalks | 209,250 | 443 | 197,775 | 419 |
| Subtotal | $5,735,298 | $12,151 | $3,751,927 | $8,045 |
| Engineering Fees (5.8%) | 332,647 | 705 | 217,612 | 467 |
| **Total** | **$6,067,945** | **$12,856** | **$3,969,539** | **$8,512** |
| Actual Difference on a per lot basis | | **4,344** | | |
| % of Conventional lot cost | | 100% | | 66% |

* 1986 dollars

ers prefer and permit PVC pipe. Most of the developing municipalities permit PVC pipe. The Rutgers ordinance permits a wide range of pipe materials including PVC, providing the materials meet AWWA standards.

**Pipe placement.** The most common placement of water mains is in the right-of-way under the sidewalk, planting strip, or roadway. However, some sources examined in the literature search caution that such placement is to be avoided because of excessive costs incurred when repair work is required.[99] Placement of water mains and other utilities within easements centered on rear lot lines is recommended as an alternative, but this practice may also cause problems. Unless the easement is sufficiently wide, maneuvering equipment may be difficult.

To avoid contamination, water lines must be separated from sewer lines, but sources differ in the amount of separation recommended. A review of the literature shows that Indiana's model

**Illustration 4–14.** *(opposite page) Water and sewer installation costs can be reduced in a cluster plan.*

**Illustration 4–15.** *Sample layout of common lateral water service (meters not indicated).*

COST EFFICIENT WATER SERVICE FOR 12 UNIT BUILDING
( Subject To Review By Local Water Supplier )

code, for example, requires water lines to be two feet above sewer lines and to be ten feet removed horizontally. HUD, by contrast, recommends a 12-inch vertical separation and an 18-inch horizontal separation.[100] The Rutgers ordinance requires an 18-inch vertical separation and a 10-foot horizontal separation, unless special precautions are taken.

As a cost savings, some sources recommend multiple water service connections to detached and row houses from a single lateral placed along the property line and/or within a perpetual easement.[101] An objection to this innovation, however, is that problems may arise in apportioning costs and responsibility for the repair and maintenance of common facilities. The cost efficiency of a single lateral with multiple connections is very attractive, however.

To summarize, a review of the literature indicates that water mains are generally placed in the right-of-way, with adequate separation from sewer lines in order to lessen the possibility of contamination. Service to multiple dwellings from a single lateral is a cost-saving innovation, but must be carefully designed so that it does not lead to later problems for homeowners.

The model ordinance attempts to address these concerns. For example, the standard specifying the separation between water and sewer lines is a reasoned compromise with some flexibility allowed as long as the public health and safety are protected. In addition, the ordinance permits common water service connections for multifamily housing—but only where there is a homeowners association to maintain these common elements.

*FIRE HYDRANTS*

Fire hydrants are generally located in the street right-of-way, and sources usually specify this placement. Standards for the *spacing* of hydrants, by contrast, vary considerably. A review of recommendations and ordinance requirements shows that spacing intervals range from a minimum of 350 feet (Indiana model code) to a maximum of 1,000 feet (Freilich and Levi). Indiana's code requires that hydrants be placed at each street intersection and spaced between 350 and 600 feet apart, depending on the density of the area serviced.

Instead of specifying spacing intervals, some sources examined in the literature search set a maximum distance between hydrants and structures: 300 feet is recommended by DeChiara and Koppelman; and 500 feet is the standard specified in Freilich and Levi's model code. However, because the loss in pressure is not significant, a maximum distance of 600 feet between structures and hydrants is not unreasonable.

An alternative approach to setting hydrant spacing standards is to require that hydrants be spaced so as to ensure the minimum fire flows discussed earlier. This approach results in a standard specifying that one hydrant is required per 120,000-square-foot area. In addition to meeting fire-flow requirements, hydrant spacing must also take into account the maximum firefighter hose lay (often 500′ to 600′). These standards are adopted in the model ordinance.

# Sanitary Sewers

Sanitary sewer systems transport the liquid and water-carried solid wastes produced in communities from residences, commercial and industrial establishments, and other sources. Like provision of water, disposal of sewage has long been a municipal concern. Construction of sewers was an engineering innovation known in ancient towns and enlarged upon on a "cyclopean scale"[102] by the Romans to serve a large urban population. The Cloaca Maxima—the great sewer constructed in the sixth century—is still in use today.[103] Despite Rome's contribution, however, city sewerage systems remained inadequate until the end of the nineteenth century.[104] Sanitary reformers and hygienists aroused public concern about the results of contamination. The result of their efforts was stricter regulation of sewerage systems.

Today in most states, standards for sanitary sewer systems are determined by state statute and regulated through such agencies as departments of environmental protection. In addition to the standards imposed by the state, utility authorities and municipal sewer departments may require certain standards in response to specific characteristics of the region or municipality. As a result there are typically variations in the standards regulating sanitary sewer systems.

A review of the literature shows that standards relating to sanitary sewer systems are concerned with two areas: 1) system strategy—determining the type of sewerage system required (i.e., public or private); and 2) system design—detailing specifications for overall designing and placement of sewer lines, pipe size and materials, and manholes and cleanouts. A summary of standards on each of these topics follows.

## System Strategy

### PUBLIC SYSTEMS

A review of the literature shows that most national authorities, model codes, and local ordinances require subdivisions to connect to a public system if one is available or "reasonably" accessible.[105] They also require connection to public systems for certain types of developments, high-density residential, and non-residential developments.[106]

If a system is to be extended at some date in the future, the authorities and codes typically require construction of a dry or "capped" system with service to each lot in anticipation of later hookups. The issue in requiring construction of a dry system is setting a limit by which time the line must be extended. Recommendations range from 5 years[107] to a more generous 15 years.[108] Others specify that plans for the extension must be part of the adopted capital improvements program,[109] or that the future public facilities will be accessible within a "reasonable" time.[110]

### PRIVATE SYSTEMS

When connection to a public system is not required—usually because housing densities are not sufficient to support a community system—a private system with its own treatment plant may be approved. Jackson, Mississippi's model code requires construction of a complete private system in subdivisions with lots under one-half acre. (Those with lots of one-half acre or more may use septic systems.) Saginaw, Michigan's model code requires that private systems be dedicated to the jurisdiction.

### SEPTIC SYSTEMS

Individual on-lot septic systems are often the preferred sewerage system strategy for residential developments with very large lots. Minimum lot sizes permitted are generally an acre or more, and density less than 2,500 people per square mile.[111] In addition, soil suitability and proper installation are critical concerns with

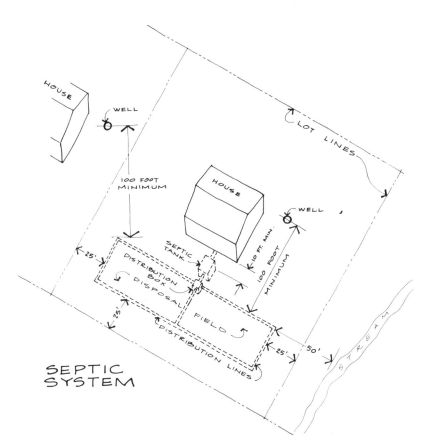

**Illustration 4–16.** *A septic system must be properly planned.*

septic systems. For this reason, most authorities and model ordinances recommend that percolation and test holes be required prior to approval and that system design be approved by appropriate officials.[112]

## System Design

*DEMAND*

Sewerage systems must be designed to handle wastes from various sources. Residential sewage flows are generally about 60 to 75 percent of the water supplied to the area. The remainder comes from industrial, commercial, or other sources or infiltration of groundwater through broken pipes, defective joints, etc.

National authorities, model codes, and local ordinances recommend that sewerage systems be designed with sufficient capacity to handle "present and future" needs.[113] "Present and

**Photo 4–18.** *Problematical septic system, Rochester, New Hampshire. (This septic tank and dry well empty into a muck and peat area. Both tanks are higher than the cellar door.)*

future" needs are variously defined as those required by the "probable future development" in the area,[114] or by the "ultimate tributary population."[115]

Field experience shows that average flow can be assumed to be 65 gallons per person, per day (without allowance for infiltration or inflow). Given this standard and the household size profiles for different types and sizes of housing units, it is possible to establish sewer-flow values for a multiplicity of housing configurations. These values are shown in Exhibit 8 of the model ordinance.

### Common Laterals

In the interest of reducing costs, HUD's *Innovative Site Utility Installations* recommends using a single sewer lateral to service multiple dwellings. However, this practice may cause problems in apportioning costs and responsibility for repair and maintenance of common facilities. While these problems must be recognized, the cost-saving advantages of single laterals are substantial.

The Rutgers model ordinance balances these concerns by permitting common sanitary service where a homeowners association or similar entity is responsible for the maintenance of the common laterals.

**Placement.** Sanitary sewer lines are generally located within street or alley rights-of-way, or in easements, if necessary. Care in placement of sewer lines must be taken to prevent contamination of the water supply by sewage: Freilich and Levi's model code specifies, for example, a 10-foot minimum horizontal separation between water and sewer lines. In *Innovative Installations*, however, HUD advocates reducing the horizontal separation between water and sewer lines, claiming that wide separation distances were instituted in the past because poor construction methods resulted in frequent leakages. "Wider separation distances made the frequent repairs easier to make without damaging adjacent

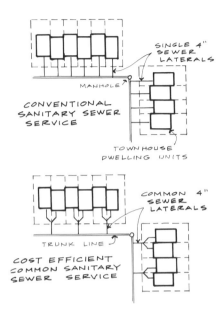

**Illustration 4–17.** *Conventional and cost-efficient common sanitary sewer services.*

**Illustration 4–18.** *Common water/sewer trench.*

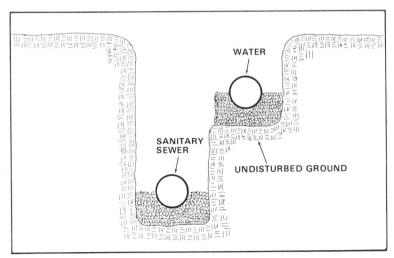

pipe lines."[116] In addition, wider separation distances between water and sewer lines lessened the possibility of contamination. Today HUD claims that better construction methods and strict inspection controls are resulting in systems requiring fewer repairs and posing few health threats. Cities cited by HUD which have reduced separation distances between water and sewer lines, without apparent problem, are Arlington, Virginia; Tampa, Florida; and Phoenix and Scottsdale, Arizona (reduction to 6 feet). The Rutgers model ordinance specifies a ten-foot horizontal separation. This standard reflects the frequent requirement by numerous state and local agencies that a ten-foot separation be maintained. Where this is not the case, the HUD recommendations should be incorporated.

**Easements.** When sewer lines are placed in easements, the easement should be sufficiently wide to permit equipment to maneuver, and access to all manholes should be required. Codes generally require easements to be located to the rear or side lot line.

The Rutgers ordinance establishes a performance standard for easements. The required easement width increases with the depth of the sanitary sewer line.

**Illustration 4–19.** *Curvilinear versus straight sewer alignment.*

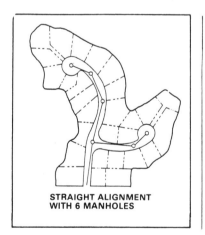
STRAIGHT ALIGNMENT
WITH 6 MANHOLES

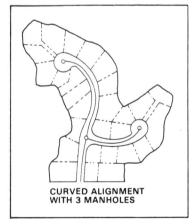
CURVED ALIGNMENT
WITH 3 MANHOLES

**Alignment.** Sewer lines are typically laid out with a straight alignment between manholes, and some model codes include this as a requirement.[117] Two HUD studies, however, recommend the installation of sewer lines along a curved alignment, citing the following advantages: installation is cheaper because the number of manholes and the length of line are reduced; other utilities are avoided more easily; the contours of the topography can be followed more readily; and hydrolic efficiency is improved.[118] Curved sewers can be constructed using either rigid or flexible pipe. "Rigid pipe...is installed by deflecting the pipe joint from a straight position....Flexible pipe...is deflected by bending the pipe itself."[119] Jurisdictions using curvilinear sewers include Phoenix, Arizona; Chicago, Illinois; Los Angeles County, California; and Riverside County, California.

The Rutgers ordinance allows curved sewers where site conditions permit and where such a layout will result in cost savings.

*SLOPE*

The slope of sewers is an important consideration in sewer design because sewers must be laid on minimum slopes in order to ensure a flow velocity which is sufficient to prevent settling of solids. Sources in the literature differ in recommendations: HUD notes that a velocity of two feet per second at full pipe flow is normally used for design,[120] whereas DeChiara and Koppelman recommend 2.5 feet per second. Freilich and Levi's model code also includes slope requirements according to pipe diameter.

HUD points out that reductions in the minimum slopes of sanitary sewer line result in less excavation and backfill and shallower sewer manholes. Cost savings are thus realized, the amount depending on the type of material being excavated (rock or soil), the allowable slope reduction, and the pipe diameter.[121] The HUD study cites the example of the city of Phoenix which has constructed gravity sewers at the slopes indicated on the table below—slopes which are less than those usually permitted.

| Pipe Diameter | *Reduced Minimum Slope in Phoenix, in ft. per 100 ft.* |
|:---:|:---:|
| 8″ | 0.33 |
| 10″ | 0.24 |
| 12″ | 0.19 |
| 15″ | 0.14 |

*Source:* HUD, *Innovative Site Utility Installations*, p. 8.

According to the study, the reduced velocities produced by shallower slopes of sewers in Phoenix have not resulted in problems with solids settling.

This model ordinance recommends that flow velocity be not less than two feet per second (to permit self-cleaning), nor more than 10 feet per second (to guard against scouring the line). It also establishes a schedule of slope standards which varies by pipe diameter—a strategy indicated in HUD's *Innovative Site Utility Installations* and also adopted by Freilich and Levi.

*PIPE SIZE*

Sources in the literature often recommend and many jurisdictions require that gravity sewer collectors be a minimum of 8 inches in diameter.[122] HUD notes that this standard sizing is used first, to prevent clogging of sewers, and second, to maintain minimum flow velocities at moderate slopes. However, HUD further points out that smaller-diameter lines could be used to transport flow just as effectively and at reduced costs. Similarly, in its study for the National Bureau of Standards, the Rice Center notes that the standards of many jurisdictions are in part based on local preferences and may not be technically optimal.[123]

Consideration should be given to using smaller lines which can transmit flow as effectively as larger lines and at reduced costs. For instance, HUD maintains that 6-inch main lines have the hydraulic capacity to handle sewage in many cases where larger lines are now specified, and notes that 3- to 4-inch lines can be used for home service laterals. Small sewers, in fact, were shown to operate efficiently without maintenance problems in a demonstration project in Las Vegas.[124] Smaller sewer lines are particularly suited in cases where the total number of connections can be determined, such as cul-de-sacs and dead-end streets. As HUD points out, "These lines cannot be extended, and therefore will not be hydraulically overloaded due to future development."[125]

The Rutgers ordinance does not specify a given minimum pipe size. Instead, it establishes a performance standard in terms of the minimum and maximum flows described earlier.

*PIPE MATERIALS*

A review of the literature shows that vitrified clay, concrete, asbestos cement, cast-iron corrugated metal, and polyvinyl chloride are all acceptable pipe materials. As noted in the section on Water Supply, however, it is likely that asbestos cement pipe will be banned as a health hazard, and it has not been included as an option in the ordinance. In addition, the model ordinance requires specific pipe materials in particular situations. For example, sewers which pass within 100 feet of a water supply well must be of steel or reinforced concrete cast iron.

*MANHOLES*

The purpose of manholes is to provide convenient access to sewers for observation, cleaning, and other maintenance. They are generally required at every change of grade or alignment, at the junction of sewers, at each street or alley intersection, and at the end of each line.[126] These requirements are specified in the Rutgers model ordinance.

For sewers 15 inches and smaller, most standards limit maximum spacing to 400 feet or less.[127] As HUD points out, this spacing criteria reflects past construction methods and materials:

*The 400 feet allowed the introduction of auger-type cleaning equipment, operating at high torques, to remove roots and other obstructions. This short cleaning distance was more manageable when irregularities were present in system alignments, such as joint separations, sumps from settlements, and cracks or breaks from improper backfilling.*[128]

HUD recommends permitting manholes to be spaced 600 to 800 feet apart where manhole access is available on both ends of a line. Increased spacing between manholes is now possible, according to HUD, because today's sewer design standards and construction techniques have reduced chances of obstruction, and modern cleaning equipment can reach greater distances than in the past. In light of these technological advances, municipalities should reexamine their manhole spacing standards.

The Rutgers model ordinance allows a 600-foot manhole spacing for larger pipe sizes (over 18 inches) where adequate modern cleaning equipment is available.

*CLEANOUTS*

Cleanouts, where permitted, serve as a substitute for manholes, providing access to sewer lines for inspections and cleaning. Freilich and Levi's model code, however, specifically prohibits them, as does Indiana's. HUD, by contrast, citing cost savings, recommends constructing cleanouts instead of manholes under certain circumstances: 1) on relatively short (200 to 300 feet) sanitary sewer lines—adequate normal maintenance access would be available through the cleanout, while access for larger procedures would be through conventional manholes on the downstream end of the line; 2) in lieu of some manholes on existing lines in need of repair; 3) in low-lying, flood-prone areas—cleanouts are less susceptible to infiltration and less expensive to install than manholes; 4) on systems where frequent horizontal bends require frequent manholes; and 5) in rocky terrain, thus reducing excavation, saving time and money.[129]

Some consideration, therefore, should be given to substituting cleanouts for manholes where possible.

# Storm Water Management

A drainage system transports storm water, surface water, street wash, and water from other sources to appropriate receiving water bodies.[130] The system itself is comprised of numerous natural and man-made elements. These include swales, which are continuous depressions that direct and divert water; ditches, which carry water; retention and detention basins, which hold and slowly release water; and curbs, which direct it to a closed conduit system of storm sewer pipes.[131] The ultimate destination of the storm flow is a permanent natural body of water such as a stream, river, or lake with sufficient capacity to accommodate the expected surface flow.[132]

A drainage system protects the public welfare by controlling runoff to prevent or mitigate physical injury, property loss, and disruption of activity which may occur after a storm. Such problems are especially pronounced after a storm of unusual intensity. This is often referred to by the frequency of such an event—for example, a storm occurring on average once every 10, 20, or 50

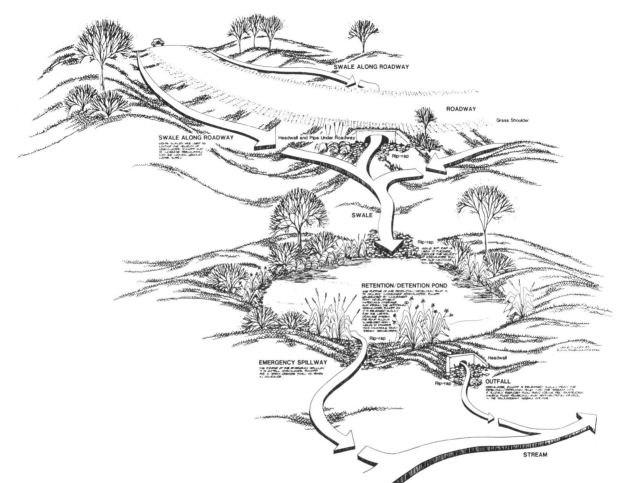

**Illustration 4–20.** *Stormwater drainage system.*

years. (Another way of stating storm frequency is to describe its probability of recurrence. For example, a ten-year storm has a statistical probability of 0.10 of recurring in a given year.) In addition to its protective function, a drainage system can enhance area water supply by enabling storm water to replenish local water resources.

Given these critical functions, it is important that a drainage system be carefully planned. This imperative does not justify, however, costly and frequently inefficient overdesign. For many years, drainage system design sought the most rapid elimination of excess water at an individual site by containing and disposing of that water through a closed system. The cumulative effect of this approach was often downstream flooding and endangered aquifers—ultimately requiring costly massive engineering works to control downstream flooding.

These problems have caused a reappraisal of the process of storm water control. The new emphasis is on designing systems for entire drainage basins, taking advantage of the non-structural system which combines natural storage, percolation, and channeling techniques. This area-wide approach may include trade-offs with temporary localized inconvenience, but solutions applied to individual sites often have the beneficial effect of lessening both long-term and short-term peak rates of runoff.

The change in drainage design philosophy is reflected in the recommendations of many of the national and model codes surveyed by Rutgers. For example, the Bureau of Standards emphasizes the need to base system design on the "potential of major storm events" rather than arbitrarily assigning specifications.[133] In *A Guide for Residential Design Review*, authors Harvey Moskowitz and Carl Lindbloom describe a "shift back to the use of swales and open drainage for storm water when feasible."[134] The Connecticut Department of Housing views storm water management as a "natural" process and emphasizes the need for a performance approach that links design specification to the magnitude of anticipated runoff.[135]

In sum, among the authorities and ordinances surveyed by Rutgers, there is growing recognition that drainage control is best approached within a regional management context, that a non-structural system be encouraged, and that system capacity reflect system demand, with system demand calculated in terms of anticipated peak rate of discharge and runoff volume.

### System Demand

Watershed storm water management requires the determination of two runoff parameters: runoff peak rate of discharge and runoff volume. Both parameters are used to compare pre-development and post-development conditions. Peak rate of discharge calculations are typically used to determine the configurations and sizes of pipes, channels, and other routing or flow control structures. Runoff volume calculations are typically used to determine the necessity for, and storage of, detention and

Photo 4–19. *Example of a swale in a planned development.*

Photo 4–20. *Pipeline under construction. Austin, Texas.*

retention facilities.

The peak rate of runoff for areas up to one-half square mile is often calculated by the Rational Formula or its derivatives.[136] The Rational Formula for estimating peak runoff rates was introduced in the United States by Emil Kuichling in 1889. Since then, it has become the most widely used method of designing drainage facilities for small urban areas and highways. Peak flow is found from:[137]

$$Q_p = CIA$$

where

$Q_p$ = the peak runoff rate in cubic feet per second (CFS)

C = the runoff coefficient

I = the average rainfall intensity in inches per hour (in./hr.), occurring at the time of concentration $t_c$ (minutes)

$t_c$ = the time of concentration in minutes (min.)

A = the size of the drainage area

The rationale for the method lies in the concept that application of a steady, uniform rainfall intensity will cause runoff to reach its maximum rate when all parts of the watershed are contributing to the outflow at the point of design. That condition is met after the elapsed time, $t_c$, the time of concentration, which usually is taken as the time for water to flow from the most remote part of the watershed.

The Rational Formula relates runoff to the characteristics and size of the drainage area and to rainfall intensity. The specific factors affecting the formula variables deserve brief discussion. For example, the runoff coefficient or C value is influenced by surface and soil characteristics, antecedent moisture conditions, and time and space relationships.

**Surface characteristics.** The peak rate of runoff from rainfall is greatest in intensely developed, high-density locations with a considerable amount of paved, impervious surfaces. Conversely, the lowest runoff coefficients are found in relatively undeveloped locations with little paving. This relationship is shown in Exhibit A-12 of the model ordinance. For example, the runoff coefficient is 0.41 for single-family homes on large lots (1 acre or greater); it is 0.45 for single-family units on lots from one-half to one acre each; and it is 0.49 to 0.76 for single-family dwellings on lots smaller than one-half acre (for Hydro Soil Group B). Even higher coefficients are found for nonresidential development, where lot coverage tends to be high and a considerable amount of parking must be provided.

**Soil characteristics.** The runoff coefficient is also influenced by soil type. The C value will be low when soil conditions are conducive to percolation as opposed to surface flow. Examples include areas with a sandy loam underbase, especially in the absence of a high groundwater table (A-type soil). By contrast, the runoff coefficient will be higher where groundwater absorption is impeded, such as in areas with clay soils found, or where there is perched groundwater table (D-type soil).

**Time of concentration.** In addition to the runoff coefficient, the remaining factors in the Rational Method equation also have a significant bearing on the peak rate of runoff. Common practice in determining the time of concentration, $t_c$, to a given design point, has been to determine a time for overland flow to reach the first inlet and then to add the time of flow in the pipe system to that point.[138] The time of overland flow can be estimated from Exhibit A-13 in the model ordinance. As indicated in this exhibit, the overland travel time varies with the slope of the land traversed by the rainfall: it is higher in instances of considerable slope, lower where the terrain is flat.

**Rainfall intensity.** Appropriate values of rainfall intensity, I, another variable in the Rational Method equation, can be calculated from data available from local studies or obtained from the rainfall intensity/frequency/duration information kept by regional monitoring stations.[139] In practice, a nomograph similar to that shown in Exhibit A-14 in the model ordinance may be used to find I. In all cases, a minimum time of concentration of 5 minutes should be used. For storm sewer design, a ten-year storm frequency should be considered as a minimum, unless special circumstances are involved, such as evidence of local flooding, inadequate downstream storm water facilities, and technical ambiguities.

**Drainage area.** The final value in the Rational Method equation is A—the size of the drainage area. It is important that this value include the full drainage basin impacting the site under review—including both upstream and downstream locations.

The Rational Method is most applicable for determining the peak rate of runoff for smaller drainage areas (i.e., up to one-half square mile). For larger areas, the Technical Release (TR) No. 55 Method is utilized.[140] The TR No. 55 Method is used to construct runoff inflow hydrographs necessary for determining basin design. The hydrograph can also be used to determine peak rate of runoff at any point in time. The TR No. 55 Method factors land use, soil type, imperviousness, and drainage area and slope.

**Runoff volume.** Runoff volume is calculated by the hydrograph analysis as outlined in the TR No. 55 Method. This method is used for watersheds with drainage areas of less than five square miles. For drainage areas of less than 5 acres, the Rational Method triangular hydrograph approximation may be used as an alternative.

The model ordinance incorporates these provisions. Calculation of drainage system demand encompasses consideration of anticipated peak rate of runoff and runoff volume. Peak rate of runoff is typically calculated by the Rational Method (for areas one-half square mile or smaller) or the TR No. 55 Method (for larger areas). Runoff volume is calculated by the TR No. 55 Method for areas of less than 5 square miles. For drainage areas of less than 5 acres, the Rational Method triangular hydrograph approximation is used as an alternative.

**Photo 4–21.** *Structural engineered stormwater system.*

## System Strategy

Strategies for dealing with storm water have been evolving over time. Years ago, the prevailing wisdom and practice were to focus on site-by-site treatment. Today there is greater acceptance of the need for a managed regional approach. Thus, in standards for system design and size, the more innovative national subdivision authorities and codes recommend a storm water management strategy for drainage, rather than construction of oversized drainage systems for separate developments.

The objectives of storm water management have also expanded. In addition to serving its traditional protective role against storm-related dangers, the drainage system is additionally now viewed as an important element in water supply and quality. The issue of water quality is underscored by court decisions finding that drainage channels can be considered as point sources of pollution.[141] With this change has come the enactment of federal and state pollution statutes. For example, the importance of drainage as it affects water quality is addressed by Section 208 of the Water Pollution Control Act.[142] In addition, numerous states have issued water management manuals specifying techniques to control storm water while protecting water quality.[143] The Rutgers model ordinance draws upon these manuals in its storm water management provisions.

**Photo 4–22.** *Non-structural natural stormwater system.*

Just as the importance of water quality is being increasingly recognized, a major emphasis is being placed on the use of non-structural engineering techniques to control storm water runoff. These techniques capitalize on and are consistent with natural resources and processes. Engineering design can be used to improve the effectiveness of natural systems, rather than negate, replace, or ignore them. As opposed to a structural system, which emphasizes rapid off-site conveyance and runoff via an enclosed pipe system, a non-structural strategy accentuates on-site drainage, percolation, open channeling, and groundwater recharge.

The national and model subdivision codes surveyed by Rutgers endorse the shift away from a totally closed pipe system. Natural overland flows, open channels, swales, and large ponds are viewed as important drainage control elements with auxiliary benefits as well. For example, retention and detention basins not only catch storm water, but can serve to mitigate pollution (i.e., by reducing soil erosion and sedimentation) while providing a recreational and visual amenity.[144]

In considering the selection of a structural versus a non-structural system, it is important to realize that the choice is not mutually exclusive: all non-structural systems contain some structural elements, and vice versa. The question, then, is one of degree. In making the choice of whether to emphasize a structural versus non-structural strategy, it is important to consider the demand to be placed on the drainage system—both peak rate of runoff and runoff volume. These values are measured using the Rational and TR No. 55 Methods previously described.

From demand one has to consider response. First, how much of the storm water can possibly be stored on-site? This can be accomplished in permanent ponds, percolation storage, dry ponds (i.e., parks and recreation areas), and even parking lots. The site has to be carefully examined as to its storage capacity, with storage capacity affected by such variables as soil type, slope, water table, anticipated physical capacity of the improvements, and so on.

Storm water that cannot be stored has to be channeled for ultimate disposition. The viability of open channeling in swales, ditches, gutters, streets, etc., as opposed to channeling in a closed-pipe system, should be considered. The hydraulic capacity of a conduit (open or closed) to convey water is calculated by the Manning Equation. The hydraulic capacity is termed Q and is expressed in discharge in cubic feet per second. This discharge is equal to the following:

$$Q = \frac{1.486}{n} AR^{2/3}S^{1/2}$$

where

$n$ = Manning's roughness coefficient
$A$ = Cross-sectional area of flow in square feet
$R$ = Hydraulic radius in feet ($R = A/P$, where P is equal to the Wetted Perimeter)
$S$ = Slope of conduit in feet per foot

This equation simply states that the hydraulic capacity of a conduit is a function of the conduit area, slope, hydraulic radius, and resistance to the flow of water as measured by the roughness coefficient.

The Manning roughness coefficient varies considerably among different conduits as shown in Exhibit A-15 of the model ordinance. Lower n values allow for faster water velocity. Thus, a faster flow will occur in a concrete-lined channel than in one lined with earth.

After the capacity of the conduit is determined, the flow velocity can be found. Typical minimum and maximum velocities for storm water are 2 feet per second (minimum) and 20 feet per second (maximum). The minimum value specifies the slowest desired flow rate—anything less will encourage siltation, clogging, etc.; the maximum value indicates the fastest permitted flow to avoid eroding or scouring the conduit. The conduit material will dictate maximum velocities. The exit velocity where a conduit empties into an open channel should be kept below the allowable soil erosion velocity for the channel lining.

Different conduits have varying minimum and maximum flow thresholds. In general, velocities in *closed conduits* at design flow should be at least two feet per second, but not more than the velocity which will cause erosion damage to the conduit. (The latter varies by manufacturer specification.) By contrast, velocities in open channels at design flow should not be less than 5 tenths foot per second and not greater than that velocity which will begin to cause erosion or scouring of the channel. (The exact maximum speed will vary by channel shape, slope, soil type, ground cover, etc.; see Exhibit A-16 in the model ordinance.)

The Manning Equation can be used to determine the applicability of a structural or non-structural system by determining the flow velocity and depth within the open channels. These values can then be compared to the channels' minimum and maximum velocities to determine their ability to convey the anticipated runoff safely. If the threshold values are exceeded, then measures may have to be taken so as to protect the channel lining. This can be accomplished through such means as planting different ground covers and regrading so as to modify slope conditions. If these measures are not feasible, then a structural system will have to be installed.

A final consideration in selecting a non-structural versus a structural drainage system is the maintenance demand. Non-structural systems require much more ongoing maintenance in the form of mowing, periodically cleaning channels, and so on. These chores are critical—if left untended, the storm water flow capacity can be severely affected. By contrast, a structural system is expensive to install, but once operational, it requires much less maintenance. Consequently, selection of a storm drainage system should consider the differing maintenance demands and the ability to meet those demands. Will homeowners or a homeowners association provide maintenance? If not, is the municipality willing and able to do so?

The Rutgers model ordinance addresses these concerns. It stresses the need to take into consideration regional drainage problems and resources as well as federal and state regulations pertaining to improved water quality. Furthermore, the ordinance emphasizes a non-structural as opposed to a structural drainage strategy—when the former is appropriate to the situation and technologically feasible.

## System Design

Once having selected an overall drainage strategy, there are many specific design considerations. The following section touches upon some of the more important such elements.

**Photo 4–23.** *Poor stormwater planning: sediment from unlined gutter plugging culvert.*

*PIPE SIZE*

Few authorities, model codes, or local ordinances specify pipe dimensions or materials. Instead, most recommend that hydrologic and hydraulic data be used to determine the pipe sizes required to carry flows and prevent clogging.[145] The hydraulic capacity can be determined by the Manning Equation, and the peak rate of runoff into the pipe system by the Rational Method. Also to be considered is the hydraulic capacity of a pipe, given its size, slope, roughness characteristics, tendency to become clogged, and self-scouring velocities.[146] In most cases, no pipe in a storm drainage system should measure less than 15 inches in diameter. Anything smaller tends to clog and poses maintenance problems.[147]

Storm sewer systems have traditionally been designed to accommodate runoff from storms occurring at various time periods. Ten-, 15-, and 25-year storms are common storm frequencies used. Some regulating agencies have required, in addition, that all pipes be increased by one size as a "factor of safety." Overdesign, however, is not only costly; it can lead to a poorly functioning system. When pipe size and design flow are not matched, velocities below the minimum may result. The design storm frequency should instead be based on the amount of protec-

**Photo 4–24.** *Proper stormwater planning: sediment will not plug culvert in a cobble-lined gutter.*

tion desired against loss of life or property. In the majority of situations, a 10-year storm frequency is adequate for storm sewer design.

The Rutgers ordinance adopts the recommendations of the national literature and bases pipe size on design runoff and hydraulic capacity, with the latter determined by the Manning Equation. For functional reasons, a 15-inch diameter pipe is required in order to avoid clogging. The ordinance adopts a 10-year storm frequency for design purposes.

*PIPE PLACEMENT AND MATERIALS*

Storm drains are generally installed in the early construction stage of residential development: Since they require gravity profiles, are located at shallow depths, and require trench backfill, the opportunity for combined trenching with other utilities rarely exists.

Careful attention should be given to discharge velocity. It is important to dissipate the water velocity at this point so as to mitigate scouring the landscape. Consequently, all discharge pipes should terminate with an end section to accomplish this purpose. The downstream channel must be lined to accommodate the flow velocity. These provisions are adopted in the model ordinance.

Materials used in the construction of storm sewers should be constructed of reinforced concrete, corrugated aluminum, or ductile iron, and should conform to pertinent standards, such as ASA, ASTM or AWWA. The least expensive materials should be permitted unless site and other conditions dictate otherwise. For example, Class III reinforced concrete pipe is acceptable except where stronger pipe is indicated (i.e., Class V may be required for pipe lines installed under traffic areas). The model ordinance reflects this performance, cost-savings approach. It provides that the "least expensive materials shall be permitted unless site and other conditions dictate otherwise."

Careful attention must be given to the pipe bedding. Typically, storm sewers should be backfilled with existing soil which is free of debris and other unsuitable material. Where subsoil is wet, a 6-inch-thick layer of broken stone should be placed beneath the pipe for support as well as to provide subsurface drainage. Where bedding with backfill is shown to be inadequate, other appropriate pipe bedding approaches should be used. These include Class B bedding, Class C modified bedding, concrete cradle bedding, and concrete encased pipe bedding. Class C modified bedding, for example, is used for rigid pipe. The model ordinance incorporates bedding specifications by pipe category.

*INLETS, CATCH BASINS, AND MANHOLES*

Design and spacing requirements governing inlets, catch basins, and manholes are intended to prevent ponding, overflow, and the flooding of intersections; to remove runoff from surfaces where the flows exceed the criteria for velocity; and to provide proper maintenance. Given these functions, catch basins should be located at low points and at other points required for proper drainage, and inlets should be placed where they can efficiently intercept and capture water flow.

The grates covering inlets should be designed to avoid blockage by debris and to consider bicycle and pedestrian safety. The latter is an issue because grates with long horizontal openings parallel to the curb present a hazard to cyclists.

Manhole spacing should be dictated by maintenance needs and the requirements of maintenance equipment. Larger pipes tend to need less maintenance as they are less prone to clogging, siltation, etc. Consequently, manhole spacing can be increased with pipe size.

| *Pipe Size* | *Manhole Spacing* |
| --- | --- |
| 15″ or less | 500′ |
| 18″ - 36″ | 600′ |
| 42″ - 60″ | 700′ |
| 66″ + | 700′ + |

All of the technical provisions indicated above are adopted in the Rutgers model ordinance.

*DETENTION–RETENTION FACILITIES*

Detention basins are not required to satisfy storm management requirements. Tanks, infiltration pits, dry wells, or gravel layers underneath paving may be used for the purpose, with appropriate consideration for length of life and feasibility of continued maintenance.[148]

**Illustration 4–21.** *Stormwater management: retention basin.*

Where detention facilities are deemed necessary, they should accommodate site runoff generated from 2-year, 10-year and 100-year storms considered individually. Detention should be provided such that after development, the peak rate of flow from the site will not exceed the corresponding flows which would have been created by similar storms prior to development. In calculating the site runoff to be accommodated by a detention facility, the TR No. 55 Method should be used. The Rutgers ordinance incorporates these standards and procedures.

Detention components (outlets, emergency spillways, dams, embankments, etc.) should be designed so as to serve the function of storing water while not posing a danger to residents; the detention system should also protect water quality.[149] Design specifications for numerous detention components are indicated in the model ordinance.

*EASEMENTS*

Drainage system components should be located within street rights-of-way whenever possible. Often, however, placement will be necessary elsewhere, thereby requiring that easements be obtained.

Easement requirements are designed to ensure access to land traversed by drainage ways or watercourses. Often codes stipulate that easements, in the case of waterways, for example, conform to the lines of the watercourse and that they be maintained in a natural state. Requirements concerning the width of easements may be general (width "to be determined"), based on a performance standard ("of such width to accommodate expected storm water runoff") or specific (range of 15´-20´ minimum). The Rutgers ordinance stipulates that the size of the easement should be dictated by working needs. To allow for a truck or backhoe, easements should generally be 20 feet in width for one utility and 5 additional feet, if practical, for each additional utility located in the same easement.

# Improvement Guarantees

## Providing Improvement Guarantees: Issues and Recommended Strategies

Improvement guarantees are subdivision regulations whose purpose is to ensure that the improvements described in the previous sections—streets, parking, utilities, and design-related improvements such as landscaping—are properly installed and maintained.[150] The need for improvement guarantees became evident after communities began adopting subdivision requirements:

*Improvement requirements quickly produced a new problem: failure of subdividers to install these improvements. An isolated problem at first, it spread steadily during the uncontrolled land boom of the 1920s and became epidemic by the end of the 1930s. . . .*

*Communities suffered a number of problems, chiefly economic, when developers failed to make subdivision improvements. Improvement guarantees were developed as a logical response to this problem. They provide the community with assurance against failure to complete the improvements, no matter what the reason. Without exception, the courts have upheld the right of communities to require this assurance.*[151]

The nature and monetary amount of improvement guarantees should reflect a balancing of interests: developers should not be required to provide guarantees that are excessive in amount, duration, or cost; yet the public must be protected from the improper installation of subdivision improvements. Designing balanced regulations that are fair to developers, yet protect communities, has been the subject of numerous reports, including *Subdivision Improvement Guarantees*, published by the American Society of Planning Officials (ASPO);[152] "Subdivision Improvement Requirements and Guarantees: A Primer," published in *The Journal of Urban and Contemporary Law;*[153] as well as others.[154] Balanced and reasonable improvement guarantees, according to these sources, are ones that meet a number of criteria: 1) the dollar amount of the guarantee will reflect the cost of completing the improvements; 2) the guarantee will be held in force only for such time needed to ensure compliance; and 3) a number of alternative mechanisms will be allowed as opposed to limiting improvement guarantees to bonds alone, which may be difficult and expensive to secure. Other alternatives include, for example, letters of credit and escrow accounts.

The advantages of permitting a range of strategies are summarized by the American Society of Planning Officials (ASPO):

*Performance bonds have proved to be difficult to obtain in many parts of the country.... The effect of these regulations has been to inhibit small-scale developers from entering the development field or surviving once they get there.... This is not a proper use of improvement guarantees.*

*A number of alternative methods to guarantee improvements... provide the community with a degree of protection.... Many of these guarantees are easier or less expensive to comply with than posting performance bonds....*[155]

This same ASPO report also stresses the importance of releasing an improvement guarantee once it has served its function:

*The prompt reduction and release of guarantees upon completion of improvements can [also] be very important in reducing costs.... The prompt release of funds guaranteeing the initial stages of development may allow those funds to be used as payment for construction costs in later stages. This faster cash flow should reduce the developer's borrowing costs.*[156]

## Model Ordinance Provisions

The requirements for performance guarantees included in the Rutgers model ordinance guarantees incorporate national recommendations for reasonable and flexible strategies. The stated goal of this section of the ordinance is indicated as follows:

*Improvement guarantees shall be provided to ensure the municipality of the proper installation and maintenance of on-tract improvements. The nature and duration of the guarantee shall be structured to achieve this goal while not adding unnecessary costs to the developer.*

To accomplish this goal, the Rutgers model permits a number of alternative methods to guarantee improvements, including security bonds, escrow accounts, and letters of credit. Letters of credit, for example, are typically less costly to the developer than security bonds, yet offer the municipality considerable protection. As discussed in the ASPO report:

*The usefulness of the standby letter of credit stems from its most important and unique characteristic: the undertaking of the issuer is absolutely independent of the underlying agreement between the account party and the beneficiary. As a result, the beneficiary of the credit, the local government, is entitled to collect on the credit prior to pursuing its claim against the developer and irrespective of the local government's ability to demonstrate the existence of a default or compensable injury. The issuer is obligated to make payment whenever the beneficiary presents the credit and any other documents required by the terms of the credit. In many cases, the accompanying document will be nothing more than the beneficiary's affidavit stating that the developer is in default.*[157]

The Rutgers model ordinance also permits subdivision improvement agreements. A subdivision improvement agreement is a comprehensive three-party agreement in which a lender promises to lend a specified amount of money to a developer for the purpose of constructing required improvements, the developer promises to use these funds to complete the improvements, and the local government promises to accept the dedication of the completed improvements.[158] As described in a recent study, this type of agreement offers the following benefits:

*1) the removal of surety bond barriers to smaller developers; 2) the savings of bond premiums; 3) the elimination of suretyship defenses; 4) the elimination of the inflexibility of the letter of credit; 5) the increase of control over security funds by a party with an economic interest in completing the improvements; 6) the decrease in the likelihood of litigation; and 7) the probability that the developer or lender actually will construct the subdivision improvements.*[159]

In addition to permitting a number of alternative methods for guaranteeing improvements, the Rutgers model ordinance incorporates other cost-saving elements while still protecting the municipality. These include a clear specification of the procedure for inspection, certification, reduction, and/or release of the guarantees. In addition, developers are given the right to have their posting of guarantees reduced as they deliver the subdivision improvements. If improvements are not made in a timely fashion, however, the municipality is given the right to apply for release of funds guaranteeing completion of the improvements.

## Notes

1. See, for example, Welford Sanders and David Mosena, *Changing Development Standards for Affordable Housing* (Chicago, IL: American Planning Association Advisory Service, 1982); Robert A. Johnston and Seymour I. Schwartz, *The Effect of Local Development Regulations on the Cost of Producing Single-Family Housing* (Davis, CA: Institute of Government Affairs and Institute of Ecology, University of California, 1984); U.S. Department of Housing and Urban Development, *Building Affordable Homes: A Cost Savings Guide for Builder/Developers* (Washington, D.C.: Department of Housing and Urban Development and NAHB Research Foundation, Inc., 1982); Department of Housing and Urban Development, *The Affordable Community: Growth, Change, and Choice in the 80s* (Washington, D.C.: Government Printing Office, 1981); and Department of Housing and Urban Development, *Reducing the Development Costs of Housing: Actions for States and Local Governments* (Washington, D.C.: Department of Housing and Urban Development, 1979).

2. Bucks County Planning Commission, *Performance Streets: A Concept and Model Standards for Residential Streets* (Doylestown, PA: Bucks County Planning Commission, 1980), pp. i-ii; National Association of Home Builders, *Subdivision Regulation Handbook* (Washington, D.C.: NAHB, 1978), p. 19; and Urban Land Institute, American Society of Civil Engineers, and National Association of Home Builders, *Residential Streets: Objectives, Principles and Design Considerations* (Washington, D.C.: ULI, ASCE, NAHB, 1974), p. 8.

3. Ibid., and National Committee for Traffic Safety, *Recommendations of the National Committee for Traffic Safety.* (NCTS, 1961); National Association of Home Builders, *Economics of Residential Street Standards* (Rockville, MD: NAHB Research Foundation, 1986).

4. Institute of Transportation Engineers, *Recommended Guidelines for Subdivision Streets* (Washington, D.C.: ITE, 1984), p. 3.

5. Michael B. Brough, *A Unified Development Ordinance* (Chicago, IL: American Planning Association, 1985).

6. See, for example, Fred A. Reid, "Critique of ITE Trip Generation Rates and an Alternative Basis for Estimating New Area Traffic," *Transportation Record* 874; and Everett C. Carter, "Databases for Traffic Impact Studies," paper presented at Rutgers University, Center for Urban Policy Research, Development Impact Analysis Conference, Washington, D.C., May 6-7, 1986.

7. Both ULI, ASCE, NAHB, *Residential Streets*, and Bucks County, *Performance Streets*, recommend a 500 ADT limit on residential subcollectors, or 1,000 ADT on loop subcollectors.

8. This figure is used as a standard for collectors by both ULI, ASCE, NAHB, *Residential Streets*, and Bucks County, *Performance Streets*.

9. Bucks County, *Performance Streets*, p. 19.

10. See Bucks County, *Performance Streets*, pp. 12-13, for a discussion on cul-de-sac length. Bucks County does not find these arguments persuasive, however, on the grounds that an ADT limitation preempts the need to establish a maximum cul-de-sac length.

11. See, for example, *DeChiara and Koppelman:* 500 feet; *Jackson, MS:* 600 feet (or as necessary by topography); *Oregon:* 400 feet (serving a maximum of 18 dwelling units); *Freilich and Levi:* 500 feet (serving no more than 14 dwelling units). Joseph DeChiara and Lee Koppelman, *Urban Planning and Design Criteria*, Third Edition (New York: Van Nostrand Reinhold Co., 1982); Syd Smith, *Subdivision Guidelines for the Jackson (MS) Metropolitan Area* (Springfield, VA: NTIS, 1973); Bureau of Governmental Research and Science, *The Development Standards Document*, Vol. 2 (Eugene, OR: University of Oregon, 1979); and Robert H. Freilich and Peter S. Levi, *Model Subdivision Regulations* (Chicago, IL: American Society of Planning Officials, 1975).

12. As an example of reduced standards in rural areas, Hamilton, New Jersey's subdivision ordinance sets the length of cul-de-sacs at 750 feet, but allows a 1,200-foot maximum length in rural developments.

13. ITE, *Recommended Guidelines*, p. 8.

14. Bucks County, *Performance Streets*, p. 13. ULI, ASCE, NAHB, *Residential Streets*, also recommends mid-block turning circles for long cul-de-sacs, pp. 35, 39.

15. Bucks County, *Performance Streets*, p. 17.

16. Lynch and Hack, *Site Planning*, p. 208, and Bucks County, *Performance Streets*, p. 8. DeChiara and Koppelman, *Design Criteria*, p. 203, allow 7-foot parking lanes, but the illustration on page 289 shows 8-foot parking lanes. Moskowitz and Lindbloom note that while 10-foot wide spaces are usually preferred, 9-foot widths are not uncommon and are adequate for residential parking which can be considered long-term parking; *Guide*, p. 94.

17. Lynch and Hack, *Site Planning*, p. 208.

18. Bucks County, *Performance Streets*, p. 8.

19. Lynch and Hack point out that traffic lanes may be up to 12 feet wide on highways, *Site Planning*, p. 208; Bucks County recommends 10-foot lanes for collectors without curbs carrying an average daily traffic of 2,000 or less (11-foot lanes if the road has curbs), and 11-foot lanes for collectors without curbs carrying an average daily traffic of more than 2,000 (12-foot lanes for road with curbs), *Performance Streets*, p. 21. The American Association of State Highway and Transportation Officials (1973) recommends 10-foot moving lanes (cited in Bucks County, p. 20); and the American Association of State Highway Officials (1971) recommends 11-foot lanes, cited in Bucks County, p. 20.

20. Welford Sanders *et al.*, *Affordable Single-Family Housing: A Review of Development Standards*, PAS Report Number 385 (Chicago, IL: American Planning Association, 1984), p. 11.

21. Bucks County, *Performance Streets*, p. 8.

22. ITE, *Recommended Guidelines*, p. 6.

23. Dimensions cited in Bucks County, *Performance Streets*, p. 12. AASHTO standard is from AASHTO, *A Policy on Geometric Design of Highways and Streets*, 1984, p. 476.

24. DeChiara and Koppelman, *Time-Saver Standards*, p. 347; Moskowitz and Lindbloom, *Guide*, p. 87; and Lynch and Hack, *Site Planning*, p. 215.

25. The sources enumerating uses of curbs and gutters include DeChiara and Koppelman, *Urban Planning and Design Criteria*, p. 281; ITE, *Recommended Guidelines*, p. 7; and ULI, ASCE, NAHB, *Residential Streets*, p. 43. Alternatives to curbing were taken from reports supplied by John E. Rahenkamp & Associates, Philadelphia, Pennsylvania.

26. ULI, ASCE, NAHB, *Residential Streets*, p. 43.

27. Ibid., p. 42. See also NAHB, *Handbook*, p. 22: "Curbs and gutters should be required only when necessary to control storm water runoff, to maintain the pavement, or to prevent deterioration of paving edge. The use of curbs and cutters should otherwise be minimized."

28. ITE points out, "The complete elimination of curbs poses a number of disadvantages, as follows:
    a. No protection is given to pedestrians, street trees, and utilities.
    b. Border area erosion is prevalent.
    c. The roadway is poorly defined at night under rainy weather when asphalt surfacing is used.
    d. Positive control of drainage is totally lacking. Open ditch-type adjacent drainage facilities are customarily employed, which leaves the subdivision with a rural appearance.
    e. Where asphalt surface is used, pavement edge ravelling poses a maintenance problem."
    ITE, *Recommended Guidelines*, p. 7.

29. Bucks County, *Performance Streets*, p. 9.

30. ULI, ASCE, NAHB, *Residential Streets*, p. 43.

31. Ibid.

32. ITE, *Recommended Guidelines*, p. 7, compares vertical and rolled curbs, citing the various advantages of each, as follows:

    Advantages of the *vertical curb* are:

    a. Pedestrians, street trees, utilities, and signs are best protected by the vertical curb.

    b. A positive limit of vehicle encroachment on the border area is established. This minimizes parkway erosion and also reduces probability of vehicles sliding off the roadway under unfavorable pavement and weather conditions.

    c. Depression of curb is required at driveways. Such depression is desirable for clear identification of driveway, which minimizes blockage by curb parkers.

    d. Excellent drainage control may be maintained by either variable height or standard height curbs.

    e. Provides improved control of potential parked runaway vehicles.

        Advantages of the *roll-type* curb are:

    a. It is slightly less expensive than the vertical type.

    b. Some persons believe that the roll type is the more aesthetically pleasing.

    c. Cheap driveway construction can be employed without curb depression. This allows the subdivider and developer certain flexibilities in their constructions, in that driveway locations are not required to be determined prior to curb installation.

33. ITE, *Recommended Guidelines*, notes these two functions of shoulders, pp. 5-6.

34. Bucks County, *Performance Streets*, p. 10.

35. Ibid.

36. Harvey S. Moskowitz and Carl G. Lindbloom, *The Illustrated Book of Development Definitions* (New Brunswick, N.J.: Rutgers University Center for Urban Policy Research, 1981), p. 171.

37. NAHB, *Subdivision Regulations*, p. 23.

38. Moskowitz and Lindbloom, *Guide*, pp. 142–143.

39. Lynch and Hack, *Site Planning*, p. 289.

40. NAHB, *Subdivision Regulations*, p. 23.

41. Four feet is the width most often recommended by authorities and required in local ordinances. ULI, ASCE, NAHB point out, however, that a sidewalk 4½ feet wide is more comfortable for passing bicycles, *Residential Streets*. HUD's *Minimum Property Standards* finds 3 feet adequate for minor walks. Freilich and Levi, *Model Subdivision Regulations*, recommend a range of sidewalk widths (from 4 to 6 feet), depending on street classification and density.

42. See appendix for construction standards.

43. Moskowitz and Lindbloom, *Development Definitions*, p. 35.

44. DeChiara and Koppelman, *Design Criteria*, pp. 309-10.

45. New Jersey Department of Transportation (NJDOT), "Bicycle Planning and Design Guidelines," *Bicycle Compatible Roadways: Planning and Design Guidelines*, NJDOT, however, assumes 12-foot lanes, recommending 24-foot roadways as a minimum width to accommodate bicycling safely.

46. DeChiara and Koppelman, *Design Criteria*, p. 309.

47. Ibid.

48. Ibid.

49. *Bicycle Compatible Roadways*, p. 12.

50. Ibid., p. 9.

51. See bibliography for complete citations.

52. At low ADT levels, bicycles can "take the lane" and vehicles can cross over into the opposing traffic lane to pass, NJDOT, *Bicycle Compatible Roadways*.

53. ITE, *Recommended Guidelines*, p. 5. See also the following, referenced in Bucks County, p. 33: James Schrader, *Street Standards in Subdivision Regulations*, PAS Report No. 183

(Chicago, IL: American Society of Planning Officials, 1965); National Committee on Urban Transportation, *Standards for Street Facilities and Services,* Procedure Manual 7a (Chicago, IL: Public Administration Service, 1958); American Association of State Highway Officials, *Geometric Design Guide for Local Roads and Streets* (Washington, D.C.: AASHO, 1971).

54. In both ordinances, higher-density areas are subject to more stringent requirements due to the greater load generated on public facilities.

55. Some sources note that in special cases, it may be necessary to reduce the minimum grade, but drainage must be positive throughout the street. See ULI, ASCE, NAHB, *Residential Streets,* p. 37, and Lynch and Hack, *Site Planning,* p. 218.

56. Lynch and Hack, for example, base maximum street grade on design speed, with grades for minor streets from 11 to 12 percent, and 9 to 10 percent for major residential streets, *Site Planning,* pp. 218, 221; Bucks County recommends a range of 8 to 10 percent, depending on road classification; and Freilich and Levi recommend standards for street grade that range from 5 to 10 percent, depending on road classification and density.

57. Lynch and Hack suggest 10 percent, p. 218; ITE recommends 8 percent, p. 8.

58. ITE, *Recommended Guidelines,* p. 8.

59. Ibid., p. 14.

60. Ibid.

61.

## BUCKS COUNTY
## MINIMUM INTERSECTION SPACING

*Major Road Type Intersected*      *Spacing (in feet)*

| | |
|---|---|
| Higher-Order Street | 1,000 * |
| Residential Collector | 300 |
| Residential Subcollector | 125 |

* Minimum spacing. Actual spacing to be determined by municipal engineer based on traffic characteristics of higher-order street.

## ITE
## MINIMUM CENTERLINE OFFSET OF
## ADJACENT INTERSECTION (feet)

*Type of Intersection*      *Spacing*

| | |
|---|---|
| Local–Local | 125 |
| Local–Collector | 150 |
| Collector–Collector | 200 |

Bucks County, *Performance Streets*, p. 31; ITE, *Recommended Guidelines*, p. 13.

62. Ibid.

63. ITE, ibid.

64. Ibid., p.13.

65. Moskowitz and Lindbloom, in *Guide*, however, recommend that standards should be spaced at a distance approximately equal to four times the height. Since recommended maximum height is 25 feet, they recommend the light standards be spaced 100 feet apart, p. 155.

66. Ibid. p. 158.

67. Freilich and Levi, *Model Subdivision Regulations*, p. 111.

68. Moskowitz and Lindbloom, *Guide*, p. 160.

69. Ibid., pp. 158-61.

70. Bucks County, *Performance Streets*, p. 40.

71. Two spaces per single-family unit appears to be the general standard, and some municipal ordinances require the same number of spaces for townhouse units. Bucks County, *Performance Streets*, p. 41, recommends that in addition to the spaces required for each dwelling unit, the following number of spillover parking spaces for visitors also be required:

| | |
|---|---|
| SF, detached | 1.5 |
| TH | 1.0 |
| MF | .5 |

72. Moskowitz and Lindbloom, *Guide*, p. 90. Moskowitz and Lindbloom, however, do not base parking requirements on house price, instead linking number of required spaces to unit type.

73. Other examples of ordinances that tie number of spaces to size of unit include:

| | |
|---|---|
| Middletown, OH: | 1.25 spaces for efficiencies |
| | 1.35 spaces for 1-BR units |
| | 1.50 spaces for 2-BR units |
| | 1.75 spaces for 3-BR units |
| | 2 spaces for 4-BR units |
| | |
| Rocky Mount, NC: | 2 spaces for 1-BR units |
| | 2.25 spaces for 2-BR units |
| | 2.50 spaces for 3-BR units |

74. Brough, *A Unified Development Ordinance*, p. 158.

75. Moskowitz and Lindbloom, *Guide*, p. 102.

76. See, for example, HUD, *Minimum Property Standards*, p. 3-16.

77. *Time-Saver Standards*, p. 414.

78. Welford Sanders and David Mosena, *Changing Development Standards for Affordable Housing*, Planning Advisory Service Report Number 371 (Chicago, IL: APA, 1982), pp. 6-8.

79. In Dade County, Florida and Des Plains, Illinois, up to 35 percent of required parking spaces may be of a size reduced for compact cars; in Newark, Delaware, when 25 or more stalls are required, up to 25 percent may be reduced dimensions; and in Seattle, Washington, at least 60 percent of the required stalls in multifamily developments must be at reduced dimensions for compact cars.

80. Moskowitz and Lindbloom, *Guide*, p. 94.

81. American Planning Association, "Zoning News," January 1984, p. 2.

82. Richard D. Tabors, Chapter 7, "Utility Services," in *The Practice of Local Government Planning*, edited by Frank S. So. et al., Washington, D.C.: International City Management Association, 1979, p. 183. Despite Rome's provision of water as a public responsibility, however, this was not always the practice. As Lewis Mumford points out, "As late as the fifteenth century, the provision of water conduits in London was a matter for private philanthropy, like hospitals and almshouses." *The City in History* (New York: Harcourt Brace Jovanovich, Inc., 1961), p. 295.

83. NALCO Chemical Company, *The NALCO Water Handbook*, edited by Frank N. Kemmer (New York: McGraw-Hill, 1979), pp. 35-41.

84. Robert W. Burchell and David Listokin, *The Environmental Impact Handbook* (New Brunswick, NJ: Center for Urban Policy Research, 1975), pp. 128-9.

85. Tabors, "Utility Services," p. 193.

86. F.P. Linnaweaver, Jr., John C. Geyer, and Jerome B. Wolff, *A Study of Residential Water Use*. Study prepared for the Federal Housing Administration (Washington, D.C.: U.S. Government Printing Office, 1967), cited in Burchell and Listokin, *Handbook*, p. 128.

87. Hittman Associates, Inc., *Forecasting Municipal Water Requirements*, Columbia, MD, 1969, NTIS No. PB 190275; cited in Burchell and Listokin, *Handbook*, pp. 128-32.

88. Burchell and Listokin, p. 128. Another approach suggested in the *Handbook* is the use of a coefficient related to total flow: Ralph Porges estimates that 13.4 percent of total flow is due to public and related water uses. See Ralph Porges, "Factors Influencing per Capital [sic] Water Consumption," *Water and Sewage Works*, Vol. 104, May 1957, pp. 199-204.

89. Tabors, "Utility Services," p. 193; and *NALCO Water Handbook*, pp. 35-1–35-2.

90. Tabors, "Utility Services," p. 193.

91. Ibid., p. 194. Tabors points out that since water systems are under pressure, increased quantities of water can be delivered with little increase in pipe size above the minimum, p. 193.

92. Connecticut, Department of Housing, *Housing and Land Use: Community Options for Lowering Housing Costs*, Hartford, CT: Connecticut Department of Housing, 1981, p. 58.

93. National Association of Home Builders, *Subdivision Regulation Handbook* (Washington, D.C.: NAHB, 1978), p. 32.

94. Ibid.

95. Freilich and Levi, *Model Subdivision Regulations*, pp. 92-3. Indiana's model code, which is based on Freilich and Levi's, contains the same provision.

96. Connecticut, *Housing and Land Use*, pp. 58-9. Connecticut's recommendations are similar to NAHB's.

97. Among sources, the following recommend a minimum size of six inches for water mains: HUD, *Innovative Site Utility Installations*; DeChiara and Koppelman; ASCE; Indiana model code; and Freilich and Levi model code. Only HUD, in seeking to minimize infrastructure costs, recommends less than 6 inches for water main diameters, and then only in cases where fire hydrants are strategically located for maximum coverage and where fire protection is not required; *Innovative Utility Installations*, p. 30.

98. U.S. Department of Commerce, National Bureau of Standards. *A Review of Standards & Common Practices in Building Site Regulation: Technical Issues and Research Needs.* Report prepared by the Rice Center, Houston, Texas. Springfield, VA: NTIS, 1981, p. 128.

99. HUD, *Innovative Site Utility Installations.*

100. HUD's recommendations reflect its interest in common trenching of utility lines as a strategy to reduce costs and construction time. HUD refers to experience with successful common trenching in San Diego County, California, in which the common trench is 24 inches wide and 48 to 60 inches deep. Gas lines there are laid at depths of 30 to 42 inches and separated from other utilities by at least 12 inches.

101. HUD, *Innovative Utility Installations*, pp. 23-27; NAHB, *Subdivision Regulation Handbook*, p. 33.

102. Lewis Mumford, *The City in History* (New York: Harcourt Brace Jovanovich, Inc., 1961), p. 214.

103. Ibid., p. 215. Mumford uses the Cloaca Maxima as an example to point out the cost-effectiveness of providing quality infrastructure: "With its record of continuous service for more than twenty-five hundred years, that structure proves that in the planning of cities low first costs do not necessarily denote economy; for if the utility needed has been soundly conceived and built, the final costs, extended over its whole prospective lifetime, are what really matter."

104. Ibid., p. 477.

105. NAHB, *Subdivision Regulation Handbook*, p. 32; Freilich and Levi, *Model Subdivision Regulations*, p. 94; Indiana, Oregon, and Escambia–Santa Rosa model codes; Hamilton, South Brunswick, and Mount Olive, New Jersey ordinances.

106. DeChiara and Koppelman, *Urban Planning and Design Criteria;* Freilich and Levi, *Model Subdivision Regulations;* and Bernardsville all recommend or require connection to a public system in high-density areas.

107. NAHB, *Subdivision Regulation Handbook,* p. 31; and Moskowitz and Lindbloom, *Guide,* p. 109.

108. Freilich and Levi, *Model Subdivision Regulations,* p. 94.

109. Mount Olive, N.J., ordinance.

110. South Brunswick, N.J., ordinance.

111. DeChiara and Koppelman, *Design Criteria.* Jackson, Mississippi's model code, however, allows septic systems on lots of one-half acre or more if approved by proper officials. Dover, New Jersey's ordinance specifies a minimum lot size of 30,000 ft.$^2$ for private systems.

112. Freilich and Levi, *Model Subdivision Regulations,* p. 94.

113. DeChiara and Koppelman, *Design Criteria.*

114. Mount Olive, N.J., ordinance.

115. Freilich and Levi, *Model Subdivision Regulations,* p. 94.

116. HUD, *Innovative Utility Installations,* p. 47.

117. Ibid., and Indiana's model code.

118. HUD, *Innovative Utility Installations;* and HUD, *Building Affordable Homes.*

119. HUD, *Innovative Utility Installations,* p. 5.

120. Ibid., p. 8.

121. Ibid.

122. DeChiara and Koppelman, *Design Criteria,* recommend a range from 8-inch laterals to many feet in diameter for large interceptors; Freilich and Levi, *Model Subdivision Regulations,* require a pipe size of a minimum of 8 inches in diameter, p. 95; and HUD, *Innovative Utility Installations,* notes that 8 inches is the standard pipe dimension required, p. 14.

123. *Review of Standards,* p. 20. It goes on to say, "Local governments' fiscal policies may call for excessive standards for pipe-sizing so as to accommodate future development without cost to the local government." Ibid.

124. HUD, *Innovative Utility Installations*, p. 14.

125. Ibid.

126. Rice Center, *Review of Standards*, p. 86; Freilich and Levi, *Model Subdivision Regulations*, p. 96; Indiana model code. HUD's *Innovative Utility Installations* calls for manholes where changes in slope occur and where lines converge or obstructions are likely, p. 16.

127. HUD, *Innovative Utility Installations*, p. 20; Freilich and Levi, *Model Subdivision Regulations*, p. 96; and Indiana's model code (although this standard applies to sewers as large as 18 inches in diameter). Jackson, Mississippi, specifies a 300-foot maximum spacing between manholes.

128. HUD, *Innovative Utility Installations*, p. 20.

129. Ibid., p. 16.

130. Rice Center, *A Review of Standards and Common Practices in Building Site Regulation: Technical Issues and Research Needs* (Washington, D.C.: National Bureau of Standards, 1981), p. 81.

131. Harvey Moskowitz and Carl Lindbloom, *A Guide for Residential Design Review* (Trenton, NJ: Department of Community Affairs, 1976), p. 112.

132. Ibid.

133. See note 130.

134. Moskowitz and Lindbloom, *A Guide for Residential Design Review*, p. 112.

135. Connecticut Department of Housing, *Low-Cost Housing Delivery*, p. 31.

136. Urban Land Institute, American Society of Civil Engineers, and the National Association of Home Builders, *Storm Water Management* (Washington, D.C.: Urban Land Institute, 1975), p. 29. See also, American Society of Civil Engineers and the Water Pollution Control Federation, *Design and Construction of Sanitary and Storm Sewers*

(ASCE and WPCF, 1969); Warren Viessman, Jr. et al., *Introduction to Hydrology* (New York, NY: Harper and Row, 1977), Chapter 11; New Jersey Department of Environmental Protection, *New Jersey Stormwater Quantity/Quality Management Manual* (Trenton, NJ: Department of Environmental Protection, 1981).

137. See New Jersey Department of Environmental Protection, Division of Water Resources, *Technical Manual for Stream Encroachment* (Trenton, NJ: Department of Environmental Protection, August 1984), p. 49.

138. Ibid.

139. Ibid.

140. U.S. Department of Agriculture, Soil Conservation Service *Technical Release* (TR) No. 55, *Urban Hydrology for Small Watersheds* (Washington, D.C. Government Printing Office, 1980).

141. Rice Center, *A Review of Standards*, p. 44.

142. Ibid., p. 16.

143. New Jersey Department of Environmental Protection, *New Jersey Stormwater Quantity/Quality Management Manual*; New Jersey Department of Environmental Protection, *New Jersey Statewide Water Quality Management Program Plan* (Trenton, NJ: Department of Environmental Protection, 1985).

144. Moskowitz and Lindbloom, *A Guide for Residential Design Review*, p. 112.

145. ULI–ASCE–NAHB, *Storm Water Management*, p. 49.

146. Ibid.

147. Ibid., p. 49.

148. New Jersey Department of Environmental Protection, Division of Water Resources, "A Draft Storm Water Management Ordinance for Municipalities," August 30, 1985, p. 4.

149. U.S. Department of Agriculture, Soil Conservation Service, *Water Management and Sediment Control for Urbanizing Areas* (Washington, D.C.: Government Printing Office, 1978).

150. See Groton, "Surety Bonds" in J. Frein (editor), *Handbook of Construction Management and Organization* (1980), p. 86. Cited in Michael M. Shultz and Richard Kelley, "Subdivision Improvement Requirements and Guarantees: A Primer," *Journal of Urban and Contemporary Law*, Vol. 28, No. 3, p. 44.

151. Brian Rogal, *Subdivision Improvement Guarantees* (Chicago, IL: American Society of Planning Officials, 1974), pp. 1-2.

152. Ibid.

153. See note 150.

154. Richard Kelley and Michael M. Shultz, "Or Other Adequate Security: Using, Structuring, and Managing the Standby Letter of Credit to Ensure the Completion of Subdivision Improvements," *The Urban Lawyer*, Vol. 19, No. 1, Winter 1987, p. 39.

155. Rogal, *Subdivision Improvement Guarantees*, pp. 4-5.

156. Ibid.

157. Ibid., p. 42.

158. Rogal, *Subdivision Improvement Guarantees*, p. 59.

159. Ibid., p. 60.

# BIBLIOGRAPHY

This bibliography is organized by the chapters of the reference section.

## Background: Evolution of Subdivision Regulation

*A. BACKGROUND AND HISTORY*

Adams, Thomas. *The Design of Residential Areas.* New York, NY: Arno Press, 1974. Reprint of edition published by Harvard University Press (Cambridge, MA), issued as Harvard City Planning Studies, Vol. VI.

American Society of Planning Officials. *Installation of Physical Improvements as Required in Subdivision Regulations.* Chicago, IL: ASPO, 1952 Planning Advisory Service Information Report, No. 38.

"An Analysis of Subdivision Control Legislation." *Indiana Law Journal,* Vol. 28 (1952).

Anderson, Robert M. *American Law of Zoning: Zoning, Planning, Subdivision Control.* Rochester, NY: The Lawyers Co-operative Publishing Company, 1986.

Anderson, Robert M., and Bruce B. Roswig. *Planning, Zoning, and Subdivision: A Summary of Statutory Law in the 50 States.* Syracuse, NY: July 1965.

Bartholomew, Harland. Chairman, "Subdivision Layout" Committee, President's Conference on Home Building and Home

Ownership, *Planning for Residential Districts*. Washington, DC: National Capital Press, 1932.

Bassett, Edward M.; Frank B. Williams; Alfred Bettman; and Robert Whitten. *Model Laws for Planning Cities, Counties, and States*. Cambridge, MA: Harvard University Press, 1935, Harvard City Planning Studies, Vol. VII.

Delafons, J. *Land-Use Controls in the United States*. 2nd ed. Cambridge, MA: The MIT Press, 1969.

James, Franklin J., Jr., and Oliver Windsor. "Fiscal Zoning, Fiscal Reform, and Exclusionary Land Use Controls." *Journal of the American Institute of Planners* (April 1976), pp. 130–141.

Lautner, Harold W. *Subdivision Regulations: An Analysis of Land Subdivision Control Practices*. Chicago, IL: Public Administration Service, 1941.

McMichael, Stanley L. *Real Estate Subdivisions*. New York, NY: Prentice–Hall, Inc., 1949.

Manuel, Allen D. "Local Land and Building Regulation," Commission Report No. 6. Cited in National Commission on Urban Problems, *Building the American City*. Washington, DC: U.S. Government Printing Office, 1969.

National Resources Committee. *Urban Planning and Land Policies*. Washington, DC: U.S. Government Printing Office, 1939. Vol. II of the Supplementary Report of the Urbanism Committee to the National Resources Committee.

Regional Survey of New York and Its Environs. *Neighborhood and Community Planning*. Vol. VII. New York, NY: Regional Plan of New York and Its Environs, 1929.

Reps, John W. *The Making of Urban America: A History of City Planning in the United States*. Princeton, NJ: Princeton University Press, 1965.

————. *Town Planning in Frontier America*. Princeton, NJ: Princeton University Press, 1965. Reprinted by University of Missouri Press (Columbia, MO: University of Missouri Press), 1980.

Sakolski, A. M. *The Great American Land Bubble*. New York, NY: Harper & Brothers Publishers, 1932.

Scott, M. *American City Planning Since 1890*. Berkeley, CA: University of California Press, 1971.

Shultz, Michael M., and Richard Kelley. "Subdivision Improvement Requirements and Guarantees: A Primer." *Journal of Urban and Contemporary Law* 28, No. 3 (1985):3.

U.S. National Commission on Urban Problems. *Building the American City.* Washington, DC, 1969.

U.S. Urbanism Committee. *Urban Planning and Land Policies: Vol. II.* Washington, DC: U.S. Government Printing Office, 1939.

Williams, Norman, Jr. *American Planning Law: Land Use and the Police Power,* Vol. 5 (1985 Revision). Wilmette, IL: Callaghan & Company, 1975.

Yearwood, R. M. *Land Subdivision Regulation: Policy and Legal Considerations for Urban Planning.* New York, NY: Praeger, 1971.

Yokley, E. C. *The Law of Subdivisions.* Charlottesville, VA: Michie, 1963.

## B.   *SUBDIVISION CONTROLS*
## 1.   Legal Perspective

Anderson, Robert M. *American Law of Zoning: Zoning, Planning, Subdivision Control.* Rochester, NY: The Lawyers Cooperative Publishing Company, 1986.

California. Office of Planning and Research. *Planning, Zoning and Development Laws.* Sacramento, CA: 1982.

Cunningham, R. A. "Interrelationship Between Exclusionary Zoning and Exclusionary Subdivision Control." *University of Michigan Journal of Law* 6 (1973): 290.

Fishman, Richard P. *Housing for All Under Law: New Directions in Housing, Land Use, and Planning Law.* Cambridge, MA: Ballinger, 1978.

Gailey, J. Benjamin. "Municipal Regulation of Housing Costs and Supply." *Zoning and Planning Law Report* 4 (February 1981).

Haar, Charles. "Enabling Legislation for Subdivision Control." *Land Use Planning.* 2nd ed. Boston, MA: Little Brown, 1971, pp. 349+.

Heyman, Ira Michael, and Thomas K. Gilhool. "The Constitutionality of Imposing Increased Community Costs on New

Suburban Residents Through Subdivision Exactions." *Yale Law Journal* 173 (1964): 1119.

Hirshon, Robert E. "The Interrelationship Between Exclusionary Zoning and Exclusionary Subdivision Control." *Journal of Law Reform* (Winter 1972): 351–360.

Johnston, J. "Constitutionality of Subdivision Control Extractions: The Quest for a Rationale." *Cornell Law Review* 52 (1967): 871–923.

Peterson, Iver. "Builders Battle Takings of Property," *The New York Times.* February 28, 1988, Section 8, p. 1.

Rose, Jerome G. "A Revolution in Land Use Regulations," *Journal of the American Planning Association* (Winter 1988): 109.

Shultz, Michael M., and Richard Kelley. "Subdivision Improvement Requirements and Guarantees: A Primer." *Journal of Urban and Contemporary Law* 28, No. 3 (1985): 3.

Siemeon, Charles L., and Wendy V. Larsen. "Exactions and Takings After *Nollan,*" *Land Use Law* (September 1987), p. 3.

Williams, Norman, Jr. *American Planning Law: Land Use and the Police Power,* Vol. 5 (1985 Revision). Wilmette, IL: Callaghan & Company, 1975.

Yearwood, R. M. *Land Subdivision Regulation: Policy and Legal Considerations for Urban Planning.* New York, NY: Praeger, 1971.

Yokley, E. C. *The Law of Subdivisions.* Charlottesville, VA: Michie, 1963.

## 2. Model Ordinances and General References

American Law Institute. *A Model Land Development Code.* Philadelphia, PA: American Law Institute, 1976.

Brough, Michael B. *A Unified Development Ordinance.* Chicago, IL: Planners Press (division of American Planning Association), 1985.

Bucks County Planning Commission. *Performance Zoning.* Doylestown, PA: Bucks County Planning Commission, 1973.

DeChiara, Joseph, and Lee E. Koppelman. *Manual of Housing/ Planning and Design Criteria.* Englewood Cliffs, NJ: Prentice-Hall, 1975.

———. *Urban Planning and Design Criteria.* New York, NY: Van Nostrand Reinhold, 1975.

East Central Florida Regional Planning Council. *Subdivision Guide.* Springfield, VA: National Technical Information Service, 1968.

Escambia-Santa Rosa (Florida) Regional Planning Council. *Model Subdivision Regulations.* Springfield, VA: National Technical Information Service, 1971.

Freilich, Robert H., and Peter S. Levi. *Model Subdivision Regulations: Text and Commentary.* Chicago, IL: American Society of Planning Officials, 1975.

Institute of Transportation Engineers. *Recommended Guidelines for Subdivision Streets.* Washington, DC: ITE, 1984.

Metropolitan Council of the Twin Cities. *Advisory Land Use Standards for Multifamily Housing.* Minneapolis, MN: Metropolitan Council, 1978.

National Association of Home Builders. *Subdivision Regulation Handbook.* NAHB Land Development Series. Washington, DC: National Association of Homebuilders, 1978.

Patterson, William. *Model County Subdivision Regulations* (HERPICC Publication, No. H-83-4). West Lafayette, Indiana: Purdue University, 1983.

Queale, William; William Miller; Robert McEldowney; and Carl Lindbloom. *Model Subdivision Ordinance.* Draft prepared for Hunterdon County and the New Jersey Department of Community Affairs, Local Planning Assistance Unit, September 1975.

Saginaw County (Michigan) Metropolitan Planning Commission. *Model Subdivision Regulation Ordinance.* Springfield, VA: National Technical Information Service, 1972.

Smith, S. *Subdivision Guidelines for the Jackson Metropolitan Area.* Jackson, MS: U.S. Department of Housing and Urban Development, 1973.

University of Oregon, Bureau of Governmental Research. *A Model Land Subdivision Ordinance Format.* Eugene, OR: University of Oregon, Bureau of Governmental Research, 1979.

(The) Urban Land Institute, National Association of Home Builders, and American Society of Civil Engineers. *Residential*

*Streets: Objectives, Principles, and Design Considerations.*
Washington, DC: ULI, 1976.

U.S. Department of Commerce, Bureau of Standards. *A Review of
Standards and Common Practices in Building Site Regula-
tion: Technical Issues and Research Needs.* Washington, DC:
U.S. Department of Commerce, November 1980.

**3.  Definitions**

Brough, Michael B. *A Unified Development Ordinance.* Chicago,
IL: Planners Press (division of American Planning Association), 1985.

Collison, Koder M. *The Developers' Dictionary and Handbook.*
Lexington, MA: Lexington Books, 1974.

Meshenberg, Michael J. *The Language of Zoning: A Glossary of
Words.* Chicago, IL: American Society of Planning Officials,
1974.

Moskowitz, Harvey S., and Carl G. Lindbloom. *The Illustrated
Book of Development Definitions.* New Brunswick, NJ: Center
for Urban Policy Research, 1981.

Schultz, Marilyn Spigel and Vivian Loeb Kasen. *Encyclopedia of
Community Planning and Environmental Management.* New
York, NY: Facts on File Publications, 1984.

C.   *IMPACT ON HOUSING DELIVERY COSTS*

Affordable Housing Task Force, Orange County (CA) Chapter,
Building Industry Association. *Manual for Reducing Housing
Costs.* Santa Ana, CA: Orange County Chapter, Building
Industry Association, January 1979.

Bergman, Edward. *Development Controls and Housing Costs.* 3
vols. Chapel Hill, NC: The Center for Urban and Regional
Studies, August 1974.

Burchell, Robert W., and David Listokin. "Improving Design Standards in Fringe Communities: Local and State Initiatives." In
Urban Land Institute (eds.), *Reducing the Development Costs
of Housing: Actions for State and Local Governments.* Washington, DC: U.S. Government Printing Office, 1979, pp. 15–
54.

———. "The Impact of Local Government Regulations on Housing Costs and Potential Avenues of State Meliorative Measures." In George Sternlieb and James W. Hughes (eds.),

*America's Housing: Prospects and Problems.* New Brunswick, NJ: Rutgers University, Center for Urban Policy Research, 1980, pp. 313–58.

California Building Industry Association. *Manual for Reducing Housing Costs.* Sacramento, CA: California Building Industry Association, 1979.

California. County of Santa Clara. Department of Planning. *Housing Development Cost as Influenced by Government Regulations and Fees: A Study of Four Cities in Santa Clara County.* Washington, DC: U.S. Department of Housing and Urban Development, 1974.

California. Office of Appropriate Technology. *The Affordable Housing Book: Strategies for the Eighties from the California Affordable Housing Competition.* Sacramento, CA: Office of Appropriate Technology, 1982.

Center for Community Development and Preservation. *Reducing Housing Development Costs: Strategies for Affordable Housing.* White Plains, NY: Center for Community Development and Preservation, 1980.

Central Naugatuck Valley Regional Planning Agency. *Least Cost Housing: Minimizing the Fiscal Impact of Zoning and Subdivision Regulations.* Waterbury, CT: 1978.

Connecticut. Department of Housing. *Housing and Land Use: Community Options for Lowering Housing Costs.* Hartford, CT: Connecticut Department of Housing, 1981.

Council of State Community Affairs Agencies. *Affordable Housing and Infrastructure: The State Role.* Washington, DC: Council of State Community Affairs Agencies, March 1984.

————. *State Actions to Promote Affordable Housing: Final Report.* Springfield, VA: National Technical Information Service, 1982.

Das, Amaiya K. *Reducing Housing Costs.* Tallahassee, FL: Florida Department of Community Affairs, 1977.

Derkowski, Andrezej. *Cost in the Land Development Process.* Toronto, Canada: Housing and Urban Development Association, 1976.

Dowall, David E. "Reducing the Cost Effects of Local Land Use Controls." *Journal of the American Planning Association* 47 (April 1981): 145–153.

Eury, Robert M. *Cost of Delay Due to Government Regulation in the Houston Housing Market.* Houston, TX: Rice Center for Design and Research, 1979.

Farr, Cheryl. *Modifying Land-Use Regulations for Economic Development.* Washington, DC: International City Management Association, 1980.

Gaffney, Mason. *Land As An Element of Housing Cost: The Effects of Public Policies and Practices.* Alexandria, VA: Institute for Defense Analysis, 1968.

Hack, Gary, and Greg Polk. *Housing Costs and Government Regulations: Is Regulatory Reform Justified By What We Know?* Cambridge, MA: Harvard–MIT Joint Center for Urban Studies, 1981.

Hershey, Stuart S., and Carolyn Garmise. *Streamlining Local Regulations: A Handbook for Reducing Housing and Development Costs.* Management Information Service Special Report, No. 11. Washington, DC: International City Management Association, 1983.

Kartez, Jack D., and Gregory Winterowd. *State Approaches to Affordable Housing: The Oregon Experience.* Chicago, IL: American Planning Association, 1981.

Leventhal, Kenneth, et al. *Bench Mark Villas: A Demonstration of Affordable Housing.* Santa Ana, CA: Orange County Chapter, Building Industry Association of Southern California, 1983.

Lincoln, James, Jr.; Dean Coddington; and John Penberth. *Summary Analysis of the Impact of State and Local Government Intervention on the Home Building Process in Colorado, 1970–1975.* Denver, CO: Bickert, Browne, Coddington and Associates, Inc., 1976.

Lozano, Eduardo E. "Technical Report: Housing Costs and Alternative Cost Reducing Policies." *Journal of the American Institute of Planners* 38 (May 1972): 173.

(Minneapolis) Metropolitan Council. Modest-Cost Private Housing Advisory Committee. *Modest-Cost Housing in the Twin Cities Metropolitan Area.* Minneapolis, MN: Metropolitan Council, 1977.

Minnesota Housing Institute. *The Multiplicity of Factors That Contribute to the Cost of Housing.* Minneapolis, MN: Minnesota Housing Institute, 1974.

Murphy, Michael. *Reforming Local Development Regulations: Approaches in Five Cities.* Washington, DC: International City Management Association, 1982.

Muth, Richard F., and Elliot Wetzler. "The Effects of Constraints on House Costs." *Journal of Urban Economics* 3 (1976): 57–67.

National Association of Home Builders. *Density Development: Cost Effective and Affordable.* Washington, DC: National Association of Home Builders, May 1982.

_____ . *Impact of Government Regulations on Housing Costs: A Selected Annotated Bibliography.* Washington, DC: National Association of Home Builders, 1976.

National Association of Home Builders Research Foundation. *The Affordable Housing Demonstration Case Study—Lincoln, Nebraska.* Washington, DC: U.S. Government Printing Office, 1982.

_____ . *The Affordable Housing Demonstration, Phoenix, Arizona: A Case Study.* Prepared for U.S. Department of Housing and Urban Development. Washington, DC: HUD, January 1984.

_____ . *Building Affordable Homes: A Cost Savings Guide for Builder/Developers.* Rockville, MD: National Association of Home Builders Research Foundation, 1982.

National Association of Home Builders and the U.S. Department of Housing and Urban Development. *An Approach for the '80s: Affordable Housing Demonstration.* Washington, DC: U.S. Government Printing Office [1983].

New Jersey. Department of Community Affairs. Division of Housing and Planning and the Tri-State Regional Planning Commission. The *Affordable Housing Handbook.* Trenton, NJ: Department of Community Affairs (1982).

New York. Westchester County. *Affordable Housing: The Westchester Approach.* White Plains, NY: County of Westchester, 1980.

Nicholas, James C., with Mary C. Olsen, Joyce Costomiris, and Adele Levesque. *State Regulation/Housing Prices.* New Brunswick, NJ: Rutgers University, Center for Urban Policy Research, 1982.

Porter, Douglas R., and Susan Cole. *Affordable Housing: Twenty Examples From the Private Sector.* Washington, DC: The Urban Land Institute, 1982.

Price, Ruth. *Housing and Land Use: Community Options for Lowering Housing Costs.* Hartford, CT: Connecticut Department of Housing, 1981.

Real Estate Research Corporation. *The Costs of Sprawl: Environmental and Economic Costs of Alternative Residential Development Patterns at the Urban Fringe.* Washington, DC: U.S. Government Printing Office, 1974.

Robinson, Jeremy. *Affordable Houses Designed by Architects.* New York, NY: McGraw-Hill, 1979.

Sagalyn, Lynn B., and George Sternlieb. *Zoning and Housing Costs.* New Brunswick, NJ: Rutgers University, Center for Urban Policy Research, 1972.

San Jose, California. *Effectiveness of Existing Residential Development Review Process and Existing Environmental Control/Protection Review Procedures.* San Jose Measure "B" Study, Working Paper No. 4, 1975.

Sanders, Welford. *The Cluster Subdivision: A Cost-Effective Approach.* Planning Advisory Service Report No. 356. Chicago, IL: American Planning Association, 1980.

Sanders, Welford, and David Mosena. *Changing Development Standards for Affordable Housing.* Planning Advisory Service Report No. 371. Chicago, IL: American Planning Association, 1982.

Schwartz, Seymour I., and Robert A. Johnston. *Local Government Initiatives for Affordable Housing: An Evaluation of Inclusionary Housing Programs in California.* Davis, CA: Institute of Governmental Affairs and Institute of Ecology, 1981.

Seidel, Stephen R. *Housing Costs and Government Regulations.* New Brunswick, NJ: Rutgers University, Center for Urban Policy Research, 1977.

Solomon, Arthur P. *The Effect of Land Use and Environmental Controls on Housing: A Review.* Cambridge, MA: Harvard–MIT Joint Center for Urban Studies, 1976.

Tick, Marvin and John Sider. *State Actions for Affordable Housing.* Prepared for the U.S. Department of Housing and Urban Development. Washington, DC: The Council, 1982.

(The) Urban Land Institute. *Affordable Community: Growth, Change, and Choice in the '80's.* Washington, DC: The Urban Land Institute, 1981.

_____. *Effects of Regulation on Housing Costs: Two Case Studies.* ULI Research Report #27. Washington, DC: The Urban Land Institute, 1977.

_____. *Reducing the Development Costs of Housing: Actions for State and Local Governments—Proceedings of the HUD National Conference on Housing Costs.* Washington, DC: U.S. Government Printing Office, October 1979.

(The) Urban Land Institute, National Association of Home Builders. *Cost-Effective Site Planning/Single-Family Development.* Washington, DC: The Urban Land Institute, 1976.

U.S. Department of Housing and Urban Development. *Affordable Housing: How Local Regulatory Improvements Can Help.* Washington, DC: U.S. Government Printing Office, 1982.

_____. *An Approach for the 80's: Affordable Housing Demonstration.* Washington, DC: U.S. Department of Housing and Urban Development [1983].

_____. *Building Affordable Homes: A Cost Savings Guide for Builder/Developers.* Washington, DC: U.S. Department of Housing and Urban Development, 1982.

_____. *Building Value Into Housing Awards.* By Barbara J. Gilbert and Judith Richland. Washington, DC: U.S. Government Printing Office, 1982.

_____. *Design for Affordable Housing: Cost-Effective/Energy-Conserving Homes.* By Steven Winter, Alexander Grinnell and Susan Rotlenburg. Washington, DC: U.S. Government Printing Office, 1982.

_____. *Final Report of the Task Force on Housing Costs.* Washington, DC: U.S. Department of Housing and Urban Development, May 1978.

_____. *Homebuilding Cost Cuts.* Washington, DC: U.S. Government Printing Office, 1983.

_____. *Housing Cost Reduction Demonstration.* Washington, DC: U.S. Government Printing Office (n.d.).

_____. *Reducing the Development Costs of Housing: Actions for State and Local Governments.* Washington, DC: August 1979.

———. *Reducing the Development Costs of Housing: Current Bibliography.* Washington, DC: U.S. Department of Housing and Urban Development, 1981.

U.S. Department of Housing and Urban Development. Office of Policy Development and Research. *Draft Ordinance for Affordable Housing* (3rd draft), 8 March 1982.

U.S. Department of Housing and Urban Development and the National Association of Home Builders. *Energy-Efficient Residence (EER-2): Final Report.* By Donald F. Livebs. Washington, DC: U.S. Government Printing Office, 1983.

U.S. General Accounting Office. *Why Are New House Prices So High, How Are They Influenced by Government Regulations, and Can Prices Be Reduced?* Washington, DC: U.S. Government Printing Office, 1978.

Weidenbaum, Murray L. "Government Regulations and the Cost of Housing." *Urban Land* 37 (February 1978): 4–5.

Wickersham, Kirk, Jr. "A Lot More Than Just an Ordinance: The Breckenridge Development Code." *Urban Land* (January 1979): 9–13.

Weitz, Stevenson. *Affordable Housing: How Local Regulatory Improvements Can Help.* Washington, DC: U.S. Department of Housing and Urban Development, 1982.

Wu, Ming-Shyong. *Public Improvement Costs for Residential Land Development: A Comparison of Five Counties in the Baltimore Region.* Baltimore, MD: Regional Planning Council, 1973.

## Administration and Procedure

Becker, Christine Schwartz. *Streamlining Governing Body Meetings.* Washington, DC: International City Management Association, 1977.

Bureau of Governmental Research and Service. *Procedures for Making Land Development Decisions—A Supplement to the Model Land Development Ordinance.* Eugene, OR: University of Oregon, Bureau of Governmental Research and Service, February 1983.

Council of State Community Affairs Agencies. *State Actions for Affordable Housing.* Washington, DC: Council of State Community Affairs Agencies, July 1982.

"Does Local 'Red Tape' Slow Down Housing? Survey Shows Only One in Five Units is Being Built." *Western City* 58 (June 1982): 6–8.

Fishman, Richard P. "Improving the Administration of Land-Use Controls." *Housing for All Under the Law*. Cambridge, MA: Ballinger Publishing Company, 1978.

Hawaii Coastal Zone Management Program. *Red Tape vs. Green Light: Proceedings of a Workshop on Government Permit Simplification, Coordination, and Streamlining*. Honolulu, HI: (n.p.), 1978.

Hershey, Stuart S., and Carolyn Garmise. *Streamlining Local Regulations: A Handbook for Reducing Housing and Development Costs*. Management Information Service Special Report No. 11. Washington, DC: International City Management Association, 1983.

Howe, Warner. "The Growing Bureaucracy of State and National Building Regulations." *Code Administrative Review* (1974): 43–51.

International City Management Association. *The Permit Application Center: Time, Money Saved*. Municipal Management Innovation, Series, No. 25. Washington, DC: International City Management Association, 1978.

_____. *Streamlining Local Regulations: A Handbook for Reducing Housing and Development Costs*. Washington, DC: ICMA, 1983. Management Information Services Report No. 11, May 1983.

Kaiser, Edward, and Shirley F. Weiss. "Public Policy and the Residential Development Process." *Journal of the American Institute of Planners* 36 (January 1970): 30.

Kolis, Annette. *Thirteen Perspectives on Regulatory Simplification*. Washington, DC: The Urban Land Institute, 1979.

Lash, James E. *Model Ordinance and Model Procedures for "One-Stop" Application for the Development of Land*. Hartford, CT: Connecticut Department of Housing, 1982.

Lauber, Daniel. *The Hearing Examiner in Zoning Administration*. Planning Advisory Service Report No. 312. Chicago, IL: American Society of Planning Officials, 1975.

Longhini, Gregory. "Streamlined Permitting Procedures." *Planning Advisory Service Memo* No. 78–79, Chicago, IL: American Society of Planning Officials, 1978.

Meshenberg, Michael J. *The Administration of Flexible Zoning Techniques.* Planning Advisory Report No. 318. Chicago, IL: American Society of Planning Officials, 1976.

National Conference of States on Building Codes and Standards, Inc. *Model One-Stop Permit Process for One- and Two-Family Dwellings.* Herndon, VA: NCSBCS, 1981.

National League of Cities. *Streamlining Your Local Development Process.* Technical Bulletin No. 10. Washington, DC: National League of Cities, 1981.

Rivkin, Malcolm B. *Negotiated Development: A Breakthrough in Environmental Controversies.* Washington, DC: The Conservation Foundation, 1977.

San Jose, California. *Effectiveness of Existing Residential Development Review Process and Existing Environmental Control/Protection Review Procedures.* San Jose Measure "B" Study. Working Paper No. 4. San Jose, CA: (n.p.), 1975.

San Mateo County, California. *Final Report on the Study of Development Review Process.* Redwood City, CA: February 1978.

Searles, Duane L., and Sharon J. Canavan. "Land Use Planning, Zoning, and the Development Process." In Annette Kolis (ed.), *Thirteen Perspectives on Regulatory Simplification.* Washington, DC: The Urban Land Institute, 1979, pp. 97–106.

So, Frank. "Tips on Cutting the Delays of Regulation." *Planning* 44 (October 1978): 26–30.

————. "Regulatory Simplification: Can the Local Administrative Process be Improved?" In Annette Kolis (ed.), *Thirteen Perspectives on Regulatory Simplification.* Washington, DC: The Urban Land Institute, 1979, pp. 107–115.

Syles, Frederick G. "Sacramento County's Dual Planning Commission: Improving the Local Planning Process." *Environmental Comment* (September 1978): 4–6.

(The) Urban Land Institute. *Reducing the Development Costs of Housing: Actions for State and Local Governments.* Germantown, MD: HUD User, 1979.

_____. "Statement/Proposed Actions to Reduce Housing Costs Through Regulatory Reform." *Urban Land* 39 (June 1980): 11–18.

Vranicar, John; Wilford Sanders; and David Mosena. *Streamlining Land Use Regulation—A Guidebook for Local Governments.* Washington, DC: U.S. Government Printing Office, 1980.

Wible, Robert. *Model One-Stop Process for One- and Two-Family Dwellings.* Herndon, VA: National Conference of States on Building Codes and Standards, 1981.

Wickersham, Kirk, Jr. "A Better Way to Regulate Development." *Practicing Planner* (September 1977): 14–16.

_____. "Breckenridge, Colorado: An Experiment in Regulatory Simplification." In Annette Kolis (ed.), *Thirteen Perspectives on Regulatory Simplification.* Washington, DC: The Urban Land Institute, 1979, pp. 85–95.

_____. "The Permit System of Managing Land Use and Growth." *Land Use Law and Zoning Digest* 30 (January 1979): 6–9.

Wright, Laurie K. "Streamlining the Permit Process." *OPR Journal* 1 (October 1978). Sacramento, CA: State of California, Office of Planning and Research.

## Design Standards

American Institute of Architects. *Design Review Boards: A Handbook for Communities.* Washington, DC: American Institute of Architects, 1974.

American Planning Association. *Site Planning for Solar Access: A Guidebook for Residential Developers and Site Planners.* Rockville, MD: National Solar Heating and Cooling Information Center, 1979.

American Planning Association and the Joint Venture for Affordable Housing. *Affordable Single-Family Housing: A Review of Development Standards.* Chicago, IL: American Planning Association, 1984.

American Public Health Association. *Planning the Neighborhood.* Washington, DC: American Public Health Association, 1960.

American Society of Landscape Architects Foundation. *Site Planning for Solar Energy Utilization.* Washington, DC: U.S.

Department of Commerce, National Bureau of Standards, 1975.

———. *Landscape Planning for Energy Conservation.* Reston, VA: Environmental Design Press, 1977.

Ashmanskas, David C. "Design and Site Review Boards: Aesthetic Control in Local Government." *Management Information Service Report 7* (No. 2, Part B), 1975.

Browne, Carolyn. *The Mechanics of Sign Control.* Planning Advisory Service Report No. 354. Chicago, IL: American Planning Association, 1980.

Buechner, Robert D. (ed.). *National Park, Recreation and Open Space Standards.* Arlington, VA: National Recreation and Park Association, 1971.

Bye, A. E. *Art Into Landscape, Landscape Into Art.* Mesa, AZ: PDA Publishers, 1983.

Carpenter, Philip L. *Residential Landscaping II: Planting and Maintenance.* Mesa, AZ: PDA Publishers Corporation, 1983.

Community Associations Institute. *Design Review.* Architectural Control Guide for Association Practitioners, Report 2. Washington, DC: Community Associations Institute, 1978.

Corwin, M. A. *Parking Lot Landscaping,* Planning Advisory Service Report No. 335. Chicago, IL: American Planning Association, 1978.

Cullen, Gordon. *Concise Townscape.* New York, NY: Van Nostrand Reinhold, 1961.

Davies, Stephen C. *Designing Effective Pedestrian Improvements in Business Districts.* Planning Advisory Service Report No. 368. Chicago, IL: American Planning Association, 1982.

DeChiara, Joseph, and Lee E. Koppelman. *Time-Saver Standards for Site Planning.* New York, NY: McGraw-Hill, 1984.

Engstrom, Robert, and Marc Putnam. *Planning and Design of Townhouses and Condominiums.* Washington, DC: The Urban Land Institute, 1979.

Glassford, Peggy. *Appearance Codes for Small Communities.* Planning Advisory Service Report No. 379. Chicago, IL: American Planning Association, 1983.

Goldberger, Paul. "Plan for Skyscraper in Brooklyn Hts. Pits Livability Against Development." *The New York Times,* October 11, 1985, pp. B1, B4.

Hack, Gary. "Research Opportunities." *Planning* (October 1984): 20–21.

Hedman, Richard, with Andrew Jaszewski. *Fundamentals of Urban Design.* Chicago, IL: American Planning Association, 1984.

Heisler, Gordon M. "Planting Design for Wind Control." In E. Gregory McPherson (ed.), *Energy-Conserving Site Design.* Washington, DC: The Landscape Architecture Foundation, 1984, pp. 165–184.

Heisler, Gordon M.; Robert E. Schutzki; Robert P. Lisa; Howard G. Halverson; and Bruce A. Hamilton. "Effect of Planting Procedures on Initial Growth of *Acer rubrum L.* and *Fraxinus pennsylvanicum L.* in a Parking Lot." U.S. Dept. of Agriculture, Northeast Forest Experiment Station, Research Paper NE-513, 1982.

Howard Research and Development Corporation. Design Department. *Guidelines for Residential Solar Collectors in Columbia, Maryland.* Columbia, MD: Howard Research and Development Corporation, 1977.

"Illustrated Guide to Parking Lot Landscaping," *Zoning News.* American Planning Association, March 1984.

Jensen, David. *Community Design Guidelines: Responding to a Changing Market.* Washington, DC: National Association of Home Builders, 1984.

Land Design Research, Inc. *Cost-Effective Site Planning: Single-Family Development.* Washington, DC: National Association of Home Builders, 1976.

Levin, Henry M. *Estimating the Municipal Demand for Recreational Land.* Washington, DC: The Brookings Institution, 1966.

Lindbloom, Carl. "The Role of Urban Design in the Planning Process." New Jersey American Planning Association *Newsletter* III, No. 3 (Spring 1985): 1–3.

Lynch, Kevin, and Gary Hack. *Site Planning.* 3rd ed. Cambridge, MA: The MIT Press, 1984.

McHarg, Ian L. *Design With Nature.* Garden City, NY: The Natural History Press, 1969.

McKeever, Ross (ed.). *The Community Builders Handbook.* Washington, DC: The Urban Land Institute, 1968.

McPherson, E. Gregory (ed.). *Energy-Conserving Site Design.* Washington, DC: American Conservation Association, Inc., 1984.

Moskowitz, Harvey, and Carl Lindbloom. *A Guide for Residential Design Review.* Trenton, New Jersey: Department of Community Affairs, Division of Local Government Services, 1976.

Moskowitz, Harvey S., and Carl G. Lindbloom. *The Illustrated Book of Development Definitions.* New Brunswick, NJ: Rutgers University, Center for Urban Policy Research, 1981.

Multnomah County, Oregon. Department of Environmental Services. *A Developer's Handbook.* Portland, OR: Multnomah County Department of Environmental Services, 1977.

National Association of Home Builders. *Land Development Manual.* Washington, DC: National Association of Home Builders, 1974.

New Jersey. Department of Community Affairs. Division of Housing. Division of Planning. *A Community Handbook.* Trenton, NJ: New Jersey Department of Community Affairs (n.d.).

Newman, Oscar. *Architectural Design for Crime Prevention.* Washington, DC: U.S. Government Printing Office, 1971.

———. *Defensible Space.* New York: MacMillan, 1972.

O'Mara, W. Paul. *Residential Development Handbook.* Washington, DC: The Urban Land Institute, 1978.

Reps, John W. *Town Planning in Frontier America.* Columbia, MO: University of Missouri Press, 1980. Reprint of edition published by Princeton University Press, Princeton, New Jersey, 1965.

Robinette, Gary O. *Plants, People and Environmental Quality.* Washington, DC: U.S. Department of the Interior, 1972.

———. *Handbook of Landscape Architectural Construction: Pavement in the Landscape.* McLean, VA: The Landscape Architectural Foundation, 1976.

Sanders, Welford. *The Cluster Subdivision: A Cost-Effective Approach.* Planning Advisory Service Report No. 356. Chicago, IL: 1980.

Simonds, John O. *Landscape Architecture.* New York: McGraw-Hill, 1983.

Schultz, Marilyn Spigel, and Vivian Loeb Kasen. *Encyclopedia of Community Planning and Environmental Management.* New York, NY: Facts on File Publications, 1984.

So, Frank S.; David R. Mosena; and Frank S. Bangs, Jr. *Planned Unit Development Ordinances.* Planning Advisory Service Report No. 291. Chicago, IL: American Planning Association, 1975.

Thurow, Charles. *Improving Street Climate Through Urban Design.* Planning Advisory Service Report No. 376. Chicago, IL: American Planning Association, 1983.

Untermann, Richard, and Robert Small. *Site Planning for Cluster Housing.* New York, NY: Van Nostrand Reinhold, 1977.

(The) Urban Land Institute. *The Community Builders Handbook.* Washington, DC: The Urban Land Institute, 1968.

_____ . *The Pros and Cons of Cluster Housing.* Washington, DC: The Urban Land Institute, 1968.

_____ . *Residential Development Handbook.* Washington, DC: The Urban Land Institute, 1978.

(The) Urban Land Institute, American Society of Civil Engineers, and National Association of Home Builders. *Residential Streets: Objectives, Principles, and Design Considerations.* Washington, DC: The Urban Land Institute, 1976.

*Urban Planning and Land Policies.* Vol. II of the Supplementary Report of the Urbanism Committee to the National Resources Committee. Washington, DC: U.S. Government Printing Office, 1939.

U.S. Department of the Interior. *National Urban Recreation Study Executive Report.* Washington, DC: U.S. Government Printing Office, 1978.

Vogel, Joshua H. *Design of Subdivisions.* Seattle, WA: Bureau of Governmental Research and Services, 1965.

Walker, Theodore D. *Residential Landscaping I.* Mesa, AZ: PDA Publishers, 1982.

Williams, Norman, Jr. *American Planning Law: Land Use and the Police Power.* Vol. 5 (1985 Revision). Wilmette, IL: Callaghan & Company, 1975.

## Improvement Standards

*A.   STREETS AND OFF-STREET PARKING*

American Public Works Association. "Why Curb and Gutter?" Washington, DC: 1988.

American Association of State Highway Officials. *Geometric Design Guide for Local Roads and Streets.* Washington, DC: AASHO, 1971.

———. *A Policy on Geometric Design of Rural Highways.* Washington, DC: AASHO, 1966.

American Association of State Highway and Transportation Officials. *AASHTO Interim Guide for Design of Pavement Structures.* Washington, DC: AASHTO, 1972.

———. *Geometric Design Guide for Resurfacing, Restoration, and Rehabilitation (RRR) of Highways and Streets.* Washington, DC: AASHTO, 1977.

———. *Guide for Development of New Bicycle Facilities.* Washington, DC: AASHTO, 1981.

———. *A Policy on Geometric Design of Highways and Streets.* Washington, DC: AASHTO, 1984.

American Society of Planning Officials. *Street Standards in Subdivision Regulations.* Planning Advisory Service Report No. 183. Chicago, IL: American Society of Planning Officials, 1964.

Boeck, Graydon R. *Residential Land Development: Planning Utilities and Streets.* Minneapolis, MN: Metropolitan Council, 1979.

Bourey, James M. "Street Design: How Wide is Wide Enough?" *APWA Reporter,* January 1985, p. 6.

Brough, Michael B. *A Unified Development Ordinance.* Chicago, IL: Planners Press (division of American Planning Association), 1985.

Bucks County Planning Commission. *Performance Streets: A Concept and Model Standards for Residential Streets.* Doylestown, PA: Bucks County Planning Commission, April 1980.

Bureau of Governmental Research and Service. *The Development Standards Document.* Vol. 2. Eugene, OR: Bureau of Governmental Research and Service, University of Oregon, 1979.

DeChiara, Joseph, and Lee E. Koppelman. *Urban Planning and Design Criteria.* 3rd ed. New York, NY: Van Nostrand Reinhold, 1982.

Feldman, William. *Bicycle Compatible Roadways.* Trenton, NJ: New Jersey Department of Transportation, December 1982.

Freilich, Robert H., and Peter S. Levi. *Model Subdivision Regulations: Text and Commentary.* Chicago, IL: American Society of Planning Officials, 1975.

Institute of Transportation Engineers. *Recommended Guidelines for Subdivision Streets*. Washington, DC: ITE, 1984.

_____ . *Transportation and Traffic Engineering Handbook*. Englewood Cliffs, NJ: Prentice-Hall, 1976.

_____ . *Trip Generation*. Washington, DC: ITE, 1987.

Lynch, Kevin, and Gary Hack. *Site Planning*. 3rd ed. Cambridge, MA: The MIT Press, 1984.

Massic, Richard L. *Subdivision Code: An Evaluation of Park and Residential Street Elements*. Little Rock, AR: Manes and Associates, 1975.

Moskowitz, Harvey, and Carl Lindbloom. *A Guide for Residential Design Review*. Trenton, NJ: New Jersey Department of Community Affairs, Division of Government Services, 1976.

National Association of Home Builders. *Economics of Residential Street Standards*. Rockville, MD: NAHB Research Foundation, 1986.

National Committee on Urban Transportation. *Standards for Street Facilities and Services*. Procedure Manual 7a. Chicago, IL: Public Administration Service, 1958.

Patterson, William. *Model County Subdivision Regulations* (HER-PICC Publication, No. H-83-4). West Lafayette, Indiana: Purdue University, 1983.

Pennsylvania. Department of Transportation. *Guidelines for Design of Local Roads and Streets*. PDT Pub. 190. Harrisburg, PA: Pennsylvania Department of Transportation, 1972.

Reid, Fred A. "Critique of ITE Trip Generation Rates and An Alternative for Estimating New Area Traffic." *Transportation Record* 874.

Sanders, Welford, and David Mosena. *Changing Development Standards for Affordable Housing*. Planning Advisory Service Report No. 371. Chicago, IL: American Planning Association, Planning Advisory Service, 1982.

Sanders, Welford; Judith Getzel; David Mosena; and Jo Ann Butler. *Affordable Single-Family Housing: A Review of Development Standards*. Chicago, IL: American Planning Association. 1984. Public Advisory Service Report, No. 385.

Schrader, James. *Street Standards in Subdivision Regulations*. Planning Advisory Service Report No. 183. Chicago, IL: American Society of Planning Officials, 1964.

Searcy, J. K. *Design of Roadside Drainage Channels.* Hydraulic Design Series, No. 4. Washington, DC: U.S. Bureau of Public Roads, 1965.

Smith, Syd. *Subdivision Guidelines for the Jackson (Mississippi) Metropolitan Area.* Springfield, VA: National Technical Information Service, 1973.

So, Frank. *The Practice of Local Government Planning.* Washington, DC: The International City Management Association, 1979.

"Standards: Is It Reasonable to Ease Up? How Far Can We Go?" *Public Works Pro-Views: Municipal Engineering,* 1st Quarter 1987/IME 87-1, p. 1–2.

(The) Urban Land Institute; American Society of Civil Engineers; and National Association of Home Builders. *Storm Water Management: Objectives, Principles and Design Considerations.* Washington, DC: ULI, ASCE, NAHB, 1975.

(The) Urban Land Institute; National Association of Home Builders; and American Society of Civil Engineers. *Residential Streets: Objectives, Principles, and Design Considerations.* Washington, DC: ULI, 1976.

U.S. Department of Commerce. National Bureau of Standards. *A Review of Standards and Common Practices in Building Site Regulation: Technical Issues and Research Needs.* Report prepared by the Rice Center, Houston, Texas. Springfield, VA: National Technical Information Service, 1981.

U.S. Department of Housing and Urban Development. *The Affordable Community: Growth, Change, and Choice in the 80s.* Washington, DC: U.S. Government Printing Office, 1981.

————. *HUD Minimum Property Standards.* Washington, DC: HUD, 1978.

U.S. Department of Housing and Urban Development. Office of Policy Development and Research. *Innovative Site Utility Installations.* Washington, DC: HUD, 1983.

————. *Reducing the Development Costs of Housing: Actions for States and Local Governments.* Washington, DC: HUD, 1979.

U.S. Department of Housing and Urban Development and National Association of Homebuilders Research Foundation.

*Building Affordable Homes: A Cost Savings Guide for Builder/Developers.* Washington, DC: HUD and NAHB Research Foundation, 1982.

U.S. Federal Highway Administration. "Street Design Elements," in *Design of Urban Streets,* p. 7–1 through 7A–4. Washington, DC: U.S. Federal Highway Administration, 1980.


## B. WATER SUPPLY

Burchell, Robert W., and David Listokin (eds.). *The Environmental Impact Handbook.* New Brunswick, NJ: Rutgers University, Center for Urban Policy Research, 1975.

DeChiara, Joseph, and Lee E. Koppelman. *Urban Planning and Design Criteria.* 3rd ed. New York, NY: Van Nostrand Reinhold, 1982.

Freilich, Robert H., and Peter S. Levi. *Model Subdivision Regulations: Text and Commentary.* Chicago, IL: American Society of Planning Officials, 1975.

Hittman Associates, Inc. "Forecasting Municipal Water Requirements." In Robert W. Burchell and David Listokin (eds.), *The Environmental Impact Handbook.* New Brunswick, NJ: Rutgers University, Center for Urban Policy Research, 1975.

Kemmer, Frank N. (ed.). *The NALCO Water Handbook.* New York: McGraw-Hill, 1979.

Linnaweaver, F. P., Jr.; John C. Geyer; and L. Wolff. *A Study of Residential Water Use.* Study prepared for the Federal Housing Administration. Washington, DC: U.S. Government Printing Office, 1967.

Mumford, Lewis. *The City in History.* New York, NY: Harcourt Brace Jovanovich, 1961.

NALCO Chemical Company. *The NALCO Water Handbook.* Ed. by Frank N. Kemmer. New York, NY: McGraw-Hill, 1979.

National Association of Home Builders Research Foundation. *Report of a National Study and Survey of Utility Design and Construction Practices for Residential Land Development.* Washington, DC: National Association of Home Builders Research Foundation, 1974.

——— . *A Summary of a National Study and Survey of Existing Utility Design and Construction Practices for Residential*

*Development.* Rockville, MD: National Association of Home Builders Research Foundation, 1974.

Porges, Ralph L. "Factors Influencing Per Capital *(sic)* Water." *Water and Sewage Works* 104 (May 1957): 199–204.

Tabors, Richard D. "Utility Services." In Frank S. So (ed.), *The Practice of Local Government Planning.* Washington, DC: International City Management Association, 1979.

U.S. Department of Commerce. National Bureau of Standards. *A Review of Standards and Common Practices in Building Site Regulation: Technical Issues and Research Needs.* Report prepared by the Rice Center, Houston, Texas. Springfield, VA: National Technical Information Service, 1981.

U.S. Department of Housing and Urban Development. Office of Policy Development and Research. *Innovative Site Utility Installation.* Washington, DC: HUD, 1983.

## C.   *SANITARY SEWERS*

DeChiara, Joseph, and Lee E. Koppelman. *Urban Planning and Design Criteria.* 3rd ed. New York: Van Nostrand Reinhold, 1982.

Freilich, Robert H., and Peter S. Levi. *Model Subdivision Regulations: Text and Commentary.* Chicago, IL: American Society of Planning Officials, 1975.

Joint Committee of the Water Pollution Control Federation and the American Society of Civil Engineers. *Design and Construction of Sanitary and Storm Sewers.* WPCF Manual of Practice, No. 9. Washington, DC: Water Pollution Control Federation, 1969.

Mumford, Lewis. *The City in History.* New York, NY: Harcourt Brace Jovanovich, 1961.

*Recommended Standards of Sewage Works* (s.l.): Great Lakes–Upper Mississippi River Board of State Sanitary Engineers, 1968.

U.S. Department of Commerce. National Bureau of Standards. *A Review of Standards and Common Practices in Building Site Regulation: Technical Issues and Research Needs.* Report prepared by the Rice Center, Houston, Texas. Springfield, VA: National Technical Information Service, 1981.

U.S. Department of Commerce. Office of Policy Development and Research. *Innovative Site Utility Installations*. Washington, DC: HUD, 1983.

U.S. Department of Housing and Urban Development and National Association of Home Builders Research Foundation. *Building Affordable Homes: A Cost-Savings Guide for Builder/Developers*. Washington, DC: HUD and NAHB Research Foundation, 1982.


D. *STORM WATER MANAGEMENT*

American Society of Civil Engineers and the Water Pollution Control Federation. *Design and Construction of Sanitary and Storm Sewers*. Washington, DC: Water Pollution Control Federation, 1969.

Becker, Burton C., and T. H. Mills. *Guidelines for Erosion and Sediment Control: Planning and Implementation*. Annapolis, MD: Maryland Department of Water Resources, 1973.

Mallory, C. W. *The Beneficial Use of Storm Water*. Washington, DC: U.S. Environmental Protection Agency, 1973.

National Academy of Sciences. *Slope Protection for Residential Developments*. Washington, DC: The Academy, 1969.

New Jersey State Soil Conservation Committee. *Standards for Soil Erosion and Sediment Control in New Jersey*. Trenton, NJ: The Committee, 1972.

Poertner, Herbert G. *Practices in Detention of Urban Storm Water Runoff*. Washington, DC: U.S. Department of Interior, 1973.

(The) Urban Land Institute, American Society of Civil Engineers, and National Association of Home Builders. *Residential Storm Water Management*. Washington, DC: The Urban Land Institute, 1975.

U.S. Department of Agriculture. Soil Conservation Service. *Water Management and Sediment Control for Urbanizing Areas*. Washington, DC: U.S. Government Printing Office, 1978.

U.S. Department of Transportation. Federal Highway Administration. *Design Charts for Open Channel Flow*. Washington, DC: U.S. Government Printing Office, 1979.

U.S. Environmental Protection Agency. *Guidelines for Erosion and Sediment Control Planning and Implementation.* Washington, DC: U.S. EPA, 1973.

Viessman, Warren Jr., et al. *Introduction to Hydrology.* New York, NY: Harper and Row, 1977.

Wright–McLaughlin Engineers. *Urban Storm Drainage Criteria Manual.* Denver, CO: Denver Regional Council of Governments, 1969.

E.  IMPROVEMENT GUARANTEES

American Society of Planning Officials. *Performance Bonds for the Installation of Subdivision Improvements.* Planning Advisory Service Report No. 48. Chicago, IL: American Society of Planning Officials, 1958.

Frein, Joseph P. *Handbook of Construction Management and Organization.* Second edition. New York, NY: Van Nostrand Reinhold, 1980.

Kelley, Richard, and Michael M. Shultz. "Or Other Adequate Security: Using, Structuring, and Managing the Standby Letter of Credit to Ensure the Completion of Subdivision Improvements." *The Urban Lawyer* 19, No. 1 (Winter 1987).

Rogal, Brian. *Subdivision Improvement Guarantees.* Planning Advisory Service Report No. 298. Chicago, IL: American Society of Planning Officials, January 1974.

Shultz, Michael M. and Richard Kelley. "Subdivision Improvement Requirements and Guarantees: A Primer." *Journal of Urban and Contemporary Law* 28, No. 3 (1975).

**Off-Tract Improvements**

Adelstein, R. P., and N. M. Edelson. "Subdivision Exactions and Congestion Externalities." *Legal Studies* 9, No. 5 (1976): 147–163.

Babcock, Richard F. (ed.). "Exactions: A Controversial New Source for Municipal Funds." *Law and Contemporary Problems* 50, No. 1 (Winter 1987).

Ferguson, J. T., and C. D. Rasnic. "Judicial Limitations on Mandatory Subdivision Dedications." *Real Estate Law Journal* 13, No. 3 (Winter 1985): 250–62.

Frank, James E., and Robert M. Rhodes (eds.). *Development Exactions*. Chicago, IL: Planners Press, 1987.

Freidan, B. J. "Allocating the Public Service Costs of New Housing." *Urban Land* 39 (January 1980): 12–16.

Gougelman, P. "Impact Fees: National Perspectives to Florida Practice." *Nova Law Journal* 4 (1980): 137–86.

Johnston, J. "Constitutionality of Subdivision Control Exactions: The Quest for a Rationale." *Cornell L.Q.* 52.

"Mandatory Dedication of Public Sites as a Condition in the Subdivision Process in Virginia." *University of Richmond Law Review* 9, No. 3 (Spring 1975), 435–61.

Nelson, Arthur (ed.). "Development Impact Fees." *Journal of the American Planning Association* 54, No. 1 (Winter 1988).

Pavelko, T. "Subdivision Exactions: A Review of Judicial Standards." *Journal of Urban and Contemporary Law* (1983): 269–94.

Sheen, J. "Development Fees: Standards to Determine Their Reasonableness." *Utah Law Review* 3 (1982): 549–69.

Snyder, Thomas P. and Michael Stegman. *Paying for Growth: Using Development Fees to Finance Infrastructure*. Washington, DC: The Urban Land Institute, 1986.

(The) Urban Land Institute. "Financing Local Infrastructure in a Time of Fiscal Constraint: Issues and Recommended Actions." In J. B. Gailey (ed.), *1984 Zoning and Planning Law Handbook*. New York, NY: Clark Boardman (1984), pp. 172–73.

# CREDITS

**Photographs**

1-1.  Tom Hoban.

1-2.  Reprinted with permission of Harper & Row Publishers, Inc. From A.M. Sakolski, *The Great American Land Bubble.* Copyright © 1932 by Harper & Brothers Publishers, New York.

1-3.  © Catherine C. Harned. Courtesy American Planning Association.

1-4.  Reprinted with permission of *American City & County.* From *The American City* (March 1936).

1-5.  New Jersey Reference Collection, New Jersey State Library, Trenton.

1-6.  Published by permission of Regional Plan Association. From Thomas Adams et al., "The Economics of Land Subdivision," in *Problems of Planning Unbuilt Areas.* Monograph in Committee on Regional Plan of New York and Its Environs, *Neighborhood and Community Planning. Regional Survey,* Vol. VII (1929).

1-7.  Reprinted with permission of *American City & County.* From *The American City* (March 1927).

1–8.    Carl Byoir and Associates (New York, New York). Courtesy American Planning Association.

3–1.    Deland. U.S. Department of Agriculture, Soil Conservation Service.

3–2.    Carl G. Lindbloom.

3–3.    Donald C. Schuhart. U.S. Department of Agriculture, Soil Conservation Service.

3–4.    J.E. Crownover. U.S. Department of Agriculture, Soil Conservation Service.

3–5.    James A. McGuire. U.S. Department of Agriculture, Soil Conservation Service.

3–6.    Gordon Maston. U.S. Department of Agriculture, Soil Conservation Service.

3–7 and 3–8.    U.S. Department of Housing and Urban Development.

3–9.    Anton Nelessen.

3–10.    Carl G. Lindbloom.

3–11 and 3–12.    Anton Nelessen.

3–13 and 3–14.    Carl G. Lindbloom.

3–15.    U.S. Department of Housing and Urban Development.

3–16.    The Urban Land Institute.

3–17a.    John Rahenkamp Consultants, Inc.

3–17b.    Carl G. Lindbloom.

3–18.    The Leigh Photographic Group. Courtesy of The Landis Group, Princeton, New Jersey.

3–19.    U.S. Department of Agriculture, Soil Conservation Service.

3–20.    U.S. Department of Housing and Urban Development.

3–21.    Keith Glanden. U.S. Department of Agriculture, Soil Conservation Service.

3–22.    U.S. Department of Housing and Urban Development.

3–23.    Courtesy American Planning Association.

3–24.    Carl G. Lindbloom.

3–25.    G.S. Smith. U.S. Department of Agriculture, Soil Conservation Service.

3-26.   Anton Nelessen.

3-27.   Carl G. Lindbloom.

3-28.   Jon Reis Photography, Ithaca, New York.

3-29.   David Listokin.

3-30 and 3-31.   Carl G. Lindbloom.

3-32.   John Rahenkamp Consultants, Inc.

3-33.   Courtesy American Planning Association.

3-34.   Carl G. Lindbloom.

3-35.   Courtesy American Planning Association.

3-36.   Orlando R. Cabanban. Courtesy American Planning Association.

3-37.   The Urban Land Institute.

3-38.   Carl G. Lindbloom.

3-39.   Alan Karchmer, Architectural View, Memphis, Tennessee. Courtesy American Planning Association.

3-40.   Courtesy National Association of Home Builders.

3-41.   U.S. Department of Housing and Urban Development.

3-42.   David Valdez. U.S. Department of Housing and Urban Development.

3-43.   The Treetops, Falmouth, Massachusetts. *Landscape Architect:* Matarazzo Design, Inc.; *Architect:* Claude Miquelle Associates, Wakefield, Massachusetts; *Developer:* The Green Company, Falmouth, Massachusetts. Courtesy National Association of Home Builders.

3-44.   Carl G. Lindbloom.

3-45.   Downing/Leach & Associates—Architects, Landscape Design. Courtesy National Association of Home Builders.

3-46 and 3-47.   Carl G. Lindbloom.

4-1.   Anton Nelessen.

4-2.   Carl G. Lindbloom.

4-3.   Courtesy National Association of Home Builders.

4-4, 4-5, and 4-6.   Carl G. Lindbloom.

4-7 and 4-8.   Courtesy American Planning Association.

4-9.   David Listokin.

4-10.   Courtesy National Association of Home Builders.

4-11 and 4-12.   Carl G. Lindbloom.

4-13.   U.S. Department of Housing and Urban Development.

4-14.   David Listokin.

4-15.   Courtesy American Planning Association.

4-16.   Carl G. Lindbloom.

4-17.   Bob Andersen, *Clayton County Register* (editor), Elkader, Iowa. Courtesy American Planning Association.

4-18.   Bennett. U.S. Department of Agriculture, Soil Conservation Service.

4-19.   Carl G. Lindbloom.

4-20.   Dennis McClendon. Courtesy American Planning Association.

4-21 and 4-22.   Courtesy National Association of Home Builders.

4-23 and 4-24.   J.H. Rogers. U.S. Department of Agriculture, Soil Conservation Service.

## Illustrations

Pages 9, 21, 37, 75, 84–85. Carl G. Lindbloom.

1-1.   Reprinted with permission of Cornell University Library. From John W. Reps, *Town Planning in Frontier America.* Columbia, MO: University of Missouri Press (1980). Map drawn by Thomas Holme. From a restrike in John C. Lowber, *Ordinances of the City of Philadelphia, 1812.*

1-2.   Copyright © Shirk Oklahoma History Center, Oklahoma City University, Oklahoma City, Oklahoma. From John W. Reps (publisher), "Historic City Plans and Views" (catalog). Ithaca, NY: Historic Urban Plans.

1-3.   Reprinted with permission of Harper & Row Publishers, Inc. From A.M. Sakolski, *The Great American Land Bubble.* Copyright © 1932 by Harper & Brothers Publishers, New York.

1-4.   Reprinted with permission of *American City & County* © 1944. From *The American City* (November 1944).

1–5.  Reprinted with permission of *American City & County* ©
       1937. From *The American City* (May 1937).

1–6.  Reprinted with permission of *American City & County* ©
       1947. From *The American City* (March 1947).

3–1.  From *Guiding Land Subdivision, Part 3: Residential Stan-
       dards.* Lansing, MI: Tri-County Regional Planning Com-
       mission, 1964.

3–2.  Anton Nelessen.

3–3.  Courtesy of Regional Plan Association. From Clarence
       Arthur Perry, "The Neighborhood Unit," in Committee on
       Regional Plan of New York and Its Environs, *Neighborhood
       and Community Planning, Regional Survey,* Vol. VII
       (1929).

3–4.  Carl G. Lindbloom.

3–5.  From National Association of Home Builders National
       Research Center, *Affordable Housing Challenge and
       Response: A Guide for Local Government and Developers,*
       Volume 1. Washington, D.C.: U.S. Government Printing
       Office, July 1987. Report prepared for U.S. Department of
       Housing and Urban Development, Innovating Technology
       and Special Project Division.

3–6.  Carl G. Lindbloom.

3–7.  Koninklijke Nederlandse Toeristenbond ANWB, the Neth-
       erlands.

3–8.  From Federal Housing Administration, *Planning Neighbor-
       hoods for Small Houses.* Washington, D.C.: U.S. Govern-
       ment Printing Office, 1939.

3–9.  Courtesy National Association of Home Builders. From
       *Cost-Effective Site Planning* (Washington, D.C.: National
       Association of Home Builders), 1976.

4–1 and 4–2.  Carl G. Lindbloom.

4–3.  The Meadows, Hingham, Massachusetts. *Architect:* Miquelle
       Associates, Wakefield, Massachusetts; *Land Planner:*
       Matarazzo Design, Concord, New Hampshire; *Client:* The
       Green Company. From *Higher Density Housing: Planning,*

*Design, Marketing.* Washington, D.C.: National Association of Home Builders, 1986.

4-4.  Carl G. Lindbloom.

4-5.  Courtesy National Association of Home Builders. From NAHB, *Higher Density Housing.*

4-6.  From National Association of Home Builders National Research Center, *Affordable Housing Challenge and Response: A Guide for Local Government and Developers,* Volume 1. Washington, D.C.: U.S. Government Printing Office, July 1987. Report prepared for U.S. Department of Housing and Urban Development, Innovating Technology and Special Project Division.

4-7.  From National Association of Home Builders Research Foundation, *The Affordable Housing Demonstration: A Case Study—Santa Fe, New Mexico.* Washington, D.C.: U.S. Government Printing Office, November 1984. Report prepared for U.S. Department of Housing and Urban Development, Division of Building Technology.

4-8.  From Harvey Moskowitz and Carl Lindbloom, *A Guide for Residential Design Review.* Trenton, NJ: Department of Community Affairs, September 1976. Report prepared for NJDCA, Division of Local Government Services.

4-9.  Andres Duany and Elizabeth Plater–Zyberk, Architects.

4-10 and 4-11.  Carl G. Lindbloom.

4-12.  Dale W. Naegle and Gary Coad, Architects. From City of San Diego, La Jolla Shores Planned District—*Urban Design Manual and Planned District Ordinance.* Prepared by the Precise Plan Committee of the La Jolla Shores Association and the City of San Diego, March 1974.

4-13.  See Illustration 4-6.

4-14.  Courtesy National Association of Home Builders. From NAHB, *Higher Density Housing.*

4-15.  Graphic by Carl G. Lindbloom. *Design:* K. Hovnanian Companies of New Jersey, Inc., Engineering Department.

4-16.  From Harvey S. Moskowitz and Carl G. Lindbloom, *The Illustrated Book of Development Definitions.* New

Brunswick, NJ.: Rutgers University, Center for Urban Policy Research, 1981.

4–17.   Graphic by Carl G. Lindbloom. Adapted from U.S. Department of Housing and Urban Development, Office of Policy Development and Research. *Innovative Site Utility Installations.* Washington, D.C.: U.S. Government Printing Office, August 1983.

4–18 and 4–19.   See Illustration 4–6.

4–20 and 4–21.   Courtesy of John Rahenkamp Consultants, Inc. (Land Planners), Philadelphia, Pennsylvania.

# INDEX

*Note: n* refers to material in notes to exhibits

AASHTO, 312, 326
Acrylonitrile-butadiene-styrene (ABS), 110
Adams, Thomas, 147*n*
Administrative officer, 4, 183
ADT (Average daily traffic). *See* Average daily traffic
Asbestos cement pipe, 347, 359
Aesthetics regulation, 214–216
Aggressive soils, 4
Aisle, 4
Alleys, 4, 51, 300–301, 311
American colonies, 132–137, 192
American Insurance Association, 345
American Planning Association, xvi, 236
American Society of Planning Officials (ASPO), 376–377
American Water Works Association (AWWA), 4, 107–108
Ancient civilizations, 131–132, 343, 351
Appearance codes, 212–214, 216–218
Applicant, 4, 184
Application for development, 4, 87–96
Applications. *See also* Documents

differentiation of, 183
for major subdivision and major site plan, 18–22
for minor subdivision and minor site plan, 16–17
procedures, 15
Approval procedures, 175–181
Approving authority, 4
Arterials, 299
Arundel County (Maryland), 180
ASCE (American Society of Civil Engineers), 4
Asphalt curbs, 55, 316. *See also* Curbs
ASTM (American Society for Testing Materials), 4
Automobile size, 69, 341
Average daily traffic (ADT), 4, 40–42, 83, 296–303
AWWA (American Water Works Association), 4, 107–108

Balled plants, 34, 242–243, 245
Bare-root plants, 34, 242–243, 245
Barrier curb, 4
Bartholomew, Harland, 143, 145*n*, 146*n*, 166, 169

Belgian block curb, 4, 314. *See also* Curbs
Berm, 4
*Berman v. Parker*, 214
Bicycle lane, 4, 98, 323, 325, 326
Bicycle path, 4, 98, 323–326
Bicycle-compatible roadway, 4, 323, 326–327
Bikeways
  construction of, 98, 326–327
  definition of, 4, 323
  location of, 324
  requirements for, 27, 62, 323
Billboards, 214
Birkbeck, Morris, 139
Blow-off, 4
Board of Adjustment, 4
Breckenridge (Colorado), 180
Brick, 39, 266, 268–272
Brough, Michael B., 165, 181, 227, 288*n*, 295, 338–339
Bucks County (Pennsylvania), 303, 305–306, 331
Buffer, 4
Buffering
  design, 261

functions of, 253, 260
materials, 261
requirements for, xix, 36–37, 261
Building design
appearance codes and, 212–214
criteria, 215–218
legal issues in regulating, 214–215
Burchell, Robert W., 158*n*
Burlapped plants, 34, 242–243. *See also* Planting requirements

California Bearing Ratio (CBR), 333
Caliper, 4, 243
Capital Improvements Program, 4
Capped system, 4, 71, 77, 346–347, 352. *See also* Dry lines
Cartway, 4, 304
Cartway width. *See also* Lane width
determining, 304-313
standards for, 47–52, 54
Catch basins, 121, 373
Centerline offset of adjacent intersections, 4, 331
Chain-link fences, 272
Channel, 4
Channelization, 4, 84, 116–120, 362, 367–369
Cincinnati, Ohio, 139
Circulation system design, 27, 205–209
Cleanouts, 360
Cleveland, Ohio, 139
Climatic zone, 35, 246–249
Cloaca Maxima, 351
Closed conduits, 116–117, 369
Closed pipe system, 367
Cluster development, 4, 25, 200–205
Collectors. *See* Residential collectors
Commercial and industrial development design, 27, 212–218
Common laterals, 4, 355–358. *See also* Sanitary sewer systems
Common open space, 4–5. *See also* Open space
Concept plan, 5, 13, 21, 87–96
Concrete block, 121, 266–272
Concrete curb, 97. *See also* Curbs

Conduits, 368–369
Conference, pre-application, 7, 13–14, 179
Conventional development, 5, 201–202
utilities cost in compared to cluster, 348
Coon Rapids, Minnesota, 236
Corporation stop, 5, 107
Corrugated aluminum pipe, 121. *See also* Pipes
Corrugated steel pipe, 121. *See also* Pipes
Cost allocation for off-tract improvements, 82–85
Crown vetch, 240–241
Cul-de-sacs
ADT on, 46
cartway widths on, 49, 51, 311–312
curbs on, 55
definition of, 5
purpose and requirements for, 301–303
right-of-way requirements on, 53–54
Cultural groups, 231
Culvert, 5, 116, 370–371
Curb radius, 52, 99, 331–332
Curbs
asphalt, 55, 316
Belgian block, 4, 314
concrete, 97
construction standards for, 97–98
definition of, 5
functions of, 313–314, 360
granite block, 98, 315
mountable, 6
parking and, 48
requirements, 52–55, 314–315
Cushions, 5. *See also* Pipe bedding

Dade County (Florida), 180, 236
Dams, 123, 374
DeChiara, Joseph, 228*n*, 251, 272, 341, 357
Dedication, 5

Demographic characteristics, 230
Density, 5, 48
Design evaluation criteria checklist, 277–282
Design flood, 5. *See also* Storm water management systems
Design and improvement standards. *See also* Improvement standards
definition of, 5
and improvement guarantees, 79–80
and landscaping, 32–40
for off-street parking, 65–71. *See also* Off-street parking
for open space and recreation, 28–32
purpose of, 23, 76–77
recommended, 143, 145
for sanitary sewers, 76–77
steps in development of, 23–28
for storm water management, 78–79
for streets, 40–65. *See also* Streets
for water supply, 71–76
Design process. *See* Site design
Detention basins, 5, 121–124, 360, 373–375
Developable areas, 25–26
Developer, 5
Development, 5
Development applications. *See* Applications
Development density, 5, 48
Development intensity, 48, 50–51
Development regulation, 5
Distribution mains, 107
Ditches, 360. *See also* Storm water management systems
Divided streets
cartway widths on, 52, 312–313
curbs on, 55
definition of, 5
purpose and requirements for, 304
Documents, xx, 87–96. *See also* Appli-

cations
Douglas Commission survey (1968), 157
Drainage. *See also* Storm water management systems
    area, 365
    definition of, 5
    on-site, 367, 368
Drainage facility, 5, 373–375
Drainage grates, 98, 327, 373
Drainage system. *See also* Storm water management systems
    definition of, 5
    function of, 360–362
    requirements, 52, 54–55
Driveway, 5, 336
Drop manhole, 5. *See also* Manholes
Drop pipe, 5
Dry lines, 5, 71, 77, 352. *See also* Capped system
Ductile iron pipe, 107, 110, 121, 347

Easements, 5, 121, 356, 375
Embankments, 123, 374
Emergency spillways, 122–123, 374
Endangered species, 26, 159
Enforcement, 2. *See also* Improvement guarantees
English settlers, 133–135
Environmental concerns
    design restrictions due to, 25
    and subdivision controls in 1960s and 1970s, 159–160
Environmental constraints, 5, 196–199
Erosion, 5, 197, 240
Escrow, 5
Escrow accounts, 86. *See also* Improvement guarantees
*Euclid v. Ambler*, 162
Exception provisions, 11
Exempt subdivision, 5

FABC, 333
Fairfax County (Virginia), 180
Federal Housing Administration (FHA), 154–156

Fees, 2
    for pre-application conference, 14
Fences
    definition and purpose of, 5, 271
    design of, 272–273
    as element of landscaping, 265
    function of, 39
    materials used for, 271–272
    placement of, 271
Final approval, 5, 20–22
Final plat, 5, 21–22
Fine specimens, 33
    protection of, 238–239
Fire flows, 72, 75, 345
Fire hydrants, 75, 76, 108, 350–351
*First Evangelical Lutheran Church v. County of Los Angeles*, 25, 162
Flexible pipe, 357. *See also* Pipes
Flood hazard area, 123–124. *See also* Storm water management systems
Flood plains, 26, 194, 196–198
    Manning's Roughness Coefficients for, 119
Floor area, 6
    in calculating daily water requirements, 74, 345
    as determinant for off-street parking, 67
Flushing, 6. *See also* Cleanouts; Manholes
Freilich, Robert H., 165, 179, 311, 346, 355, 357, 360
Frontage, 6. *See also* Streets
Functional standards, xviii–xix. *See also* Design and improvement standards; Improvement standards; Site design

Garages, 68, 336, 339
General Development Plan (GDP), 6, 18, 87–88, 183–184
Governing body, 6
Grade, 6, 99, 332. *See also* Street grade
Graded area, 61, 97–99, 197, 319–323
Granite block curb, 98, 315

Grass, 240
Grid pattern, 150, 207–208
Ground cover, 6, 240–241, 248
Gutter
    definition of, 6
    function of, 313–314
    requirements for, 52–55, 314–315

Hack, Gary, 194*n*, 203, 207, 230, 305, 320
Hardy Cross method, 6, 107, 347
Hedman, Richard, 192–193
Historic district, 6
Historic site, 6, 194, 197
Hittman coefficient, 74, 344–345
Homeowners association, 31–32
    and role in common open space ownership, 234
House service connections, 107
    common lateral, 349–350
    placement of, 348
Hydraulic capacity of a conduit, 115–116, 368
Hydrologic response, 6

Illuminating Engineering Society (IES), 6, 63
Illumination. *See* Lighting requirements
Impervious surface, 6. *See* Soil
Impoundment, 6, 368. *See* Detention basins; Retention basins
Improvement guarantees, 375–378
    maintenance and performance, 79–80
Improvement standards. *See also* Design and improvement standards
    for sanitary sewers, 351–360
    for storm water management, 360–375
    for streets, 293–342. *See also* Streets
    for water supply systems, 242–351
Improvements
    definition of, 6
    guarantees of, 79–80
    off-tract, 81–86

*Indiana Law Journal* survey (1952), 152–154, 157
Individual sewage disposal system, 6, 352, 354. *See also* Sanitary sewer systems
Industrial development design, 27
Information signs, 335
Inlets, 121, 373
*Innovative Site Utility Installations* (HUD), 355
Institute of Transportation Engineers (ITE), xvi, 7
    definitions of land uses, 43–44
    guidelines for subdivision streets, 295, 302–303
    trip generation rates, 40–42, 297
Intersections, 63, 99–100, 331–332
Interpretation, 3
Island, 6, 318. *See also* Divided street
ITE. *See* Institute of Transportation Engineers

Joint Venture for Affordable Housing, xvi, 165, 236
Junkyards, 214
Jurisdiction, 2, 10

Koppelman, Lee E., 228*n*, 251, 269, 272, 341, 357
Kuichling, Emil, 363

Land acquisition economics, 146
Land Ordinance of 1785, 137
Land Planning Bulletins, 154
Land use approval procedure
    problems regarding, 175–176
    recommendations and actions for reform in, 176–181
Land use definitions, 43–44
Landscape design
    approach to, 211
    functions, 209–211
    importance of, 27–28
    plant materials used in, 211–212
Landscaping. *See also* Planting requirements

adding additional, 241–242
    definition and purpose of, 235–236
    materials, 236–237
    parking lot, 262–264
    paving material used in, 265–270
    plan for, 33, 237
Landscaping standards, 32
    buffering, 36
    parking lot, 38
    paving materials and, 39
    plan, 33
    purpose of, 32–33
    site protection and general planting requirements of, 33–35
    street furniture and, 39–40
    walls and fences and, 39
Land-use regulations, xv–xvi
Lane numbers, 47, 306–307
Lane width. *See also* Cartway width
    on divided streets, 52
    explanation and standards for, 47–49
    on marginal access streets, 52, 312
    moving, 47–52, 305–306
    parking, 47–52, 305–306
    on residential access streets, 50, 307–310
    on residential collectors, 51, 310
    on special purpose streets, 51, 310–313
    on stub streets, 52, 313
    on subcollectors, 50–51
Lateral sewers, 6. *See also* Sanitary sewer systems
Lautner, Harold W., 152*n*
Laws of the Indies, 132–133
Legal issues, 161–163
Levi, Peter S., 165, 179, 311, 346, 355, 357, 358, 360
Lighting requirements, 63, 101, 105–106, 334–335
Linnaweaver Method, 344
Lindbloom, Carl, 228*n*, 235, 264, 362
Listokin, David, 158*n*
Los Angeles County (California), 180

Lot, 6
Lot area, 6
Lot frontage, 6, 48
Lynch, Kevin, 194*n*, 203, 207, 230, 269*n*, 305, 320

McMichael, Stanley L., 156
Main, 6
Maintenance guarantees, 6, 79
Major site plan, 6, 18–22
Major subdivision, 6, 18–22
Manholes, 5, 6, 110–111, 121, 359, 373
Manning equation, 6, 115–119, 368, 369, 371, 372
Marginal access streets
    cartway widths on, 52, 312
    curbs on, 55
    definition of, 6
    purpose and requirements for, 303
Master plan, 6
Median, 6
Minor site plan, 6, 16–17
Minor subdivision, 6, 16–17
*Model County Subdivision Regulations* (Indiana), 179
*Model Land Development Ordinance* (Oregon), 179
Model subdivision ordinances
    history of, 163–166
    and improvement guarantees, 377–378
    processing recommendations incorporated in, 179–180
*Model Subdivision Regulations* (Freilich and Levi), 165
Montgomery County (Maryland), 180
Moskowitz, Harvey, 228*n*, 235, 263–264, 362
Mountable curb, 6
Moving lane
    definition of, 7
    widths, 47–52, 305–306
Mulch, 7, 240

National Association of Home Builders (NAHB), xvi, 320, 346

National Board of Fire Underwriters, 345
National Cooperative Highway Research Program Report Number 187, 297
National Recreation and Park Association (NRPA), 220, 222
  recommended standards for local developed open space, 223
  suggested facility development standards, 224–226
Neighborhood compatibility, 198
Neighborhood unit, 200–201
New England colonies, 133–134
New Jersey Municipal Land Use Law, 191
Noise, 260
*Nollan v. California Coastal Commission*, 162
Nomograph, for determining time of runoff concentration, 113
Nonresidential off-street parking, 67, 339, 341–342. *See also* Off-street parking

Off-site, 7
Off-street parking. *See also* Parking lots
  function of, 336
  improvement standards for, 65–71
  location of, 341
  nonresidential, 67, 339, 341–342
  residential, 66, 336–339
  reasonable walking distance for, 70
  requirements for, 65–68, 336–341
  sizes of spaces for, 69, 341
Off-street parking space, 7
Off-tract, 7
Off-tract improvements
  cost allocation for, 82–85
  definition and principles of, 81
  escrow accounts used for, 86
  purpose of, 81
Oklahoma City, Oklahoma, 136
On-site, 7

On-site drainage, 367, 368
On-street parking space, 7
On-tract, 7
Open space
  common, 4–5
  cultural groups and use of, 231
  defined, 7, 221
  importance of, 219–220
  improvement standards for, 28–32
  minimum requirements for, 221–222
  ownership, 234
  parcels, 233–234
  standards, 28–32
  total land area requirements for, 222–233
Orange County (California), 180
Ordinances, 1, 130
Overhead wiring, 334
Overlay map technique, 195

Parking, off-street. *See* Off-street parking
Parking lanes, 47–52, 303–306
Parking lots. *See also* Off-street parking
  design for, 342
  landscaping in, 38, 262–264
Parking standards, 65–68
Parks. *See also* Open space
  influence on development of, 220
  NRPA recommended standards for, 223
  provisions for, 154
  responsibility in providing, 28
Pavement
  construction standards for, 101, 102
  definition of, 7
  edge, 314
  requirements, 63
  thickness, 332–333
  type, 333
Paving materials
  definition and purpose of, 266
  design of, 270

  as element of landscaping, 265
  relative strengths of, 104
  types of, 266–270
Peak hour trips (PHT), 83
Peak rate of discharge, 111, 362–365
Penalties, 2
Penn, William, 134–135
Perc test, 7
Performance guarantees, 7, 79
Performance standards, xix–xx, 160–161
*Performance Streets* (Bucks County Planning Commission), 165, 294–295
Perimeter strips, 264
Pervious surface, 7
Petaluma, California, 159
Philadelphia, Pennsylvania, 134–135
Pipe bedding, 110, 121, 372–373
Pipes
  asbestos cement, 347, 359
  corrugated, 121
  drop, 5
  ductile iron, 107, 110, 121, 347
  flexible, 357
  materials, 107, 109–110, 115, 121, 347, 349, 358–359, 372
  placement of, 349–350, 372–373
  rigid, 357
  size of, 107, 115, 347, 358, 371–372
  systems, 367
Planned unit development (PUD), 7, 87
Planning Advisory Service (PAS), 214, 215, 307
Planning board, 7, 10
Plant hardiness zones, 35, 38, 246, 247
Plant species, 246–249
Planting requirements, 33–35, 211–212. *See also* Buffering; Landscaping design; Landscaping
  for balled and burlapped versus bare-root plants, 242–243
  for protection of existing plantings, 238–239
  for slopes, 240–241
  size, 243

and topsoil preservation, 238
for trees and shrubs, 243–246
Plat, 7
Polyvinyl chloride sewer pipe (PVC), 107, 110
Population density, 230–231
Potable water supply, 7
Pre-application conference, 7, 177, 179
Pre-application procedure, 13–14
Preliminary approval, 7
Preliminary subdivision plat, 7
Premature development regulation, 159
President's Conference on Home Building and Home Ownership (1932), 143
Procedural improvement, xx
Procedures
    for application, 15
    for major subdivision and major site plan applications, 18–22
    for minor subdivision and minor site plan applications, 16–17
    need for reform in, 176–181
    pre-application, 13–14
    recommendations to expedite reform in, 181–184
Processing fees, 2
Public Administration Service (PAS) survey (1941), 151–153, 157
Public open space, 7
Public response time limits, 184
Public welfare, 1
PUD (Planned-unit development), 7, 87

Rainfall intensity, 111, 114, 365
Ramapo, New York, 159
Rational method, 7
Rational Formula calculation, 111, 115, 363–366, 368, 371
Rational nexus test, 81
Reasonable relationship test, 81
Recommendations of the National Committee for Traffic Safety (NCTS), 294
Recommended Guidelines for Subdivision Streets (ITE), 295

Recreational facilities. See Open space
Regional Plan of New York and Its Environs (1929), 143, 150
Regional recreational preferences, 231
Reinforced concrete pipe, 109, 115
Reps, John, 192
Residential access streets. See also Streets
    cartway width on, 50, 307–310
    curbing on, 54
    definition of, 7, 297
    functions and requirements for, 40, 298
    right-of-way, 56–57
Residential collectors
    cartway widths for, 51, 310
    curbs or shoulders on, 55
    definition of, 7
    purpose and requirements for, 299
    right-of-way profiles of, 60
Residential density, 7
Residential development design
    clustering in, 201–205
    neighborhood unit in, 200–201
    standards, 26–27
Residential off-street parking, 66, 336–339. See also Off-street parking
Residential street hierarchy, 8, 9, 40, 45–46. See also Street hierarchy; Streets
Residential Streets, 294
Residential subcollectors. See also Subcollectors
    cartway widths for, 310
    definition of, 7
    purpose and requirements for, 298–299
    right-of-way profiles on, 58–59
Retaining wall, 8
Retention basins, 8, 360, 373–375
Rice Center, 358
Right-of-way
    definition of, 8, 328
    profiles, 56–60
    requirements and dimensions,

53–54, 62–63, 328–329
Rigid pipe, 357
Runoff peak rate of discharge, 111, 363–365
Runoff volume, 111–112, 362–365
Rural residential lanes, 51, 300, 310–311
Rutgers Subdivision and Site Plan Handbook
    goals of, xvi–xvii, 165–166, 377–378
    open space standards in, 230
    processing procedure recommendations in, 181–184
Rutgers University survey (1979), 157–159

Sanitary sewer systems. See also Sewers
    background, 351–352
    common laterals in, 355–358
    design and placement of, 76–77, 353–355
    function of, 76–77
    requirements for, 107–111
    strategy, 352–353
Schools, 154
Screen, 8
    for parking lots, 262–263. See also Buffering
SCS (Soil Conservation Service), 8, 120n, 122, 124
Sedimentation, 8
Separability provision, 3
Septic systems, 8, 76, 352–353. See also Sanitary sewer systems
Septic tank, 8
Setback, 8
Sewage generation, 77
Sewers. See also Sanitary sewer systems
    definition of, 8
    flow, 73
    lateral, 6
    slope of, 357–358
Shade trees, 35. See also Trees

areas for, 327
definition of, 8
planting procedures for, 246,
    250–253
for street planting, 254–259
use of, 35, 62
Shared parking, 65, 336, 337
*Shared Parking* (Urban Land Institute),
    68
Shoulder
    definition of, 8, 316–318
    materials for, 318–319
    requirements for, 55–60, 317
    uses of, 52
Shrubs
    planting procedures for, 243–246
    recommended, 248–249
Sidewalk
    construction specifications for,
        97–98, 322–323
    definition of, 8, 319–320
    location of, 321–322
    requirements for, 61, 320–321
Sight triangle, 8, 99–100, 332
Signs, 65, 335
Site analysis, 24, 193–195
Site design. *See also* Design and
    improvement standards
    and building design guidelines,
        212–218
    circulation system, 205–209
    definition of, 192–193
    difficulties in, 189–192
    evaluation criteria checklist, 277–
        282
    landscape, 209–212, 235–277.
        *See also* Landscape design;
        Landscaping; Landscaping stan-
        dards
    for open space, 219–234. *See also*
        Open space
    residential, 200–205
    site evaluation and layout steps in,
        193–199
Site layout, 196–199
Site plan, 6, 8

Site plan application procedure
    major, 18–22
    minor, 16–17
Sketch plan, 8
Slope plantings, 240–241
Slope standards, 26, 108, 109
Small, Robert, 203
Socioeconomic characteristics, 230
Soil
    aggressive, 4
    berm, 4
    runoff coefficient and characteris-
        tics of, 364–365
    and protection of existing plant-
        ings, 238–239
    topsoil, 9, 33, 238
Soil cement, 8
Spanish settlers, 132
Special purpose streets. *See also*
    Streets
    alleys, 4, 51, 300–301, 311
    cartway width on, 51, 310–313
    cul-de-sacs, 5, 51, 301–303, 311–
        312
    curbs on, 55
    divided, 5, 52, 55, 304, 312–313
    marginal access, 6, 52, 55, 303,
        312
    rural residential lanes, 51, 300,
        310–311
    stub, 8, 52, 55, 304, 313
Specifically and uniquely attributable
    test, 81
Stabilized turf (earth), 8
Standard City Planning Enabling Act,
    142
Stankowski Method, 115
Storm water detention, 8
Storm water management systems
    background of, 360–362
    demand, 362–366
    design of, 370–375
    detention facilities, 121–124
    inlets, catch basins, and manholes
        for, 121
    pipe capacity, materials, and

placement, 115–121
protecting water quality in, 124
requirements for, 78–79
strategy, 113, 366–370
Storm water retention, 8
Street frontage strips, 264
Street furniture
    definition of, 8, 274
    design of, 275–277
    as element of landscaping, 265
    placement of, 274–275
    requirements for, 39–40
    types of, 236
Street grade, 63, 98–99, 330
Street hardware, 8, 236, 333. *See also*
    Lighting requirements; Signs; Wir-
    ing
Street hierarchy, 8, 9, 60, 296–297.
    *See also* Residential street hierarchy
Street lighting. *See* Lighting require-
    ments
Street loop, 8
Street name signs, 335
Streets
    arterials, 299
    and cartway width, 47–52, 54,
        304–313
    definition of, 8
    early recommended standards for,
        147
    hierarchy system of, 8, 40–46,
        165
    improvement standards reduction
        for, 293–296
    and intensity of development on,
        48, 50–51
    regulation of, 40
    residential access, 7, 40, 54, 56–
        57, 297, 298, 307–310
    residential collectors, 7, 51, 55,
        56–57, 60, 299, 310
    special purpose. *See* Special pur-
        pose streets
Stub streets, 8
    cartway widths on, 52, 313
    curbs on, 55

definition of, 8
purpose and requirements for,
  304
Subcollectors. *See also* Residential sub-
  collectors
    cartway widths on, 50–51
    curbs on, 54
Subdivision, 6, 8
Subdivision application procedures
    major, 18–22
    minor, 16–17
Subdivision controls, xviii
Subdivision costs (historic), 143, 144,
  146, 152, 153, 158
Subdivision regulation
    description and importance of,
      129–131
    in ancient civilizations, 131–132
    legal basis and reexamination of,
      161–163
    in 1928–World War II, 142–150
    in 1960s and 1970s, 157–160
    in 1980s, 160–161
    nineteenth century, 137–141
    post World War II, 151–157
    town planning in colonies, 132–
      137
Subdivision and Site Plan Committee
    definition of, 8–9
    establishment of, 12, 183
*Subdivision and Site Plan Handbook.*
  *See* Rutgers *Subdivision and Site*
  *Plan Handbook*
Subgrade, 9, 101, 103, 322–323
Swales, 52, 54, 360, 367, 368

Tanbark, 39

Technical Release (TR) No. 55 Method,
  365, 368
Topographical features of development
  sites, 231
Topsoil. *See also* Soil
    definition of, 9
    preservation of, 238
    requirements, 33
Townships, 137
Traffic control signs, 65, 335
Traffic patterns, 27, 205–209
Traffic volume, 47–48
Tree canopies, 250, 251
Trees. *See also* Shade trees
    planting procedures for, 243–246
    protection of, 25–26, 238
Trip, 9
    peak hour, 83
Trip generation rates, 40–42, 297
Turf shoulders, 319

Underground wiring, 62, 64
Underdevelopable areas, 25–26
*A Unified Development Ordinance*
  (Brough), 165, 181, 295
U.S. Supreme Court decisions, 25, 162,
  214
Untermann, Richard, 203
Urban Land Institute (ULI), xvi, 9,
  176–177, 235–236
    survey (1950), 153, 157, 159
USCGS (United States Coast and Geo-
  detic Survey), 9
Utility areas, 327
Utility lanes, 62

Valves, 107, 108

Variance, 9
Vehicle size, 69, 341

Waiver provisions, 11
Walker, Theodore D., 247n
Walkway systems, 27
Walls, 39, 265, 270–273
Water
    demand for, 71–76, 344–345
    quality of, 124, 367
    sewage generation and consump-
      tion of, 77
Water mains, 107
Water meter, 107
Water Pollution Control Act, 366
Water supply system
    background of, 342–344
    demand, 71–76, 344–345
    design and placement of, 107–
      108, 347–351
    improvement standards for, 342–
      351
    strategy, 346–347
Wetlands, 25
Williamsburg, Virginia, 133, 192
Wiring
    overhead, 334
    underground, 62, 64, 327
Woonerf concept, 207
Work Projects Administration (WPA),
  143, 148–149
Wrought iron fences, 272
Wye, 9
Wye connections, 9

Zoning, 162
Zoning board, 184